THE
Edwardian
COUNTRY HOUSE

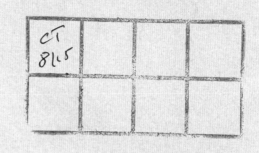

THE Edwardian COUNTRY HOUSE

Juliet Gardiner

First published in 2002 by Channel 4 Books, an imprint of
Pan Macmillan Ltd, 20 New Wharf Road, London N1 9RR,
Basingstoke and Oxford.

Associated companies throughout the world

www.panmacmillan.com

ISBN 0 7522 6166 5

Text © Juliet Gardiner, 2002

9 8 7 6 5 4 3 2 1

A CIP catalogue record for this book is available from
the British Library.

Design by Isobel Gillan
Illustrations by Amanda Patton
Photography © Simon Roberts/Growbag, © Simon Grossett,
   © Mark Pinder and © Debi Treloar
Colour reproduction by Aylesbury Studios Ltd
Printed by Butler and Tanner, Frome, Somerset

〰 This book accompanies the television series
The Edwardian Country House made by Wall to Wall
for Channel 4.
Executive producer: Emma Willis
Series producer: Caroline Ross Pirie

CREDITS
While every effort has been made to trace copyright holders
the publishers will be glad to make proper
acknowledgements in future editions of the book in the event
that any regrettable omissions have occurred at the time of
going to press.

L B Chappell: 15; Simon Grosset: 8, 10, 55, 68, 75, 76, 77, 78,
79, 83, 87, 117, 125, 140, 142, 144, 147, 149, 150, 151, 154, 156,
157, 162, 163, 169, 174, 175, 182 (right), 187, 203, 225, 248
Hulton Getty: 179, 221, 241, 269; Isobel Gillan: 16; Mary
Evans Picture Library: 244, 271, 272, 274; Lord Palmer for
permission to reproduce photography from the Manderston
family albums: 2, 11, 20, 22, 23, 24, 40, 71, 73, 74, 107, 108, 118,
158, 170, 176, 181, 182 (left), 188, 195 (inset), 196, 215, 218, 222,
224, 226, 227, 230, 233, 237, 238, 256, 264; Mark Pinder: 208,
209, 255, 256, 257, 260, 262, 263; Simon Roberts: 7, 13, 17, 18,
21, 26, 28, 30, 31, 32, 33, 34, 35, 36, 37, 38, 39, 41, 42, 43, 44, 46,
48, 49, 50, 51, 52, 53, 56, 57, 58, 59, 60, 64, 65, 66, 82, 86, 88, 89,
92, 95, 96, 97, 100, 102, 103, 106, 110, 115, 121, 122, 123, 124,
126, 127, 128, 129, 130, 132, 133, 134, 135, 136, 139, 166, 167,
171, 172, 180, 184, 185, 192, 193, 194, 195, 199, 200, 201, 206,
207, 210, 211, 214, 229, 243, 245, 247, 249, 251, 254, 267, 268,
277, 278; Fritz von der Schulenburg: 19 ; Debi Treloar: 62, 85,
90, 98, 104, 152, 161, 164, 252, 259

'Huntin', Shootin' and Fishin' (p. 178) reproduced by
permission of A. P. Watt Ltd on behalf of Mrs Teresa
Elizabeth Perkins and Jocelyn Hale.

Thanks to Paula Pryke Flowers for recreating the table
flowers (p. 90) and the table centrepiece (p. 259), Denis
Dubiard for creating the jelly (p. 85), Sugar Mountain,
Hawick, Scotland for supplying sweets (p. 152), Caroline Rose
at Rose & Co Apothecary for supplying the beauty remedies
(p. 104) and floral bath soaks (p. 161).

Contents

Introduction

The stately homes of England
How beautiful they stand!
Amidst their tall ancestral trees
O'er all the pleasant land...

FELICIA HEMANS

John Betjeman wrote, 'The Edwardian was the last age in which a rich man could afford to build himself a new and enormous country-house with a formal landscape garden, a lily pond and clipped hedges.'[1] Such country houses, which became the markers of society's 'Saturday to Monday' house parties (Monday being the significant day since anyone who could regularly be at leisure on a weekday must not *need* to earn a living), have come to epitomize the years between the Boer War and the Great War: the Edwardian era in which the privileges of the rich were made possible by the labour of their servants, an age when the inequalities of wealth and poverty were starkly delineated and the conventions of class were still rigidly, if complexly, defined.

The period from 1905 to 1914 is the subject of this book, involving a unique social experiment in Edwardian living. Manderston, a large, beguiling, classical-style house on the Scottish borders near Berwick-upon-Tweed, rebuilt by an Edwardian plutocrat in 1905, was the container for the experiment. The house, which still functions today as the family home of the descendants of the Edwardian owner was taken over by the television production company Wall to Wall. They chose a family, the Olliff-Coopers, to live 'upstairs', and recruited a dozen or so individuals who were prepared to live 'below stairs' as servants for three months.

However, this was to be no 'upstairs, downstairs' costume drama, but as faithful a re-creation as possible of the way in which such a wealthy household would have functioned in the Edwardian era. Manderston is virtually unchanged in all the essentials from that time, and it was possible to reconstruct the material conditions with authentic Edwardian cooking facilities, food, clothes, toiletries and remedies, the lavish entertainments and the endless, menial work, while the social 'rules of engagement' that framed Edwardian lives were replicated from household manuals, reference works and memoirs of the time.

The intention was to see how a set of twenty-first-century individuals, comprising a range of people from a variety of jobs and modern ways of life, would interrogate the Edwardian way of life, how they would cope with the various demands put upon them – whether cleaning grates or dealing with visiting cards – negotiating a very different set of social mores, and accepting or rejecting the rules and regulations that pertained both upstairs and down a century ago. The Edwardian country household was described by its contemporary admirers as a 'well-oiled machine'. This did not refer just to the organization of the household but to social arrangements too, the acceptance of hierarchies, of place and of class distinctions. How that 'machine' ran, how smooth was its operation and if and how and why grit got into the workings causing it to judder uncomfortably, or even to throw into reverse, is the subject of both this book and of the television series.

CHAPTER ONE

The Golden Years

Over the past century, the Edwardian era has assumed a crystalline fragility. The long decade is caressed with a nostalgia for time stood still, for innocence, and for a world lost; in the words of Samuel Hynes, it is viewed as a 'leisurely time when women wore picture hats and did not vote, when the rich were not ashamed to live conspicuously, and the sun really never set on the British flag'.[1]

The years from 1901 to 1914, which constitute what is now designated the Edwardian period, are of course an infinitely less static and more complex time than that suggested by the clichés of sunlit lawns, games of croquet and tennis, tinkling bone china teacups, twirling lace parasols, fox fur stoles and sprays of Parma violets, frock coats and tweed Norfolk jackets, shooting and boating parties, fabulous wealth and conspicuous display. Indeed, not all the summers were golden – rather the reverse. In 1901 the weather was near perfect, and in 1911 the sun shone almost continuously, but in the years between, summer skies were often grey and lawns were rained on rather more than they were anointed with the sun's rays.

An enthusiastic welcome for the Edwardian era: Sir John Olliff-Cooper (left),
Mr Jonathan, Master Guy, Miss Anson and Lady Olliff-Cooper.

The nostalgia for this era is occasioned largely by the contrast between the periods that preceded and succeeded the Edwardian years, and which seem to endow it with a shape and a completeness denied to other epochs. When Victoria died she was the longest-reigning monarch in British history, and the succession to the throne of her overweight, much-pleasured, many-mistressed fifty-nine-year old son, after more than half a lifetime spent in the wings, seemed to suggest a trepanning of the oppression of the Victorian era. 'The queen is dead of an apoplectic stroke and the great Victorian age is at an end,' noted the poet Wilfrid Scawen Blunt in his journal. 'This is notable news…it will mean great changes in the world.'[2]

On 4 August 1914 Britain declared war on Germany. Nothing that had happened before that event had made it possible to predict or imagine the harsh and terrible reality of the Great War that scythed a generation of young men, either in its almost unendurable longevity, or in its unprecedented and unrelenting carnage. As well as all the myriad other things that the First World War was, and represented, it became a distorting optic. It is impossible to focus the Edwardian period other than through this prism. This gives those years a sharp poignancy and an undercurrent of melancholy that is the very substance of nostalgia and regret. It makes their glitter appear tawdry at the same time as rendering it strangely and compellingly innocent.

The ex libris *of Lady Eveline Miller, wife of Sir James Miller who rebuilt Manderston, showing the house and its gardens.*

It is facile to envision the Edwardian period as unique, as wholly different from what preceded and succeeded it, and to focus on the detail is to dissolve the picture and reconfigure it in a different, more nuanced pattern, one of contrast and plurality. Much from the Victorian century persisted well into the Edwardian period and beyond: many of the currents of 'modernism' apparent after 1918 were clearly eddying before 1914. The First World War was less of a terminal event or a watershed, than an accelerator of change, or, in some instances, even an inhibiter of progress in the social, political and economic affairs of Britain. As Jose Harris points out in her survey of British social history of the period:

> Many features of pre-war society – changes in the structure of family life, the emergence of the labour movement, the challenge of feminism, the investigation of poverty, the rise of aesthetic modernism, and the growth of religious and moral uncertainty – seem to anticipate concerns of the later twentieth century…[while] other aspects of Edwardian life – the fashionable predominance of a leisured aristocracy, the sheer immensity of the poverty of the poor, the omnipresence of infant death, the restricted scope of central government, and the ingenuous confidence in the future of the British Empire (and indeed of European civilization in general) – seem so utterly remote from a later age that it is tempting to see them as part of a wholly vanished society…[3]

The word that echoes down the years from the Edwardian era is 'golden'. Gold glows, it gleams, it glitters, and it glistens. The rays of late summer afternoon sun burnish the landscape with a lingering golden glow that seems reluctant to fade. Gold is the hue of sunlight – and of display.

Gold conjures up secured wealth and fortunes of avarice; it connotes investment and acquisition, nuggets and money markets, the exchange of fungible assets rather than the stability of the settled old money of land. 'The Bank of England gives gold unconditionally and exchanges its notes for gold, therefore international trade can rely that all claims on London will be paid in gold, and as gold is, among all circulating mediums, the least subject to fluctuations, for this reason bills on England are negotiable everywhere...' explained a foreign investment banker to a meeting of the Institute of Bankers in March 1907.[4]

Gold has become a seed-metaphor for the Edwardian age. The historian of the City of London, David Kynaston, writing in the final decade of the twentieth century, calls the volume that covers the near-quarter of a century from 1890 until the outbreak of the First World War, *The Golden Years*. As he points out, one of the most popular books at the time by the author of *Wind in the Willows*, Kenneth Grahame, was *The Golden Age*, 'little though it touched on monetary matters'.[5] The 1911 edition of the *Encyclopaedia Britannica* explains that 'gold [has] been valued from the earliest ages on account of the permanence of its lustre...gold is the universal symbol of purity and value...when pure [it] is the most malleable of all metals. It is also extremely ductile.'

In the popular imagination, the golden image is still potent. The novelist and critic Marghanita Laski, who was born the year after the Edwardian age came to its tragic end, suggests:

> In so far as any single group in a community imposes a popular image of its domestic life on an age, for Edwardian England that group was the very rich...[leaving] a crude impression of an aristocracy and a plutocracy whose gay and often gaudy glitter was maintained by hierarchies of submissive servants, of homes adorned – as George, Duke of York [later to be George V] wrote to his wife in 1901 – 'with all that Art and Science can afford', the background for gargantuan dinner parties and gorgeous balls in the metropolis, and for weekend parties of near-feudal splendour in the country. Because it is the rich who impose this image and because it is the rich who can take fullest advantage of the new range of choices – social, technological, aesthetic – that the age has to offer, any account of Edwardian domestic life must give to the rich more attention than their numbers might seem to warrant.[6]

And it was 'the home adorned' that seemed to exemplify these riches. Property underpinned all other social institutions in Edwardian Britain, and mapping who owned what and how they acquired it and in what manner they held it became a preoccupation of the late Victorians' and Edwardians' curiosity about their nation's prosperity. The value of land, the traditional focus of property ownership, had been in decline, particularly after the agricultural depression of the 1880s. Britain's land had been worth around £2,000 million in the late 1870s; by 1914 it had fallen steadily to a little over £1,000 million, and by then it constituted only around a twelfth of the national wealth compared to a quarter some forty years earlier. In contrast, the value of housing and business premises rose from around £1,000 million in 1865 to nearly £3,300 million in 1909.[7] And in the place of land, other forms of property came to embody the indices of wealth, the bestowal of rights (such as the vote), privileges and citizenship, and connotations of thrift and of moral rectitude that had previously adhered to it.

Despite the increase in taxation as part of the spread of the tentacles of the administrative state, a huge amount of property remained in private hands – and much was concentrated in a few. The age of opulence was an exclusive one. In 1905, the aptly named economist, Sir Leo Chiozza Money, explained that 'more than one third of the entire wealth of the United Kingdom is enjoyed by one thirtieth of its people…the wealth left by a few rich people who die approaches in aggregate property possessed by the whole of the living poor'. Four Edwardian plutocrats who died between 1906 and 1911 left estates valued in excess of £5 million (somewhere around £300 million in today's money) which were fortunes without precedence. Yet of the 343,000 deaths in England and Wales in 1901, only 33,400 (17 per cent of the population) left anything at all other than a few chattels.[8] More recent calculations by historians, far from contradicting these Edwardian figures, have suggested that the situation was if anything more acutely unequal. These suggest that for the years 1911 to 1913, 10 per cent of the adult British population owned 92 per cent of the nation's wealth, making Edwardian Britain one of the most unequal societies in early-twentieth-century Europe in terms of access to property, and possibly (though this is harder to determine) less equal than at any other time in Britain's history.[9]

And the Edwardian rich in many cases were of a different order, as a character in W. H. Mallock's satire *The Old Order Changes* makes clear: 'You, the gentleman of the country, the old landed families…you no longer stand on your own proper foundations. You are reduced financially to mere hangers-on of the

Deliveries for the big house: vegetables await the kitchen maid's attention.

bourgeoisie. Your material splendour, which once had real meaning, is still, no doubt, maintained. But how?…The yellow stucco of ninety years ago has given place to the towers of a Gothic castle…[but only because] his Grace…has five million dollars' worth of railway stock in America…You could no longer live like seigneurs if you were not half tradesmen.'[10] The new plutocrats were outrunning the aristocrats in the gold stakes with money made from finance and investment, fortunes built on trade and manufacture and spent on property not in the form of land from which to draw income, but on building or acquiring or extending houses as showcases for their wealth and the fabulous lifestyle it enabled. 'In King Edward's reign,' wrote John Betjeman, the poet, nostalgist and conserver of things Victorian and Edwardian, 'most British people regarded architecture as an expensive luxury. They liked expensive luxuries.'[11] And there were plenty of luxurious houses, many 'with an Osbert Lancaster touch to them',[12] such as those built for the Rothschilds at Waddesdon, Mentmore and Tring; Château Impney in Worcestershire built for a salt manufacturer 'in the style of a grand hotel'; Overstone Park in Northamptonshire built for a banker (or rather his wife's fancy) which Pevsner cited as an example of 'asymmetricalissime', and of which the owner himself was not proud. 'I am utterly ashamed of it,' he raged. 'I grieve to think I shall hand such an abortion to my successors… [We might as well] have undertaken to whitewash a blackamoor'; and there was Alfred Rothschild's Halton House in Buckinghamshire which was described as 'memorably vulgar…a combination of a French Château and a gambling house…gaudily decorated…hideous…the sense of lavish wealth thrust up your nose',[13] though its owner seemed pleased enough as he trotted round his home in a dog cart pulled by two zebras.

These plutocratic residences may not all have been architectural gems: Lord Leverhulme employed half a dozen different architects to design Thornton Manor in Cheshire, admitting that his taste ran to a preference for 'Georgian dining rooms as the rooms in which to give large dinners. For small dining rooms I prefer Tudor. For drawing rooms I prefer what is called the Adam style; for entrance halls the Georgian.'[14] But however eclectic, even vulgar, the aesthetic of such establishments, leisured lives were congenially spent in them hosting fabulous balls and fancy dress parties, shoots at which game rained down in convoys, more than ample breakfasts, formal lunches and multi-course dinners, with champagne awash 'at moments when a glass of barley-water might have been acceptable' as J. B. Priestley observed.[15] There was an indulgence of (or turning a blind eye to) a degree of sexual licence (and sexual double standards), an enthusiasm for hunting, shooting, fishing, boating and gambling. And to keep this life afloat, a troop of servants labouring below stairs and toiling in the grounds was a necessity.

But, as are most societies at most times, Edwardian society was in a state of flux. The era was to witness the election of a Liberal government that was to mount a gradual assault on 'unproductive wealth' in the interest of the social welfare of the many; the development of the Labour Party, representative of the interest of the working man in Parliament; industrial unrest and the consolidation of trade union rights; the arrival of the 'new woman' with her demand for education, the vote and changed economic and legal status; the stirring of nationalist movements throughout the Empire, and its implacable demands in Ireland; threats to the balance of power which, exacerbated by the ultimately bruising experience of the Boer War, reconfigured British foreign policy in Europe, and would bring about the Great War.

The Edwardian country house, that quintessential icon in the gilded portrait of early-twentieth-century England, did not escape the breezes of change. As the economic historian Martin Daunton has written, 'The tax system is a very effective way of articulating assumptions about the market, consumption and social structures.'[16] In the mid 1850s Gladstone had recognized that 'the operation of income tax is severe on intelligence and skill as compared to property',[17] and had always hoped to be able to abolish income tax and transfer the burden of taxation to death duties which would have hit the landed estates hardest. In 1890, the American economist Henry George's influential work, *Poverty and Progress*, argued that land was failing to pay its proper contribution to the national community. What was required was an increase in taxation on property and on unearned income. 'For many years,' remarked the son of the Chancellor of the Exchequer, Sir William Harcourt, 'the budgets have been more or less rich men's budgets; it is time we had a poor man's budget' – and the 1894 budget consolidated the duties paid on death in ways that penalized large estates. One per cent was levied on estates of £100 to £500, and this rose to a maximum of 8 per cent on estates over £1 million; increases in land value where no improvements had been made were taxed, and graduated income tax rose. It was not as powerful an assault on property as it might have appeared at the time, and it was not until Lloyd George's 1909 'people's budget' or, as he called it, 'war budget…for raising money to wage implacable warfare against poverty and squalidness' that most of the tax increases fell on the wealthy and unearned income, but it was a substantial straw in the wind for the wealthy and the propertied.

A silver stairway to a golden age: the staircase at Manderston which prior to the First World War took three men three days to dismantle, polish and put back.

In addition 'the servant problem' was beginning to make itself manifest. Between the census of 1891 and that of 1911, although the number of domestic servants in England, Wales and Scotland fell only marginally from 1,949,606 to 1,822,169[18] (in a ratio of roughly two-thirds female servants to one-third male), there were far more families seeking servants than there were servants to fill the vacancies, and after 1911, the situation got worse – as far as employers were concerned.[19] It was, in fact, a problem that affected the middle-classes more than the rich, but it was a potent augury of changes in society. In Vita Sackville-West's *roman- à-clef, The Edwardians*, this was portended when Wickenden, the head carpenter at Chevron, comes to see the young master, Sebastian; his 'eyes swimming with tears', he says:

> 'It's my boy, your Grace – Frank, my eldest. Your Grace knows that I was to have taken him into the [carpenter's] shops this year. Well, he won't come. He wants to go – I hardly know how to tell your Grace. He wants to go into the motor trade instead. Says it's the coming thing. Now your Grace knows…that my father and his father before him were in the shops, and I looked to my boy to take my place after I was gone. Same as your Grace's son, if I may make the comparison. I never thought to see a son of mine leave Chevron so long as he was fit to stay there.'[20]

The Edwardian country house, while not sheltering the poorest in the land (indeed, it was frequently pointed out that most domestic servants were better off than their counterparts in industry, retail or commerce since they had room, board and in some cases uniforms provided), can be seen as an exemplar of many of the features and tensions of those years. It serves as an index of the shift in financial and thus political and social power, the shift from old to new money, and the social conventions and aspirations that accompanied these. It exemplifies the change in the perception of aristocratic property as being a local landmark, a part of the national heritage and thus of legitimate interest to the public, to functioning increasingly as a private home, excluding all but the invited.[21] It regularly staged a variety of occasions of ostentatious consumption, it formed a staging post in the social circuit of the wealthy, it made manifest the evolution of class as a powerful social category with the calcification of social distinction not just between masters, mistresses and servants, but also among gradations of servants. The Edwardian country house thus stands as a micro-society by which to describe and interrogate fundamental aspects of Edwardian life.

The genuine article: Christine Mason, a Scottish Edwardian parlour maid.

But though the buildings and their artefacts may still be extant, the residents are long gone. The project of the Channel 4 series, *The Edwardian Country House*, was thus to people as authentic a house as possible, representative of the home and habits of an Edwardian plutocrat, with modern-day 'explorers'. Dressing in the clothes, eating the food, and using only the things that would have been available at the time, guided by the conventions and mores of such a society and regulated by the rules inscribed in contemporary memoirs and manuals, a collection of twenty-first-century individuals would move into an Edwardian country house for three months and live out an experiment in Edwardian living to the best of their ability. There would be a real family upstairs serviced by an appropriate number of 'servants' downstairs, and each would strive to absorb and re-create their understanding of Edwardian society within the parameters provided by the house and its contents, and the recollected experiences of the early years of the 1900s.

After a great deal of searching, considering and rejecting, the house was selected: Manderston, near Duns in Berwickshire close to the Scotland–England border. And after even more advertising, reading, sifting, meeting and interviewing, a family, the Olliff-Coopers, was invited to live upstairs, a 'tutor' was engaged, and twelve (later to rise to thirteen) individuals from different parts of the country and from a variety of walks of life, none of whom had ever met before, were engaged to work downstairs. The experiment began on 21 August 2001.

The house is marvellous, it's wonderful, it is simply better than anyone could possibly have imagined. It's so *huge*,' enthused the elegantly attired Lady Olliff-Cooper, as the gleaming Napier swept her and her family through the heavy wrought-iron gates and drove slowly up the long drive to Manderston, an imposing neo-classical country house set in 56 acres of formal gardens and parkland on the Scottish borders.

As the car scrunched to a halt on the gravel, the front doors opened and a pewter-haired butler emerged, followed by two footmen. Mr Edgar stood at the top of the steps to the porticoed entrance to welcome his new master, Sir John Olliff-Cooper, while the two footmen hurried down the stone steps to open the car door and assist the family to alight. The Napier had been built in 1903, and at the time was in the same league as a Rolls Royce or a Lanchester. A seven-seater with a six-cylinder, 45-horsepower engine, it is capable of a maximum speed of 40 mph; it sold for £495 plus an extra £25 for the hood.

The disembarkation did not go quite as smoothly as it would have done in a period drama since the family were as yet not fully conversant with the niceties of Edwardian etiquette and precedence, and all were anxious to get a closer look at the stately pile that was to be their home for the next three months. But soon Sir John, his wife Anna, their sons Mr Jonathan (known to the family as Jonty) and Master Guy, and Lady Olliff-Cooper's sister, Miss Avril Anson, managed to scramble out, and stood gazing in awe at the façade of Manderston, which has more the dimensions of a terraced street than a family home.

Exploring the territory: the Olliff-Cooper family stroll in the grounds of the Edwardian Country House.

*The butler, Mr Edgar, welcomes the Olliff-Cooper family
to their new Edwardian domain.*

Gathering up their skirts, the ladies followed Sir John up the steps and were led into the house. Mr Edgar introduced them to the waiting staff, who lined up to give a bow or bob, before conducting the family through the marble-floored and -pillared hall, opening doors to offer the family glimpses into a bewildering array of grand rooms all 'filled with wonderful antiques', as Lady Olliff-Cooper gasped. There was the dining room with its ornate ceiling featuring a relief of Mars, the Roman god of war, in the centre and with the largest private collection of 'Blue John' (*bleu-jaune*), a valuable, semi-precious stone mined only in Derbyshire) in Scotland – urns, obelisks and candelabras – arrayed on the mantelpiece and sideboards. A full-sized slate and green baize billiard table dominates the library, the walls of which are lined with leather-bound volumes. The romantic ballroom is decorated with panels depicting Venus, goddess of love, with cherub-filled roundels at the corners and a ceiling showing the sun god, Apollo, with his cupids, from which hangs a pair of magnificent Italian crystal chandeliers. Finally, the Olliff-Coopers trooped into the drawing room with its pastel-tinted Adam ceiling, and fireplace over which hangs a Madonna and child painted by Murillo, where the footmen served them afternoon tea.

The sense of awe that the Olliff-Coopers felt on first seeing the house that was to be their home was similar to the impressions of a young reporter on the local Berwickshire newspaper as, bored with dancing, he had wandered round Manderston on the night of a 'house-warming' ball held at the house in 1905:

> You roam say for an hour, through halls, in and out of rooms. Through vestibules and along corridors, up superb staircases and through more corridors and chambers. Returning, you are startled to find new beauties crowding themselves on you from out-of-the-way corners – places that you have missed – and you get lost, and you want to begin all over again. Presently, it dawns upon you that it is absurd to attempt to do the place in an hour, and that it is necessary to do it in instalments, a little at a time in order to appreciate in any adequate way the exquisite treasures with which the mansion is literally deluged.[22]

In that year, 1905, the Russo-Japanese war was raging, and there were already signs of unrest in the great Russian Empire that would erupt into revolution a little more than a decade later: 22 January 1905 was to go down in history as Russia's 'Bloody Sunday', when troops of Tsar Nicholas II fired on peaceful protesters led by a young priest, Father Gabon, who were making their way to the Winter

Palace in St Petersburg with a petition for the Tsar – 500 strikers were killed. In June that year mutinous sailors aboard the battleship *Potemkin* attacked their officers and, shouting 'Liberty, Liberty', threw them into the Black Sea and ran the Red Flag up the pole.

At home Edward VII was on the throne. His mother, Queen Victoria, had died in January 1901 aged eighty-one, and the next year Edward was crowned, king at last after the longest-ever reign of a British monarch: sixty-three years. The accession of the late-middle-aged playboy King promised a transformation from the 'dullness and decorum' of the Victorian court into the 'glitter and vivacity' of the Edwardian era. There was certainly little sign that the 'smart set' of plutocrats and socialites (sometimes of dubious social origin) that had surrounded Edward when he was Prince of Wales would be likely to moderate their behaviour – an endless round of pleasure, comprising parties, balls, theatre visits, dinners, country house weekends, gambling, cards, horse racing, illicit love affairs – now that he was king. There was political change afoot too. In December 1905 the King invited a lowland Scottish Liberal, Sir Henry Campbell Bannerman, to form a government after the resignation of the Conservative Prime Minister, Arthur Balfour, his party in disarray over tariff reform. The following February the Liberals were to have a landslide victory at the general election, reducing Tory representation in the Commons from 401 to 156 seats, and – a portent of things to come – the Labour Representation Committee, the forerunner of the Labour Party, led by Keir Hardie, won 30 seats and trebled its share of the vote.

The year 1905 saw the completion of the rebuilding of Manderston – hence the celebratory ball. It had taken two years, and when it was finished the house was a masterpiece, a near-flawless example of the finest Edwardian craftsmanship, and a monument to the riches and excess of those gilded years

An Edwardian vista: the Robert Adam-inspired hall at Manderston.

between the death of Victoria, who symbolized the bourgeois propriety and sober industry of the nineteenth century, and the Armageddon of the Great War. The first house on the site, near Berwick-upon-Tweed, just over the English–Scottish border in fine fishing country, was built in the late 1780s for a Mr Dalhousie Watherstone. Watherstone had bought the land from an East India Company surgeon, John Swinton (Swinton village is a few miles from Manderston). The architect was either Alexander Gilkie or John White (drawings by both of a proposed house exist).[23] In 1853 the square, stone house was sold to Richard Miller, and on his death his younger brother, William, bought the estate from Richard's widow for £78,050. Descendants of William have lived in Manderston ever since, and his great-great-grandson, Lord Palmer, is the present owner.

William Miller was a rich man. He had made his money in the Baltic trade in hemp and herrings, and after spending sixteen years in St Petersburg as the British Consul, he returned to Manderston and was elected as Liberal Member of Parliament, first for Leith and later for his home county of Berwickshire. More of a constituency politician than one active in the House, Miller was created a baronet by the then Prime Minister, William Gladstone, in 1874 in gratitude for the political dinners he hosted in the Liberal interest.

The rebuilding of Manderston, the Edwardian Country House, took two years from 1903 to 1905.

Sir John and Lady Olliff-Cooper

John Olliff-Cooper (or John Cooper as he is more usually known), a former Lloyd's 'name', has run his own successful flooring company for the past thirty years. Aged fifty-six, he has a love of the Edwardian period stretching back many years, and is a connoisseur of Edwardian fishing – restoring antique fishing rods is one of his hobbies. 'I am completely 1905 between the ears,' he admits. But in his twenty-first-century mode, John writes on fishing and travel for an Internet magazine. He has two adult sons from a previous marriage, who did not take part in the project, though one of them managed to pay a couple of visits to his temporarily ennobled father and stepmother.

Anna Olliff-Cooper, who is fifty-two, works part-time as a doctor in the casualty department of Southampton General Hospital. She also runs the family home (in the New Forest in Hampshire), looks after her two sons and in her 'spare' time is studying for a philosophy degree with the Open University. She was quite clear why she had wanted to take part in the experiment: she was at something of a crossroads in her life and had begun to feel that she was on a treadmill of relentless hard work. She felt exhausted most of the time and yet somehow unfulfilled: she desperately wanted a change. When she saw the advertisement for people to live in the Edwardian Country House for three months, it seemed like the answer. She thought she would apply to be a servant – after all, she thought ruefully, she was pretty used to looking after other people. But a moment's further thought made her realize that that just wouldn't be possible. Guy was only nine; he still needed her. But if they *all* went as the family upstairs…

Sir William had already started to enlarge the modest Georgian house, adding a Doric *porte-cochère* to the existing Ionic pillared entrance porch, a French Renaissance-style mansard roof and additional bedrooms for the servants.[24] Tragically, his heir, William, choked to death on a cherry stone while still a schoolboy at Eton in 1874, so on Sir William's demise, the baronetcy, the estate and the fortune all passed to his second son, James, who was twenty-four at the time.

Sir James was the perfect country landowner of the 'new money' variety: a career soldier (though he had failed the 'examination' for the Blues which probably indicated that he was not out of the top drawer socially), he was also an excellent shot, good at sport, a fine horseman and generally popular – 'Lucky Jim' was the nickname his friends gave him. He was also, as the magazine *Vanity Fair* pointed out in 1890, 'one of the most wealthy commoners in the country [his horse racing activities added a total of £118,000 – over £7 million in today's money if one uses a rather crude and not entirely accurate

Sir William Miller Bt. M.P., the wealthy merchant who bought Manderston from his brother, and left it to his son...

multiplier of 60 – to James's inheritance] and a bachelor' – a very eligible young man indeed. Predictably, he married well. The bride he took in 1893 was the Hon. Eveline Curzon, the fourth (and supposedly the prettiest) daughter of Lord Scarsdale (who could trace his family lineage back to the Norman Conquest). Her older brother was George Nathaniel Curzon, who was Viceroy of India from 1899 to 1905.

Lady Miller's father's seat was Kedleston Hall in Derbyshire, a magnificent eighteenth-century house designed by the architect Robert Adam. Sir James was determined that his new wife would have a home to match her father's. Indeed, when he had ventured to Kedleston to ask for Eveline's hand in marriage, he had replied to the traditional paternal inquiry: 'Can you keep my daughter in the manner to which she has become accustomed?' in the affirmative, adding quietly, 'perhaps even a little better'.

On 27 May 1901, Sir James, by now an officer in the 11th Hussars, returned from fighting in the Boer War. His route from the railway station was decked with flowers, and by the South Lodge entrance had been erected an evergreen arch from which hung a golden M for Manderston (and Miller) framed by tulips. Here the horses were uncoupled and the carriage pulled triumphantly up the beech-lined drive by a team of his tenants led by members of the Volunteer Band from Duns, the nearby small town. Looking afresh at his rather modest home and mindful of his promise, Sir James set about making his boast to his father-in-law a reality. The next month he engaged the services of one of Scotland's foremost architects, John Kinross, the son of a Stirling coach builder who had served part of his apprenticeship with an Edinburgh firm, Wardrop and Reid, which specialized in Scottish baronial homes.

When he was twenty-five, Kinross had borrowed £250 from his mother and set off for Italy, where he spent two years studying Renaissance architecture and immersing himself in Italian culture, life and language. It was here that he acquired a cosmopolitan outlook that he was never to lose, and his 'inherent aristocracy of taste' flourished.[25] On his return, Kinross paid back his mother (with interest) and published a limited edition of a distillation of his Italian architectural education, *Details from Italian Buildings Chiefly Renaissance* in 1882. This volume bought Kinross to the attention of the eccentric third Marquess of Bute, a scholar, linguist, devout Catholic and one of the richest men in Britain, who owned some 117,000 acres. At only eighteen years of age, Bute had become the patron of the architect William Burges, the foremost exponent of the Gothic Revival in Britain and designer of Cardiff Castle and Castell Coch. Burges died in 1881 and Bute transferred his patronage to Kinross, providing him with commissions for the next fifteen years, including the restoration of a priory, an abbey, a friary, and of Falkland Palace which was unfinished on Bute's death in 1900.

In 1901, a year after his patron's death, came the commission from Sir James Miller's to rebuild Manderston. Miller knew Kinross already. The architect had built a neo-baroque house for the baronet's sister at nearby Thurston in the 1890s, then was commissioned to design a boathouse at the edge of the lake at Manderston to celebrate the marriage of James and Eveline; and in 1895 he had designed a palatial stable block for the Manderston horses. Before starting the new work, Miller sent Kinross to Kedleston to see what he had in mind. When Kinross returned with his sketches, he began to draw up plans to transform the rather austere Georgian mansion into a neo-classical masterpiece to rival – if not surpass – his client's father-in-law's home (though on a smaller scale). It was to be grand enough for formal entertaining and large enough for the small army of servants that such lavish hospitality required. There was sufficient space for twenty-two live-in servants, and others would have been brought in for special occasions. To Kinross's enquiry about what the budget for the rebuilding was to be, Sir James replied airily, 'It doesn't really matter.'[26] It must have seemed the ideal brief for an ambitious architect – but could have been a disaster of excess in less sensitive hands.

The house was to be in the Georgian style, in tune with the fashion of the time as well as in imitation of Adam's Kedleston, and it was also influenced by French neo-classicism. Kinross removed the 1870s additions and built in the style of the eighteenth century. In effect, he combined 'scholarship and eclecticism to make something new',[27] producing an Edwardian version of a Georgian house for Sir James. It 'perfectly represents', as J. Mordaunt Crook has written, 'the Classicizing (or socializing) of new money'.[28] The whole main part of the house was reconstructed: one room was added, others enlarged; a new wing was added for gentlemen with 'bachelors' bedrooms', a gun room and office; the old stables to the west of the house were converted into a laundry and servants' quarters; and the attic storey (also for servants' accommodation) was rebuilt. The original south front overlooking the garden remained but was refaced, while the north entrance façade was demolished and the roof removed and rebuilt to deepen the house.[29] The coat of arms of the Miller family is over the main entrance door. It bears the family motto *Omne Bonum Superne* – All good comes from above – which, as the guide book points out, is a generous acknowledgement, since the fortune that allowed for this building came from herring caught in the deep.

The interior of Manderston owes a great deal to the Adam revival, too – though the arrangement of the rooms was specified for Edwardian entertainment rather than for Georgian verisimilitude, with a ballroom and drawing room of identical size adjacent so that the double doors between them could be flung open for dancing. The

Sir James Miller who gave his architect, John Kinross, a free rein – and an open cheque book – to rebuild his country house heritage.

walls of both were covered in primrose and white, the racing colours under which Sir James's horse, Sainfoin, won the Derby in 1890 – at odds of 25 to one. Rock Sand, sired by Sainfoin won the Triple Crown (the Two Thousand Guineas, Derby and St Leger) in 1903 – the year that the rebuilding of Manderston had started. The entrance hall was lined in marble, as was the much larger hall at Kedleston, and the pattern on the marble floor was identical. The ceilings in particular were in the style of Adam, the most magnificent of which adorned the drawing room, the ballroom (a replica of the dining room ceiling at Kedleston) and the dining room. Much of the furniture is a quotation from Robert Adam's designs, from the heroic busts adorning the bookcases in the library to the soaring organ pipes in the hall, while the frieze in the hall was derived from Adam's design for the entrance hall at Syon House in Middlesex. Indeed, so indebted to Kedleston was Manderston (albeit constructed on a more modest scale) that when Lady Miller's brother, Lord Curzon, was recovering from a motoring accident, he elected to spend his six-month convalescence at Manderston, and gave his sister an old English well – which she sited in the formal Japanese garden – in thanks.[30]

As the eighteenth century gave a 'civilizing' lexicon to *nouveau riche* British taste, so too did a European aesthetic. This was absorbed both from the art and architecture of Renaissance Italy, a stop on the Grand Tour that young aristocrats undertook to complete their education, or the excesses of *Ancien Régime* France, and both styles are found at Manderston. Kinross, of course, had his own particular portfolio of Italian Renaissance influences. The circular morning room, with its views of the

The funeral of Sir James Miller (1906). The wealthy owner of Manderston left
a year's salary in his will to all his servants and employees.

Cheviot Hills, is probably modelled on a similar room in the Palazzo Massimo Colonne in Rome by Peruzzi; the radiator grilles in the dining room and below the organ case are copied from Verrochio's Medici tomb in the church of San Lorenzo in Florence; and the large, translucent alabaster vases set in the arches outside the dining room, placed to reflect the setting sun, reprise the blind, semicircular archways of San Miniato al Monte (also in Florence). It was, however, from pre-revolutionary France that Kinross took his most flamboyant reference, and one that trumpeted Sir James's lack of concern with budgetary constraints. The cantilevered silver (plated) staircase that leads from the marble hall to the first-floor bedrooms is an almost carbon copy of the staircase in the Petit Trianon at Versailles planned by Madame de Pompadour, the courtesan and mistress of Louis XV.

But sadly, Sir James did not have long to enjoy his splendid new house: just three months after Manderston's completion, he caught a chill travelling from London to Scotland on the overnight sleeper, insisted on hunting the next day, the chill turned to pneumonia, and he died aged forty-one in January 1906.

In 2001 it was Manderston that Caroline Ross Pirie, the series producer and director from Wall to Wall, chose as the laboratory for the great 'Edwardian experience' to be filmed for Channel 4. In the two earlier series, *The 1900 House* and *The 1940s House*, when modern-day families 'lived history' by bringing their twenty-first-century experience and sensibilities to the material conditions of the past, Channel 4 had purchased the houses to be used, and experts had restored them to the original condition of the period, buying contemporaneous furniture, equipment and artefacts before the Bowlers moved into the 1900 house in Charlton in South London, and the Hymers to the 1940s house in West Wickham, Kent.

With Manderston it would be different. Manderston is a stately house that is open to the public to view as it was when it was rebuilt in 1905: the decoration is as it was when John Kinross had finished, the furniture and works of art as they were when Sir James and Lady Miller selected them. But it is also a home, lived in by descendants of Sir James Miller, Lord Palmer (of the biscuit-manufacturing family Huntley and Palmer), his wife Cornelia and their three children, who vivify the Edwardian setting. The task for Wall to Wall was thus one of assemblage. They would be using only part of the house for the programme to make it a feasible proposition for the 'servants' who were to be employed, yet the production designer, Maggie Gray, was able to plunder the whole 109-roomed house for the things she needed to recreate Manderston exactly as it would have been in 1905, sourcing extras that had long ago disappeared like a silver phonograph in the ballroom and hip baths for the servants' ablutions.

The social historian and curator of the Armley Mills Museum in Leeds, Daru Rooke, who had advised on the 1900 house and who had recommended Manderston, travelled to Scotland to help Maggie and the chief researcher on the project, Mark Ball, reconstruct artefacts and plan the layout of the interiors of rooms that had long fallen out of use, such as the ice room for storing blocks of ice before gas and electric refrigerators, and renovate the huge coal, and wood-burning cooking range that had long been superseded by modern stoves. Daru cast his historian's eye over what was being used in the house today and banished vacuum cleaners (unusual before the First World War), replacing them with bristle brushes and Ewbank carpet sweepers; he insisted that detergent and scouring powder should be binned, and poured away washing-up liquid, replacing such modern materials with soda crystals and Monkey Brand soap which contained sand and was used instead of scouring powder; this was too harsh for washing clothes, for which soft green soap was to be used. Plate powder and tins of Brasso were imported for the endless tasks of cleaning cutlery, condiments and ornaments, and boxes of matches, candles and tapers stacked up, though Manderston had electric light in 1905.

Sadly, the great drying racks in the basement laundry were damaged beyond repair, so it was decided that the dirty clothes and household linen would be packed in wicker laundry baskets and sent

The upstairs family: Sir John and Lady Olliff-Cooper seated with Master Guy.
Behind the sofa stand Miss Anson and Mr Jonathan.

out to a local laundry as would have happened in many Edwardian houses. Maggie was delighted to find piles of linen – sheets, pillow cases and tablecloths – stacked neatly in a linen cupboard off 'pug's parlour', though much of it was yellowing and too fragile for the robust wear that three months' daily use would subject it to, and had to be replaced. Crystal glasses for wine, port, champagne, aperitifs and digestifs were supplied from the Stuart Crystal company's collection and lined up by size in the housekeeper's pantry. Fine china for the upstairs table was supplied by the china manufacturers Wedgwood – Rococco for daily use, and Madeleine for grand occasions – and white earthenware crockery selected for the servants' daily use. Houseplants popular in Edwardian times were placed in urns and cachepots. There were palms for upstairs while downstairs wide-leafed aspidistras were a particular favourite, and were hardy enough to survive the gloomy rooms in the basement.

This was the habitat that the Olliff-Cooper's, a busy, professional family from Hampshire, was to 'inherit' and inhabit for three months. It was not simply the house and all the accoutrements, the grounds, the stables, the dairy, the gardener's house – they were to assume the lifestyle of a very wealthy Edwardian family. They would wear the clothes of the era, eat the food that would have been served, and be constrained by what would have been available, whether for washing their hair, medicating minor illnesses, or attending to personal hygiene and appearance. The novels that they would find in the house would be only those popular at the time. They would navigate the wider world with the help of early-twentieth-century magazines and newspapers. The family would have a fast learning curve of Edwardian social etiquette, and given the wealth and status they had acquired (Mr Olliff-Cooper was elevated to the baronetcy for the duration) and a house run by servants, their social relations would be calibrated entirely differently from the ways they were when the family first arrived at Manderston. The Olliff-Coopers would move differently, talk in different voices and of other topics, their recreations and amusements would be entirely changed and their responsibilities of another order altogether. They would have obligations to themselves, to each other, to their household and to the local community that would frame their time in the Edwardian Country House.

But it was not just the 'future' from which the Olliff-Coopers had been transported, it was also from the past. If the Edwardian period seems in so many ways like another country to us at the start of the next century, it seemed something of a new terrain for those living through it, cut off in style, manner, mores and expectations from the decades that had preceded the accession of Edward VII. Indeed, it was the last time a historical period has become known by the name of its monarch. There has been no second Georgian age and the 'new Elizabethan Age' never caught currency. We name later times as decades – the twenties, the thirties, the sixties.

Manderston epitomized the Edwardian era. It was built for it. The great house was again to host a leisured, privileged, gracious life that has now passed. And this was the world that the Olliff-Coopers were to inhabit for three months. How would the family translate to a century ago? How would they find living in one of the grandest houses in Scotland? How would three over-busy adults and two fully occupied young people fill their days with none of the imperatives and pressures of their daily lives in the twenty-first century? How would they manage with the clothes, the food, the social expectations of a wealthy Edwardian family? And above all, in a time of cheap labour when the luxury of one class was made possible by the work of others – 'hands' in factories and servants in domestic establishments – how would *they* find living with servants? Would they find it embarrassing to be waited on hand and foot? To expect their every whim to be met, their orders obeyed instantly by people whom, if they met them in their ordinary lives, they would recognize as equals? Or would they find it all too easy to slip into a master/ or mistress/servant relationship?

CHAPTER TWO

Below Stairs

A week before the Olliff-Coopers swept up the drive to the Edwardian Country House, a horse-drawn wagonette had bumped through the North Gate and made its way towards the house. Sitting on the slatted wooden seats were three 'servants' arriving to take up their positions in the 'big house'. As they clutched the boxes that contained their worldly possessions in one hand and hung on to the sides of their jolting transport with the other, the maids craned for their first glimpse of the house that was to be their home for the next three months. As they rounded a bend, the imposing façade of Manderston hove into view. 'It's *huge,*' gasped Jessica, who had come to take up an appointment as second housemaid. It was exactly the same reaction that Lady Olliff-Cooper was to have at her first sight of Manderston, but then Jessica added, 'And we've got to clean all that!'

Below stairs at the Edwardian Country House. The servants assemble in order of status: the upper servants, the butler, lady's maid, housekeeper and the chef, at the front, the lower servants ranged behind.

As if to emphasize the difference that the house represented to those 'upstairs' and those 'downstairs', the wagonette sheered sharply right away from the raked gravel drive that led to the porticoed front entrance, and drove under an arch to clatter through the brick courtyard. It drew up in front of the plain wooden door that led down a flight of stone steps to the basement: the servants' quarters.

The footmen, Rob and Charlie, hurried out to help the maids clamber down. Smoothing down their skirts and cramming on their bonnets, Antonia, the kitchen maid, Becky, the first housemaid, and Jessica gazed around the courtyard, glimpsing marble statuary through an upstairs window, before following Rob and Charlie down the stairs to the gloom of their new habitat.

Just like the Olliff-Coopers upstairs, those downstairs at Manderston had been among almost 7,000 people who had seen the advertisement calling for volunteers for the Edwardian Country House and sent for further information – and suprisingly far more had wanted to try life below

Dressing the part: the second footman, Rob, adjusts the bow tie of the first footman, Charlie.

stairs than above. They had been attracted not by a life of luxury and leisure, but by curiosity about one that held out the prospect of unremitting hard work, of discipline, and of learning a new vocabulary of service and obedience. According to the 1901 census, the servant class was among the largest group of the total population of some 32 million in Britain, and of these over 100,000 were aged between ten and fifteen years,[1] the youngest being the age of Master Guy.

In his account of domestic service, Frank Dawes quotes the example of the Duke of Portland who, at the beginning of the twentieth century, had an establishment that comprised a steward, wine butler, under butler, groom of chambers, four footmen, two steward room's footmen, master of the servants' hall, two pageboys, head chef, second chef, head baker, second baker, head kitchen maid, two under kitchen maids, sundry vegetable maids and scullery maids, head stillroom maid, hall porter, two hall boys, kitchen porter, and six odd-job men. He also employed a head housekeeper, a valet, a personal maid for the Duchess and another for his daughter, head nursery governess, French governess, schoolroom footman, and fourteen housemaids; and there was a head window cleaner and two under window cleaners. Outside, some thirty servants were employed in the stables and the same number were at work in the newly installed garage, while other servants worked in the grounds, the laundry, the home farm and the gymnasium. The steam-heating plant and electricity generator required a staff of six engineers and four firemen, and the newly installed telephone exchange in the house required a telephone clerk and assistant plus a telegrapher. The whole empire was guarded by three nightwatchmen.[2]

Such an establishment was at the summit of the servant-employing class, and few households matched such a vast number of servants, or such a specialized calibration of roles. Indeed, the majority of servants were likely to be employed in middle-class villas where a cook, a maid and a scullery maid

The housekeeper

Jean Davies, who is sixty, learned her housekeeping skills growing up during the Second World War. She is an enthusiastic cook, gardener and poultry-, goat- and donkey-keeper. For a time she and her husband, Peter, ran a silver service restaurant but now they specialize in 'living history', going round to primary schools showing children all about life in nineteenth-century England. She felt that taking the job of an Edwardian housekeeper would be 'a fantastic experience'. Peter too was interested, and had applied to be butler at Manderston – though such a couple would be unusual in an Edwardian household. She did not relish their separation, but it would be worth it, she kept reminding herself in the first few days when it all seemed very strange and she felt extremely homesick. 'It will be an opportunity for a total immersion in the Edwardian experience.'

Mrs Davies was unfazed by the size of Manderston – 'It reminds me very much of Tatton Park near us in Cheshire, where Peter and I have done demonstrations' – but 'I *am* rather daunted about all the work that's going to be involved.' She had also heard that the chef was French and she knew all about French temperaments in the kitchen from her days in the restaurant business. She wondered how she would get on with the butler – would he be domineering? And then there was the question of discipline, which, for the female staff, was firmly in her domain. 'The young people are going to find it very hard, but that's how it was in Edwardian times. My goodness, I'll keep them busy. But I hope that I can be a person the young ones can turn to if they are in any sort of trouble, or want some advice.'

would be the most the family could afford. Employment was most sought after in the grandest establishments, though. It was not simply the prestige of the name and how it would look on a servant's 'character' (reference). It was the opportunity to work in often beautiful surroundings and to enjoy the camaraderie of a downstairs colony, rather than the intense loneliness of a 'maid of all work' or 'cook general' in a lower-middle-class household.

On arrival at the Edwardian Country House, the maids' first duty was an interview with the housekeeper, Mrs Davies. As housekeeper, 'the sole management of the female servants rests with [her]: it is her duty to engage and dismiss them, with the exception of the nurse, lady's maid and cook, whom the mistress of the house herself engages'.[3] A housekeeper was required 'to have methodical habits, to be firm and impartial in her dealings with under servants, although strictly exacting respecting the due performance of their duties, as she, in all respects, represents her mistress, and is invested with her authority'. The interview was conducted in Mrs Davies's downstairs sitting room, which was known as 'pug's parlour' (since an upper servant was irreverently called a 'pug' by the lower servants) and occupied a prime location in the bow of the house just below the morning room.

It is a pleasant room, large enough to entertain visitors, an abode befitting the 'upper servant' who was second only to the butler in the below stairs hierarchy, and in charge of all the female servants in the house. It is richly furnished in crimsons and dark greens, with a deeply padded sofa and horsehair-stuffed armchairs, and a fire burning in the grate against the late summer chill. (The fire had not been easy to achieve, as the chimney had not been swept for over forty years – two chimney sweep's poles were broken in the attempt and a jackdaw's nest landed on the hearth.) Mrs Davies had brought a number of framed photographs of her Edwardian ancestors to hang in her parlour. A chenille cloth-covered table stands in the centre of the room and it is here that the upper servants proceed in strict order of precedence, with the housekeeper following the butler into her 'own' room, to eat pudding and take cheese after lunch or dinner in the servants' hall. It was here too that Mrs Davies could sit and talk to her fellow upper servants, the butler, Mr Edgar, and the lady's maid, Miss Morrison, in the evening when the work of the house was finally done. She might well be busy, though, with some household mending as the small party gossiped and speculated about life upstairs.

To one side of the room is a desk where the housekeeper prepares for her daily meeting with the lady of the house to receive her instructions for the day, checks the household accounts (which her mistress may wish to see), oversees the orders for supplies of meat, fish, fruit and vegetables and dry goods from the kitchen, tots up the invoices sent in by local tradesmen and deals with any staffing matters that arise, just as her Edwardian counterpart would have done. On a shelf are ranged cookery books such as *Mrs Beeton's Book of Household Management* (an 'entirely new, revised and greatly enlarged' edition of the original 1861 version had been published in 1901); Eliza Acton's cookery books; *Domestic Cookery* by Mrs Rundell; *Warne's Model Cookery and Housekeeping Book*; advice

Lady Olliff-Cooper met with the housekeeper, Mrs Davies, every morning to order the smooth running of the house.

manuals such as *Cassell's Household Guide: Being a Complete Encyclopaedia of Domestic and Social Economy, and Forming a Guide to Every Department of Practical Life* (c. 1900–11); *Everywoman's Encyclopaedia* (8 volumes, 1910); and *The Housewife's Friend: A Treasury for Every Household to which is added hints for domestic servants*. Mrs Davies had been informed when she arrived, in words taken from an Edwardian manual for servants, 'As housekeeper you must be accountant, diplomat and task master all rolled into one.' And as another manual warned, 'The office of housekeeper is no sinecure, more especially in the country, when the heads of establishments entertain largely, and when the house is, during the winter months, more or less full of guests.'[4]

The tentacles of status reached down to the linen cupboard where family and servant's table linen was strictly separated.

The room also serves as the housekeeper's storeroom. The walls are lined with floor-to-ceiling cabinets housing the family's finest china and porcelain. The china closet is the responsibility of the housekeeper and she must oversee the washing, drying and replacement of all the china in the closet after meals, checking for breakages or any damage. Hers is also the responsibility for distributing the household linen from the airing cupboards for making up beds and laying tables.

Additionally, the housekeeper has the task of ordering and doling out household supplies such as candles, matches, soap, cleaning materials, polishes and waxes, and toiletries from a small room off the parlour. An Edwardian housekeeper would also have had herbs such as thyme, rosemary and sage dried in the oven to be kept corked in glass bottles; made pot-pourri to make the rooms fragrant by drying rosebuds and petals, violets, orange blossom, jasmine, lavender and orris root, and maybe including a clove-studded orange;[5] she would have distilled rose water of dark, damask roses, made lavender water, and stuffed small muslin bags with rose leaves, cloves, cinnamon, coriander seeds and mace to perfume linen and underwear. She would have dispensed medicine to the servants, such as lozenges for sore throats, inhalations for chesty coughs and healing balms and ointments, and made up her own remedies on occasions, maybe applying a small bag of heated salt to relieve neuralgia as recommended by *The Servant's Own Paper*, or dripping chloroform on to cotton wool to ease earache, handing out spoonfuls of castor oil, recommending a warm mustard bath for chilblains and the application of a bruised poppy leaf for wasp stings. In short, her aim should be to earn the Edwardian accolade that approves:

No better keeper of our store
Did ever enter at our door.
She knew and pandered to our taste
Allowed no want and yet no waste.

It was the housekeeper's task to prepare tea to be taken in the drawing room. This was often a sociable occasion, served when ladies in the neighbourhood paid an afternoon call. She would cut dainty sandwiches and bake scones, fancy cakes and biscuits. Mrs Davies found that her cherry or sultana fruit scones served with jam and her Scottish shortbread were the family's favourites, while the servants were particularly fond of her oat flapjacks which she had to make almost daily.

When visitors came to stay, the housekeeper would take charge of the arrangements, organizing the disposition of bedrooms – in consultation with her mistress, since in Edwardian times this could be a delicate matter, particularly among the bed-hopping 'fast set' that surrounded the King.

Above all, as housekeeper, Mrs Davies's role was to ensure the smooth running of the household and to maintain discipline among the female servants. But she could expect status and service as well as responsibility and hard work. In a house the size of Manderston in 1905, Mrs Davies could have expected an annual salary of some £50 with 'all found', and she would have privileges to match her responsibilities not enjoyed by those lower down the servants' ladder. Apart from the luxury of her own sitting room, the lower servants would wait on her to an extent – a bell pull hangs by the fireplace in her parlour and this peals one of the fifty-six bells in the corridor outside. (Indeed, it was through waiting on the upper servants that the lower were supposed to learn their trade and be pronounced fit to serve the family upstairs.) In common with her fellow upper servants, the housekeeper would not be expected to do any dirty or menial work. Her life would be much more self-regulated than those who were below her in the rigid hierarchy that pertained below stairs, and whose lives she effectively ruled in conjunction with the butler. The housekeeper could arrange her own time off – providing this in no way incommoded the smooth running of the household – and the time at which she retired to bed was her own concern and not prescribed as it was for the lower servants. As housekeeper, she would have been accorded the courtesy title of 'Mrs' regardless of her marital status.

The summons: the row of bells in the Edwardian Country House exemplified the
upstairs/downstairs system by which those above stairs commanded the services of those below.

The housemaids

Rebecca Smith, the first house-maid, had read history at Reading University, and now, at twenty-six, was back in her home city of Liverpool. 'I've always had an affinity with the past. When I went round stately homes as a child, I'd always be thinking, "How did they actually live? How would they clean all this stuff?"' But it was her grandmother's stories that really inspired Becky. 'She was in service. She was only fifteen when she first went away – she was scared, but she had to. Her father had died and they needed the money… She'd lost all feeling in her hands and she was quite proud of that because it showed how hard she worked. I remember thinking that I wouldn't want to work that hard.'

An injury put paid to the early hopes of Jessica Rawlinson, the twenty-three-year-old second housemaid, to be a dancer. She now works in Kent and enjoys clubbing and whizzing around in her car. In fact Jess thought that she was probably 'a bit nutty wanting to do this. I love modern life – there's so much freedom.' But the lure of the past was strong. 'I *think* I know quite a lot about the period. I've seen films and television series, but you never see what really goes on, how hard they had to work, how unremitting it was. If I'm honest, I'm wondering if I've got the stamina to do it.'

Erika Ravitz, the third housemaid, is a graduate in textile design from Hertfordshire. She joined the project halfway through and was thrilled to take on a new challenge. Erika is a fitness fanatic but imagined that she'd have little opportunity for kick-boxing in the Edwardian Country House: her exercise would be more likely to be carrying buckets of coal.

Having concluded her interview with the new first housemaid, Becky, Mrs Davies now turned to Jessica, the second housemaid, while Antonia the kitchen maid waited nervously on a hard bench in the corridor.

Mrs Davies began. 'It's a delicate question, I know,' she said to Jess, 'but it has to be asked: are you pregnant?'

'Absolutely not, no way. No, no,' insisted a startled Jess.

'You're sure?' queried the housekeeper, before going on to ask her if she was strong (since there would be lots of heavy work) and healthy (since it would be hard and the hours would be long). Then it was time to remind Jess that she was subordinate to the first housemaid and that Becky would delegate duties to her and that Jess should look to her, Mrs Davies, as well as to Becky 'to learn the skills of her trade'. She was given a list of her daily duties starting with the instruction to rise at 6.30 a.m. and present herself downstairs ready to start work washed, dressed 'and with your hair tied neatly back under your cap' half an hour after rising. She was instructed how to address the upper servants, and, if essential, members of the family – though in the general course of her duties she should try never to let them set eyes on her. She was allowed only one bath in a tin bath in her room each week and this was to be filled by carrying up jugs of hot water, and then carrying down jugs of dirty water. Nevertheless, she was expected to be 'clean, neat and presentable at all times' so should 'wash her face, feet and underarms each morning before dressing'. She was forbidden to wear make-up, jewellery or silk stockings.

Finally, Jess was issued with a length of white muslin and a length of elastic and shown how to construct washable sanitary wear to be used during her 'monthlies'. It was always possible that the housekeeper might demand regular inspection of this article to satisfy herself that the maid had not fallen pregnant.[6]

The second housemaid (like her fellow lower servants) might have free time between half past two and four o'clock in the afternoon 'providing your work has been completed', though she might be 'obliged to do some ironing or light needlework' during this time – and this was to prove illusory since 'the work is *never* done'. The second housemaid's day, which started at 6.30 a.m., would end after she had helped Becky to fill the stone hot water bottles to be placed in the beds of the family, their guests and the upper servants. Coverlets had to be turned down and the bedrooms tidied while the family was at dinner. She and Becky were then free, unless, of course, 'the family has any further requirements'.

'Teach me to be humble, O Lord'. The servants at morning prayers in the hall.

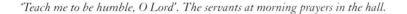

There was no time for reflection on their new surroundings for Antonia, Becky and Jess: the family were expected in less than a week, and there was a great deal to be done in preparation for their arrival. At Manderston in 1905 there had been thirteen female servants: three laundry maids, six housemaids, three scullery maids and a cook.[7] The re-creation of the Edwardian Country House in 2001 had shut off a large number of rooms so that the servants' task of cleaning the house and looking after the family, though demanding, was possible given that their number matched the number of rooms in use, and the relatively small size of the 'upstairs' family. The present-day female staff consisted of a housekeeper, a lady's maid, two housemaids, a kitchen maid, and a scullery maid (who had not yet arrived), and later a third housemaid was appointed.

First the maids climbed the four, long flights of stone stairs – ninety-seven in all, as they soon came to realize – to their attic bedrooms to leave their luggage. The servants were segregated in their sleeping arrangements, and as much as possible in their household duties too. It used to be accepted that there was a general stiffening in moral rectitude in the Victorian era after the relative licence of the eighteenth century, and the endorsement of a strict moral code of family values meant that extramarital sexual congress of any sort was made as difficult as possible. But historians now are more likely to emphasize the fact that extramarital sex was likely to lead to marriage, and this is why employers, anxious not to lose a good servant to wedlock and motherhood, were strict in their policing of their servants' sexual activities. Followers were forbidden and as many obstacles were put in the way of one of the footmen seducing one of the maids – or any other possible permutation that below stairs life might suggest.[8] 'If one of the menservants was ever found anywhere in the women's section after they had retired for the night, he was instantly dismissed without a reference,' wrote Margaret Powell, who had been a housemaid in Hove in Sussex. [9]

All the female staff slept upstairs in small rooms under the eaves. The housekeeper had a bed-sitting room with a fire, small table and comfortable chair where she could sit in the evening if she chose, rather than downstairs in 'pug's parlour'. Unlike the lower servants, the housekeeper would be free to take a bath whenever she wished in the upper female servants' bathroom (since the rebuilding had provided Manderston with indoor plumbing and sanitation and these had been extended to the servants' quarters – which was not always the case). She shared this bathroom with Miss Morrison, Lady Olliff-Cooper's maid, whose rooms were along the corridor. Miss Morrison had a sitting room and workroom combined where she could attend to her mistress's clothes, ironing, sewing, darning and mending by her fire, and a small bedroom.

The maids' rooms might seem cramped by modern standards, with sloping ceilings and small

At ease: the kitchen maid, Antonia, and the first footman, Charlie.

Jess, the second housemaid, dresses in her attic bedroom for her day's work.

windows, but by Edwardian working-class standards they were positively spacious, and a housemaid used to sleeping three or four (or more) to a bed at home would have felt privileged indeed to share a room – rather than a bed – with only one other person, or even have her very own room as Antonia, Jess and Becky did at Manderston (until Becky and Jess decided it was more companionable to share). The rooms had not been used for years now that Manderston survives with only a caretaker couple, plus help from the estate on big occasions. They were covered with years of grime and cobwebs which had to be cleared away so that the furniture appropriate for Edwardian servants could be collected from the mass of stuff piled up in every storeroom. Local women who worked at the house were employed to help, and soon the rooms were ready for their new occupants. In accordance with the times, they had been plainly furnished with a simple wooden chest (if a maid was lucky; if not, she would keep her meagre possessions in the tin trunk she had arrived with), a hanging cupboard, a single, narrow iron bed with a ticking-covered horsehair or flocking mattress and a cotton coverlet.

The furniture in a servant's room accorded to his or her status in the household: the more elevated the servant, the better quality his or her furniture was and the more likely the washbowl and jug were to match rather than being odd, cracked pieces. The furniture would be second-hand articles that had seen service in the main part of the house, while a strip of thin, worn carpet often failed to cover the wooden floorboards. In most households the small fireplace would probably have been lit only if the maid was ill, but in Edwardian times Manderston had been renowned for providing each servant with a bucket of coal every day. In imitation, the maids in the Edwardian Country House sometimes used to light a fire in one of their rooms, and all would sit up there to talk in the chilly Scottish evenings when they wanted to get away from the eagle eye of the butler in the servants' hall.

There was a washstand with a china basin and jug standing ready for morning ablutions (and evening if the maid didn't fall into bed exhausted without attending to her toiletries). An improving thought or biblical quotation would be framed on the wall, and a small table or chair stood by the bed for a candle (in fact Manderston had electric light installed when it was rebuilt, though it could be erratic in the early days) and a Bible or other improving book – not that there promised to be much time to read. And under each spartan bed stood a chamber pot since 'water closets should not be used during the night'.

It was the servants' quarters that had proved a key factor in the choice of Manderston for the Edwardian Country House programmes: they were – and remain – a superb example of the sophisticated domestic arrangements of an Edwardian country house. Stretching almost the entire length and breadth of the house, they are almost exactly the same now as they were when the rebuilding of Manderston was completed in 1905. Despite their size, it was intended that the servants' quarters should be as 'invisible' as the servants themselves. At Manderston, the basement – which literally functioned to 'underpin' life upstairs – was not visible either when approaching the front entrance, or when looking back from the gardens. Robert Kerr, who was Professor of the Arts of Construction at King's College, London, and himself an architect (though with a not very successful practice), advised in his influential work *The Gentleman's House, or how to plan English residences from the Parsonage to the Palace* (published in 1864), that the first step in building a country house should be to work out how many servants the clients could afford and then plan from that basis, and at Manderston in 1905 that had meant twenty-two.

Then: an Edwardian kitchen maid prepares food at Manderston.

A wide, white-tiled corridor runs the length of the house and from it open the kitchens, storerooms, larders, an ice room (the forerunner of the modern-day fridge and essential in summer), the still room, the servants' hall, the housekeeper's parlour, and the butler's rooms and his pantry, plus sleeping accommodation and washing facilities for the single male servants and any men servants brought by visitors to the house.

The kitchens were also designed by John Kinross: they have black and white ceramic tiled floors, and the ceiling beams are painted with a plaited ribbon pattern which continues into the scullery. Pride of place in the kitchen goes to the state of the (Edwardian) art cooking range housed in a separate unit in the centre of the room. Made by G. Drouet of the Ateliers Briffault in Paris, it provided four ovens of varying temperature as well as a hot plate on top, an open fire for spit roasting and a bread oven. An underground flue leads from the range to a chimney in the boiler house at the other end of the house. Learning the vagaries of this massive furnace would be one of the main tasks of the *chef de cuisine*, M. Dubiard, and keeping it alight would be the round-the-clock (or so it seemed) duty of the scullery maid – of whom there were to be several in the course of the 'Edwardian experiment'.

The kitchen at Manderston is large, with high ceilings and a floor space that seemed like a cricket pitch to tired servants and entailed a great deal of walking during the course of a working day. But a cavernous kitchen was recommended, since the heat and steam and vapour could be overpowering, largely emanating from the range which was a challenging and demanding appliance, but not necessarily a very efficient one. A large range could easily burn a hundredweight of coal a day, but at the beginning of the twentieth century coal was cheap at around £1 a ton and regulations governing pollution non-existent. As late as 1920 it was

…And now: the chef, M. Dubiard tackles the Edwardian Country House cooking range.

estimated that only about 3 per cent of the heat generated from the coals was used to heat food, while another 7 per cent went to produce hot water. Of the remaining heat, 35 per cent was absorbed in the brickwork, 25 per cent was lost in flue gases, and at least 30 per cent went into heating the kitchen – all year round.[10]

Deliveries to the house had been well planned. There was a telephone on a hook in a small kiosk in the corridor – something of a novelty in 1905 – from where Mrs Davies would place orders for the house with local suppliers after consultation with the chef over menus. Tradesmen had a separate entrance and a separate corridor, and when the scullery maid heard the bell ring, she would open the door by pulling a lever outside the scullery, which saved her a long walk. She would then direct food

Plucking game: Kenny, the hall boy, and Ellen, the scullery maid, stoically undertake one of the least favoured tasks in the Edwardian Country House.

into whichever of the larders – white-tiled to keep cool – was appropriate: raw meat in one, cooked in another, game, fish, ice, pastry – all had their own place of preparation and storage. When the tradesman had sorted out his deliveries he would come to the scullery door – no further – to help himself to a mug of beer from the pitcher that stood on the table for that express purpose.

The designation of individual rooms for specific purposes had reached its apogee in the 1870s when it was reported that at Kimmel Park at Clwyd in Wales, a special room had been set aside for ironing newspapers. By the late nineteenth century, the gradual decrease in the number of domestic servants had led to a certain rationalization of 'all those places with interminable corridors and little rooms'.[11] In those days, when the control of disease was increasingly being linked to higher standards of cleanliness and hygiene, yet before effective refrigeration, the separate pantries at Manderston were a model of rational planning for the segregation of food storage and preparation.

Adjoining the kitchen is the scullery, for food and vegetable preparation and washing-up. This is where Antonia would spend most of her days in the heat and steam, supervised by M. Dubiard, and helped – intermittently – by a scullery maid. With an upstairs household of four adults, a child and a tutor, and an eventual downstairs complement of thirteen, it was clear that with all the skinning and plucking and boning and peeling and chopping and kneading, not to mention the endless piles of dirty pots, pans, plates and dishes that keeping them fed entailed, the scullery was going to represent 'home' to the kitchen staff for much of the three months that they were to live at Manderston.

Through a door at the far end of the servants' corridor was a small brick yard to which the new downstairs residents would try to sneak for a quick cigarette, or snatch a moment's fresh air and a chance to look at the sky, since the basement windows kept their quarters gloomy and the electric light needed to be on all day. Beyond the yard was a small grassy lawn where clotheslines had been erected. In earlier days this drying ground, 'well open to the sun and… sheltered from high winds… and the attentions of wandering poultry… and the incursions of pigs, puppies and calves',[12] would have been used to bleach linen, which was laid on the grass to whiten in the sun and was turned several times and sprinkled with warm water or dilute lye until a satisfactory brightness was achieved. Then the sheets and tablecloths and napkins would be rolled up and left until it was time to iron the linen.

'Whiteness' has always been associated with cleanliness and, according to the historian Pamela Sambrook, it became something of an obsession in the nineteenth and early twentieth century. This method of spreading linens on the grass – preferred because grass was a natural oxidizing agent and the springiness allowed air to circulate (though sometimes the linen might have been draped on hedges and bushes) – was practised well into the 1930s by those with space to do so.[13] For country houses with a large stock of linens, a professional 'whitener' who specialized in bleaching linen might have called to provide this service on a regular basis. It was not unusual, particularly after the development of the railways in the mid-nineteenth century, for laundry to be sent from a family's London establishment to their country house to be dealt with in the commodious laundries there, and then returned clean and ironed by rail to the metropolis.

Today there are optic brighteners in detergents to achieve the 'blue whiteness' that is supposed to signal good housewifery (and of course automatic washing machines that deliver clean clothes at the flick of a switch). The Edwardians had moved away from earlier practices of steeping linen in lye or urine to clean it; they now soaked their linen in washing soda and lime, or a concentrate of potash or borax, and added a squeeze of Reckitt's Blue into the final rinse of whites – or even crumbling up the blue paper that wrapped loaves of sugar if the laundress was particularly economical. But laundry was still a toilsome and exhausting business. After the washing came the mangling, the starching (there were still instructions for making starch out of potatoes or rice in late-nineteenth-century household manuals that would have been in use in the twentieth, though proprietary brands were by then readily available), and the endless labour of ironing with irons weighing some 8 or 20 pounds each. These irons had to be made hot on special stoves such as the one in Miss Morrison's room, and were used on a low, long wooden table covered with calico-covered blankets, with a hard 'polishing board' for ironing stiff shirt fronts. Goffering tongs (similar to hair curling tongs) were heated on the stove, to deal with the frills and ruffles on blouses and petticoats, and the caps and aprons housemaids wore in the afternoon.

The lady's maid dealt with her mistress's personal laundry and the Edwardian Country House servants, who used their clotheslines only for the odd rinsed-through tea-towel, could not imagine how they could have added laundry to what they considered to be an entirely chore-filled new life. Rather than employ additional staff as

The household laundry awaits collection at the servants' entrance.

laundry workers, or bring in a 'freelance' each week, the unusable state of the laundry equipment at Manderston meant that Jess's laundry duties were to be confined to collecting, listing, packing, unpacking, checking and distributing the household's laundry sent out to a commercial laundry – and that seemed task enough to her.

The arrangements of the servants' working quarters were well organized: 'Every servant, every operation, every utensil, every fixture should have a right place and no right place but one,' approved Kerr. And in that way, as in others, the servants' basement made concrete the Edwardian social hierarchy. As in wider society, so below stairs strict boundaries were observed, and the grander the house, the more formal and rigid the below stairs hierarchy was likely to be: indeed, the lines could be drawn even more strictly than among those they served. Each job was clearly demarcated and, for example, the footman would not have been expected to take on any of the housemaid's responsibilities, and the 'lower five' would be obliged to respect and obey the orders of the 'upper ten' (though the ratio was entirely misleadingly named) and address them strictly according to status and custom.

It was not only what they had to do and the conditions under which they had to do it that would prove irksome to the Manderston staff. For the women, it was the clothes they had to wear too. The laced-in corsets made it painful, if not impossible, to bend down to clean grates or scrub floors. The metal stays dug into the women's hips and stomach and the tight lacing at the waist made it hard to eat enough at mealtimes to sustain the energy the servants needed for their physically demanding work. As Antonia pointed out, for everyone with more than a 32-inch bust, 'your tits were pushed right up and out and it made you looked enormous, really pigeon-chested'. These garments hardly facilitated the endless bending and stretching and getting down on their knees that were the daylong activities of the maids. But there was no hope of discarding the much loathed corset for, without the nipped-in figure that it achieved, the dresses of the period could not be done up.

Ellen (left) and Antonia snatch a brief respite from their duties in the basement kitchen.

Each maid had two print working dresses, and two black dresses for afternoons and evenings, plus one for best. Her working clothes got filthy very quickly, what with dusting and scrubbing and washing floors. The Edwardian clothes came from a variety of sources. Rosalind Ebbutt, the costume designer for the Edwardian Country House, purchased some clothes and hired others from theatrical costumiers. Sometimes they were original garments carefully preserved for a century, but more often they were exact replicas which were trimmed whenever possible with original Edwardian lace, braid, feathers, beads and buttons. But sometimes

Rosalind, or her assistant, Amanda Keable, decided to have clothes made to designs inspired by drawings from the period in fashion magazines, from photographs taken at society balls and parties or country house events, sketches from catalogues or garments directly copied from originals. They sought out fabrics that would have been used for clothes at the time: cotton, woollens, serge, cambric and muslin for downstairs and tweed, alpaca, fur, linen, silks, satins, taffeta, chiffon and lace for the drawing-room set.

'There was no question of using original clothes for the servants,' Rosalind explained. 'On the whole they just haven't survived. Servants' clothes were worn until they'd been mended and patched so much that they fell apart. And the clothes the twenty-first-century servants wore were going to receive pretty punishing treatment. So everything was made new. The maids' dresses were in discreet colours that would not draw attention to them as the went about their work; blue and grey for the kitchen maids and pink prints for the housemaids to merge with the décor upstairs. Mrs Davies's dresses were mainly black, and Lady Olliff-Cooper's maid, Miss Morrison, was fitted out in shades of blue and green.

'I had some great good fortune with the servants' dresses since, as I said, there aren't many examples still around to copy. It turned out that there were some wonderful photograph albums at Manderston and I pored over those showing the servants from around 1905 until the First World War, and had some dresses made that were as near as possible to the originals. Then I plundered the archives at Petworth House in Sussex, where there is a whole series of photographs of the servants there taken in their off-duty clothes at exactly this period, which was another serendipity.

'We had the greatest problem with shoes – for the young people in particular. People today who have been used to wide-fitting shoes from an early age and now wear trainers most of the time find it very painful to cram their feet into much narrower, tighter Edwardian leather shoes, and as the servants were on their feet so much of the time, this became a real issue. I know they found the corsets restricting too. The servants had it harder than the ladies upstairs because their stays were steel rather than the more pliant whalebone. Each one was individually made to measure, and if the women put them on over cotton interlock vests that were becoming popular in the early years of the century, they shouldn't have rubbed too much. I think after a bit the maids did manage to get the hang of lacing them and things got a bit better on that front. They wore bloomers of course, which were cotton and quite loose so they didn't cause a problem.'

Just as Antonia, Becky and Jess were beginning to find their way around their new working quarters that first day, it was time for dinner. The young women filed silently into the servants' hall. The butler, Mr Edgar, stood stiffly at the head of the table while Mrs Davies took her place at the other end. The female servants lined up on one side in gradually descending order of status, the men on the other, and all stood behind their chairs while Mr Edgar said grace.

There was an empty chair at the end of the female line. 'Where is the scullery maid?' enquired Mr Edgar sharply.

'She was certainly expected today,' replied the housekeeper, 'and I've had no word.'

This was alarming news, since there was so much to do before the family arrived. At that moment the front door bell sounded through the basement and, surprised at the thought of 'someone of quality' calling when the family were not yet in residence, Mr Edgar hurried upstairs. He opened the heavy front door and there stood Lucy, the new scullery maid. Mr Edgar looked pained and called for one of the footmen to escort her to the servants' door. After dinner he summoned her to his room: 'The front entrance,' he explained firmly, 'is *not* for the likes of us.'

CHAPTER THREE

The Butler's Pantry

This is the first day that we are together and I must impress on the staff that there is going to be no idle chatter at table. The servants are there to eat their meal and they should only speak when spoken to,' explained the butler, reflecting on the first lunch that the servants had taken together in the house.

The housemaid, Becky, thought that it 'was the worst meal time that I have had in my entire life. You could have cut the atmosphere with a knife. I was so scared.'

'All I could think of was "What question might he ask me?"' added Jess. 'His look is definitely scary. It could turn you into a block of salt. I addressed him as "Sir" and apparently that was wrong. He said that it should have been "Mr Edgar". It's very confusing. He is in charge and I am really scared of him and the silence as everyone eats is just unnatural. I am a gobby person and having to be quiet all through the meal was just so abnormal.'

'I realize that the staff are probably all saying "this man is quite awful",' admitted Hugh Edgar, 'but I lived like that myself. When I used to go to tea with my grandfather, he would sit at the head

The servants at table: dinner presided over by Mr Edgar, with Mrs Davies at the other end, and the rest of the servants seated according to rank.

The butler

Hugh Edgar, a consultant architect who advises on cultural projects, was brought up in Edinburgh and now lives in Surrey. He has worked all over the world, including for the Hashemite royal family, and has built a mausoleum mosque for the late wife of King Hussein of Jordan.

'I am very interested in how Edwardian society worked,' he said. 'I am interested in class and how it operated. I am fascinated by a society in which the boundaries were so clearly defined, when everyone knew their place and knew what was expected of them, and in a way I think that made life easier. I have some experience of Edwardian life because my grandfather was very much an Edwardian and for him discipline was all-important.

Mr Edgar knew that the lower servants would not find the hard work and the long hours easy, and that 'I will have to establish my authority from the start. I am going to see that we run the Edwardian Country House as near as possible to how it would have been run then.' He was also apprehensive about his relationship with his master: would they establish a bond? He was delighted to find that after a time, 'Sir John and I sometimes find ourselves talking man to man, though I never forget that he is the master and I am the servant.' He stoutly maintained that 'Our job here is to serve the family. There is no other reason for our being here,' and was rewarded when Sir John referred to his sixty-five-year-old butler as 'a tower of strength'. At the conclusion of the Edwardian experiment, Mr Edgar reflected: 'This was an era when everything became bigger and more extravagant – and the Edwardian Country House reflected that. Gambling became a craze upstairs and downstairs and then when the war came in 1914, that was a terrible gamble too!'

of the table at tea time and insist "children should be seen and not heard". And that's how it was. All you would hear was "Would you pass the bread and butter, please?" Apart from that, the meal was eaten in total silence. No doubt as time goes by we may be able to relax here in the Edwardian Country House and allow some chatter. But I have to set a standard. If one evening I tell someone that they have to keep quiet, I mean it and it doesn't matter why. I am at the head of the table and so I'm the one who determines who will speak, how much will be said and what will not be said. I appreciate that sounds harsh, but how else do you establish your authority with new staff in a new house? We have to start as we mean to go on. Sir John and his family will be arriving in a few days, so there will be a lot of pressure from the family, there'll be no time for chatter. We will need to have our meal as quickly as possible and then get on with the task in hand.

'I presume that is where my grandfather was coming from in his day. He died when he was eighty-four and he was a very busy man – he worked up to his dying day, he simply had no time for fripperies at teatime. He'd be polite and ask how I was getting on at school. And I'd reply, "All right,

The trio known as the 'upper ten', the butler, Mr Edgar, the lady's maid, Miss Morrison (centre),
and the housekeeper, Mrs Davies, confer.

Grandpa" and that was it. He'd recognized that I was at the table, but that's all he'd done. My father told us that he really loved us children, but frankly I was terrified of him.'

'The office of butler is…one of very great trust in a household,' wrote Isabella Beeton in her *Book of Household Management*, which first appeared in thirty threepenny monthly supplements to the *Englishwoman's Domestic Management Magazine* run by her husband, Sam. The work began in 1859, when Mrs Beeton was just twenty-three, and took her 'four years of incessant labour'. It was published as a 1,000-page book in 1861 – the most comprehensive work on domestic affairs ever to be attempted. The encyclopedic book was an immediate best-seller, running to many editions after Mrs Beeton's death in 1865 from puerperal fever following the birth of her fourth child; she was only twenty-eight. Her book's value as a domestic *vade mecum* persisted in many households until the First World War – and beyond. [1]

Mr Edgar was to assume his role with the utmost gravity, always aware of his position and mindful of his responsibilities. A slim, wiry man who walks everywhere at an extremely brisk pace, breaking into a trot when matters appear urgent, he had shaved off his customary beard in keeping with the times and perennially appeared neat and dapper in his black trousers, black tailcoat, starched white shirt, stiff white wing collar and black bow tie. It was essential that he should always appear formal, but some households preferred that the butler should commit some sartorial solecism – maybe the wrong trousers for the coat he was wearing – to make sure no one mistook him for a gentleman.[2]

As butler, Mr Edgar was the highest-ranking household servant: he was in charge of all the male servants, as the housekeeper was of the female staff, and he took precedence over Mrs Davies at table and in the 'pug's parade' to her sitting room after meals. She would defer to him in other matters, too. He had taken to heart the dictates of the ex-butler to the 'Duke of Romsey' (a pseudonym to disguise the employer's true identity), who had written a guidebook for his fellow servants that they might profit from his experience:

> In all establishments, it is [the butler's] duty to rule. In large establishments it will be greatly required; for under-servants are never even comfortable, much less happy, under lax management. Order in this sense means mutual comfort. What the butler has to do and avoid to secure this object must be determined by himself; but one thing he must never fail to do, viz., to notice faults on their occurrence, and after a firm caution, if the fault is repeated, to bring the culprit before the notice of the head of the house. Let the butler neglect this, and farewell to his rule.[3]

The butler was the person who had most to do with the family 'upstairs'; it was an important and complex relationship. As the anonymous author of *The Servants' Practical Guide* published in 1880 laid down, 'A butler who knows his duties, and performs them with zeal, integrity and ability, cannot be too highly prized by judicious heads of families.'[4] On the butler's ability above and below stairs rested the good order of the household, the comfort of the family and also, to no small degree, its social reputation.

Butlers were expected to be bachelors without the distractions and temptations of a family of their own, and Mr Edgar (or Edgar as he was called by the family) might even be addressed as 'Olliff-Cooper' below stairs should he accompany the family on a visit to another great house, so completely was his identity sunk into theirs. The butler's suite of rooms was positioned as near as possible for access to the principal rooms, particularly the dining room, so that when about his regular duties, or when summoned by bells, he could bound up the stairs to appear in minutes. The butler acted as valet to the master of the house in an establishment the size of Manderston, laying out Sir John's clothes for the day, brushing and

'At first rising it is the duty of the butler where no valet is kept, to manage and arrange his master's clothes'.

sponging them when necessary, polishing his shoes and shaving his master with an open cut-throat razor which he would strop on a leather strap. Safety razors had been available since the 1880s but were still looked on as a bit cissy, and not capable of giving such a close shave. As Mrs Beeton pointed out, 'gentlemen are sometimes indifferent as to their clothes and appearance'[5] – not that this was the case with Sir John – and should this be the case, it was the valet's duty to keep his master 'up to snuff', ensuring that he was neatly, and correctly, dressed for every occasion. An untidy master reflected badly on his servant.

The butler's location near the stairs from the basement to the ground floor indicated that he had easy access to supervise the laying of tables and the serving of meals, and to open the front door to visitors and announce their presence, or accept a visiting card if the family was 'not at home' or chose to pretend that it was not.

Mr Edgar's personal domain included an office that was the hub of the organization of the household, where he implemented the plans and activities of the day that he had discussed with Sir John at their daily morning meeting. It was here, peering through sometimes two pairs of gold-rimmed spectacles, and using his draughtsman's skills and neat, spidery handwriting, he drew up detailed timetables for all the staff, specified special duties for the day for the footmen, pored over seating plans for lunch and dinner, and orchestrated major social events such as fêtes, balls, weekend shooting parties and the like. On his walls a butler would be likely to have an improving tract, framed, or perhaps a discreet watercolour. On his shelves would be lined up the essential works of reference for his position:

Edwardian multi-tasking. Mr Edgar in his role as valet gives Sir John his morning shave (left) and in his capacity of butler, polishes a silver tray from the safe.

a copy of the Bible, the Book of Common Prayer, manuals with advice for the efficient running of a house and the proper conduct of servants, a last-year's copy of *Burke's Peerage* (since the current one would be in use upstairs) for when visitors came, and probably a copy of *Bradshaw's Railway Guide* for those occasions when his master wished to venture to London, or visit relations or friends a steam train journey distant. It was here that the butler interviewed new male staff, enquiring about their previous experience and often about the occupation of their father, as well as reading the 'character' supplied by their previous employer and noting their personal appearance and mien. It was to this room that he would summon the household servants to lecture them with little homilies, discipline or, in extreme instances of transgression or insubordination, dismiss them. The grave remark 'I will see you in my room later' sent a tremor down the spine of a lower servant – as it was intended to.

The butler would also have been in charge of the cellar – this had been his primary function in earlier times; indeed, Mrs Beeton considered that 'the real duties of the butler are in the wine cellar: there he should be competent to advise his master as to the price and quality of the wine to be laid in'.[6]

A gentleman's gentleman: Mr Edgar discusses household matters with Sir John at their regular morning meeting.

He would ensure that the cellar was properly stocked with bottles of fine wine, champagne, port, 'malt liquors', sherry, brandy and any other fashionable liqueurs that took the family's fancy. He would store the bottles in the correctly labelled bins and, in consultation with the master of the house, decide on the wines to be served at lunch and dinner and carefully note in his cellar notebook those bottles drunk. Traditionally, empty wine bottles (and no doubt the few inches left in the bottom) were the perquisites (or perks) of the butler, who could sell them for pin money. The butler's responsibility for the wine cellar made it imperative that a master should satisfy himself of the man's good habits on appointment, since 'insobriety is a very common failing among butlers…and the inconvenience to which a master and mistress are subjected when they are unfortunate enough to engage a butler addicted to drink, is of a serious nature'.[7] And indeed the temptations offered by the wine cellar were adduced as another reason why it was not a good idea to employ a married man in the position of butler. Should the butler's wife be 'ailing and very much in need of strengthening things…half bottles of wine and whole bottles of wine are under such circumstances not unlikely to find their way to the butler's home; while he justifies himself for this lapse of trust by the specious reasoning that a bottle or two of wine can make no possible difference to a master whose cellars are so bountifully stocked, while to his wife it makes all the difference in the matter of regaining health and strength'.[8]

A plainly furnished (and always impeccably tidy) bedroom led off one end of Mr Edgar's office and adjacent to his rooms was the butler's pantry where silver and plate were washed and polished. Next to that, tucked away with no access from the servants' corridor, was the silver vault where the valuables were stored and to which only the butler had a key. At Manderston, the butler had been the best-paid of all the servants (as would have been the case in all but the largest houses where a steward would have been employed). The leatherbound *Servants' Book* from the house reveals that William Tait, a thirty-five-year-old butler who left the Millers' service to work for Lord Kinross in August 1903, had received an annual salary of £60. Often a butler, at the top of his professional tree, would be 'suited' for life, a stalwart of the household, 'as solid and reliable as the Bank of England',[9] but this does not appear to have always been the case at Manderston. In December 1909 George Smith (who by this time was paid £65 a year) seems to have left after only two days, and his successor, Frank Ricketts, 'went abroad' after only two months, though it looks as if the unnamed butler who came next stayed right through the First World War, when the entries cease.

Folding clothes

'A valet's duty,' warned Mrs Beeton's guide in 1901, 'leads them to wait on those who are, from sheer wealth, station and education, more polished, and consequently more susceptible of annoyance.' To avoid any possibility of this, Mr Edgar, who acted as Sir John's valet as well as his butler, copied out copious notes on how to fold his master's clothes in the correct manner.

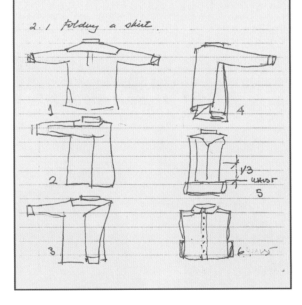

He rises as late as possible, he exerts himself as little as he need; he declines to take up the governess's supper or to clean her boots…several times a day he partakes freely of nourishing food, including a surprising quantity of beer…a jolly, magnificent fellow is the flunkey,' wrote Lady Violet Greville in an article on 'Men-Servants in England' published in the *National Review*.[10] For 'governess' read 'tutor', and could Lady Greville's description fit the case of Charlie and Rob, the two footmen in the Edwardian Country House? Both were aged twenty-three and both thought that being a footman for three months might be 'a bit of a laugh'.

Rob had worked for a time in a hotel in Torquay, where he learned all about silver service waiting – a useful apprenticeship for his Edwardian Country House role. He admits to being 'something of a peacock – I have been known to strut', which again was a quality not unimportant in the lexicon of footmanly skills. As well as having to work hard downstairs under the direction of the butler, footmen had an ornamental role upstairs, serving at table, assisting guests, riding at the back of the carriage in imitation of their forebears who would run alongside their master's vehicle, partly for security, largely for display. On top of this, Rob carried out the duties of a valet for Master Guy while Charlie performed the same function for Mr Jonathan and any visiting gentlemen staying at the house.

The speeding footman: Rob hurries along the interminable corridors and flights of stairs to get food from the kitchen to the dining room upstairs.

The footmen

Charlie Clay, the first footman, expected life in an Edwardian Country House to be like his public school. A former area salesman, the twenty-three-year-old from Nottingham has spent some time travelling around America and hasn't entirely lost his wanderlust. He is not reticent about his charms. 'I've done some modelling, and I rather like to be the centre of attention,' he confessed engagingly. Like most of the younger servants he wondered how he would get on without clubs and bars, but reckoned that he could provide some entertainments for his fellow below stairs staff. Taking orders, though, was not his strong suit. It had got him into trouble at school – how would he adapt to Edwardian discipline? In fact, Charlie soon became quite a favourite with the butler, who thought of him as 'confidant'.

Rob Daly, the second footman, who is also twenty-three, has a degree in genetics from London University, but he hasn't quite found his vocation. Born and brought up in south Devon, he too admits to a liking for attention. He had been looking forward to the Edwardian experience, and was certainly prepared for hard work. Nearing the end of his spell of servitude, Rob reckoned that Sir John 'thinks that we footmen do our jobs well because we want to impress the family, but I am not sure that's the case. We do our menial tasks to the best of our ability because it is the only way of maintaining our self-respect. In an odd way the hierarchy and the restrictions are liberating. You don't have choices and you don't have to make decisions. It takes away a lot of responsibility.'

He concluded, '"Rob the footman" will always be with me' – and Charlie agreed that whatever he did in later life, his Edwardian persona would forever be part of him too.

Footmen brought prestige to the families they worked for. As Pamela Sambrook explains, 'being waited on at dinner by a manservant carried higher status than a mere parlour maid'.[11] A tall, handsome, liveried footman, his posture erect, his hair powdered on grand occasions, who was confident in the rules of etiquette and served adroitly but with something of a theatrical flourish at table, brought glamour to a household. So it was not surprising that when Mr Edgar first interviewed the two young men, he was mentally comparing their height, assessing the set of their jaw and the curve of their calves. In his survey of *Life and Labour of the People in London* conducted in the 1890s, Charles Booth reported that a footman's wages were related to his height: a first footman who stood 5ft 6in would earn from £20 to £22, whereas one who could draw himself up to 5ft 10in, or even attain 6ft, could command from £32 to £40.[12] For aesthetic reasons, footmen of very similar height were preferred to present a pleasing symmetry at table.[13] The livery they wore was intended to indicate to visitors how far they were removed from any connotation of menial work (which is not how it felt to Rob and Charlie), since their braided, gilt-buttoned, eighteenth-century-style jacket, breeches and white gloves would have been entirely unsuitable. Furthermore, his employer invariably provided a footman's livery whereas the maids had to purchase their own uniform. It was another example of the gender difference whereby male servants were paid more than their female equivalents, and, since their roles made them visible to the family and guests, were more individualized and enjoyed a higher status than the 'invisible' servants who laboured to help produce what the footmen served and clean where they served it.

Finally the butler pronounced: Charlie, who had done some modelling and engagingly confessed that he rather liked to be centre stage, would be appointed first footman. 'I think Charlie's a bit of a perfectionist, like me,' Mr Edgar assessed. Rob would be second footman – a post that entailed, among other things, taking charge of Mr Edgar's chamber pot.

As well as the ceremony, there was the skivvying. As Mrs Beeton pointed out, 'the footman…is expected to make himself generally useful…his life is no sinecure; and a methodological arrangement of his time will be necessary, in order to perform his many duties with any satisfaction to himself or his master'.[14] Charlie and Rob's 'many duties' below stairs, which necessitated 'rising early to get through all the dirty work before the family are stirring', included a considerable amount of menial work. Coal had to be carried upstairs for the fires and blocks of ice manhandled into the storeroom; and although pots and pans and the servants' crockery and cutlery were scoured by the scullery maid

Dressing for dinner: Rob stands in for Charlie as Mr Jonathan's valet.

Charlie selects the Wedgwood china for tea, to be taken by the Olliff-Coopers in the drawing room, from the store cupboard situated off the housekeeper's room.

in the scullery, Rob and Charlie were charged with washing up the glasses, fine china, the silver and plate that the family used, in the butler's pantry. This proved to be no sinecure either: scouring agents such as the ubiquitous Monkey Brand soap were expensive and considered too coarse for fine things, so a few crystals of soda would be added to the hot water to give a sparkle and items washed in strict order starting with the glasses. Lead shot or fine ash was recommended for cleaning the inside of decanters, or later bleach was employed to get rid of the stains, but in both cases 'the decanter must be *very* thoroughly rinsed and upended to dry'. A footman recalls that a relatively modest dinner for ten people required 324 items of glass, china and silver – and that didn't include the saucepans and dishes washed up in the scullery.[15]

The household manuals in use in the Edwardian Country House all included recipes for making cleaning agents, polishes and other household necessities. But in the Edwardian period things were changing: proprietary brands of household products were beginning to be advertised in the newspapers or magazines that proliferated at the beginning of the century. Many of the names are not unfamiliar to the middle-aged today: Johnson's or Ronuk furniture polish, Bluebell metal polish and Goddard's powder for cleaning plate, Sunlight soap, Nugget boot polish and Meltonian cream for shoes.[16] Obviously households varied, depending on the inclination of the mistress of the house, the butler or the housekeeper: some were eager to try out new products, while others insisted that the old ways were the best. No doubt in the majority of households the new and old methods co-existed for many years.

Footmen spend a lot of their time in the basement with arms plunged up to the elbows in soapy water, or polishing plate. Cutlery, cruets, sauceboats, serving dishes, soup tureens, coffee-and teapots were cleaned with jeweller's rouge made from powdered rust mixed to a paste with ammonia, which was smoothed with bare fingers over scratches and finished off by polishing with a chamois leather.[17] This was regarded as one of the hardest jobs 'behind the green baize doors' of the servants' quarters: if the endless washing-up gave the servants chapped hands, the silver cleaning developed painful blisters, but perseverance soon developed hardened 'plate hands' which could be regarded as one of a footman's 'badges of office'.

Knife-cleaning was regarded as the footman's province too. With their delicate ivory, bone or mother-of-pearl handles, knives could not just be plunged into hot water along with the other cutlery. Writing in 1842, Anne Cobbett stated authoritatively that 'it is next to impossible for a woman to clean them well'. In her day knives were cleaned on a knife board covered with the reverse side of leather pulled tight, and rubbed with a paste that included emery powder or ground chalk and

The footmen unfold a tablecloth in preparation for laying for dinner, checking that it is the right size depending on the number of guests.

hartshorn – hart's antlers ground to provide ammonia – mixed with lard. Knives (and forks) were often finished by being plunged into earth or fine sand mixed with moss or hay; when not in use, they were stored covered in lard and wrapped in brown paper.[18] By the turn of the century, however, knife-cleaning machines were common in most comfortably off households and these were a boon – indeed, one version was even patented under the trademark 'The Servant's Friend'. The most widely used model was made by William Kent and was a round drum-shaped wooden container on a cast-iron stand: it had first excited attention at the Great Exhibition in 1851 but was still recommended as 'being very good' in 1902.[19] The knives were washed carefully and then pushed into slots, emery powder was poured in and rotating brushes buffed the knives to perfection as the handle was turned. As well as removing rust and polishing the blades, the action sharpened the knives; but for a really cutting edge, a grindstone would need to be used, or knives were often sharpened on the stone sink in the scullery.

Mirrors (or looking glasses) for some reason were considered to be the special responsibility of footmen and 'being very costly should be cleaned with great care' explained *The Complete Servant*, an indispensable manual written by Samuel and Sarah Adams, both of whom had been in service for many years, in his case rising from footboy to house steward, and in hers from maid-of-all-work to housemaid, lady's maid and finally housekeeper. 'First, take a soft, clean sponge, just squeezed out of water, and then dipped in spirits of wine, rub the glass over with this, and then polish off with fine powder blue or whiting, tied up in muslin, quickly laid on, and then rubbed off, with a clean cloth, and afterwards with a silk handkerchief.'[20] As was explained in *The Footman's Guide,* 'It is generally understood to be the peculiar duty of men-servants to look after the cleaning and dusting of the tables, sideboard, chairs, trays and all other articles of mahogany furniture in the parlour or drawing room.'[21] They should be polished with oil or wax of an 'appropriate colour to the wood', using 'two pieces of woollen cloth…one to put it on, and the other for polishing' and a 'piece of soft cork' could be used to 'rub out stains'.[22] It was not, however, just the preparations that ensured a good shine, admonished *The Footman's Guide,* but rather 'be assured, whatever you have heard to the contrary, that *arm-oil* or *elbow-grease*, is the finest thing in the world for giving and preserving a fine polish'.[23]

There was one traditional footman's chore that Charlie and Rob were glad to be spared: cleaning lamps. When paraffin or oil lamps lit great English houses, this was an onerous task and often a special 'lamp room' was set side for its performance. As many as seventy lamps had to collected from all over the house. The brass had to be polished, the glass chimney or globe carefully cleaned with leather pads on sticks (washing the glass should be avoided, according to Mrs Beeton, 'as it causes them to crack when they become hot'),[24] the wicks had to be trimmed, 'cut even at the top' to minimize smoking and ensure a steady flame, the oil changed once a week, and the whole reassembled and replaced in the rooms. It was also the footman's task to go round the house at night to check that all the lamps had been

'I nearly told him where he could stuff it'. The 'silent and discreet' footmen relive incidents of the day in their basement bedroom.

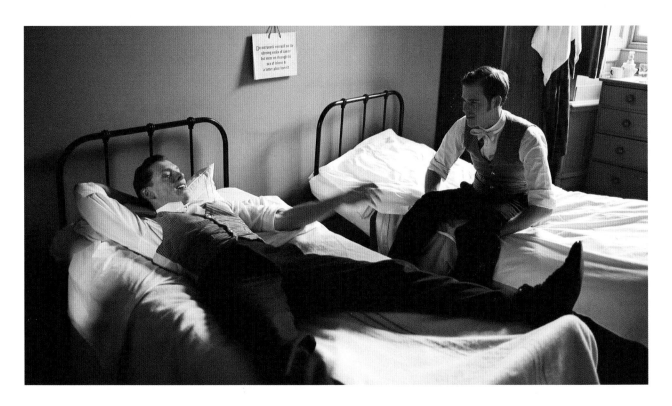

extinguished, since they represented a considerable fire hazard if left unattended. But Manderston had been electrified when the house was rebuilt.

In 1878, the American, Thomas Alva Edison and the Englishman, Joseph Swan, both invented incandescent carbon-filament lamps suitable for domestic use, and three years later Lord Kelvin lit up his Glasgow house with over a hundred incandescent electric lights fitted into former gas burners.[25] Electricity in the early years of its use could be erratic and it could be dangerous. At Hatfield House, Lord Salisbury and his family hurled cushions at the electric plugs that periodically emitted sparks. But when Manderston was completed, one of Sir James Miller's proud boasts was that his was one of the first houses in the country to have the luxury of an electric light controllable from the bed – including in the butler's bedroom.[26]

Another modern invention – the telephone – had also lightened the footman's load. Alexander Graham Bell, an Edinburgh-born teacher of the deaf, was the first person to transmit recognizable speech in 1875 via fluctuating electric currents. He patented his invention and, after several court battles with his rival, Joseph Alva Edison, Bell's company merged with Edison's in 1889 to form the United Telephone Company in London. House telephones were still a novel convenience at the turn of the century, but a most welcome one since their installation made it possible to place orders for the household with local suppliers and convey messages, all without the need to send a footman on an errand.

But there was still the non-automated task of cleaning boots and shoes. This would have involved leather riding boots and stout walking shoes which required the use of 'three good brushes and good blacking: one of the brushes hard, to brush off the mud; the other soft to lay on the blacking; the third of a medium hardness, for polishing; and each should be kept for its particular use'. Arthur Inch, the son of a butler, who has worked in some of the grandest houses in England, including at Londonderry House and as first footman at Blenheim Palace (and had advised Mr Edgar on his duties before he took up his position in the Edwardian Country House), insisted that it took at least half an hour spent on each shoe to properly clean and polish to a conker-like sheen a pair of men's leather shoes – and that included taking out the laces, washing and ironing them.

Small wonder then that Charlie and Rob would agree with the *The Complete Servant* that 'the business of the Footman is…multifarious and incessant'.[27] Unlike Mr Edgar, the footmen would be addressed by their first names by the family upstairs – or at least by *a* first name. The most usual appellations were Charles (which was fortunate), James and John (or John Thomas until, as E. S. Turner reminds us, D. H. Lawrence made that name unusable).[28] In some houses the first footman might always be called Charles even if his parents had christened him Sam, the second footman James and so on. It was another example of the objectification of those below stairs. But the footmen in the Edwardian Country House were at least accorded their own names.

The main complaint of a footman, apart from the long hours and the lack of freedom, was perhaps not so much the hard physical work, which perversely was more the lot of the female servants, but the monotonous and repetitive nature of their days and the fact that it was ultimately unproductive, as a former footman sadly reflected: 'It is like throwing a stone in a pond, rings are formed in the water which eventually fades [sic] quite away. So that at the end of his day's work [the footman] can show nothing that he has done. He has made nothing, produced nothing, yet he has been constantly on the alert all day, not knowing where his next job will spring from.'[29]

In the strict hierarchy that pertained below stairs, the first footman was obviously inferior to the butler – and might indeed strive to be 'industrious, attentive, and disposed to make himself useful'.[30]

Rag rugs

A rag rug would be just the sort of thing that an Edwardian servant might have made for her room in the evenings, picking up the work when she had a few minutes to sit down.

'Rag rugs are a craft born of necessity'.[31] In the mid nineteenth century, sacking was imported from India and because of the suitability of this material for making rag rugs, this craft became a popular activity.

There are a number of types of rag rugs: in Britain the most popular variety are prodded (or poked) rugs, while hooked rugs are particularly favoured in North America. There are also rugs made from strips of braided fabric stitched together, usually in an oval or circle shape, and appliquéd rugs made by stitching thick fabric shapes onto a firm fabric backed by sacking.

Rag rugs are made by cutting up strips of fabric and pushing them through a sacking or hessian backing. They were to be found in Victorian and Edwardian bedrooms and in front of the hearth in the kitchen. Rag rugs appealed to people's sense of thrift, since they used up material from worn-out clothes, and they gave artistic licence in the choice of colours and arrangement of patterns. Different regions would have traditional local patterns, and in its lifetime a rag rug would have several incarnations: first as a heavy bed covering in winter, then, as it got a little old and soiled, as a bedroom mat before ending life in front of a coal fire downstairs.

The popularity of rag rags declined when commercially-made rugs and carpets became cheaper in the twentieth century, but interest in crafts and the desire to recycle materials has led to a revival of interest in this appealing form of home production.

To make a prodded rag rug today, you need a piece of firm sacking or hessian (square, oblong, circle or half moon in shape), with the edges hemmed or bound with tape. Cut the fabric for the pile – worsted or woollen cloth is best – into strips about 2cm x 10cm (1in x 3 ½in), making sure that they are all exactly the same length. Using a sharpened wooden clothes peg as a 'prodder', force a small hole in the sacking, push the fabric through and bring it back through another hole about 5mm (⅛in) away, ensuring that both ends are of equal length. Push in another strip as close as possible to the first – the more densely packed the strips, the more hard-wearing the rug will be. Work out a pattern in advance and sketch it on the sacking with a felt pen or tailor's chalk. You could use blocks or stripes of colour, or aim for a random speckled effect – maybe with a diamond shape of solid colour in the centre. Or you could even design a simple picture such as a ship or sun design.

Trim the 'pile' with a pair of scissors to give an even finish. A backing of a toning fabric such as linen or firm cotton can be sewn over the sacking if you like. Alternatively, a layer of latex or adhesive can be used to coat the underside of the rug to prevent it from slipping, and also making it impossible for the rag strips to pull out.

A weary Rob reflects on the footman's lot.

and learn all he could from him in order that he might aspire one day to apply for a butler's position himself – and the second footman was inferior to the first. As footmen, they were accorded a higher status than the housemaids since they were men and they had direct contact with the family, and they were definitely superior in status to two other servants: the hall boy and the scullery maid.

Hall boy was a fit designation for Kenny since that was where he slept, in a wooden box bed that folded out of a cupboard in the basement hallway, his privacy ensured only by a folding screen. His role was the male equivalent of a maid-of-all-work. He had to hang around the hall waiting for orders. Essentially he did the jobs he was given by Mr Edgar or the footmen – and they were usually the most menial, the dirtiest and the most physically taxing. As *The Complete Servant* explained, the hall boy 'is expected, and indeed engages to do that part of the business of a footman, which is deemed the most laborious'.[32] Kenny had arrived at a moment when work in the Edwardian Country House was threatening to overwhelm everyone, but in Edwardian times he would have most likely either to have got the job through connections his family might have had with other Manderston servants, or by answering an advertisement for 'a strong, respectable lad used to hard work…' 'On first entering service,' advised a manual, 'the lad should consider himself upon trial, and endeavour with all his might to arrive at the right conclusions with regard to all matters concerning his duties, by watching those around him and taking their advice.'[33] Once appointed he would find himself bringing in the coal to fill the scuttles, chopping logs and kindling for the fires, shovelling snow in winter, helping wash up, cleaning boots, grinding coffee, moving any furniture that required shifting, taking out the rubbish, sweeping the service yard, running errands and trudging to the post office in nearby Duns with the household letters and parcels.

In the Edwardian period, eighteen-year-old Kenny would probably have entered service at about fourteen or fifteen years old and, like Samuel Leachy who joined the Manderston staff as a hall boy in 1911, could have expected to earn round £16 a year – though if this was his first position (unlike Leachy, who had come from the Caledonian Hotel in Edinburgh), it might be a little less. He would have considered himself lucky to find a position in a house with the standing in the community of Manderston (though he might have to keep reminding himself of this good fortune as he unblocked drains on a freezing February morning), since this would give him a good start up the long ladder that might one day lead to the dizzy heights of butlerdom. But in his immediate sights would be the hope that if he worked hard and kept out of trouble, he could expect to get an under footman's job in a few years. 'He, of all others,' encouraged the 'Duke of Romsey's' ex-butler, 'has the prospect and opportunities of preferment to a higher and better sphere. He is not bound to clean boots or knives and forks all his life. Service is a perfect ladder; and by a willing and obliging disposition, a habit of doing the right thing at the right time, anticipating the wants of those by whom he is surrounded, and taking necessary pains to master all the technicalities of his profession, he may rise from boy to butler.'[34]

But would Kenny have behaved in this exemplary manner? He found life in the Edwardian Country House hard and lonely at first. He had arrived several days after the other servants and, as hall boy, 'I have to sit at a table on my own at mealtimes. I'm not allowed at the table with the other servants, and no one is allowed to speak unless they're spoken to at meal times. I'm not sure if the butler is a power-hungry monster or a slave-driver, or just trying to get into the rhythm of things. We'll see. And it's tough having to sleep in the hall on a mattress that's made of straw. It's a bit like being in a boot camp. I've got quite a strong character, and not being able to speak up for myself is hard. I hope I can stand it and it won't knock me down too much. I can see myself having joined a trade union if I'd lived in Edwardian times and had this sort of life…'

But if Kenny found life tough, Lucy, the first scullery maid to be employed in the Edwardian Country House, quickly found it insupportable. A former waitress who found it punishingly hard to get up in the mornings, eighteen-year old Lucy was determined to make faith triumph over reason – at first. She wasn't quite sure what a scullery maid's duties were but 'my mum said it would be scrubbing floors and peeling vegetables and that sort of thing'. Lucy hadn't got off to a very good start by coming to the front door of the Edwardian Country House, but this did not dent her determination: 'The way I see it, the next three months are going to be really hard but when I get back I'm going to be so appreciative of what I have and the value of money and the value of everything, so it'll be a really good lesson.'

Jack-of-all-trades. Kenny, the hall boy, chops up logs with an axe for the Edwardian Country House fires.

But within a day or so it was obvious to Lucy that she was 'absolutely at the bottom of the scale in this great big house'. She would have earned about £12 a year and her 'line manager' was the kitchen maid and ultimately the *chef de cuisine* who ruled the kitchen department. She was expected to be prepared to assist them in any task they saw fit, though her 'chief responsibility is to clean, scour and scrub the pots and pans' used to prepare the family's and the servants' meals as well as the crockery and glasses used by the servants. 'Your domain is the scullery,' Lucy was told, and that was certainly the case, usually up to her elbows in greasy washing-up water since when she wasn't helping prepare vegetables or ensuring that 'the kitchen is kept spotless at all times', she was 'constantly washing up after both the kitchen maid and the chef as they prepare meals'. The scullery maid had the smallest bedroom, ate with the hall boy on a separate table from the other servants at first, would 'only ever be allowed upstairs for morning prayers' and on top of everything the huge Edwardian house terrified her. The first few nights Lucy was there, the other maids' sleep was disturbed by her screams: she was convinced that she had seen a ghost, and insisted that she could not sleep alone. She got Becky and Jess to push their beds together so she could snuggle in too, which meant not much rest for anyone.

It was soon apparent that Lucy would be the first Edwardian Country House deserter. And, after only three days, she went to see Mr Edgar in his office to announce she was going home.

Two down: Kelly, the second scullery maid to leave, packs her bags.

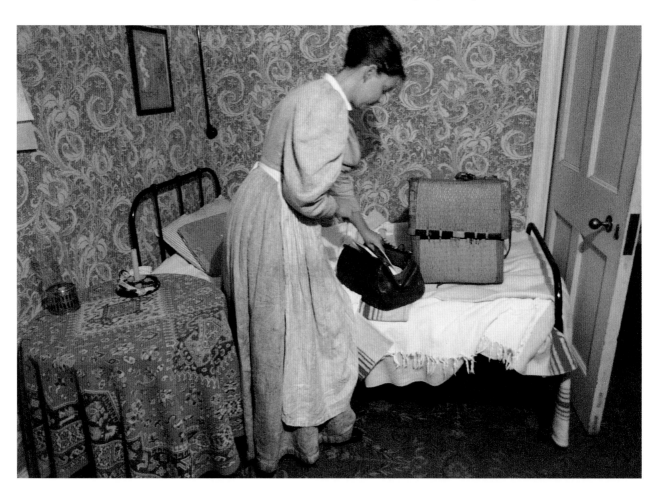

'I was just so tired, the days are so long, these poxy corsets are agony, we all look pregnant, my skin's come up in blotches. I don't get on with the chef which is a problem because we're together all the time. He's always criticizing me and he makes me feel stupid. I was supposed to be downstairs at 6.30 in the morning and I wasn't so the ovens weren't lit and I got told off for that. I'm not a spoilt brat, but I've just never had to do things like this before. I've never cooked, or cleaned or done washing or anything. My mum does everything. I miss my boyfriend, and I can't even phone him which I do all the time at home when I need some comfort, and it's all terrible and I've made up my mind I'M GOING HOME. I'm sure it would do a lot for my character to stay, but I just can't take it any more.'

So Lucy was put on the train back home to Harpenden in Hertfordshire, presumably to a welcoming if not overjoyed reception from her family. This would not have been the case with her 1905 counterpart: poor families were invariably reliant on the money their sons and daughters in service were able to send home, as well as their absence meaning one less mouth to feed, and a bit more space in the bed for the other siblings. A fourteen-year-old Norwich girl quoted by Pamela Horn went into service in Beckenham in Kent, and was desperately homesick. She sent pleading letters to her mother, begging to be allowed to come home. Her mother 'wrote back and said be thankful you've got a bed to lie on and a good home'. The girl never asked again, and out of her wages of 8 shillings a week, managed to send 2s 6d a week home.[35]

The other servants greeted Lucy's departure with mixed feelings, but little surprise. 'I don't think she'll stick it out,' the chef had opined on Lucy's second day. 'She's scared of the dark and she's scared of hard work.' Becky and Jess had tried 'talking to her' and reassuring her about the ghost (which turned out to be partly the chef, M. Dubiard's fault: he had told Lucy that an old house like Manderston was bound to have a ghost – Mr Edgar was *not* amused). 'But we knew she wasn't going to last. She was really homesick, and she kept saying how tough she found it and how her family had always done everything for her. And I must admit,' said Becky, 'she didn't stick to what she was meant to be doing. She'd just wander off.'

Antonia agreed: 'She was lovely, but she was more feisty than a scullery maid would normally be, and she'd just down tools when she'd had enough. And so I had to scrub the sink because she hadn't done it, and that's not really my job as kitchen maid. She was a bit of a skiver, and she was always crying, but now she's gone I feel completely shafted. I am just afraid that I am going to have to do her job as well as mine and I've got too much to do anyway, We must have a new scullery maid as soon as possible, we desperately need another pair of hands.'

What gave Antonia's anxiety an edge was the fact the Olliff-Coopers would be arriving in a couple of days. There seemed to be an enormous amount of work to do in the house already. How on earth would the servants manage when the family was in residence? 'I've never met Sir John and Lady Olliff-Cooper before,' explained Mr Edgar 'and I am very concerned about what they will think of us and whether they will be expecting more than we have done, and whether we have really got absolutely everything ready for them as we they would like. It'll be a big day and I *am* fearful.'

'We're all apprehensive,' agreed Becky. 'There are so many rooms to clean, so many ornaments and trinkets to dust, but on the other hand, it's exciting. We've worked it all out on paper, how we are going to manage. We've formulated a plan, but until they actually get here, we won't know if it'll work. Things could go either way. The family might be really nice and considerate to us, or they might make our lives a total misery. We're just going to have to wait and see.'

CHAPTER FOUR

Up to Snuff

The first dinner party,' wrote Lady Greville in her work of information and exhortation, *The Gentlewoman in Society*,[1] 'causes a tremor to the stoutest heart. No really first class entertaining can be done where money *is* an object. It is not necessary to be ostentatious or lavish, but all perfection must be paid for and requires a great deal of care and forethought. How few are the really good dinners we can look back to with satisfaction at the end of the season! Two or three perhaps; for where the food was excellent and well served, the company often proved tiresome. It does not lie in everyone's capacity to organize a really successful dinner…'

There were, she explained, several kinds of dinner parties, ranging from the large dinners or banquets to private dinners, which fell into two categories. 'The spreads…given on strictly reciprocal principles or "cutlet for cutlet" as a great lady of my acquaintance once called them. Here, again, no enjoyment is expected or received: a duty to Society is simply fulfilled. So many people have dined or danced you; so many people must be dined in return.' On such occasions, Lady Greville writes:

> There will be a profusion of retainers dressed in the traditional costume of satin breeches and silk stockings with powdered hair…Dinner tables now resemble either flower gardens and hothouses, a jeweller's emporium, or a window in Liberty's shop with silks of all colours freely and tastefully displayed. The exact proportion in which floral and silver decorations should be used is known only to the elect souls…A few prefer baskets of lovely fruit only…[though] too much conventionality still prevails on all these points where individual taste and feeling only should decide. Large dinners generally break up early; the hostess and her friends respectively feel they have done their duty.[2]

Then there are 'small dinners [which] require even greater care in their management, but when properly carried out are perfection. It has often been said that the numbers at table ought never to exceed that of the muses' (nine), but Lady Greville was inclined to 'extend the number to twelve who can be well seated at a round table'. The guests at 'a *diner intime*, as the French call it, require to be even more carefully chosen than the *menu*…the women must be pretty and agreeable; the men, noted in some way…'[3]

Vita Sackville-West described the syndrome in her novel *The Edwardians*.[4] 'Those meals! Those endless extravagant meals in which they indulged all year round,' sighed Sebastian, 'the darkly handsome…patrician adolescent' master of Chevron, the hero of the novel. Chevron stands in for Knole, the great Elizabethan house in Kent with its reputed 365 rooms, one for every day of the year, and the 'self-contained little town' of servants needed to sustain it. Knole was the central passion of Vita's life, the house that, under its terms of settlement, she as a woman could never inherit.

> How strange, Sebastian mused, that eating should play so important a part in social life! They were eating quails and cracking jokes. That particular dish of the Chevron chef was famous: an ortolan within the quail, a truffle within the ortolan, and *pâté de foie gras* within the truffle…From his place at the head of the table, Sebastian watched the jaws going up and down…they were all people whose names were familiar to every reader of the society titbits in the papers…he was obliged to admit that they were very ornamental. They seemed so perfectly concordant with their setting, as though they had not a care in the world.[5]

Sir William Miller MP, the father of the man who had rebuilt Manderston, had been given a baronetcy for his service to politics by the Liberal leader and four times Prime Minister, William Gladstone, in his dissolution honours in 1874. His honour, however, came not as a reward for his political activities in the House of Commons, for it is said that he never once spoke in the chamber. Rather, it was for what would today be called networking: the grand political dinners Sir William gave with the intention of consolidating support for the Liberal Party in the Borders, winning converts to Gladstone's causes. These causes were financial liberalism, a commitment to parliamentary reform, and a vehement denunciation of the 'forward' foreign policy in the Balkans and Afghanistan of his Conservative partner in the musical chairs of late Victorian politics, Disraeli. This was to reach a moral crescendo during Gladstone's 'pilgrimages of passion' against 'Beaconsfieldism' in the nearby seat of Midlothian in the 1879–80 election campaign, which the Liberals decisively won.

At such dinners the food and wine would have been of the finest quality and likewise the guests chosen – and placed – with great regard for their status and their influence. Status was the pivot on which much of Edwardian high society turned, for in many cases its membership was no longer burnished with the patina of age. Since the middle of the nineteenth century the old British aristocracy of birth and land had been gradually giving way to a new aristocracy of money: the Edwardian plutocracy. It no longer 'took three generations to make a gentleman': it took wealth to live like one. The process had been noted by *Punch* in its monthly series 'The Side Scenes of Society' which chronicled

Social setting: the dining room with its depiction of Mars, God of War on the plasterwork ceiling.
The portraits hanging on the wall were acquired to give the impression of a distinguished ancestry.

the doings of the Spangle-Lacquers, a *nouveau riche* family who had made their fortune from 'soap, gin, tallow, rags or something equally interesting, by a process of alchemy which leaves all the old philosophies far behind'. The Spangle-Lacquers' friends were much the same: 'you can assign [them] no fixed position in society [since they are generally met with] in places where distinction was acquired by paying for it'.[6]

This was not a new situation: all 'old money' had been new once and from medieval times the ranks of the British landed classes were sustained with new recruits, and anyone who made a sufficient fortune would try to buy an estate or build a country seat in order to stake their claim to a position of power in the upper echelons of society. In the 1860s, Lady Stanley of Alderley encapsulated such social mobility in a terse comment: 'Half the peerage have no grandfathers.' It was the acceleration of this tendency after the agricultural depression of the mid 1870s that was so striking. The price of land fell alarmingly (between 1875 and 1897 the value of agricultural land had fallen from £54 to £19 an acre) and the fusion between land and commerce increased. By 1900 'the new rich were setting up in country houses, being given titles and continuing to take the train up to their offices in order to deal in newspapers, ships, tobacco, coal, gold or linoleum'.[7]

The architectural historian Joe Mordaunt Crook writes: 'By the end of the First World War, in London, in the shires, the ascendancy of money was indisputable. A new type of élite had been established…the Edwardian period was the age *par excellence* of the *arriviste*.'[8] It was an unsettling experience: Lady Dorothy Nevill, who had been at court, wrote in 1910 regretting that when she had first known London society it was 'more like a large family than anything else':

> Everyone knew who everyone else was…mere wealth was no passport…in the [eighteen] forties none of the millionaires had yet appeared. There were rumours of Hudson, the railway king, and his wife, but they were never in Society…[but] very soon the old social privileges of birth and breeding were swept aside by the mob of plebeian wealth which surged into the drawing rooms, the portals of which had up till then been so jealously guarded. Since that time not a few of the mob have themselves obtained titles, and now quite honestly believe that they are the old aristocracy.[9]

'The advance of new money can be measured even more clearly by the dramatic spread of the Edwardian baronetage,' wrote Mordaunt Crook. There had been Victorian baronets with a background in trade, but in the Edwardian period the baubles rained down on new money. In 1905, eight millionaires were nominated, their wealth made from lace, cotton, coal, US property, banking and shipping.

The 'mere wealth' of this 'new aristocracy' was remarkable. The word 'millionaire' was a nineteenth-century coinage – or rather import from France – and was used to label those who had made their fortunes in the Industrial Revolution, but between 1809 and 1858 only ten non-landed millionaires were recorded: wealth was still in land. Just after the First World War the balance had tipped decisively. Between 1860 and 1920, 188 non-landed millionaires had died and these men represented 'new money'. When income tax was eight pence in the pound they left their legacies in cash, shares and bonds rather than land. Of the very richest who left over £5 million, Charles Morrison was a warehouseman and merchant banker, Henry O. Wills was a tobacco magnate, and Alfred Beit and Sir Julius Wernher were both gold and diamond magnates, though the Dukes of Derby and Westminster – traditional aristocrats whose money was in land and property – also got in above the £5 million wire.[10]

With their new riches, the men who had not made it from land determined to buy land and build houses on it to emulate the landed aristocracy, or surpass them in the size and grandeur of their homes. It was, as the economic historian W. D. Rubinstein has written, the respect wealth paid to status.[11] Of those one hundred or so new peers created from non-landed backgrounds between 1886 and 1914, about a third had 'compensated for their origins by buying big estates', in Mordaunt Crook's words.[12] Land was traditionally regarded as 'safe': 'It was impossible for land to burn down, or be stolen, or blow up, or sink at sea,' writes Mark Girouard.[13] Land was reliable, it was prestigious and it gave a fellow a permanent stake in the country. It was not, however, the best return on investment for most of the nineteenth century, and by the 1880s it turned out not to be safe at all.

With declining agricultural prices, due largely to the influx of cheap corn from the US and to falling rents, and trumped by the introduction of graduated death duties which rose to a maximum of 8 per cent on fortunes in excess of a million by the Liberal Chancellor of the Exchequer Sir William Harcourt in his 1894 budget, confidence in the land among those who had traditionally owned it was dramatically eroded.[14] In the words of Oscar Wilde's Lady Bracknell: 'What with the duties expected of one during one's lifetime and the duties exacted from one after one's death, land has ceased to be either a profit or a pleasure. It gives one a position, and prevents one from keeping it up. That's all that can be said about land.'[15] Though this view of the effects of death duties and other forms of taxation was greatly exaggerated prior to Lloyd George's 'people's budget' in 1909, squeezed between a world economy that was distinctly to their disadvantage and a government that seemed distinctly unwilling to make concessions, all but the super rich among the aristocracy found it necessary to retrench, curtail spending and sell off land, art – and houses. In the years between the accession of Edward VII and the First World War, Holbeins, Rembrandts, Raphaels, Canalettos, Gainsboroughs and works by lesser artists from private aristocratic collections all went under the hammer, as did silver, gold, china, furniture, books and jewels. From the 1880s landed families sold off their town houses, their subsidiary land, and often their houses on the land too. Wings that had been added in the golden age of Victorian optimism and prosperity were demolished – and sometimes whole houses too. Between 1879 and 1914 some seventy-nine great houses were destroyed and the figure continued to rise after the First World War.[16] By 1914 around 80,000 acres of English land had changed hands for some £20 million including large tracts belonging to the Duke of Bedford. As the *Estates Gazette* noted, 'the unanimity of large English landlords in selling their estates clearly points to some great change in the condition of affairs in this country', with 'the slicing off of large portions of ancestral

'A fabulous animal having the head and wings of an eagle and the body and hind quarters of a lion'. The Griffin gate at Manderston.

and extensive domains'.[17] It was much the same in Scotland: the Marquess of Queensbury sold half his holdings of land in Dumfriesshire in 1897; the Duke of Argyll disposed of the Island of Tiree; the Duke of Fife sold off vast tracts of his land between 1880 and 1889; and the Duke of Sutherland put 330,000 of his Scottish acres on the market.[18]

If they did not sell their houses, then – strapped for cash – the landed gentry were increasingly unable or reluctant to extend their existing residences, or build new ones. Well over half the large houses that had been built between 1835 and 1874 were at their behest, but from 1875 to 1914 the proportion fell to less than one-fifth.[19] A number of great houses did find buyers among the new plutocracy. Sir Julius Wernher bought Luton Hoo, designed by Robert Adam and built for the 3rd Earl of Bute, Prime Minister to George III, in 1767, the gardens laid out by 'Capability' Brown; the Guinness family bought Elveden Hall in Suffolk (from a wealthy – and extravagant – Indian maharajah); the soap-boiler Joseph Watson bought Compton Verney from the 19th Baron Willoughby de Broke; in 1904 Apethorpe Hall near Peterborough was sold to the grandson of the railway contractor Sir Thomas Brassey; and the heir to the Glasgow chemical manufacturer, Sir Charles Tennant, whose hydrochloric-acid belching chimney rose above the city 'higher than the campanile at Cremona',[20] commissioned Lutyens to build him a house at Rolveden in Kent

Lady Miller's London house, 45 Grosvenor Square in Mayfair, decorated for the coronation of George V in 1911.

(1907–1909).[21] The hugely wealthy American plutocrat, William Waldorf Astor, whose wife Nancy Astor would become the first woman to take her seat in House of Commons, bought two: in 1893 he acquired Cliveden on the Thames in Buckinghamshire, which had been rebuilt to the design of the architect Sir Charles Barry by the fabulously wealthy Duke of Sutherland in 1850–1; and in 1903 the thirteenth-century Hever Castle in Kent, the childhood home of Anne Boleyn.[22]

But in many cases the new 'super wealthy', or even the very rich, did not buy the seats of those above them on the social ladder: they purchased part of the estate of the landed gentry and built, or rebuilt, their own houses. 'Turning to the present time,' wrote an architect (and future President of the Royal Institute of British Architects) in 1908, 'probably more country houses are being built and more money and thought expended on them, than at any time since the days of the Stuarts.'[23] The houses represented notable commercial success and the consolidation of this success through investment in land – or rather the countryside. The town house enabled the pursuit of business and the participation in the London season, which ran from the start of the new parliamentary session in

February (or April or May if a family had no contact with political life) to late July when there was a general exodus to the sea – yachting at Cowes, maybe, or a *séjour* on the French Riviera – the country and the grouse moors followed by a spot of partridge shooting, and then the hunting season began.

Sir James Miller owned a house at 45 Grosvenor Square in Mayfair in addition to Manderston. The country house was intended for leisure, the semblance of a rural life to enable country pursuits like hunting, fishing and shooting. Such houses usually stood in fairly extensive grounds but were ornaments on the land rather than deriving an income from it, as aristocratic landed families had in earlier times. In the Edwardian period, the country houses of the *nouveaux riches* were devoted to pleasure and conspicuous consumption: they were set up for entertaining. Who knows, one day Edward VII and the smart set that eddied around him (many of them such as the tea king, Sir Thomas Lipton, and the financier Sir Ernest Cassel were very notably 'new money' men themselves) might include such a house on their social peregrinations. In 1896, the then Princess of Wales for the first time ever stayed in a commoner's home, West Dean Park in Sussex. The magazine *World* noted this social landmark: 'Until this surprising "end of the century" not even a Prince had stayed in any but the most important houses. At one time the visit of a monarch or an heir apparent made the greatest of great ladies, great statesmen or great courtiers, greater. But by degrees the line has been drawn lower and still lower, until at last of very few rich people can it be said that they have never had royalty under their roofs.'[24]

The carriage driver, Tristan, stands at the front door to assist a dinner-party guest to alight from a horseless carriage.

With its 109 rooms, its commanding position, its imposing façade, its 56 acres of formal gardens with manicured lawns, a sinuous lake, and pleasant garden walks – only the distant Cheviots on the horizon look wild and untidy – Manderston is a paradigm of such an Edwardian monument to money and the pleasures it can buy. Inside, the impression is reinforced to the power of ten. It did not need the sociologist Thorstein Veblen, writing in 1899, to point out how precisely material goods were coming to represent the status of their owners, or, the hopes of their owners, the correlation between emulation and consumption.[25] Anyone could read the alphabet of aspiration from Sir James Miller's essay in Classicism in the hallway with its vistas of marble. It was a hallway for show whose use was redundant from its construction, since the introduction of bells throughout the house did away with the necessity for servants to lurk permanently in that grand space. But it was floored with a magnificent roundel of inlaid marble (based on the one at Kedleston Hall) and housed a marble statue of Miriam and the infant Moses by Franco Barzaghe, and from it rose the famed silver staircase with crystal stair rods leading to the first floor where a silver-plated bath reposed in the master bedroom suite. There were Adam-style plastered ceilings and Wedgwood bas-reliefs, solid rosewood doors and then there were the furnishings. '[Manderston] arguably contains the most extravagant and best-preserved examples of Edwardian upholstery in Britain,' conceded *Country Life*, which first appeared in 1897 to feed the British (and overseas) romanticism about the countryside in general, and the house in the country in particular. It is where 'luxury and opulence are matched by quality in every detail'.[26]

Dinner party guests entering the dining room, the entrance to which is flanked by the two impassive-looking footmen in Charles and Robin mode.

The furnishings and decoration of Manderston had been placed in the capable hands of the fashionable London firm of Charles Meillier & Co., the company that had completely redecorated Sir James's Grosvenor Square house in 1897.[27] The firm was probably established in the 1860s and continued in business until the 1930s. At the time of Manderston's rebuilding, smart money had a taste for Louis XV- and Louis XVI-style interiors, and this is what Meillier provided for Sir James's country seat. They also provided the high-quality reproduction furniture – chosen not on the grounds of cost (or if so, inversely so), since for example a reproduction Louis XV Régence cupboard with marquetry inlay was for sale in 1905 for £2,400. Meiller & Co. provided floor plans, drawn to scale, to show how they expected their furniture to be displayed. For example, the highly formal furniture – chairs, small tables, commodes and screens – that furnishes the living room was to be disposed around the room with an insouciant disregard for symmetry and an almost minimalist approach in comparison to the over-stuffed rooms of the high Victorian period less than a decade or so earlier. The curtains in the ballroom were woven with gold and silver thread, which sparkled under the huge crystal chandelier, while the wall hangings there and in the ballroom were 'an immense extravagance',[28] made of brocatelle (a more dramatic – and expensive – fabric than damask) figured in white satin, and cut velvet, with the exceptionally large repeat patterns that were so fashionable in the Edwardian era, replete with draped valances, flounces and tassels, all hung from heavy brass poles, while the Louis Seize chairs in the drawing room and ballroom were covered in rich silk and brocade.

With its impressive exterior and awe-inducing interior, its eighteen bedrooms for family and guests, and including a 'bachelors' corridor' (a self-contained little colony of four bedrooms with their own bathrooms for unmarried men whose late-night revelry and strong cigarettes were shut off

'Dinner stands alone as an institution sacred to the highest rites of hospitality'. Sir John braces himself for the ordeal.

from the rest of the house), it was hardly surprising that Sir John Olliff-Cooper, the temporary legatee of Manderston, should wish to show off 'his' house. Some three weeks into the family's stay at Manderston, Sir John decided that the time had come for him to host a political dinner party for what he called 'the great and the good' among his Scottish neighbours, and invite political opinion-formers from across the border too.

A book of *Etiquette, Rules and Usages of the Best Society* published in 1886 instructed that 'those invited should be of the same standing in society. They need not necessarily be friends, nor even acquaintances, but, at dinner, as people come into closer contact than at a dance, or any other kind of party, those only should be invited to meet one another who move in the same class of circles.'[29]

I t's an absolute minefield,' Lady Olliff-Cooper sighed as she sat at her desk wrestling with whom to invite, and how to seat them, writing names on small cards and inserting and reinserting them into a red velvet simulacrum of the oval-shaped Manderston dining table. At her elbow lay an open copy of *Burke's Peerage*. Invitations should be sent out 'from two to ten days in advance', insisted one contemporary guide to etiquette (which seems rather short notice for anyone with an active Edwardian social life). Another, written by Mrs Humphry (who, as 'Madge', was the guru of the magazine *Truth*, and a contributor to *Everywoman's Encyclopaedia*), advised:

> The usual length of an invitation to dinner is three weeks, but this is by no means a fixed rule. In the height of the season it may be abridged or extended, according to circumstances. Sometimes a hastily got up dinner might be given for someone who is passing through London, or visiting some provincial town. Foolish indeed, and inexperienced in the ways of the great world, would be the person who would take exception to a short invitation in these circumstances. In the same way a distant date is sometimes fixed at a time when everyone may be supposed to be fully engaged for several weeks to come and a dinner invitation has been received as much as six weeks in advance of the date fixed. This is, of course, very exceptional.[30]

Informal invitations ran along the lines of 'Dear Mrs Green, Will you and Mr Green dine with us in a friendly way on Tuesday, 9th July at eight o'clock?'[31] This easy spontaneity, however, was not permitted for formal invitations, which could be written 'on notepaper of the small size known to stationers as "invitation notes". Or they could be cards: 'the usual size is 4½ by 3½ inches, and the printed characters are copperplate'. They are 'issued in the name of the gentleman and lady of the house:[32] 'Sir John and Lady Olliff-Cooper request the pleasure of the company of…' Mrs Humphry

'The man of "perfect manners" is he who is calmly courteous in all circumstances'. Lord Steel arrives at the political dinner party.

points out that 'it will be seen that the only items to be filled in are the name or names of the guests, the date and hour. Sometimes "honour" is used rather than "pleasure" and occasionally the "R.S.V.P" is replaced by "An answer will oblige", an ungrammatical sentence which some persons prefer to the initial letters of the French phrase,' sniffed the etiquette-meister. 'The form of invitation cards varies slightly,' she prescribed, 'but the simplest are those used by persons of the highest rank. Those who do not care to copy the customs of the aristocracy often have their crests in gilding on their invitation card' and, she added with disdain, 'I have even seen two crests ornamenting one card.'

Clearly, there was no question of that: the Edwardian Country House might not be a ducal seat but there would be no vulgarity in any communications that issued from *its* portals. The requisite-sized, simple cards were ordered in raised, black copperplate. They could, after all, be used for the variety of social events that were envisaged for the coming months by filling in 'dinner', 'ball', 'fête' or 'shoot', to indicate precisely at which function a guest's pleasure (or honour) was requested.

Receipt of such an invitation placed a complex social responsibility on the invitee too. 'An answer should be returned at once, so that if the invitation is declined the hostess may modify her arrangements accordingly. The mode of replying is regulated by that of the invitation. It would be a great mistake to answer a friendly note with a formal one, and though not nearly so heinous a crime, replying to a formal card by a note in the first person is sometimes misunderstood.'[33] Acceptance was simple: to decline posed a trickier problem. The excuse should be couched in the third person, something along the lines of 'Mr Anstruther regrets very much that he will not be able to accept Sir John and Lady Olliff-Cooper's kind invitation for the 7th as he will not be in the country, having previously arranged to spend a week with friends in Monte Carlo' should be acceptable. The commonplace 'owing to a previous engagement' was considered to be so overused as to constitute an example of 'studied incivility', other than in the 'most formal cases, or where the acquaintance is very slight' when presumably the inviter would be uninterested in the minutiae of the invitee's daily round.

How to invite, and *when* had now been established. But *who* to invite was no easier. The general guidelines were clear: 'A host and hostess generally judge of the success of a dinner by the manner in which conversation has been sustained. If it has flagged often, it is considered proof that the guests have not been congenial; but if a steady stream of talk has been kept up, it shows that they have smoothly

'It is not correct' instructed an etiquette manual 'to forget that if dinner is the important meal of the day in the matters of food and wine, so it is in courtesy, conversation and geniality'.

amalgamated, as a whole.'[34] It was all a question, as Mrs Beeton sagely remarked, of 'care being taken by the hostess, in the selection of invited guests, that they should be suited to each other'.[35]

The Edwardian Country House was to host a political dinner, so it would be politicians around whom the event would revolve, interspersed by local people of note and interest to ensure a lively, but not contentious, evening of good conversation. The oval mahogany table in the Manderston dining room could be extended to seat twenty people with ease, and so, counting the family as four, Sir John and Lady Olliff-Cooper, Miss Anson and Mr Jonathan (Master Guy would certainly not have been included, as no one under fourteen would be seen at the dinner table), that meant drawing up a list of sixteen people to invite – with a handful of names in reserve in case some on the A list were 'otherwise engaged'. Soon invitations were written and posted, and prompt replies received.

Sir David Steel, ex-leader of the Liberal party, was coming, with his wife. He had been a Westminster MP for border constituencies from 1965 to 1997, and is now a Liberal Democrat Scottish MP, and the Scottish Parliament's first presiding officer. The MP for Berwick-upon-Tweed and deputy leader of the Liberal Democrat party, Alan Beith, and his wife, Baroness Maddock (herself a former Lib-Dem MP), had accepted, as had Lord Deedes, a grand old man of British politics and journalism who was born in 1913. From a landed Kentish family, Deedes, a former editor of the *Daily Telegraph* and a Conservative MP for twenty-four years, was both the supposed model for Evelyn Waugh's intrepid Boot, and the recipient of the 'Dear Bill' spoof letters from Denis Thatcher that enjoyed such success in *Private Eye*. The final politician was David Mellor, once in the House as Conservative member for Putney; he had put his various political and personal vicissitudes behind him and is now a broadcaster, sports columnist, chairman of the government's task force on football, and a sought-after guest in political salons. In addition to the political contingent, Lady Chelsea, who is herself a modern-day authority on etiquette, would be coming (and would be eagle-eyed in noticing if the parvenus were 'up to snuff' in their first major social test in the Edwardian Country House). Some local guests had been invited, including Mr Liddell Grainger and Lady De La Rue, from nearby Ayton Castle which the Olliff-Coopers had visited, along with personal friends of the Olliff-Coopers, including Baron Bentinck and his wife, who were travelling up from Hampshire for the occasion, and Mr Jonathan had been allowed to invite a friend of his own age.

Lady Olliff-Cooper carefully copied the names of the guests on to small place cards – and then began the delicate business of constructing a table plan. It wasn't just common-sense courtesies like seating people next to those with whom they were likely to have something in common, yet not know so well that they would have nothing new to say. Husband and wife combinations were, of course, to be avoided, and the sexes interspersed. In addition there were the rules of rank and precedence and these were labyrinthine. Manuals for butlers and footmen would have routinely printed tables of precedence, and familiarity with these would have been expected in the competent servant. This was no easy task in the Edwardian period. In the reign of Edward VII the annual number of new barons quintupled from that of his mother, Queen Victoria, within a generation. And the creations were overwhelmingly *nouveau riche*. In 1905, for example, the Tory government nominated eight millionaires for elevation.[36] To help anxious hostesses cope with the influx of newcomers (of which they themselves might be one) to high society, Burke (of *Peerage* fame) published a *Book of Precedence* in 1881 which contained an alphabetical list with a key number by each entry. These 'indicate at a glance the position of the various grades in society',[37] for those for whom such information had not been imbibed with their mother's (or possibly wet nurse's) milk.

The greatest complexity lay in the fact that protocol of precedence had to be maintained within each hierarchical institution, and problems could arise when these cut across aristocratic definitions of place.[38] Gwen Raverat, a granddaughter of Charles Darwin and thus a member of the 'aristocracy of intellect', recalled the difficulties of a Cambridge dinner party:

> The guests were seated according to the Protocol, the Heads of Houses ranking by dates of the foundations of their colleges, except that the Vice-Chancellor would come first of all. After the Masters came the Regius Professors in the order of their subjects, Divinity first; and then the other Professors according to the dates of the foundations of their chairs, and so on down all the steps of the hierarchy. It was better not to invite too many important people at the same time, or the complications became insoluble to hosts of ordinary culture. How could they tell if Hebrew or Greek took precedence, of two professorships founded in the same year? And some of the grandees were very touchy about their rights, and their wives were even more easily offended.[39]

It was unlikely that a sister of Lord Curzon would have been so rigid in her *placements* at Manderston, but as newcomers the Olliff-Coopers were determined to play by the book and, according to their manuals, some rules were immutable: the principal female guest – 'the lady to whom [the host] wishes to pay most attention' according to Mrs Beeton, 'either on account of her age, position, or from her being the greatest stranger to the party'[40] – would be seated on the right of the host (and be led into dinner by him), while her husband (if she had one and he was present) would escort the hostess into dinner and sit himself on her right. So Lady Chelsea sat to Sir John's right and, since she was unaccompanied, Lord Steel was to Lady Olliff-Cooper's right, Lord Deedes on the other side while Lady Steel was placed to the left of Sir John. The rest of the company are seated 'as specified by the master and the mistress of the house, according to their rank and other circumstances which may be known to the host and hostess'.[41]

'A lord takes precedence over a baron, doesn't he?' pondered Lady Olliff-Cooper (though in Britain the titles are interchangeable). 'But what if he's a foreign baron?' she wondered further, thinking of the Dutch Baron Bentinck. 'Then Lord Deedes fought in the Second World War and Jonty knows quite a bit about the military from his time in the Cadet Force at Winchester, so it might be nice to seat those two together. And then Jonty is going up to Oxford to read history, and hopes to take some politics too, so maybe he could have Alan Beith on his other side?'

Lady Greville reminded hostesses that 'though the viands are good, they are but accessories; it is especially the bringing together of congenial spirits that is aimed at. A man must not be too great a talker, nor a woman too much taken up with herself; each must contribute his share to the general fund of conversation, and each must come with the determination to appear at his very best and brightest.'[42] But Lady Olliff-Cooper was 'not quite sure yet who's who in that respect. And now I've got two women sitting next to each other and that'll never do. I'll have to start all over again,' she said, pulling all the cards out.

Then there were decisions to be made about what food and wine to serve. Wearily, she reached across her now cluttered desk and rang for the chef.

It is,' explained a new edition of *Mrs Beeton's Household Management* published in 1888, 'in the large establishments of princes, noblemen and very affluent families alone that the man-cook is found in this country,' and indeed Queen Victoria had had a male chef, M. Menager, who was a very superior person himself, living in a smart London house, travelling to work by hansom and coining £500 a year (roughly £32,500 in today's terms), when an apprentice cook could expect to earn about £15 per annum.[43] She also employed a number of sous-chefs, an Italian confectioner and an Indian cook for the curries.

By the Edwardian age, a French (or at least French-trained) chef was what 'very affluent' families aspired to. France suggested Paris and that suggested Second Empire luxuries such as truffles, oysters, game, patisseries, fine chocolates and champagne. There was great cachet in a French menu, and dinner guests would be impressed to hear that it was not just the ingredients that had been imported, but the man to prepare them as well. After all, 'the art of cookery, or *gourmanderie*, is reduced to a regular science in France, where an egg may be cooked half a hundred

The chef

M. Denis Dubiard, the French chef in the Edwardian Country House, was taught to cook by his grandmothers, who both lived in rural France. His grandfather was also a truffle hunter, who managed to find truffles without the help of either pigs or dogs snorting out the delicacies. 'My grandfather just used his nose. He would go out early in the morning and come back laden with truffles. It was amazing.'

It was from his grandmothers that M. Dubiard inherited his instinct for food and his love of cooking, and learned the rudiments of his craft – including cooking on an open coal fire. 'I love cooking traditional dishes, slowly on an open hearth. That is one of the reasons why I wanted to come to cook in an Edwardian house. I am fed up with modern technology, I wanted to come to the countryside and cook in the old ways again, taking ingredients from nature. I have already found

game, pigeons, chickens and lots of rabbits and a plentiful supply of herbs and vegetables.'

M. Dubiard, who is thirty-eight, now lives on the edge of London with his wife and two small sons. He was born in Paris and trained at the famous Maxim's restaurant, and since then has worked in some of the finest restaurants in London.

In the vast Edwardian kitchen, he had to learn the intricacies of the range – and persuade or bully others to share the task of keeping it alight. The Olliff-Coopers had a steady stream of guests and were proud to show off their French chef's culinary prowess with elaborate dinners, plus breakfasts and lunches. And as well as cooking, M. Dubiard ministered to the servants when they were sick, compiling recipes of infusions and poultices that were 'guaranteed' to cure anything from a common cold to heartache.

ways, so those who can afford large families of servants, and give frequent entertainments, consider a man-cook as economical, because [in theory] he produces an inexhaustible variety without any waste of materials, and that elegance and piquancy of flavours which are necessary to stimulate the appetites of the luxurious'.[44] When the Olliff-Coopers arrived at Manderston, they found to their delight that they had just such a master craftsman in their own kitchen. M. Denis Dubiard was trained at Maxim's in Paris, in the tradition of the great French chefs, Escoffier and Carême, and he has subsequently worked in the finest London restaurants and various private houses.

A chef's pay varied from house to house but *The Servant's Practical Guide: a Handbook to Duties and Rules* published in 1880 gives a male cook's earnings at between £100 and £150 a year (and that did not include perks), which compared with around £60 for the butler and was higher than a female cook could have commanded. The cooks employed at Manderston appear all to have been women between 1901 and 1914, and their wages ranged from £40 to £50 a year, depending presumably on their experience and former positions. And of course there would be fierce competition for the services of a fine French chef, and the master and mistress of the house would have no desire to see their star performer lured away by higher wages and better conditions offered elsewhere.

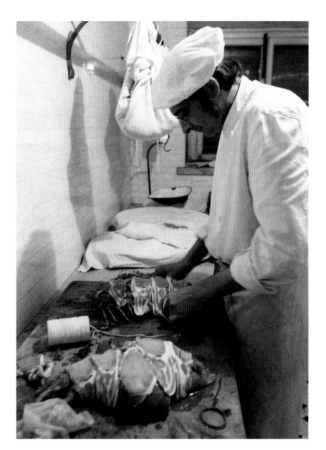

M. Dubiard prepares meat for dinner in the pantry set aside specifically for such a task.

Food served at the Edwardian dining table not only had to taste delicious, it had to look enchanting too. Snowy, damask-clothed tables, glittering with silver and crystal, would display pheasants dressed with their tail feathers, fish in aspic primped with herbs, a glazed and decorated boar's head, hocks of breadcrumbed and clove-studded ham, candied fruits or frosted grapes piled high on *tasses* (stemmed dishes), small hillocks of bonbons and sugar-spun confectioneries, cream gâteaux decorated with curls of bitter chocolate and candied violets, epergnes filled with exotic fruits or marzipan *petits fours*. There would be raised meat pies, the pastry glazed with egg, the edges crimped and decorated with pastry leaves; jellies turned out from elaborate copper moulds that made them look like shimmering, translucent castles, some with the different flavours layered in jewel-like layers of ruby, emerald and amber, others with perfect nasturtiums or pelargoniums encased in the gelatine, or with creams or fruit piled in a hollow centre; tiny pastry *bateaux* filled with raspberries or wild strawberries in season; asparagus wrapped in damask napkins and laid on silver platters; lobsters decorated with seaweed; silver lattice baskets of perfect, darkly speckled quail's eggs; and, on the grandest of occasions, a centrepiece carved from a block of ice – swans were particularly favoured.

Jellies

'Take some fine soaked and blanched calves' feet,
and set them to cook in one and three-quarters pints of water apiece.
Skim as thoroughly as possible; cover, and then cook very gently
for seven hours,' instructed the great French chef, Escoffier,
in the 1907 version of his Guide to Modern Cookery.

This method would produce the gelatine required for making the fruit and savoury jellies that were so much a feature of the Edwardian dinner table. But the 1901 edition of *Mrs Beeton's Book of Household Management* suggested that 'calves' feet are very rarely used now for the making of stock for jellies. By means of Swinborne's Patent Refined Isinglass, jelly may be made with the greatest facility in a few minutes, possessing the nutriments of calves' feet without the impurities.'

Fruit and wine syrup

Makes approximately 2 pints (around a litre).

1 pint (450ml) water
1lb 4oz (550g) granulated sugar or loaf sugar
½ lemon and ½ orange
2 star anis
4 cloves
20 coriander seeds
2 sprigs of mint and a sprig of thyme or lavender
½ vanilla pod
½ cinnamon stick
1 pint (450ml) dry white wine

Put the water and sugar in a pan, slice the lemon and orange thinly and add to the water with the remaining ingredients (except the wine). Bring to the boil, turn down the heat and allow to simmer for about 20 minutes. Add the wine and bring back to simmering point for a further 5 minutes, before removing from the heat. Leave to cool while the flavours infuse.

Strain the syrup through a fine sieve.

Pineapple and mint jelly

M. Dubiard's recipe for this jelly was highly acclaimed by the Olliff-Coopers and their guests.

½ peeled ripe pineapple
About 15 mint leaves
1 pint (450ml) cold water
¼ pint (125ml) M. Dubiard's fruit and wine syrup
½ oz (10g) powdered gelatine
A little crystallized ginger, finely chopped
Green food colouring
Peppermint food flavouring

Cut the pineapple into cubes, and place them in a saucepan with the mint leaves and cold water. Heat this, and simmer for about 10 minutes. Then add the syrup, and simmer for a further 10 minutes.

Leave it to cool and infuse before straining. Add the gelatine to the strained mixture, whisking as you do so. Put the pan on a moderate heat to dissolve the gelatine, carrying on whisking gently. Remove the pan from the heat when it reaches simmering point.

To make a layered jelly, pour the mixture into two separate bowls; add the crystallized ginger to one, and a few drops of the green food colouring and peppermint food flavouring to the other.

Pour a layer of one coloured jelly in the bottom of a copper or china jelly mould, which has been rinsed in cold water. Wait until it has just set and pour on a second layer of the contrasting jelly. Continue with alternate layers until the mould is full. Put into the fridge to set completely.

The Edwardian dinner table was a highly regarded art form. A chef was considered to be a culinary artist, and the creative temperament was only to be expected – particularly when this was spiced with coursings of Gallic blood. The oft-heard complaints about these super chefs were that they were demanding, had short fuses and were not above screaming at their helpers, flinging terse, heavily accented orders over their shoulders as they rushed from storeroom to stove, throwing pots across the kitchen and storming out at the height of preparation for dinner. And that while they might truly be geniuses when it came to dealing with crustaceans, icing delicacies, concocting rich sauces or judging the right moment to remove a soufflé from the oven, cooking the 'good, plain food' required by the servants to fuel their hard daily labours was another matter altogether.

It was the same in the Edwardian Country House kitchens. 'The chef's ordering langoustines and lobsters and seagulls' eggs and goodness knows what else for upstairs, while he basically serves us gruel, night after night,' complained the footmen and the housemaids. 'Vegetables floating in broth, or a tiny piece of pork that has gone grey with age. We need proper meals if we are to do our work properly,' Becky insisted, 'particularly these growing lads' – gesturing to Charlie, Rob, Kenny and Tristan (the groom and carriage driver who lived at the stables but joined the indoor staff for meals and relaxation). And for Becky it was particularly hard for she was a vegetarian. This is a fairly unremarkable stance today, but was unusual in Edwardian times and was often dismissed as the preserve of those with advanced sexual views and unorthodox dress codes, though in fact since the 1830s there had been a tradition of nonconformist vegetarianism. And it was certainly not, in his view, M. Dubiard's role to 'pander to the dietary peccadilloes of the servants' (a very authentic Edwardian attitude). So at first Becky literally had a very lean time.

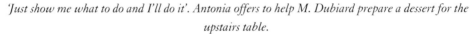

'Just show me what to do and I'll do it'. Antonia offers to help M. Dubiard prepare a dessert for the upstairs table.

A kitchen maid's endless task: Antonia peeling potatoes – again.

After a few days' discontent, and consultations between Mr Edgar and Mrs Davies, it was agreed that in future Antonia, the kitchen maid, would take over the responsibility of cooking for the servants, and she would give a list of the ingredients she needed to the housekeeper. Antonia was quite prepared to rustle up baked potatoes, macaroni cheese and the like for Becky. It was further decided that, since they had all started work at 7 a.m. if not earlier, the servants would have their main meal at 12 noon and the evening meal would be a lighter affair, sometimes using up leftovers from upstairs eked out with extra vegetables or stretched by putting them in a pie. Matters improved immediately as far as meal times below stairs were concerned.

Like all fine cooks, M. Dubiard has a visceral approach to his art: 'I chose this job because I like cooking old, traditional dishes. I enjoy getting to understand the vagaries of a coal range. I like to hear the noise it makes and to control the intense heat, juggle with the various ovens and the hotplates. And I like the countryside too. I like to get out in the fresh air and wander around or go exploring on my bicycle. I look out for birds and I enjoy plucking poultry and game, trapping rabbits and skinning them for the pot.'

But the Manderston kitchen posed some challenges: the range in particular. At first, despite everyone's best efforts it had been unused for so long that it proved impossible to get going. A number of experts were consulted and the hugely long flue that ran 15 feet horizontally under the kitchen, before striking vertically up through the house to the chimney on the roof, had to be laboriously cleaned out. When the house was first built this would have been a scene reminiscent of Charles Kingsley's *The Water Babies* with a sweep's skinny boy from Edinburgh sent wriggling along the dark, sooty flue with his brushes.

The range almost put the whole Edwardian Country House project in jeopardy. 'If we hadn't been able to cook on it we wouldn't have been able to feed either the Olliff-Coopers or the servants,' explained the senior Wall to Wall researcher on the Edwardian Country House, Mark Ball, who had spent anxious days as various experts scratched their heads at its intransigence. Finally the furnace on one side of the huge, free-standing range was lit – and stayed alight. 'When the house was built, the cook would have used one half for three months, and then used the furnace on the other side for the next three months, turn and turn about,' explained Mark, 'but as we were only here for three months we decided one side was enough.'

The great range was the heart of the kitchen, but it was a demanding, consuming presence. As a novelist explained in 1886: '[ranges] are like organs, only to be played upon by one who knows the stops'.[45] It needed to be kept alight twenty-four hours round the clock, for if it went out, it took considerable time and effort to get started again and there would be no hot water for the family's (or the servants') morning tea. It was the scullery maid's job to get up early and put coal on the smouldering embers to make sure that

'We'll experiment' instructed the chef.

it flared up in time for the other servants' arrival in the kitchen. Without a chimney above the range, as would have been the case in earlier periods, the ovens of these closed, or 'self-acting', ranges were regulated by opening or closing the flues. It was always much harder to get a good fire going when the weather was still and they wouldn't 'draw'. On the day of an important dinner party, everyone in the kitchen would be praying for a brisk wind.

It wasn't just a question of heaping on more coal either – the ash had to be cleared out and carried down the long corridor for disposal, and coal had to be carted in from the yard to be stacked in the coal hole off the kitchen to ensure an endless supply for the ravenous furnace. But neither Lucy, nor her successor Kelly, was much good at early mornings and M. Dubiard found that he was getting up at 5 a.m. to coax his range into life, until he declared firmly that a master chef would not have considered this to be part of his duties. Then Kenny, the hall boy, took over the responsibility, as well as fetching in the coal, returning to his hall cupboard bunk for an extra hour's sleep once he was sure the range was properly alight.

It was hot and heavy work in the kitchen dealing with the range, learning to judge the heat of the various ovens. It was hard for Antonia and the succession of scullery maids, preparing pounds of vegetables, ensuring that the permanently bubbling stockpot on the top of the stove was kept replenished with bones, scraps of meat and root vegetables, scrubbing a seemingly never-ending stream of pots and pans, and washing up all the implements the chef used in his cooking and the servants' crockery and cutlery – all without the aid of modern detergents and scouring powder. 'We tried to use Monkey Brand soap because this is what seems to have been used in most Edwardian kitchens,' explained Antonia, 'but it left a residue of soap on everything so we just use soda crystals and hot water. That seems to work best, but it's *very* hard on your hands.' But M. Dubiard had shown expertise here too, mixing halves of lemons with flour, salt and vinegar to ferment in a somewhat malodorous gunge kept in a pail under the sink. This proved to be a miracle cleaner for copper, bringing the saucepans up shining with not much effort, and getting rid of the verdigris that could stick to the insides of copper pots and pans, and was such a dangerous ingredient in careless Edwardian cooking.

We are arranging a dinner party for next Friday,' Lady Olliff-Cooper explained to her chef as he came through the door of the morning room in response to her summons. 'It'll be a formal occasion – we are inviting about twenty guests, and my husband is anxious to make quite an impression,' she added. The dinner party would be the first real test of the chef: a lot would be riding on its success, and it would be a challenge for all the servants too since the family was new to the area and their visitors would be curious about how the Edwardian Country House was run, its standards of cuisine, service and conversation. Did the Olliff-Coopers run an establishment commensurate with their status as one of the major country house 'owners' in the Borders?

'I was wondering what menu we might serve?' ventured Lady Olliff-Cooper.

M. Dubiard looked resolute. 'I think eight courses,' he said. 'We will start with a *consommé de boeuf*, well-laced with sherry, followed by warm oysters. Then we'll have something to refresh the palate before the fish course. I am thinking of a champagne sorbet followed by Filet de Sole Véronique. The main course, given the hunting season, should be roast venison. For dessert I will make Pêche Sara Caroline – that always creates a stir – to be followed by a good cheese board with celery and raisins and finally some *bonnes bouches* – petit fours, little trifles like that.'

'That sounds all right,' said Lady Olliff-Cooper faintly, 'but small portions, I think. Don't forget the ladies in their tight corsets and how difficult it is for them to eat much,' she added feelingly.

A master chef enjoyed more status, independence and money than the other servants, and foolish indeed would be the lady of the house who interfered, or tried to interfere, with her maestro's productions. She would expect to receive her chef's written suggestions for the lunch and dinner menus from the housekeeper at their daily meeting, and would usually expect to consult directly with the chef only on important occasions such as the Olliff-Coopers' upcoming political dinner. She would recognize that the kitchen was his fiefdom: there was no question of his mistress descending to the basement kitchen (or any other of the servants' quarters) to confront the chef in what Mrs Beeton called his 'sanctum sanctorum' – other than in exceptional circumstances. Like so many other functions of the Edwardian Country House, it was the wish of those upstairs that their every gastronomic whim was satisfied – how, and at what cost, was simply not seen as their concern.

Antonia trying out the sorbet-making machine.

Table flowers

*'Hostesses in the season vie with each other as to whose table
shall be the most elegant, and are ready to spend almost, if not
quite, as much upon the flowers as upon the food itself,
employing for the floral arrangement people who devote their time
to this pleasant occupation,' proclaimed the 1901 edition of
Mrs Beeton's Book of Household Management.*

The containers were important: some people 'prefer low decorations, others high ones, but there is one rule that should always be in force, and that is that the flowers and their receptacles should never interfere with the line of vision…the great objection to epergnes …was that they hid the guests from one another.'

For the political dinner party, the flowers were chosen to complement Lady Olliff-Cooper's dress. The containers were wicker baskets painted gold then rubbed with silver leaf and burnished with graphite so they looked suitably old; they blended well with the soft pink and reds of the chosen roses – full-blown Bourbon and Gallicia variety. Fronds of asparagus fern were studded between the roses, and the baskets were edged with *Alchemilla mollis* in three different shades of pink, while swathes of small-leaved tree ivy trailed across the table. Any small gaps were covered with damp moss and the arrangement placed on a glass plate to protect both the mahogany table and the white damask cloth. It would also have been usual to use fruit – pineapples or waxy apples or velvet-like peaches – which would have been wired into containers with flowers.

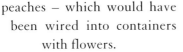

In Edwardian times, the flowers would have been secured by tying small bundles of rosemary or lavender twigs with raffia and packing them into the container vertically. Individual stems and foliage would then be pushed in between the twigs to keep them upright, and water poured in to the container.

In country houses, the gardener would have been in charge of tending the flowers and cutting blooms to decorate the table every day. For a dinner party, the head gardener would be informed of what colour flowers were required and either he, or someone skilled in floral arts, would make up the arrangements in the greenhouse or potting shed. The finished decorations would be carried in through the servants' entrance for the butler or footmen to place where required.

For very grand occasions, when the whole house was to be decorated with flowers, a team of gardeners would arrive at the crack of dawn to ensure that all was ready before the master and mistress came downstairs.

CHAPTER FIVE

Dressing
for Dinner

Eva Morrison was a natural choice as a lady's maid: 'I knew she was absolutely right the moment I saw her,' enthused Rosalind Ebbutt, the costume designer, who had been present at the auditions since she knew better than anyone the range of skills that a lady's maid in a grand Edwardian country house would need to possess. *The Complete Servant* spelt out what those were:

> A lady's maid is generally to be near the person of her lady; and to be properly qualified for her situation, her education should be superior to that of the ordinary class of female servants, particularly in needlework, and the useful and ornamental branches of female acquirements. To be peculiarly neat and clean in her person, is better than to be tawdry or attractive, as intrinsic merit is a much greater recommendation than extrinsic appearance. In temper she should be cheerful and submissive, studying her lady's disposition, and conforming to it with alacrity. A soft and courteous demeanour will best entitle her to esteem and respect. In fine, her character should be remarkable for industry and moderation, her manners and deportment, for modesty and humility, and her dress for neatness, simplicity and frugality.[1]

Miss Morrison (or Morrison as she was known upstairs) is a Scot who had trained and worked as a hairdresser for many years, and had recently honed her sewing skills in the haberdasher's shop she and her mother own. Coupled with Miss Morrison's enthusiasm for the period and her delight in rich Edwardian fabrics – flurries of silk, satins, chiffon, tussore, faille, crêpe de Chine, mohair and cashmere – and trimmings of lace, fur, feathers and braid, there was no doubt that she would be able to offer invaluable assistance in matters sartorial as well as practical to the two women participants in the Edwardian 'experiment', Lady Olliff-Cooper and her sister Avril.

A lady's maid enjoyed a high status in the hierarchy of Edwardian servants. She was one of the 'upper ten' and would enjoy their privileges; she was not expected to wear a pinafore as she would not be undertaking any menial or grimy tasks. She would take dessert with the butler and the housekeeper in 'pug's parlour', and have morning tea brought to her by the first housemaid, while the second housemaid followed behind to make up the fire in her room. A lady's maid would have her room cleaned for her by the housemaids, she would be free to take a bath as often as she wished in the female upper servants' bathroom rather than a tin tub that was the lot of the lower servants – and may well have been given some perfumed unguents or salts by milady to pour in the water. She would be well dressed herself since one of her perks would be to have some of her mistress's clothes handed down to her once they had seen out a season, and her dexterity with needle and thread would mean that she could alter them to suit her size and personal style. A lady's maid would frequently retire with the housekeeper to either of their comfortable upstairs bedsitting rooms at the end of the evening to gossip by the fire, while the lower servants indulged in more boisterous activities in the servants' hall in the basement.

Her responsibilities were to her mistress: her first duty was to wake the lady of the house with tea and toast, or an arrowroot biscuit, draw the curtains in the bedroom and discuss with her mistress what her plans were for the day and which clothes she would be requiring. The maid would then draw her mistress's bath, or pour out the water she had brought up from the kitchen into a china bowl for washing, lay out her mistress's clothes – including underwear (if she had not done so the night before) – and then help her to dress.

Her mistress would then sit down at her dressing table and busy herself with her toiletries while her maid dressed her hair. First Miss Morrison would brush Lady Olliff-Cooper's hair, which she had plaited the night before, and then tease her long, blonde tresses into an elaborate Edwardian roll swept off her collar. To achieve the necessary fullness that was fashionable at the time, she would wind the hair around what were inelegantly called 'rats'. In her novel *The Edwardians*, Vita Sackville-West described them as 'unappetizing objects, like last year's bird's-nests, hot and stuffy to the head, but they could not be dispensed with, since they provided the foundation on which the coiffure was to be swathed and piled and into which innumerable hairpins were to be stuck. It was always a source of great preoccupation with the ladies that no bit of the pad should show though the natural hair. Often they put a tentative hand up to feel, even in the midst of the most absorbing conversation.'[2]

The lady's maid

Eva Morrison was in no doubt why she had volunteered to come to the Edwardian Country House as a lady's maid. She wanted to pay homage to her hard-working grandmother, who had been in service as a kitchen maid with the Earl and Countess of Antrim, leaving her East Lothian home to voyage to Ireland as a young girl just before the First World War. She had stayed at Castle Antrim for three years until she had to return to Scotland to nurse her sick mother. 'My mission is to relive my grandmother's life,' Miss Morrison said resolutely. She had no doubt that that was the position she wanted in the project, and she was ideally qualified for it. She had had her own hairdressing salon, and now runs a soft-furnishing and haberdashery shop with her mother on the outskirts of Edinburgh. Miss Morrison does alterations and mends fine garments in a workroom at the back.

Her student daughter was incredulous: 'Why do you want to work as someone's maid?' But when Miss Morrison watches films, she 'never watches the actresses, all I look at are the costumes', and she knew that she was in her element from the moment she started to unpack Lady Olliff-Cooper's dresses, shaking out the creases and hanging them up, brushing coats, smoothing out feathers and furs, sorting the intricacies of Edwardian corsets and underwear… But it was soon apparent that Miss Morrison's skills would be in great demand from upstairs and down – washing underwear and blouses, even scrubbing corsets, mending clothes, cutting hair and powdering the footmen's hair for formal dinners. 'Accolades to her virtues fall readily from my pen,' wrote Lady Olliff-Cooper in a reference, should her lady's maid ever think of making the higher reaches of domestic service her lifetime career.

Morrison had a solution: she had read that an Edwardian maid would nightly collect the loose hair from her lady's hairbrush and form this into rolls to bulk out the elegant hairstyle she was creating. These elaborate styles provided the ideal platform for the elegant picture hats that are so redolent an image of the Edwardian period. These were huge, often anchored by vicious-looking hat pins with jewelled or enamelled ends; decorated with lavish trimmings such as osprey or ostrich feathers, they could cost as much as 50 guineas (around £3,000 at today's prices). Miss Anson had a modern, short, layered hairstyle, which defied any attempt to fashion it into a credible Edwardian coiffure, so she wore a wig, and the care and styling of that fell to Miss Morrison too.

Washing hair was a problem in the Edwardian Country House: at first Miss Morrison had followed a recipe for shampoo that involved lemon juice and egg yolk but, far from conditioning the hair, it made it dull and sticky. Further experiments adding vinegar were more successful and Sir John was happy with that. But Lady Olliff-Cooper disliked the smell of vinegar about her person, and contented herself with Miss Morrison's 'dry shampoo' method – talcum powder rubbed into the hair and then brushed vigorously out again every four or five days.

For grand occasions, a maid might dress her mistress's hair with a tiara, or, for slightly less formal occasions, a jewel-studded comb, or maybe she would weave lace or ribbons or artificial leaves into the hair. One night when Lady Olliff-Cooper set off for the opera in nearby Berwick-upon-Tweed, Miss

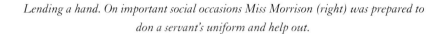

Lending a hand. On important social occasions Miss Morrison (right) was prepared to don a servant's uniform and help out.

*'Everything does up at the back!' Miss Morrison helps
Lady Olliff-Cooper dress.*

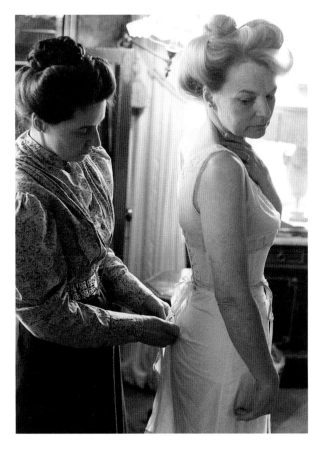

Morrison stood just inside the front door and proudly watched her mistress get into her carriage wearing a marabou-trimmed pink taffeta cape over her dress, with a 'fascinator' in her hair consisting of a spray of osprey feathers, to complete the elegant outfit.

A lady's maid needed nimble fingers for hairdressing and sewing, and also to do up all the hooks on the corsets and the dresses and high-necked blouses that Edwardian women wore, for these did up at the back, making the wearer entirely dependent on help in getting dressed. Miss Morrison would lace Lady Olliff-Cooper's corset, pulling in the waist as tight as was bearable on formal occasions, since in Edwardian times a curvaceous figure was much admired. A new design of corset introduced in 1900 was intended to be more 'natural' and 'healthy' than Victorian ones that exerted great pressure on the waist and diaphragm. It produced an S-shaped figure by forcing the bust forward and the derrière out. But in more Junoesque women the effect was rather more a 'kangaroo stance' with an overhanging 'balcony bust' which was a good foot ahead of the rest of the body.[3] The earliest memory of the photographer Cecil Beaton (who was born in 1904) was of ladies 'laced into corsets that gave them pouter-pigeon bosoms and protruding posteriors'.[4]

New technologies made it more possible to mould women to this much-coveted sinuousness in the Edwardian period than it would have been a century earlier. The corsets were extra-long and flat fronted and the metal hooks could be subjected to what amounted to almost mechanical force, and metal eyelets allowed laces to be yanked in much further than had been the case with stitched silk eyelets.[5] Vita Sackville-West described the elaborate process:

> Buttons [the lady's maid] knelt before her, carefully drawing the silk stockings on to her feet and smoothing them nicely up her leg. Then [the Duchess] would rise, and, standing in her chemise, would allow the maid to fit the long stays of pink coutil [a strong cotton fabric], heavily boned, around her hips and slender figure, fastening the busk down the front, after many adjustments; then the suspenders would be clipped to the stockings; then lacing would follow, beginning at the waist and travelling gradually up and down, until the necessary proportions had been achieved. The silk laces and their tags would fly in and out, under the maid's deft fingers with the flick of the skilled worker mending a net. Then the pads of pink satin would be brought and fastened into place on the hips and under the arms still further to accentuate the smallness of the waist. [6]

Hair ornaments

By the reign of Edward VII, Society women's hats
had reached almost ridiculous proportions on some occasions.
Massive creations perched on top of elaborate hairstyles and were
weighed down with feathers, braid, lace, artificial flowers and fruit
and were sometimes kept on with a long chiffon scarf that
tied under the chin.

No Edwardian lady would have ventured outside without a hat, and since hats were so decorative and also so hard to put on, they were frequently worn indoors on social occasions – including at the lunch table. Even young girls would never go out bare-headed.

These elaborate hats were usually secured by beautiful, though lethal-looking hat pins made of steel anchored through non-too clean hair (since freshly-washed hair was too soft and floppy to provide a satisfactory base) and with decorative ends made of jet, pearl or lacquered enamel.

However, for evenings, when hats were not worn, a decoration of feathers or ribbons might be worn in the hair. The elaborate hairstyles of the Edwardian era meant that it was easy to secure such decorations with wire, but with today's less formal styles, they can be attached to hair combs or to 'scrunchie' bands used to tie hair into a bunch.

Ostrich, peacock, marabou or pheasant feathers can be wired on, as can small bunches of tiny fabric flowers, while adhesive face and body 'tattoos', or paste diamante can be glued on to combs.

Despite the popularity of feathers on millinery and hair decorations, and on the bodices of dresses sometimes, there was a movement against the mass slaughter of birds in order to provide decoration for the heads of society women which was already gaining momentum. In 1889, various 'fur and feather' groups (in this context, fur meant down rather than animal skins) came together to form the Society for the Protection of Birds, which received a Royal Charter from the game-shooting Edward VII in 1904. As a result of the society's lobbying, the Importation of Plumage (Prohibition) Bill was introduced in 1908, but did not become law until 1921.

In the Edwardian Country House, the women found that tight lacing placed restrictions on breathing and movement – and women's magazines were loud in their condemnation of this practice. 'It is a great mistake to think it is ever necessary to tight-lace,' fulminated *Woman's Life* in 1906. 'It is always undesirable and always inartistic. More ruined digestions, more red noses, more weak hearts, more agonies of pain…have been caused by this than anything.'

'I can only perch on hard chairs, I certainly can't relax into sofas or armchairs and I can hardly bend down to cuddle Guy, my corset is so constricting,' Lady Olliff-Cooper regretted, while the whalebone stays chafed so unmercifully that she would slip a fine cotton or silk vest next to her skin. Edwardian underwear was made of cotton – and was saucy in that the bloomers were crutchless to make it possible to use the loo without a major production, though some had a buttoned flap (or trapdoor) for the same purpose. Silk stockings would be fastened on to the corset's suspenders and next came cotton petticoats, usually trimmed with Brussels or Honiton lace in the case of the 'upstairs' contingent, then an underskirt. It was then time to put on the dress, or blouse and skirt if it was to be a quiet day without visitors. If the maid was dressing her mistress for a grand dinner or ball, precious jewellery would be fetched from the safe in the butler's room, but otherwise appropriate pieces would be chosen from the casket on milady's dressing table. The lady of the house was then ready for breakfast, and she swept downstairs, while her maid would tidy her dressing table and collect any

'A [lady's] maid who wishes to make herself useful', suggested Mrs Beeton,
'will study the fashion-books with attention, so as to be able to aid her mistress's judgment
in dressing according to the prevailing fashion'.

dirty clothes for washing. She would gather up the shoes for polishing, check that any outdoor clothes needed brushing or sponging, and gather up the garments that needed running repairs or alterations.

Then it was back to her room, with armfuls of flounces, and the Edwardian lady's maid started her daily round of washing, mending and sewing in her work room. At Manderston, Miss Morrison was fortunate to have a walled balcony with a wonderful view of the grounds: the formal rose gardens, the lawn fringed by the lake and the view framed by the purple haze of the Cheviots. She had rigged up some clotheslines on this balcony so that she could hang the clean, white bloomers and petticoats to blow dry in the wind, hidden from view of anyone walking in the grounds below – she hoped. She would rinse out the vests and silk stockings, using some Lux soap flakes that Mr Edgar had found in the house and given to her. She might have to wash the ladies' corsets too, which could be a major job, scrubbing the fabric with a nail brush and then having to twist and ease the stays back into shape. Then she would wash the cotton garments using carbolic soap, rinse them and then add some Reckitts blue to the water to brighten the whites before wringing the clothes out by hand and hanging them on the line. 'I get real satisfaction from seeing the clothes blowing on the line on a good drying day – and you get a lot of wind in Scotland – so you know that the clothes are really fresh. It's somehow more rewarding than just shoving clothes into an automatic washing machine.'

Miss Morrison's heavy irons were kept hot on a small iron stove in the fireplace which she kept burning all day. She would use them in rotation every time she needed to iron – which was frequently. She also had a small iron heated by methylated spirits, but once she had got the hang of getting her 'iron stove' really hot, she preferred to use this. She would hang fine chiffons, silks and velvets in the steam of a kettle to get the creases out, but that still left piles of cotton and linen from Lady Olliff-Cooper and Miss Anson to iron every day and all the frills and pleats and ruffles, of which there were many, needed the attention of a goffering iron. Miss Anson had a particular fondness for linen clothes which were a devil to iron, until Miss Morrison remembered one of the tips that her grandmother, who had been in service herself, had passed on: 'Sprinkle the fabric with water, roll it up tightly, and then it'll be much easier to iron.'

Alterations and trimmings seemed to take a lot of her time, particularly those of Miss Anson, who would want a collar changed here, a sleeve altered there, even her bloomers made more streamlined on one occasion – 'She has alterations on alterations,' sighed Morrison. And in order to give variety to the outfits, Morrison experimented with making new belts and trimming blouses and dresses with different ribbon or lace, adding feathers and stitching net and artificial flowers to hats. She had intended to run up some new clothes for her mistress herself, but found that in all the time she was in the house, she only ever had time to make one skirt. As soon as she sat down at her sewing machine (a revolutionarily useful

---

How to wash corsets

Corsets loomed large in the lives of the female members of the Edwardian Country household, and laundering these unlovely garments presented Miss Morrison with something of a challenge. She copied down instructions in the back of the journal she kept:

First, take out the laces and wash them. Lie the corset on a flat surface, and scrub thoroughly with a small brush using soft green soap (or white if you have it) and tepid water. When clean, rinse repeatedly under cold running water and pull into shape lengthways. Lie flat to dry, pulling into shape at regular intervals. When the corset is dry, rethread the laces. Do not iron.

'The lady's maid should be properly qualified for her situation…particularly in needlework'.

machine with its ability to 'tuck, frill, gather, quilt, braid and embroider' – as well as stitch – first introduced in Britain in the 1850s), the bell that she had placed at the bottom of the staircase leading from the Olliff-Coopers' floor would ring. She would hurry down the stairs to find that Lady Olliff-Cooper needed to change her clothes again, perhaps to receive a visitor, pay a call or go riding. Her corset needed to be relaced to suit whatever clothes she was wearing, and her hair redone.

If Lady Olliff-Cooper was calling on a nearby country house, Miss Morrison would be expected to accompany her in the carriage, to carry any small gifts she might want to take, arrange her clothes and help her on and off with her outer garments. Miss Morrison's Edwardian counterpart would have welcomed these excursions as much as she did, since they got her out of the house and provided an opportunity to meet and talk with other ladies' maids in the houses she visited.

A lady's maid worked long days, and for this reason (and for the dexterity of their fingers) younger women were often preferred. A lady's maid was at the beck and call of her mistress until the mistress retired for the night: she would have helped her dress for dinner and have waited for the summons to undress her, plait her hair, make sure that her nightwear was aired, and help her into bed at the end of the day, and this could be well past midnight if the family was entertaining or attending a function.

In addition to her duties as hairdresser, seamstress, dresser and escort, a lady's maid would have been expected to be a mine of information about medical matters, beauty aids – and stain removal. She would have made her own potions using lemon juice to whiten hands, known a recipe for a pomade for removing wrinkles with onion juice, honey and wax, be confident about how to get rid of ink stains as well as brightening tarnished pearls, banishing moths (camphor bags or turpentine soap wrapped in brown paper) and a host of other useful things.

Inevitably a degree of trust and closeness developed between a lady and her maid: it is hard to attend to the intimate toiletries of a person without getting to know them fairly well. Lady Olliff-Cooper was no exception: 'My maid Morrison is a truly wonderful person. She is teaching me all manner of useful things and she has a delightful sense of humour. She is a real treasure. I have come to value her greatly. And I think that Morrison is thoroughly enjoying serving me, and takes as much pride in turning me out as a cook would take pride in turning out a wonderful meringue gâteau, or something like that.' Most ladies' maids became the confidantes of their mistresses, sharing not only snippets about clothes and beauty, but gossip, excitements, anxieties and heartaches too. Miss Morrison was privy to Lady Olliff-Cooper's anxieties about how she was coping with her new world, listened to her concerns about Guy, and was discreet about the fact that on many nights Sir John did not sleep in his own bedroom down the corridor, but spent the night in his wife's bed. A lady's maid was expected to be discreet, and sometimes wise beyond her years, yet never forget her station. She could give advice when asked but never proffer it uncalled for.

In the eighteenth and early nineteenth centuries, French maids (like French chefs) had been considered the pinnacle of elegance with their supposed insider knowledge of Parisian haute couture, and their 'charming' broken accents, though Germans and Swiss were recognized as being more practical. But during and after the Napoleonic wars it was considered unpatriotic – and maybe a little risky – to employ a French maid in such a close capacity. In Frances Hodgson Burnett's novel *The Making of a Marchioness*, published in 1901, Lady Maria Bayne, the mentor of the heroine, Emily Fox-Seton, advises her: '[Jane – who had applied to be Miss Fox-Seton's maid] would probably be worth half a dozen French minxes who would amuse themselves by getting up to intrigues with your footmen. Send her to a French hairdresser to take a course of lessons, and she will be worth anything. To turn you out properly will be her life's ambition.'[7] In any case, Miss Morrison was indignant at the very idea: 'French maids! I'll show them that there are no maids finer than Scottish maids,' she asserted stoutly.

The intimate apparel of the ladies of the Edwardian Country House blows in a
'good drying wind' outside Miss Morrison's attic room.

Beauty remedies

*Caroline Rose has her own apothecary shop in Haworth, the
Yorkshire village which was made famous by the Brontës. It is
fitted out in a style that would make an Edwardian feel instantly at
home, with glass-fronted mahogany cabinets, large chemist's bottles
filled with strange-coloured liquids, wooden counters, old-fashioned
metal cash registers, and boxes and jars of home-made lotions and
potions and remedies piled from floor to ceiling.*

The Roses (Caroline's mother, Patricia, is also involved in the shop) travelled to Manderston to bring a range of their wares to sell at the bazaar, and stayed on to advise Miss Morrison and Mrs Davies on how to make Edwardian preparations for use in the house. Two recipes in particular are easy to make today with ingredients that are readily available.

Rose and glycerine hand salve

Little less than ³/₄ oz beeswax
30ml coconut oil
30ml vegetable oil
10ml castor oil
5ml glycerine
4ml otto of roses

Melt the beeswax and coconut oil with the vegetable oil in a double boiler. When melted, remove from the heat and add the castor oil and glycerine, stirring well. Add the otto of roses and continue stirring as the mixture cools. Beat well when the ointment begins to set, and continue beating until a smooth consistency is achieved. Pour or spoon into waxed ointment boxes, or small tins or jars, to set.

Cool cream

*This is one of the oldest beauty creams and can be
used to remove make-up, but also as an intensive
night-time cream.*

3 teaspoons beeswax
¹/₄ cup mineral or almond oil
2 or 3 drops rose oil
1 drop red cochineal

Melt the beeswax with the mineral or almond oil over a double boiler. Stir while cooling and add the rose oil and red cochineal. When cool, whip until smooth and light. Spoon into glass or ceramic jars.

The lady's maid 'is generally to be near the person of her lady…her education should be superior…in the ornamental branches of female acquirements'.

But however charmed the life of a lady's maid might appear to the other servants, it was not altogether a happy one. Apart from the long hours, and the need always to appear bright and friendly, it was a life lived vicariously. A 'friendship' based on servitude, and sinewed by the cash nexus, meant that should a lady's maid's employment be terminated for any reason, the closeness a maid believed she enjoyed with her mistress made such an act feel like a poignantly painful rejection.

Though a maid was always a servant, albeit a trusted one, to her mistress, she was often regarded with suspicion by her fellow servants, who suspected that her loyalties lay with milady rather than with them, that she enjoyed special privileges, and the currency in which she paid for these was by telling downstairs tales upstairs. 'Everything we say,' complained Antonia, the kitchen maid, 'whether it's to her individually, or something she overhears in the servants' hall, gets taken upstairs with Miss Morrison's slant on it. I know that she's on our side really, but she has a different agenda from everyone else. When Kenny went fishing in Sir John's lake, which he'd been forbidden to do, it was Miss Morrison who told Sir John. So now Kenny has been threatened with the sack if he ever does it again. She freely admits that she is working for the family, and that at the end of the day, it's the family who are her priority, not us at all. It feels a bit like having a traitor in our midst.' And when she did spend time with the other servants, Miss Morrison's conversation was somewhat guarded, for she was mindful that the conduit could never be from upstairs to down. If an Edwardian lady's maid was found to have indulged in loose talk about anything she had heard or observed in the drawing rooms and bedrooms of the gentry, she would face instant dismissal with no hope of a 'character' which she would need to find another position. So the life of a lady's maid's could be an isolated one, fully accepted by neither the society above stairs, nor that below, while her career prospects led up something of a cul-de-sac. She could expect to earn about £30 a year, with her board and food, and in general her clothes would be 'found' from among her lady's cast-offs. But a lady's maid was unlikely to have acquired the kitchen skills that were necessary to reach the summit of a female servant's ambition: the housekeeper's role.

There was a great deal of advice on choosing dresses, as there was on most aspects of an Edwardian lady's life. Colour was important: 'any colour, whatever may be suited to certain persons, and be injurious to the beauty of many others. It is therefore necessary to choose not only the colour adopted by the tyranny of fashion, but that which best suits the complexion,' instructed *The Duties of a Lady's Maid*.[8] That useful duo Sarah and Samuel Adams were of the opinion that 'females of fair complexion ought to wear the purest white: they should choose light and brilliant colours, such as rose, azure, light yellow, &c. These colours heighten the lustre of their complexion, which if accompanied with darker colours, would frequently have the appearance of alabaster, without life and without expression.'[9] On the contrary, however, a 'woman of dark complexion' should avoid these colours for fear they might cause her to look 'tanned' which would never do since it suggested that she might have had to labour in the fields in the sun rather than spending her time reposing under a parasol in the shade. Lady Greville, writing in the 1890s, was equally prescriptive: 'the fat woman should wear black; the blonde mauve and pale blue; the brunette orange, and red and vivid green'.[10] For the political dinner Lady Olliff-Cooper, wisely in view of these strictures, had decided to wear fashionable 'sweet pea' colours, a pale lavender dress trimmed with dove grey. Miss Morrison relayed this information to Mr Edgar so that he could co-ordinate the flowers for the table with her mistress's outfit.

On the night of the dinner Miss Morrison hurriedly finished her own meal in the servants' hall before going upstairs to run Lady Olliff-Cooper a bath, help her attend to her toilette and dress. Vita Sackville-West describes just such an occasion: 'the maid gathering the lovely mass of taffeta and tulle, held the bodice open while the Duchess flung off her wrap and dived gingerly into the billows of her dress'.[11] An Edwardian lady married to a wealthy man might expect to buy her finest dresses from Paris, the mecca for fashionable women at the beginning of the twentieth century.[12] The apogee of the Parisian couture houses was Worth, a 'veritable Temple of Fashion' founded by a Lincolnshire man. Here the American heiress and notable beauty, Mary Leiter, who had married George Curzon (the brother of Lady Miller, the wife of the owner of Manderston), regularly shopped for evening dresses that could cost 'hundreds even thousands of pounds'.[13] Such creations were fragile concoctions of delicate chiffon, silk, lace and net, and might only be wearable on a couple of occasions before they

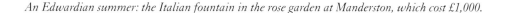

An Edwardian summer: the Italian fountain in the rose garden at Manderston, which cost £1,000.

*Fashion plates: a page from a Manderston photograph album showing what the well-dressed
Edwardian country house party guest was wearing.*

began to wilt like hothouse flowers. Less ethereal beings would have their clothes made by a
dressmaker working in her (or his) own salon.

The most fashionable London modiste of the period was Lucile, the sister of the novelist Elinor
Glyn, who set up in Old Burlington Street before moving to Hanover Square, and in 1900 married
one of her directors, Sir Cosmo Duff Gordon. A divorced woman who had started to make clothes
to support herself and her daughter, her fame was soon international and she numbered Margot
Asquith as one of her clients along with the Duchess of Westminster – and, inevitably, Lillie Langtry.
The mannequins Lucile employed, however, were 'big girls' with 'fine figures', not one of them less
than six feet tall or tipping the scales at less than eleven stone – and clearly the ideal of Edwardian
beauty, for many landed a millionaire as a husband.[14]

In straitened circumstances the Edwardian lady might resort to clothes run up by a nimble-
fingered maid using a paper pattern. Or she would buy them ready made, from one of the smart
department stores, their windows filled with 'innumerable whim-whams and fribble-frabble of
fashion',[15] which had expanded from haberdashers or drapers in London, Edinburgh and the other
provincial cities and towns during the nineteenth century.

The growth in conspicuous consumption was one of the most striking aspects of the Edwardian
age. As the first industrialized nation with a growing empire, London was the undisputed capital
market of the world, following the collapse of the Paris money market after the Franco-Prussian war

in 1870 and the migration of many European financiers and bankers to the metropolis. In the words of the socialist artist and designer William Morris in 1880, it was 'the richest city, of the richest country, of the richest age of the world'.[16]

There had been an economic downturn in the last two decades of the nineteenth century with the agricultural depression, falling land prices and declining share prices, but by the death of Queen Victoria in 1901, there was a renewed blaze of economic prosperity – though it was not one at which the entire nation could warm its hands. The inequality of wealth was greater in Edwardian Britain possibly than anywhere at any time in the world, and there was great poverty amidst this growing plenty. For the next decade, with a few hiccups, the upward trend in unevenly shared economic prosperity continued. By 1900 the total value of British exports (including the re-export of imported produce largely from the Empire) was valued at £354 million: by 1913 it had risen to £635 million, of which over £500 million represented home-made goods, an expansion that was twice as vigorous as in the preceding twenty years. In addition, for the first time in half a century, exports grew faster than imports, leading to a very satisfactory balance of payments.[17]

The portents were far from favourable for the long term, however. By 1900 Britain's outputs of coal, iron and steel had been surpassed by those of Germany and the United States, and by 1914, although Britain's share of world trade in manufacture remained the largest of any country, competition – again from Germany and the United States – was challenging this hegemony. But it is still very possible to reflect that 'surely there was never such a time in the life of the world when it was so good, in the way of obvious material comfort, to be alive and fairly well-to-do as it was before the [First World] War'.[18]

The impression of Edwardian prosperity was greatly enhanced by the increasing wealth of London, the entertainments it offered and the fabulous range of wares for sale in its shops. From 1801 to 1841 the population of London doubled from just over a million to over two million, and thereafter it increased by around a million every decade until the First World War, when it stood at just over 7 million.[19] The spread of railways networking the country from the 1840s made the metropolis and other large cities more accessible. The Great Exhibition of 1851 had proved a magnet to the provinces, and from then onwards, the growth of retail establishments to cater for the growing prosperity of the middle and upper classes was remarkable.

Fashion preoccupied many Edwardian women, had they the means to follow it. Fashion was 'a badge of social status and its devotees regarded it with high seriousness and full absorption', explains the fashion historian Elizabeth Ewing.[20] Alexandra, both as Princess of Wales and Queen, was a leader of Edwardian fashion with her elegant slim figure, beautiful clothes, high-piled hair and distinctive multi-stranded pearl chokers. She was 'dazzlingly beautiful, whether in gold and silver at night, or in violet velvet by day, [and she] succeeded in making every other woman look common beside her', exclaimed Lady Oxford in 1906.[21]

Edwardian beauty

'A first-class maid is expected to be a thoroughly experienced one: to be a first-class hairdresser, experienced in dressing a lady, and a good packer, mistress of everything that appertains to her offices,' decreed *The Duties of Servants*. And that includes making beauty aids from ingredients easily found in the house. Anxious to attain these high standards, Miss Morrison copied out a tip on how to darken eyebrows and eyelashes by rubbing them often with elderflower berries, or, if these were unavailable, with a burnt cork or a clove singed in a candle's flame.

*Dressed in style for the races: Sir John
and Lady Olliff-Cooper.*

Lady Olliff-Copper was soon to find that she was no exception to this interest in modish dress. 'My family arc a bit puzzled by me and say I am turning into a mindless doll, though Jonty kindly indulges me by saying that I am just getting in touch with the female side of my personality. They see me taking an interest in female sorts of pursuits, which is not my normal role at all. I had no idea how much time one *could* spend thinking about dresses, what colours go best with what, what trimmings to add, what jewellery to wear,' marvelled the modern-day casualty doctor. 'I don't spend much time on my appearance at home, and my clothes by and large come from charity shops because I think they're good value, and I get quite a kick out of searching for things and making the best of them. But here I think my husband is quite overwhelmed by seeing me dressed up like that. He keeps saying "you look so beautiful" – in tones of slight surprise, actually. It's not quite so flattering but there you are, and I think he feels it reflects on him. I imagine it was like that in Edwardian times too. Men dressed up their wives as much as possible to reflect their status. That was the wife's role. I feel that I am living in a Mills & Boon romantic novel. It's a woman's fantasy of beautiful clothes, and jewels and carriages, and judging by my husband's reaction it's a man's fantasy too, corsets and crotchless underwear and suspenders.'

Mrs Humphry decreed: 'The object of a fashionable woman in dressing, is to make herself distinctive without becoming conspicuous – to excel by her union of graceful outline and fidelity to the fashion of the moment (no easy task), and while offering no striking contrast to those around her. So to individualize herself that she is one of the few who remain in the memory, when the crowd of well-dressed women is recalled only as an indistinguishable mass.'[22] It was hardly surprising that women spent time poring over the plethora of illustrated magazines that were available – and which disseminated high fashion beyond the realm of the very rich. Between 1880 and 1900, forty-eight new titles appeared. Sam (widower of Isabella) Beeton's monthly *Englishwoman's Domestic Magazine*, the blueprint of modern-day women's magazines, had ceased publication in 1879, to re-emerge in 1881 *as Milliner, Dress-maker and Draper*, while another of Beeton's titles, *The Queen*, merged with another magazine in 1863 to become *Queen, the Ladies' Newspaper*. From the 1880s a series of new magazines emerged, aimed at 'women of taste' who had an interest in society – royalty in particular – fashion, home and family. *The Lady's Pictorial* (which Oscar Wilde complained was devoted to 'mere millinery and trimmings')[23] ran from 1881 to 1921. *The Lady*, subtitled 'A Journal for Gentlewomen', was first published in 1885, but it was not until 1894 that its circulation took off when an ex-nanny introduced a small-ads section and soon the magazine had become what it remains today – 'a sort of *Exchange and Mart* for nannies'.[24] Then there were the penny (as opposed to sixpenny) weeklies, *Forget Me Not* and

Home Sweet Home, both launched in 1893, and the hugely popular *Woman at Home* merged with the mass circulation penny paper *Home Notes* which started publication in 1894 and eventually became *Woman's Own* in 1957. *Home Chats*, which was unlikely to have graced the Manderston bedside table since it was aimed at 'women who actually did some, if not all, their own domestic work',[25] thrived from 1894 until 1957, while *Woman's Weekly*, with its knitting and sewing patterns and romantic fiction, first appeared in 1911, and the similar *My Weekly* the previous year.

'I think it's a tribute to how much we have become involved in the project that I have become really interested in women's magazines of the period,' said Lady Olliff-Cooper. 'I have just been sent a copy of *Weldon's Ladies' Journal* for 1910 and I am scanning the pages for new ideas for dresses and hairstyles and hats. The Edwardians were obviously very keen on wearing bits of animals, feathers – osprey feathers, ostrich fathers – and masses of furs which were very *à la mode* in 1910. But what I need now clearly, is half a seagull. Half a seagull was a real fashion statement in 1910. They are simply everywhere.'

As well as gazing at fashion plates in magazines, a well-to-do Edwardian woman could have attended one of the newly popular fashion shows, window-gazed – or simply have gone on a shopping expedition to one of the many department stores that were particularly instrumental in extending fashion's domain to the middle classes. The fashionable shopping hours were between two and four in the afternoon. Omnibuses mingled with hansoms, and shop delivery vans, instructed to move at a snail's pace so that passers-by could read their advertising slogans plastered on their sides,[26] clogged up the London streets packed with ladies intent on a day's shopping in the new department stores. It was a similar story in Manchester, Birmingham and Edinburgh.

'Half a seagull is quite the thing.' A sampler of New Year fashions from Weldon's Ladies Journal *(1910).*

In London's Knightsbridge, a small grocer's shop was expanded by the son of the owner into a department store in 1861. Unlike most previous fashionable retailers, Harrod's business was founded on an unusual 'cash only no credit' principle to avoid the disastrous cashflow problems that were liable to bankrupt many retailers. By the time of the publication of its Jubilee booklet in 1909, the shop was able to boast 'Harrod's is widely known as THE SHRINE OF FASHION. We adapt beautiful Continental Creations to English tastes and conditions, and supply the most exclusive creations in fashionable attire at moderate prices.'[27] It employed 'living models' instead of wax mannequins and organized fashion parades in its restaurants. The store, whose telegraphic address was 'Everything, London', had eighty departments spread over a shopping area of 30 acres.

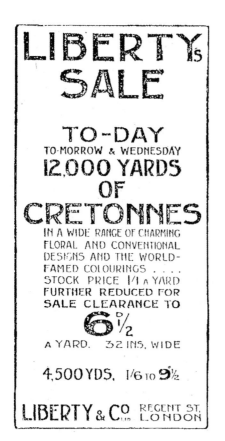

Also in Knightsbridge was Harvey Nicholls, which had started life as a linen draper's shop in 1813, while in Kensington a trio of ex-drapers was to survive into the 1960s: Derry & Toms (founded 1862), Pontings Brothers (1873) and John Barkers (1870). A perceptive haberdasher from Wakefield in Yorkshire had noted the potential that customers arriving at Paddington railway station could have for the retail trade, and opened his eponymous shop in Bayswater selling ribbons and lace – which included jabots, collars, cuffs, *fichus*, handkerchiefs and all sorts of trimmings and fancy goods. But soon William Whiteley had added dresses, millinery, silks and furs to his shop's range, and by the end of the century the greatly expanded store was able to designate itself as the 'Universal Provider' since it also provided hairdressing, catering, dyeing and dry cleaning services as well as selling books, food and ironmongery.[28] In the West End could be found Marshall & Snelgrove (1848), Dickins & Jones (which had been founded as Dickins & Smith as early as 1790), Peter Robinson (founded in 1833, by 1900 the company occupied a large island site at Oxford Circus and had three other shops including a 'Mourning Warehouse' in Oxford Street), Debenham & Freebody, Bourne & Hollingsworth (in Oxford Street from 1902), Swan & Edgar (1812) and D. H. Evans (1879). In 1864, Somerset-born John Lewis, who was buyer of silks and woollens for Peter Robinson's, set himself up in business a stone's throw from his original employers; and round the corner in Regent's Street, there was the exotic shop that Arthur Lasenby Liberty opened in 1875, calling it 'East India House' and filling floors with richly coloured stuffs and artefacts from India and the Orient.

In the provinces there was Caley's of Norwich, in Manchester Kendal Milne & Faulkener (1837), and in Newcastle upon Tyne there was Bainbridge (1830), and also Fenwicks (which ambitiously opened a branch in London's fashionable Bond Street in 1891); there was Lewis's of Liverpool (1856) and Jessops of Nottingham (1860). Jenners in Edinburgh was an upholstery and fabric shop when it opened in 1838, but when it was rebuilt in 1895 after the original shop was destroyed by fire, it became Edinburgh's smartest department store, situated in fashionable Princes Street.

In 1909 Gordon Selfridge, late of Marshall Field's department store in Chicago, opened the largest purpose-built shop in England in Oxford Street, where he employed people whose sole task was to dress the windows which were kept illuminated until 12 o'clock every night. The store comprised 130 departments and thus its advertising slogan, 'Why Not Spend The Day at Selfridges?', did not seem impractical. Department stores were able to buy in bulk and thus reduce prices, and this, coupled with their comprehensive range, accounted for their popularity with the discerning shopper. A number of these shops sold not only fabrics and ready-to-wear clothes, but also part-made garments which a lady's maid could finish – and customize. In 1908 Harrods was still advertising their 'ever-popular unmade robes' while Peter Robinson's 'unmade dresses…only required joining up at the back' – very useful when sizing was as rudimentary and haphazard as it was until the 1920s.[29]

An Edwardian lady would also be able to buy her clothes from such emporia from an illustrated mail order catalogue, a recent innovation at the time, and one most welcomed by ladies from out of town. Indeed, as the fashion historian Jane Ashelford recounts, Marshall & Snelgrove's Country Room received over 1,000 letters a day and had to employ more than one hundred clerks and accountants to process and dispatch orders.[30] Until the middle of the period, Elizabeth Ewing explains, those dresses advertised by mail order invariably meant a made-up skirt and material for the bodice. She quotes a 1906 Marshall & Snelgrove catalogue offering 'a handsome lace robe in ecru or ivory, including full material for the bodice', while in 1907 Swan & Edgar's catalogue featured a 'smart silk robe (unmade) easily adapted to any figure'.[31]

But while the Edwardian lady might well shop in London during the season, or in the case of the occupants of Manderston travel to Edinburgh to visit stores or dress-making establishments and milliners, or be taken in the brougham to the nearby small town of Duns for fabric or trimmings from the haberdasher's, she was still very dependent on her lady's maid for many additions to her wardrobe, adaptations, alterations and running repairs. This was a fact that Lady Olliff-Cooper reflected on the night of the political dinner, as Miss Morrison handed her mistress her white kid gloves before she slowly descended the silver staircase to greet her guests.

In the eighteenth century, dinner would have been taken at around two in the afternoon; during the nineteenth it edged towards the late afternoon and by the turn of the century the rise and rise of 'new money' (and the introduction of effective and efficient artificial lighting) had indicated a different imperative. Men 'at business' were working something approaching an eight-hour day. They needed to get home in time to bath and change before setting out for a social event, so dinner was increasingly served at 8 p.m. It was essential that the hostess was present in the drawing room, resplendent in her evening finery, at least a quarter of an hour before the first guest arrived. Guests knew that 'to be punctual at the hour mentioned is obligatory. If you are too early, you are in the way; if too late you annoy the hostess, cause impatience among the assembled guests, and perhaps spoil the dinner'.[32] On arrival, they would have been ushered into the drawing room by the butler or the first footman, and, at a dinner of more than six or eight, the men would have been handed a place card with the name of the woman next to whom he was to be placed at dinner. If the man was not acquainted with his dinner companion he would go over to introduce himself and, when the gong sounded at exactly 8 o'clock, would rise and offer her his arm. The party would then process into the dining room in strict order of precedence, led by the host and the principal female guest. This would be 'the eldest lady or the greatest stranger, or, if there is a bride present, precedence is given to her, unless the dinner is given for another person, in which case he escorts the latter…Husbands should not escort their wives, or brothers their sisters as this partakes of the nature of a family gathering'.[33] The procession would be brought up by the hostess on the arm of the 'gentleman of most importance present – that is, of most importance socially'.[34]

Mr Edgar flung open the heavy rosewood doors and Lady Olliff-Cooper drew in her breath when she saw how beautifully the staff had laid the table with a fine white damask cloth, a battery of crystal glasses and regimented silver cutlery, placed just so, in order that plates and bowls could be put directly in front of each diner without having to rearrange the cutlery between courses. The mahogany table had been wound apart by brass handles and extra leaves slotted in to accommodate the twenty diners. A napkin, folded into an elaborate mitre shape by Rob and Charlie (or Robin and Charles as Sir John had decided they should be known above stairs), stood by each place 'making an ornament to the table'. Silver condiment sets for salt, pepper and mustard were placed at regular intervals along the table. Heavy silver candelabras burned softly at either end of the table, wound round with ivy and small flowers. The three footmen (Kenny the hall boy had been dragooned into service for the evening – and renamed Kenneth for the occasion), wearing livery, their hair powdered, their patent, buckled slippers gleaming, stepped silently forward to pull out the chairs and seat the guests at table, Sir John, as host, sat at the head of the table with his back to the fireplace. It is to be hoped that the female guests would have remembered that 'gloves are kept on till the wearer seats herself at table. They may or may not be resumed after dinner, though usually the right-hand glove is put on previous to hand-shakings and goodbyes before the party breaks up. At very formal houses where the hostess is a dragon of social etiquette, one dares not relax the slightest rule…'[35]

Dinner was to be *à la russe*, a style first introduced in the 1820s which remained the fashion in the Edwardian era. As Mrs Beeton explained, 'It differs from dinners in the mode of serving the various dishes. In dinner *à la russe*, the dishes are cut up on a sideboard, and handed round the guests, and each dish may be considered a course…a menu or bill of fare should be laid by the side of each guest'.[36] Before that innovation, dinners were usually served *à la française*; the host had carved at table and two large courses, each with a great variety of dishes, were put on the table one after the other. A gentleman would help himself and offer his neighbour dishes that were within his reach, and ask for other dishes to be passed either by another diner or a footman. A soup and a fish course would have been on the table at the same time and would have been removed when the entrées (cutlets, fricassées, boudins, sweetbreads or pâtés) were served followed by the roast. The new style was

Table napkins

As ever, Mrs Beeton had advice for this area of etiquette and decoration. 'In ordinary family use,' she wrote, table napkins or serviettes 'are sometimes folded smoothly and slipped through "napkin rings" made of bone, ivory or silver…each member of the family having his or her own ring.' Those required for dinner parties and other formal occasions, however, 'should be neatly and prettily folded'. The napkins need to 'be slightly starched and smoothly ironed…a small dinner-roll…should be placed in each napkin, and such patterns as "Mitre", the "Neapolitan" or the "Rose" and the "Star" are convenient shapes, [and] the appearance of the dinner table will be greatly improved by putting a flower or small bouquet in each napkin.'

THE MITRE

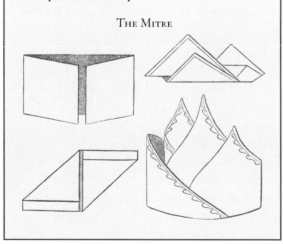

recommended since 'it gives an opportunity for more profuse ornamentation of the table, which, as the meal progresses, does not become encumbered with partially empty dishes and platters'.[37]

By 1905 meals were simpler, but the Olliff-Coopers' political dinner still consisted of eight courses, all to be expertly served by tyro footmen serving soup from a solid silver tureen and handing round vegetables in solid silver dishes (since at the last moment the chef's aesthetic had revolted at the prospect of china, and silver had had to be fetched from Edinburgh). The plates were Wedgwood in Madeleine design, and each footman was assigned to a particular section of the table, in a plan carefully drawn up in advance by Mr Edgar, so there would be neither collisions nor guests left waiting to be served.

As was correct according to Mrs Beeton, 'the master of the house should be answerable for the quality of his wines and liqueurs' and Sir John, mindful of his responsibility, and of the impression he was anxious to make, had consulted with a St James's wine merchant that had been founded in 1698. 'I think you should serve champagne with the oysters – Ruinhart champagne was very popular with the Edwardians and it's beginning to make a comeback,' Simon Berry advised. 'Then a Riesling

Mr Edgar carefully ladles out soup in the dining room.

with the fish would be appropriate. The Edwardians drank far more German wines than we do today, though Chablis was on our list in 1910 if you prefer that. To do justice to the venison, how about one of the great reds – a Brane-Contenac perhaps, a claret from the Margaux region?' But the real *pièce de resistance* came when Mr Berry produced from his cellars a genuine 1905 bottle of Tokay (or Tokjai as it is now usually known), a legendary wine that was supposed to have anointed the lips of the dying Tsars and rulers of the Ottoman Empire. 'It comes from Hungary, and was expensive since it's the essence of the grape. They are not crushed, the juice is extracted by force of gravity. Tokay wasn't imported into Britain until the beginning of the twentieth century, but because it has a high sugar concentrate, it is one of the few bottles of wine that was laid down in 1876 that is still drinkable today. I *think* I could let you have a couple of bottles.'

Sir John's eyes gleamed. 'We'll treat it like port and serve it when the ladies have left the table,' he decided.

In Vita Sackville-West's novel, the heir of Chevron describes a dinner party there: 'The jewels of [the guests] glittered, the shirt-fronts glistened; the servants came and went, handing dishes and pouring wine in the light of the many candles. The trails of smilax wreathed greenly in and out among the heavy candelabra and the dishes of grapes and peaches.'[38]

The first formal dinner was a taxing occasion for the Edwardian Country House footman, who should 'wear thin-soled shoes that their steps may be noiseless, and if they should use napkins in serving (as is the English custom) instead of gloves, their hands and nails should be faultlessly clean…and [a footman] should wrap one corner of a damask napkin around the thumb, that he may not touch the plates and dishes with the naked hand. A good servant is never awkward. He avoids coughing, breathing hard or treading on a lady's dress; never lets any article drop, and deposits plates, glasses, knives, forks and spoons noiselessly.'[39]

There were rules for guests too, including:

> Greediness should not be indulged in. Indecision must be avoided. Do not take up one piece and lay it down in favour of another, or hesitate. Never allow a servant…to fill your glass with wine that you do not wish to drink. You can check him by touching the rim of your glass…Bread is broken at dinner. Never use a napkin in place of a handkerchief for wiping the forehead, face or nose. Everything that can be cut without using a knife should be eaten with the fork alone. Never lay your hand, or play with your fingers upon the table. Do not toy with your knife, fork or spoon, make crumbs of your bread, or draw imaginary lines upon the tablecloth.

As for the hostess, she 'should not express pride regarding what is on her table, nor make apologies if everything she offers you is not to her satisfaction. It is much better that she should observe silence in this respect, and allow her guests to eulogize her dinner, or not, as they deem proper. Neither is it good taste to urge guests to eat, nor to load their plates against their inclination.'[40]

In the Edwardian Country House that night, the service was impressively adroit (though etiquette decreed that 'a master or mistress should never censure the servants at dinner, however things may go wrong'),[41] the food delicious – and spectacular to look at. The conversation ranged widely, laughter punctuating the talk of sport, social events, and the opinions of those round the table of the politics of the Edwardian era.

In the Victorian period, a dinner could well have lasted for three hours, but the wife of Edward VII, Queen Alexandra, when she was Princess of Wales, had introduced the fashion for shorter dinners with fewer courses (relatively speaking). Some complained, though, that this gallop through a *repas* made it necessary 'to skip at least two courses if [one] wishes to make a few remarks to the lady whom [one] escorted to table'. Dinner would end when 'the signal to leave the table is given in the merest nod or smile to the lady who has been taken down by the host. She is sure to be on the look-out for it; but if she is not, it is sufficient to rise, whereupon all the ladies get up at once. It is well, however,' warned the etiquette guru, 'to make a decided effort to catch the eye of the principal lady, as she might consider it a slight if the hostess were to make the move without the usual co-operation. It might be put down to ignorance.'[42]

The conclusion of dinner was a delicate matter. The signal must not be given at the very moment that one of the guests 'has just laid down a knife or fork or a wine-glass, lest it might appear that the whole party had been waiting for the conclusion of that one individual's meal'. Equally, 'if any one is in the midst of an animated or interesting conversation, the move must be deferred until it slackens off a little. On the other hand, should any disagreeable or unwelcome topic arise, the signal is sometimes prematurely given in order to make a diversion'.[43] The ladies withdrew from the dinner room to take coffee in the drawing room, leaving in the same order in which they had entered, while the men enjoyed port and brandy, cigars and more political discourse at the table before rejoining them.

'If an aristocracy keeps too tight a hold like in France,' Jonathan Olliff-Cooper suggested, 'then society comes back to bite it.'

'But we're not talking about an aristocracy here,' interjected David Mellor crisply. 'These people were merchants who were ennobled and their house can been seen as a monument to the British ability, even within the restraints of that time, to be a meritocracy.'

When Sir John fulminated on the effect that rising taxation was having on country houses at the time, Alan Beith demurred: 'It was a pittance compared with the wealth many people were able to enjoy,' he said, looking round the lavishly appointed dining room.

As he sipped his port, Lord Deedes could be heard describing the then Prime Minister H. H. Asquith as 'a static Liberal' while conceding his foresight in giving 'Lloyd George his head in trying to liberalize our society'. But the spectre of Liberal decline and the rise of the Labour Party hung in the air. 'As Engels said, you can't agitate a man with a full belly,' reminded David Mellor, replete after the six-course dinner, 'but there were plenty of people around with empty bellies.'

It was the former Liberal Party leader, David Steel, now the Liberal Democrat Lord Steel of Aikwood, who sounded the knell, reminding his fellow diners of the words of Lord Grey (the Liberal Foreign Secretary from 1906 to 1916): 'If the Tory Party represents the haves and the Labour Party represents the have nots, then the outlook for the Liberal Party is pretty poor.'

There was no question of the footmen being 'stood down' that evening. The invitation had specified 'carriages at midnight', and as the guests departed, Charles, Robin and Kenneth handed out coats and wraps, gloves and fur stoles (and secretly hoped for a tip to be pressed in their palms). Mr Edgar stood gravely at the great porticoed doorway to bow the guests into the night, before turning on his heels to oversee the clearing-up, the washing-up, the drying-up, the putting-away, that would go on below stairs long after those above had drifted off to sleep in their feather beds.

The dishwasher(s), Edwardian model. Jess (left), Erika and Becky dry up the dinner party silver.

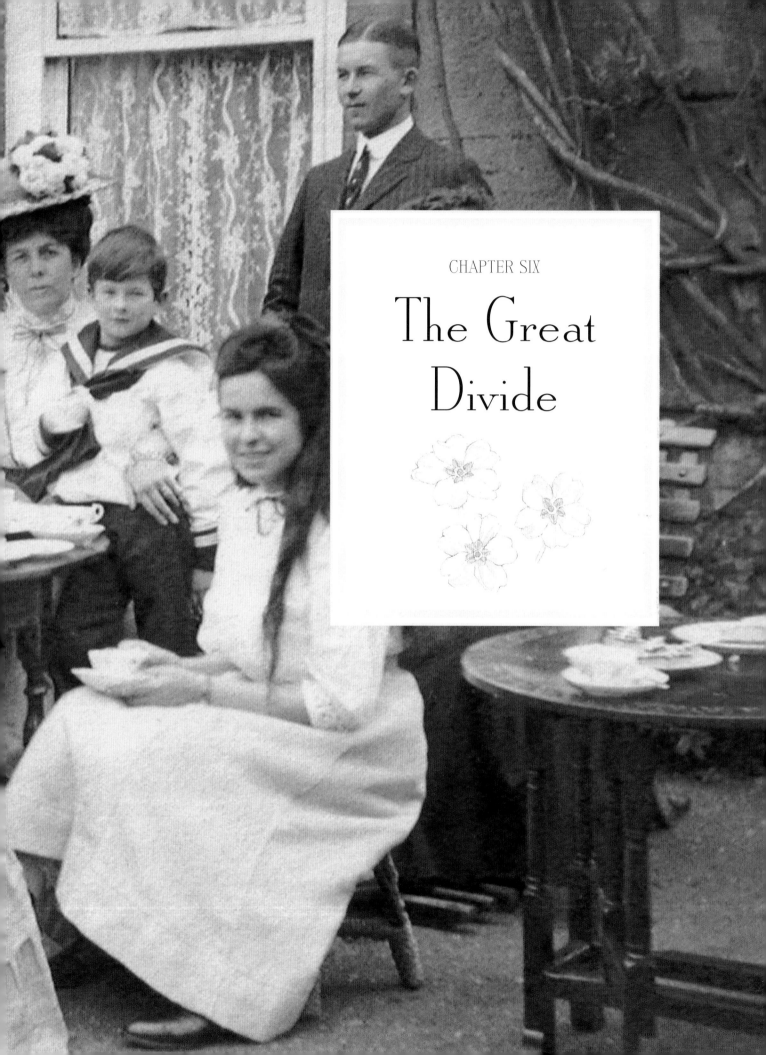

CHAPTER SIX

The Great Divide

In an Edwardian country house, the architect Robert Kerr insisted, 'the family constitute one community; the servants another. Whatever may be their mutual regard as dwellers under one roof, each class is entitled to shut its doors upon the other, and be alone…what passes on either side of the boundary shall be invisible and inaudible on the other.'[1] This social segregation was planned into the very fabric of the house, with the servants' quarters layered around those of the owners, their children and their guests. The 'family' occupied the ground and first floors; the servants worked below them in the basement and slept above them in the attics. Just as boundaries were never to be blurred in social behaviour, so there were to be no spatial ambiguities. Those who lived above stairs did not venture below. The master and mistress of an Edwardian country house almost never set foot in the kitchens that produced their food, or the laundry that did all their washing, and knew only by report the conditions in which their servants lived. Upper servants such as the butler, housekeeper, the lady's maid and the chef would appear in the family's quarters only when summoned, or for pre-arranged meetings. Apart from the footmen who ushered in guests and served at table, the lower servants would rarely have had any direct contact with the family at all.

The respectful distance that the servants were required to keep was evident in many ways, but it was particularly exemplified in one small act. If a letter arrived for a member of the family, or a visitor left a calling card, the butler or a footman would take it to the appropriate person, but he would not make physical contact by handing it over from his gloved hand to his master or mistress. Rather, he would put the object on a small silver salver kept expressly for the purpose, and the addressee would take it from the tray to read and place any answering communication on the tray.[2] No contamination between the world of work associated with grease and grime (though not a speck would have been present on the footman's impeccable uniform) and that of the fragrant, leisured classes would have occurred. Other servants would be expected to be as invisible and as inaudible as possible. 'Always move quietly about the house, and do not let your voice be heard by the family unless necessary. Never sing or whistle at your work where the family would be likely to hear you,' advised a manual for servants published in 1901. 'Should you be required to walk with a lady or gentleman, in order to carry a parcel, or otherwise, always keep a few paces behind…'[3]

It was in the nineteenth century that this stratification of the domestic community, had formalized the situation of the previous century where family, children, guests and servants had been more likely to have been jumbled together as part of the informal, organic whole, into one in which roles were rigidly defined and hierarchies firmly adhered to. With the social changes of the late century, when unpropertied wealth rather than land and pedigree became the indices of status among many of the new country house owners, these distinctions were maintained, even calcified, by a class that, in many cases, was only the first or second generation to live to the manor born. While there can be no single model for how a country house was organized, the most appropriate description in many instances in Edwardian times was less of the household as a community than as a well-oiled machine with its specialized functions separated, each 'cog' meshing smoothly to ensure that the whole 'ran like clockwork'.

The country house way of life could not exist without a raft of servants. Staff were needed to cook, clean, garden, valet, and look after the children and the horses in these commodious establishments. The number of rooms, the cluttered, fussy style of furnishings, and the intensely social way of life made country houses extremely labour-intensive to run. Standards of housekeeping were high; meals were extensive, elaborate and frequent. The family changed clothes several times a day – six was not unusual for the women – and became accustomed to a gilded bubble of gracious living, cosseted with fresh flowers everywhere, their whims answered at the ring of a bell, their newspapers ironed and sometimes even their coins washed.[4] The country house way of life of conspicuous consumption required an appreciative rotating audience of guests partaking in a series of events – dinners, shoots, parties, balls, weekend house parties – all of which added greatly to the work of the servants. And the servants themselves created work, needing to be cooked for, washed up after, and their laundry dealt with. The suburban middle classes might have kept a maid-of-all-work; the aristocracy of money kept an establishment of specialists where duties were strictly defined and compartmentalized – and demarcation was rigorous. It was not solely the work to be done that dictated the number of retainers, however. An Edwardian country house was not simply required to

'I am having a really good time horse riding. I've learned a lot and I really enjoy it,' enthused Mr Jonathan.

be run with discreet efficiency; it needed to advertise its wealth through display – including the display of servants. This entailed a full 'front of house' cast, consisting of a distinguished butler, liveried footmen and coachmen, a range of personal servants – ladies' maids and valets – and, when needed, nannies, nursery maids, governesses or tutors for the children.

Rank and income influenced how many servants a family might keep, and manuals gave advice on this to those new to employing servants; the criterion was less the size of their houses, and thus the work that needed to be done, than the size of their incomes. In general, it was considered that around 12 per cent of income should go on servants' wages with an additional 10 per cent required if horses and carriages were kept and servants needed for those duties.[5] This total would have been increased by the wages paid for casual staff recruited locally to help out on special occasions – a wedding or a christening, a large ball, a shooting party or a servants' ball – or for specific tasks of maintenance and repair around the house or seasonal work in the grounds.

Writing on how to plan *The Gentleman's House* in 1864, the architect and academic Robert Kerr suggested the first task should be to work out how many servants the client could afford, not, as one might have expected, what work needed to be done and therefore how many servants would need to be employed to do it.[6] So the planning of the 'domestic offices', in his view, did not start from the desire to make work as labour-saving as possible, but rather to accommodate a given number of servants and allow them adequate space to carry out their duties. This arrangement was possible because labour was in plentiful supply, and thus cheap – more so in the country than in town. Domestic servants were largely drawn from rural areas.

The Edwardian housemaids' routine: Becky sweeps a rug with a dustpan and brush

It is sometimes difficult to build up an accurate picture of life below stairs since few servants wrote their memoirs, or left any written record, though those who did have left an illuminating and poignant legacy. A vivid picture has also been built up in recent decades from oral sources, historians and journalists interviewing those who were in service in the late Victorian and Edwardian period, and beyond. Further insights can be gleaned from the numerous manuals that were produced for the instruction of servants, from comments from employers in memoirs, diaries and letters, from recipe books, contemporary novels, magazines and newspapers. For accurate statistical information, the census returns are an invaluable source of information about the conditions of domestic service. The census was taken every decade and it was a criminal offence not to make a return. However, because of the nature of the material revealed and the possibility of identifying the respondents, census returns are confidential for a hundred years. The 1901 census was taken in March that year, only weeks after Edward VII had been proclaimed king. It went online in January 2002, but the work of analysing the data and establishing patterns of the very start of the Edwardian period will take time.

…while Erika dusts the dressing table and polishes the bedstead.

Employment categories changed to some extent after the 1871 census and it is much harder to extricate precise information about domestic servants after that date. Doubt has also increasingly been thrown on the census enumerators' returns: some enumerators tended to interchange the words 'housekeeper' and 'housewife', and women's part-time work was frequently not entered in the returns.[7] It is possible to use the 1871 census material as a basis and add to this the various surveys of domestic service – both governmental and by other organizations – published between then and the First World War. The 1871 census showed that 79 per cent of all those working in domestic service came from rural areas,[8] though as the rural population shifted to cities and towns this became less the case and has been advanced by historians as one of the reasons for the slow decline of those entering domestic service. However, employers tended to prefer country lasses (and lads) who they believed to be healthier and stronger, with better morals and more willing to take orders. There were, of course, far fewer job opportunities in the country than in towns and cities, and there would be a tradition of service in the neighbourhood 'big houses'. A son might well serve where his father had, and employees frequently recommended their relatives when a vacancy came up where they were working.

Domestic service provided training, and a career structure of sorts. For girls it encouraged housewifely skills (though these were likely to be in excess of the abilities needed to run their own modest homes when they married) and for both sexes a form of apprenticeship. Mary Russell Mitford,

The kitchen maid

The kitchen maid in the Edwardian Country House has a very responsible job in 'real' life. Antonia Dawson works as a Police Control Room Officer responding to 999 calls in central Nottingham police station. Fortunately for those below stairs, she also has a qualification in catering and hotel management. 'I live a very modern lifestyle. I've got my own house, my own car and I look after myself. So it would be really interesting to see what it would have been like for a woman living in the Edwardian period – to be told what to do, how to talk to people. I know that if I *had* been born then, this is the sort of job I probably would have done, given my class. I imagine that I would have considered myself very lucky to be employed in a grand house like this. I'm thirty now and that's quite old not to be married – or it certainly was then – so I'd be hoping for promotion to a cook, or something like that.'

writing about life in the Berkshire countryside in the nineteenth century, recalls how farmers' daughters went 'into service at fourteen and stayed till they married, learning there lessons of neatness, domestic skill and respect for quality of all kinds'. In this regard, things had not changed much in the countryside in the Edwardian period – except that education had been made compulsory until the age of thirteen in 1880 (raised to fourteen in 1918), though there were many exemptions for child workers and in general girls did not enter service until they were sixteen or seventeen.[9] In 1901, of 4 million women in employment, nearly half were in domestic service[10] and they formed around 11 per cent of the total work force.[11] In 1912 Lady Willoughby de Broke was still valiantly commending domestic service in terms that 'a well-trained domestic servant is of real value to the nation, she makes the best possible wife and mother, as she has acquired a good knowledge of housewifery and habits of cleanliness, punctuality, and, to some extent, hygiene'.[12]

A scullery maid might have been expected to achieve the position of a housemaid by the time she was twenty, and a hall boy who had failed to achieve the status of footman by the time he was twenty 'was destined to remain a lower-class servant',[13] whereas it is likely that he would not have attained the maturity and experience necessary to be a butler before his thirties. The 1871 census revealed that less than 10 per cent of ladies' maids were over forty. The majority of female servants would hope to 'marry out' before they were thirty, or, if not, have attained the respectable status of housekeeper. Such a woman might hope to remain in this position until she was too old to work, and then, if she was fortunate, be looked after in her infirmity by a grateful family; if not, the workhouse loomed. Almost all female servants were single: the census recorded only 3 per cent who admitted they were married, and a number of these were living apart from their husbands. Very occasionally a husband and wife might be employed as butler and housekeeper, and widows were sometimes hired as housekeepers, governesses or nurses.

The housemaids would have their work planned so that they would open the shutters, set the fires, sweep, dust and polish the living rooms before the family was up in the morning. As soon as the family had gone downstairs for breakfast, the housemaids would tidy and clean the bedrooms and bathrooms, making sure that they had finished before anyone returned upstairs. Should a maid encounter a member of the family in the corridors or on the stairs, she would lower her eyes to the ground, or even turn her face to the wall, so that there was no possibility that she would have to be acknowledged by an employer who chose to think of his or her lower servants as household functionaries rather than sentient beings helping the family.

'She knows that I work for her,' sighed Becky, duster in hand, shrinking into the shadows as Lady Olliff-Cooper came expectedly out of her room and swept down the silver staircase to the morning room. 'She could at least acknowledge my presence. How does she think everything gets done if she never sees any of us working?' But if one metaphor that describes the Edwardian country house is that of a smoothly running machine, another is of a gliding swan: the elegant serenity of upstairs made possible only thanks to the frantic, but unseen, footwork going on below. The world below stairs was separated as effectively as possible from that above and the separation was made apparent in every material detail. It would have been perfectly possible to visit most large country houses, and Manderston was no exception, without ever being aware that there *was* a 'downstairs' and certainly not what went on in those nether regions, while enjoying the distillation of all that effort. Heavy mahogany doors sealed the basement off from the ground floor, and while the side that faced the family's part of the house was elaborately carved, the reverse side that the servants saw was plain and functional, in some houses covered in green baize to further muffle sound from below.

Charlie, wearing white gloves so as not to mark the silver, lays the table for dinner with the precision expected of a first footman of quality.

The domestic offices were planned to immure the family from reality, to nurture the illusion of effortless production. The tradesmen's entrance at Manderston was set back and to the side of the house so that no one glancing out of the window in the main house need ever catch sight of the delivery of food destined for their table or the carting away of detritus generated by their luxurious consumption. The self-contained world of downstairs meant that staircases climbed from the basement to the attic floors via ninety-seven stone stairs, entirely bypassing the circulation system of the main house, so that the lower servants would pass their daily lives unseen and unheard by those they served. The bells that jangled incessantly, set off by peremptory pushes and pulls from upstairs, were a one-way communication: the only response possible was a leap to action. The kitchen was situated in the middle of the basement complex so that cooking smells wafting upstairs would be minimized. This was no easy task in days when it was recommended that cabbage should be boiled for half to three quarters of an hour with the lid off, when game was hung until it was so high as to be almost rank (any maggots perished in the cooking), and, without effective refrigeration, keeping milk, cream and cheese from going rancid (particularly in the summer months) was a constant problem – though there was a rather primitive chest ice box at Manderston, which helped.

The arrangement of the kitchen might have partly solved one problem, but it exacerbated another: heavy trays of food had to be carried from the kitchen, along the servants' corridor and up a steep flight of stone stairs where, at the top, stood a butler's tray stand where the trays could be balanced for a moment before Mr Edgar or the footmen pushed open the heavy door and carried the food into the dining room. It was back-breaking work. The food lift in operation when Manderston was rebuilt had

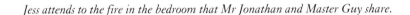

Jess attends to the fire in the bedroom that Mr Jonathan and Master Guy share.

long been removed; neither was there a 'dumb waiter'– a serving duct that ran between floors enabling plates to be loaded on one floor and winched up or down to the next – so sixty-five-year-old Mr Edgar and the footmen had to carry a succession of heavy trays piled with crockery, glasses, cutlery, tureens and serving dishes full of food, up and down stairs for breakfast, lunch, tea, dinner and any other occasion that took upstairs' fancy. In addition it meant that the food was often half cold after its lengthy journey along corridors and up staircases, and then standing outside the dining room until all the dishes had been assembled for serving. This, as with the odours of cooking pervading the house, was a perennial problem. The Prime Minister, Benjamin Disraeli, was reported to have murmured, 'At last, something warm,' as champagne was served at dinner in a country house one evening.

As the material aspects of the house connived at the family's comfort upstairs, so the daily routines of their servants were dictated entirely by the requirements of their master and mistress. The lower down the pile you were, the earlier you were expected to get up. As Kenny went back for a snatched sleep in his hall cupboard bed after stoking up the fire, the scullery maid, up in her attic room, tried to ignore the alarm clock that was insistently ringing – providing she had remembered to wind it up the night before. 'I never rely on the alarm clock,' said Becky, the conscientious first housemaid in her room next door. 'I listen for the grandfather clock chiming on the floor below. If it chimes six, I'm all right, because Jess [the second housemaid] and I are supposed to get up at half past, but if it strikes seven then we're in big trouble.' The female lower servants would get out of bed, feeling for the thin carpet strip with their bare feet, pad along the corridor to fetch water from the tap to fill their pottery jugs and then take them back to their rooms. Then they would pour the water into a bowl

Eyes demurely lowered, Becky hurries along the hall in response to the family's latest request.

for a quick wash of face, hands, underarms and private parts before getting dressed. 'At first it took me ages to get my corset on, but now I'm much quicker,' said Becky, 'and I don't need help any more.'

Each maid had arrived at the house with her uniform in a black tin trunk. Unlike the men servants whose uniforms were supplied by their employer, a girl entering service was required to buy or make her own uniform. She would need to have three sets of clothes – print dresses for the mornings for doing the dirty work, a black dress and a white cap and apron for afternoons, and her own clothes for outdoors and church on Sundays. She would be expected to wear a hat at all times outside and generally to look 'clean and decorous'. An article in *The Girl's Own Annual* in 1890 detailed exactly what 'a young servant's outfit' should consist of and totalled the cost at £3 11s 4¾d – no small consideration when this represented something in the region of a scullery maid's wages for six months. It meant that a girl entering service either had to do some other work beforehand to save up sufficient money to equip herself to be a scullery maid, or she would have to borrow the money from family or friends (providing *they* could find it) and pay it back from her meagre quarterly pay packet. Sometimes, an employer would provide the uniform and then deduct the cost from the maid's wages. She would also of course have to provide her own underwear, shoes and stockings, which cost about 4½d a pair and were usually so darned that it was not clear which (if any) was the original lisle.[14] A particular irritation was the employer (and there were many) who 'generously' gave her maids a length of cotton each for Christmas to have made up into a working uniform – at the maid's expense.

Once hastily dressed, the maids hurried downstairs, hoping to find the range blazing and the kettle boiling so that Becky could make tea and toast for Miss Morrison and Mrs Davies, who enjoyed this privilege as upper servants. The scullery maid had disappeared into her eponymous domain by this time, to make sure all the washing-up from the night before had been done and the floor was swept, and to help get ready for breakfast before the chef, M. Dubiard, enjoying his privilege of a later start, emerged. He would then begin to prepare a full Edwardian breakfast for the family, consisting of fruit, eggs – that might be boiled, coddled, poached or scrambled – sausages, perhaps a pair of kippers, or maybe a chafing dish of kidneys.

At 8.15 a.m. the bell for the servants' breakfast sounded and upper and lower servants all gathered in the servants' hall to be served bowls of porridge, cups of tea and bread and butter prepared by the kitchen maid, Antonia. By the time that she sat down for breakfast, Becky would have already opened the shutters in all the rooms on the ground floor – a job she particularly relished – opened the windows

Ever eager to learn, Ellen (left) tries out her culinary skills, watched by Miss Morrison.

to briefly air the rooms, tidied, dusted and polished the furniture and run the Ewbank sweeper over the carpets in the morning room, the dining room and the drawing room. Meanwhile, Jess, as second housemaid, had attended to the fires, a very necessary job in a large, cold Scottish country house. There were small store rooms on each floor where the maids concealed their cleaning equipment and materials, and where coal and wood for the fires was stored – providing that Kenny had remembered to bring in the coal from the coal hole and hauled the buckets upstairs, and chopped logs and kindling so that Jess could fill the scuttles and lay the fires. Before she came to Manderston, Jess had never lit a fire in her centrally heated life. Now she was expert at it, sweeping out the ash and cinders before building criss-crossed pyramids of kindling, rejecting those logs that were too green to burn before tipping on the coal. 'Light with a Lucifer match – use Bryant and May's, because theirs will *not* ignite unless they are rubbed on their own box, and thus are less dangerous than those which will kindle by stepping on…' advised *Warne's Model Cookery*, yet another book of advice for servants.[15] It was dirty work, for which she wore a black dress and dark brown apron to hide the coal dust, but her hands were permanently engrained with black no matter how hard she scrubbed, and she wondered if this badge of office would be permanent. Apart from lighting the fires, Jess had to monitor their progress, checking every hour whether they were still burning, and she found to her amazement that this responsibility made her reluctant to leave the house for lengthy periods since she felt that no one else possessed the incendiary skills she had acquired.

In addition to Becky and Jess, there were soon two more female servants in the Edwardian Country House. Lucy had been replaced as a scullery maid by Kelly, and though at first, it looked as if Kelly would

The scullery maid

Ellen Beard was the third scullery maid to come to the Edwardian Country House, and she was the one to stay the course – and find romance. Twenty-two-year-old Ellen (or Carly, as she is known in the modern world) is a farmer's daughter from North Devon. She studied countryside management at college and then moved to Exeter. Ellen had been planning to travel when the Edwardian Country House opportunity came up, but she put her plans on hold in order to test whether she was looking at the past – helped by the reminiscences of her grandmother – through rose-tinted spectacles. She thought it would be good to be more appreciative of what she enjoyed in the twenty-first century – comfortable beds, telephones, text messaging her friends…and the hardships of Edwardian life would certainly achieve that.

stay, she too found the endless monotony of 'doing nothing but washing up pots all day long' too much and, on the evening of the political dinner party, as the other servants formed a human chain to deliver the meal, Kelly went quietly to her room, packed her belongings ready to leave. The revolving door of scullery maids had to stop, decided Lady Olliff-Cooper, and so she joined the housekeeper, Mrs Davies, in interviewing for Kelly's replacement. Her ladyship had also acceded to her servants' pleas that there really was too much work for only two housemaids, particularly as the Olliff-Coopers were living in fine Edwardian style and entertaining with an open-handed generosity and a wish to dazzle that threw a heavy burden on the staff. So as well as appointing Ellen as the scullery maid, a third housemaid, Erika, joined the staff at the Edwardian Country House.

Ellen is a farmer's daughter from Devon and hopes were high that she'd 'know what hard work meant' and get on and do it. Although Becky and Jess had campaigned for an addition to their team – and with winter coming on, Jess's fire duties would prove all-consuming – they found it hard to work with Erika at first. Becky decided that rather than feeling that she had to train Erika into the exact routine that she and Jess had established, and then check up that she'd done the work to Becky's now exacting standards, she would have her own areas of responsibility – the corridors and staircases, the servants' quarters and helping dry up in the butler's pantry when needed.

As soon as breakfast was finished, Miss Morrison, who had already taken tea and toast to Lady Olliff-Cooper in her bedroom, hurried upstairs to run a bath for her mistress, help her dress and do her hair. Becky slipped upstairs too to do the same for Miss Anson, Lady Olliff-Cooper's spinster sister who did not have a lady's maid of her own, while Mr Edgar, who had presided at breakfast, knocked on Sir John's door prepared for his morning role as valet and barber.

At 9.15 the bell rang for family prayers. The family gathered around Sir John, who read the first prayer. The servants had left what they were doing and stood silently. Family and servants were brought briefly together in the hall as one community with the spiritual and temporal authority of the master asserted. Sir John then often turned to his direct representative below stairs to read the next prayer. As he did so, the butler looked meaningfully over his wire-framed spectacles. The servants could be sure that whichever prayer Mr Edgar had selected 'as being appropriate to the household that day' from the small leather-bound volume of *Helps to Worship. A Manual for Holy Communion and Daily Prayer* (1909) that he carried in his breast pocket, it would be a coded message by which he wished to convey a reprimand that the culprit could not fail to understand.

There was the time when all the lower servants had gone into the nearby town of Duns to celebrate Charlie's birthday and Charlie and Kenny had got very drunk and so hungover the next day that they had crept away to sleep it off by the lake. Mr Edgar had felt deeply betrayed by their behaviour when he finally found them, and remembering his own father's strict regime, resolved that 'discipline will have to be tightened in *this* household'. The next morning, he read the prayer for temperance and the miscreants shuffled uncomfortably. As the Edwardian Country House experiment continued and tempers below stairs sometimes became frayed,

Becky uses the carpet sweeper in the morning room while the family is at breakfast.

accusations flew and offence was taken, there were several occasions when Mr Edgar felt it appropriate to read the prayer for friendship: '…help us in this world to love each other in Thee and for Thee'. On occasions he had also selected the one for truth, when it felt it had been violated – on either side of the baize door: 'O Lord God, Who knows the very secrets of our hearts; root out of my heart all hypocrisy and deceit that I may be truthful and upright in all that I do…' And the prayer for humility: 'Almighty God, who resistest the proud, but gives grace to the humble; grant that I may never be lifted up by pride, nor exalt myself above others…' was one he frequently proclaimed, looking solemnly around the assembled company as he did so.

Prayers were a time for Sir John to demonstrate the paternalism that characterized the Edwardian country house, a legacy from the Victorian era. They were a time for announcements, congratulations on duties well performed, on birthdays celebrated that day, and for admonitions. 'I used to hate morning prayers. I thought they were condescending and something we didn't need to do,' confessed Antonia after a few weeks in the house, 'but now I love going to prayers. It sets the mood of the whole house. It lets the servants know how the family really are, and lets the family know how the servants are by the prayers that are said.'

As soon as prayers were over, the family went in for breakfast, which had been laid and was served by the footmen while the rest of the servants returned to their morning tasks. In the kitchen the housekeeper, Mrs Davies, was kneading bread, dodging the chef as he whirled from the range to the table making a roast for the family's lunch. She hoped that the range would be hot enough for the loaves she was making for the table upstairs and down and that there would be an opportunity to get them into the oven before it was needed to roast the lamb.

Vails

Vails, an eighteenth-century form of largesse (which could be so onerous that, as one visitor complained, it would have been cheaper to stay at a tavern), were revived in the form of tips in the Edwardian period. Their distribution remained a delicate business. 'The amount given as a tip depends on circumstances and particularly on the social standing of the visitor,' explained 'Madge' (Mrs Humphry) in an article on 'Country House Visits' in *Everywoman's Encyclopaedia* (1910).

Just before 10.30 Mrs Davies would have to wash her hands, go to her parlour to change into a clean apron and tidy her hair before going upstairs for her daily meeting with Lady Olliff-Cooper to discuss the day's business. How many were there to be at lunch? What was the chef proposing to cook that night? Please remind him that Guy's tutor, Mr Raj Singh, does not eat meat and M. Dubiard must cook fish for him for luncheon *and* dinner. Lady McEwen from nearby Duns will be calling at tea time tomorrow. Could Mrs Davies please make sure that there was some raspberry jam to have with the scones, and a rich fruit cake would be nice. How was the new scullery maid doing? Was she turning out to be a good worker? My sister and Mr Jonathan wish to ride this afternoon. At 3 p.m., I think. Will she please make sure that Tristan has the horses ready.

At the same time that Mrs Davies was taking her orders from Lady-Olliff Cooper, Mr Edgar was closeted with Sir John in his business room. This was the second time that servant had seen master that day. The butler would have taken tea to Sir John, run his bath, laid out his clothes for the day and deftly shaved his master using a cut-throat razor.

'I need to discuss arrangements about the shoot with you, Edgar.'

'Yes, Sir John.'

'I was concerned about the servants' behaviour at prayers this morning. I noticed that Antonia was not present and that Kenny had his hands stuffed in his pockets and a smirk on his face.'

'Antonia is unwell, Sir John, and she is in her room. I will make sure to speak to Kenny myself.'

In her workroom Miss Morrison was washing her mistress's clothes and those of her sister before settling down to trim the hat that Lady Olliff-Cooper had decided to wear to the forthcoming fête to

Miss Morrison interrupts her sewing to respond to a summons from Lady Olliff-Cooper.

be held in the grounds of Manderston, and to wrestle with Miss Anson's wig. 'I learned how to do what was called board work when I was at hairdressing college. It was very tedious at the time, and most people didn't bother to do it. They weren't interested in wigs and thought they'd never need to know about them. But I stuck at it, because you never know when it might come in handy. That was twenty-five years ago, and I'm so glad that I did. It's given me the confidence to tackle these Edwardian wigs here now,' recalled Miss Morrison. But as she worked, her ear was cocked in case the bell at the foot of her stairs summoned her to her ladyship's bedroom.

On the floor below, Becky was cleaning the bedrooms while the ladies breakfasted. The housemaids swarmed silently in the wake of the family all day: when they left a room, the servants would go in to restore it to its pristine state, tidying papers and anything the family had used, plumping cushions that bore the imprint of their presence, and then slip quietly out again unseen, unacknowledged and unthanked.

Morning cleaning ran to a tight schedule, an almost impossible one if there were several guests occupying the first-floor bedrooms. First Becky opened the windows to air the room. The carpets had to be swept either with a carpet sweeper or with a stiff brush, and the wood surround mopped. The curtains were heavy, as were the wall drapes around the bed, and Becky battled with dust endlessly. She had been advised that if she washed the paintwork with a mixture of vinegar and water this would stop the dust from settling, and she thought that she might try that. Fortunately for her since there were numerous bathrooms on the first floor for family and guests at Manderston – including a priceless silver-lined one in Sir John's bathroom – she did not have to deal with the chamber pots by emptying their contents into a covered slop bucket as happened in the servants' quarters. Ever vigilant for bed bugs that thrived in horsehair, she checked the mattress and finally made the bed (*The Complete Servant* recommended the housemaid should change into a clean apron before doing so, but Becky certainly didn't have time for that), plumping up the pillows and the quilted satin eiderdowns. Then it was the bathrooms to clean, rubbing the porcelain with coarse salt in the absence of scouring powder if scum proved stubborn. Edwardian housemaids would 'turn out' a different room on a rota basis each week, moving the furniture to clean under it.

The hierarchy of servants' tasks was subtly calibrated and unwritten: while Becky would have cleaned and tidied Lady Olliff-Cooper's room, she would not have touched her ladyship's dressing table. That was the privilege of the lady's maid, just as downstairs, while the housemaids would clean the reception rooms, they were forbidden to touch the writing desks which would be dusted by the butler.[16]

Major cleaning in an Edwardian country house would have to wait until the family left for the London season. Then windows would be left open to air the rooms; curtains would be taken down, brushed and sponged; windows cleaned; brocade wall hangings brushed with a soft brush then gently rubbed with tissue paper and a soft silk cloth; and wallpaper blown free of dust with a pair of bellows and then lightly rubbed with a stale loaf of bread torn into pieces. In the days before the invention of the 'puffing billy' vacuum cleaner in 1901 and its slow adoption into British households, tea leaves (or even sand or grass) would be scattered on carpets to absorb the grime before a stiff brushing; wooden floors would be scrubbed with soap or soda and water or dry-scrubbed using sand; paintwork wiped with a mixture of soap and beer, or grated potatoes made into a paste with water if the paint was white, and buffed with a chamois leather; grates would be blacked with powdered blacklead mixed to a paste and then burnished with three separate brushes till it gleamed and the slate hearth polished with hot mutton

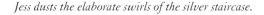

Jess dusts the elaborate swirls of the silver staircase.

Mister Jonathan reads in his room.

fat. The furniture would be polished with a home-made product, a mixture of beeswax and turpentine; the china ornaments and glass vases would be carefully washed; footmen would perch precariously on stepladders to wash the crystal drops of the chandeliers; drawers and cupboards would be tidied and lined with fresh, scented paper. During this time when the family was away and food would not have to be bought and prepared for them, the servants would have been paid 'board' wages, a cash payment to buy their own food, and beer. It was presumed that women would eat less than men and by the Edwardian period women lower servants might expect to receive around 10–12 shillings a week and men a shilling or so more.

Guy had celebrated his tenth birthday a few days after the family had arrived at Manderston. The servants had pooled ideas of how this could be celebrated. They were keen to make the young boy, who had been volunteered for the Edwardian Country House far from his school, his friends and his Gameboy, feel more at home. They had come up with the inspired idea of a paper chase that led to the prize which was Guy's birthday present – a pony of his own – and Mrs Davies and the housemaids had organized it, tying coloured crêpe paper round trees as markers.

Originally, it had been intended that Master Guy was to be educated at home. The services of a tutor, Mr Raj Singh, had been procured and a schoolroom equipped with books, maps, globes, arithmetic tables and educational models. But, unlike an Edwardian schoolroom in which the children of a large family would have been taught, Guy was on his own – and lonely. It was decided that he should go to school in Berwick. Mr Singh supervised his homework and took him for nature walks in the grounds, but it was Rob who played board games with him, gave him supper in his room, read him stories before he went to sleep, and made sure he was awake in the morning to go in to see his mother before going to school.

After his discussion with Sir John, Mr Edgar went back to the basement to implement his master's wishes: he called in the staff for instructions, praise or remonstration. He wrote out rotas for time off and a list of duties for the forthcoming week; he penned letters; consulted with the chef (though he found M. Dubiard 'a law unto himself'); and then went along to the butler's pantry to see how Charlie and Rob were getting on with washing up the breakfast silver and dishes and getting ready to lay for luncheon. All china and silver had to be checked in and out by the housekeeper from her cupboards, and breakages reported and listed, so it was a long process. Later Mr Edgar would decant any wine, sherry or port for dinner and make sure that the champagne was on ice. And every day there would be special duties to attend to, occasioned by the social arrangements of those on the floors above. Throughout the day he would be alert for the summons of the bell, listen out for the sound of a carriage on the gravel and the clang of the front door, which he would answer, showing expected visitors into the morning room, and seating 'persons' (a local official perhaps, or an 'agent for somebody's tea') in the hall to wait. He would prowl round the house checking that all was in order, that the blinds were down to protect the pictures hanging on the walls if the sun was strong, that all was tidy and tranquil and that his staff had discharged their duties *almost* to his satisfaction.

In the corridor outside, Jess had taken time out from checking on the fires and was sorting through the laundry that was collected and delivered to the house twice a week. Every week something seemed to go missing and Mr Edgar was complaining that he was down to his last pair of socks. When the huge wicker baskets were delivered Jess and Mrs Davies sorted the linen in 'pug's parlour'. At the request of the footmen, they measured all the tablecloths so they could pin a label on each to indicate its size; then the footmen would be able to take one to fit the dining table, according to how many leaves were in place for a particular meal, without having to unfold each white damask cloth.

Meanwhile in the kitchen it was hot, steamy and a hive of activity. Mrs Davies had phoned her food orders to the suppliers and deliveries had been made into the cool, tiled larders. M. Dubiard was preparing lunch and planning ahead for dinner at the same time. That day he was going to cook a turbot so he took it along to the end of the corridor to wash and fillet it in a tiled room with a huge sink. The sink was irrigated by a punctured metal tube that ran round the perimeter so that water poured continuously on to the marble slab and made the preparation of fish both easy and hygienic. Antonia was making dinner for the servants. The midday meal, the main meal of the day for those below stairs, was called dinner while upstairs it was a lighter meal than the evening meal and was referred to as luncheon. Today the servants would be having steak and kidney pie, but it wasn't easy to cater for so many.

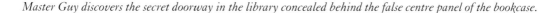

Master Guy discovers the secret doorway in the library concealed behind the false centre panel of the bookcase.

'Frankly, we've got a bunch of fussy eaters here,' said Antonia. 'Mr Edgar can't eat eggs, cream, butter, milk, rice, potatoes, or meat the majority of the time, but he does like pulses. He'd eat them at every meal. Then Becky is a vegetarian, and I am worried that she is not getting enough to eat, she was thin when she came, but she is stick thin now. Jess doesn't like meat much either, she loves rice and pasta and veggies. Charlie doesn't eat broccoli, cabbage or cauliflower. He has to have a baked potato every day. Kenny will eat any lean meat without fat between two great doorsteps of bread. He'll eat anything between bread, I think he'd eat a spaghetti bolognese sandwich. Tristan doesn't like mushrooms or gravy, he doesn't much care for puddings or fish either and he won't eat hot things, spicy curries and that sort of thing. Rob will eat pretty well anything but he talks so much that it all gets cold and then he doesn't want it. But Ellen is fantastic, she'll eat anything that's put in front of her and Mrs Davies is much the same, but she never makes any comment on my cooking which is a bit scary as she's the housekeeper!'

There was no time to make a pudding: 'We'll have fruit today,' Antonia decided, 'and maybe I'll make a tapioca pudding for tonight.'

Kenny was bringing in the coal and filling the scuttles, sweeping the yard and giving a hand in the kitchen. And Ellen was peeling potatoes in the scullery and waiting for the next load of washing-up to arrive, having just finished scouring the pots she'd had soaking overnight from dinner. Ellen's

Fire drill: Jess watches with satisfaction as the fire in the morning room blazes.

day was largely spent washing up the pots and pans used in the preparation of meals, and then washing up the things used in eating the meals, with some vegetable preparation in between. Maybe she might be told to pluck and dress a grey partridge, a duck or a pheasant: 'To pluck either game or poultry, have a bird upon a board with its head towards you, and pull its feathers away from you, which is the direction they lay in; many persons pull out the feathers in a contrary direction, by which means they are likely to tear the skin to pieces, which would very much disfigure the bird for the table,' advised *The Gastronomic Regenerator*.[17] This didn't worry Ellen too much since she'd lived all her life on a farm, but she knew how excruciating Becky had found it when she'd been asked to help. 'But though she can't bear the idea of meat, and it took her ages, she did it. I really admired her for that.'

The last job of the day for Ellen was to sweep and mop the black and white tiled floors in the kitchen and scullery, which got filthy with all the traffic and food dropped during the day – but they never seemed clean enough for the chef, which was rather dispiriting, Ellen thought. Sometimes Kenny would help her with the washing-up, but he had other jobs to do, Mr Edgar needed his help, and Charlie and Rob called on him to do their bidding in the butler's pantry. But M. Dubiard had promised that he would show her how to make ice-cream. 'I've come here to learn,' insisted Ellen.

After a few days Mr Edgar had relented and allowed conversation at the dinner table providing that it was decorous. If voices were raised or opinions got heated, he would rap out 'Silence, sir', or 'Silence, miss' and that was – usually – sufficient. Although it was the servants' main meal of the day, it was not one to linger over since the family had lunch at 1 p.m. and Mr Edgar, the footmen and of course the kitchen staff were all involved in that.

After lunch, the meal had to be cleared and the washing-up done in the butler's pantry while Ellen washed the servants' crocks in the scullery, then everything had to be put away again. Jess checked on her fires, Miss Morrison obeyed a summons upstairs to help Lady Olliff-Cooper change into her tea gown (which was always a relief since it was loose and flowing and did not require a corset to be worn). Becky went to Miss Anson to help her get ready to go riding, which meant taking off her wig since it would not fit under her hard hat, and lacing up her tight leather boots. Charlie went to help Mr Jonathan get ready for riding too since he was to escort Miss Anson; and down in the stables, Tristan was saddling the horses.

Mrs Davies had probably done a quick tour of the upstairs rooms when she was sure the family was out of the way, as would her Edwardian counterparts, to check that 'her' housemaids had done their work properly – though within a short time she realized that this was no longer necessary: the maids were highly conscientious and efficient. She would also make sure that there was fresh water in the vases and check other small items of household concern. It was standard practice in service for the housekeeper – or the mistress of the house – to test the maid's work by hiding small coins about the rooms, under a chest of drawers, on a picture rail. If they pocketed the money, maids would be sacked for dishonesty: if the coins were not discovered, they would be accused of negligence and severely reprimanded. At first, Becky had suspected that Miss Anson was testing her domestic skills by concealing screwed-up pieces of paper in unlikely places in the Edwardian manner.

After lunch the housekeeper went into the kitchen to start making scones and some 'fancies' for tea in the drawing room. Her cherry or sultana fruit scones with jam were a particular favourite upstairs and Mrs Davies made some most days, while downstairs the servants were particularly partial to her oat flapjacks so they were regularly prepared. This would be the time when she might bottle some fruit, make chutney or jam, usually from produce gathered from the kitchen garden or orchards of the estate.

A housekeeper would be expected to know rudimentary first aid and distil simple remedies – though in the Edwardian Country House, it was the chef who produced comforting infusions and embrocations when staff fell sick. M. Dubiard experimented with burdock seeds for throat and chest ailments, and a paste of rosemary for eczema, while an infusion of honeysuckle was supposed to help asthma and hyssop for a cold, though it was also reputed to be good in a paste for insect bites and burns. Pennyroyal was supposed to be soothing for headaches, elderflower tea for throat infections, brewed fennel seeds for indigestion, watercress for coughs. The flowers of golden rod could be made into a poultice for arthritis, or an infusion for digestive upsets, while thyme infusions were an excellent pick-me-up, as was summer savory. Sage had many uses – to relieve menstrual pains, help circulation, calm nervous anxiety, and, with its antiseptic properties, as an effective gargle for laryngitis or tonsillitis.

The hours between three and five *might* be a lull in the day for the servants, a brief time to sit around the servants' hall and chat, catch up on some mending or even 'knit dish cloths from the string tied round tradesmen's parcels' if they were feeling particularly industrious. If they had time, they could amuse themselves with embroidery or carving wood, or maybe playing the old piano that had been provided for the servants. They could go to their rooms to read or write letters home, or more likely catch up on the sleep of which they felt they were so grievously deprived. M. Dubiard liked to take some fresh air whenever possible, so after lunch most days he would try to find time to change out of his white chef's uniform, put on his tweed coat and go for a bike ride through the neighbouring countryside.

But the interlude could not be guaranteed: it was quite likely that a member of the family would ring the bell to summon a servant to take a letter to post, sponge a coat or clean some shoes that had got muddy – and then the front door bell might sound. The afternoon was when the local ladies might pay a visit, or leave their card. And then tea had to be served in the drawing room at 4 p.m. The housekeeper would make the tea and arrange cakes and pastries on plates and cake stands, and the footmen took it up to the drawing room, often the only occasion when this formal room – with its spindly, uncomfortable upright chairs and scattered small tables and screens – was used. It was the meal the footmen 'hated

Mrs Davies's recipes

The housekeeper, Mrs Davies, made this traditional treacle toffee for Bonfire Night (and parkin too), which everyone munched as they watched the guy go up in flames.

Treacle toffee

1lb (450g) black treacle
1lb (450g) golden syrup
1lb (450g) demerara sugar
8oz (225g) butter
half a cup of water
1 dessertspoon of vinegar

Melt all the ingredients in a saucepan over a medium heat, stirring gently.

Boil hard, without stirring, for about 20 minutes, until the mixture reaches 260°–270° (if you are using a sugar thermometer). Alternatively, drop a small amount from a spoon into cold water – if it forms a hard ball, it is ready.

Pour into a buttered flat tin and mark into squares while still warm.

Break into pieces when cold and wrap in greaseproof paper.

(NOTE: in Edwardian times, imperial measures would have used; metric equivalents are given here – for best results, one system only should be used consistently.)

with a passion. All those little plates, and knives and napkins and scones and cake and butter and jam and cream and there's nowhere to put anything down properly. It's ridiculously long-drawn-out affair, it seems to go on for ever, and if the family don't ring when they've finished, we're so busy getting our own meal and preparing for dinner that we forget to clear. So it's a disaster all round,' concluded Rob.

Domestic service was vestigial of earlier patterns of pre-industrial employment when, in effect, most workers were servants living in their master's house and bound together by reciprocal obligations, as the historian Jessica Gerrard reminds us.[18] The terms of their employment remained pre-industrial, with hours of work unregulated by legislation; they were paid quarterly out of their master's or mistress's personal income, with board and lodging as part of their remuneration. Since they lived in their employer's house, their time was at his or her disposal and they were subject to any legal demand the employer cared to place on them. Thus servants were not *entitled* to any time off, and indeed, the obligatory attendance at church on a Sunday morning was regarded by some employers as time off from work. But by the Edwardian period it had become customary for a servant to have a half day off a week and a full day off once a month. In the early days at the Edwardian Country House, there had been no official time off either, and this had occasioned a near revolt of the servants when M. Dubiard had broken all the rules of etiquette by insisting that Lady

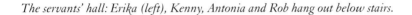

The servants' hall: Erika (left), Kenny, Antonia and Rob hang out below stairs.

Olliff-Cooper came below stairs to see the conditions in which the servants were working. She and her sister had been appalled at the amount of work that the servants were required to do and how exhausted they all were – though they were also rather shocked at the conditions in the kitchen with somewhat dirty, unswept floors and a roller towel that made Miss Anson, as a microbiologist, feel almost faint. The situation had led Mr Edgar to discuss the matter with Sir John and it was agreed that all servants could take half a day a week as free time (which meant from the time they had finished their chores after lunch – probably around 3 p.m. – until 10.30, when they were obliged to be in and the door would be locked) and every other Sunday. It was stressed that this concession was not a right, but a privilege that could be revoked at any time for any reason – the requirements of the household, or the servant's own misdemeanours.

The younger servants seized the opportunity to get out of their basement confine and would walk into Duns where the routine was always the same: tea and cakes at the Pewter Plate, buying sweets at Candy Corner, a drink at the Whip and Saddle, dinner at the Swan and then back to the Whip and Saddle for more drinks before hurrying back the two miles through dark country lanes home. But it was hard for Miss Morrison to take a predictable day off, as her work was so intimately bound up with the activities of Lady Olliff-Cooper, and it would not have been proper for any other servant to have performed the personal tasks Miss Morrison did, so she was only able to snatch time off if her ladyship was away or out for the afternoon. Yet, as Miss Morrison herself pointed out, she got rather more outings than the other servants since as a lady's maid she would accompany her mistress on social calls and shopping expeditions, and would help in her charitable activities.

Charlie teaches Kenny footmanly skills for when extra help is needed upstairs.

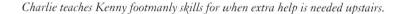

By 5 o'clock the basement was a hive of activity again: the servants ate supper at 6 p.m., and dinner was served upstairs at 8 p.m. This usually consisted of between four and six courses if the family was not entertaining, and almost double that number if they were. It was not always easy to know how many were to be at table, and that made life for everyone downstairs very difficult. The chef did not know how much food to prepare and the footmen did not know how many places to lay for. If there were one or two extra or missing guests at the last moment, it could throw everything into confusion since etiquette absolutely forbade an unused place at table, and extra places meant the whole business of laying the table had to start again from scratch.

As first footman, Charlie sounded the gong at 7 o'clock to alert the family and their guests that it was time to go up to dress for dinner, and then sounded the dinner gong at exactly 8 o'clock. Whereupon the butler would fling open the double doors of the morning room and announce, 'Dinner is served, m'lady.' Or that was the theory. To Mr Edgar's ongoing distress, dinner was often delayed. 'One minute late is too much,' he would fume, and it was frequently rather more than that. As the butler represented the family to the servants, so he was the public face of those below stairs and anything that went wrong in the discharge of their duties, he regarded as his fault. Any criticism of the servants was a criticism of him. It is the butler, explained Mrs Beeton, who must see that the duties of the male house-servants 'are properly performed, that they do not rob their master of either time or service'.[19] So Mr Edgar had cast a critical eye over the table to make sure that it was laid correctly before he allowed the gong to be struck, and he lit the candles just before the diners entered. Now he oversaw the meal, carving the joint, hovering to pick up a dropped napkin here, fill a wine glass there, help a lady with her wrap, all as unobtrusively as possible. When he was satisfied that all was running smoothly, the butler took up his position behind Sir John's chair, stepping forward to ring the bell as Rob and Charlie (or Robin and Charles as they were known upstairs) cleared one course to alert the kitchen staff to start to dish up the next.

Laying the table

Before a dinner party at the Edwardian Country House, Mr Edgar planned the operation with near-military precision, and sketched the table plan to ensure that the footmen would get it right. He followed Mrs Beeton's instructions:

It is usual to lay two large [knives and forks] flanked on the right by a fish knife and a soup spoon and on the left by the fish fork; other knives and forks are supplied with the plates for the different courses. The question of what wine is to be drunk at dinner will determine what glasses will be wanted, as the glasses used for dessert are put on afterwards. Supposing sherry, champagne and claret are to be served, put the proper glasses for each to the right side of each person, setting them in a triangle with the sherry glass (the first used) at the top, just reaching to the point of the knife, but at a convenient distance from it.

The footmen served wine from the right and food from the left and, Mrs Beeton instructed, each should 'hold [the dish] so that the guest may take it with ease. In lifting dishes from the table, he should use both hands, and remove them with care, so that nothing is spilt on the tablecloth or on the dresses of guests.' Throughout the whole meal, when they were not serving or carrying trays up and downstairs, Charlie and Rob had to stand to attention watching the diners so they knew when to clear and when to refill wine glasses. But like the legendary brass monkeys, the footmen were supposed to hear and see and speak no evil – or anything good or amusing – as they gazed impassively into the middle distance. 'Do not smile at droll stories told in your

À la russe: *Rob and Kenny (promoted to third footman for the occasion) serve at a dinner party.*

presence, or seem in any way to notice, or enter into, the family conversation, or the talk at table, or with visitors…' decreed *Rules for the Manners of Servants in Good Families* (1901).

After dinner was finished, cigars smoked, *digestifs* imbibed, coffee drunk and guests ushered out, Charlie and Rob went wearily downstairs again. If they were lucky they might have been 'stood down' after Lady Olliff-Cooper turned to her husband and said, 'I don't think we need Charles and Robin any more this evening, do we?' and they waited with bated breath to hear if the master of the house agreed. But this was only likely to happen if it was a family-only dinner – when guests were present, so were the footmen, for the duration.

Dinner over, it was washing-up again: it had been decreed by Mr Edgar that Kenny would start as the dirty dishes came down between courses, so that there was not such a pile to tackle at 10 or 11 at night. But it didn't always work out. While the family had been at dinner, Becky had done the rounds of the bedrooms again, clearing up discarded clothes from the day, closing the shutters, drawing the curtains, switching on bedside lights, laying out dressing gowns and nightdresses, turning down the bed covers and slipping a stone hot water bottle between the crisp linen sheets as the nights grew colder. If there were female guests who had come 'unmaided' then their night-time comforts would be the housemaid's responsibility too, as any male guest's would be the footmen's. Miss Morrison had to stay up until the ladies were ready to retire, and when the bell rang, she would go to help Lady Olliff-Cooper to prepare for bed, and maybe hear some titbits from the evening as she brushed her ladyship's hair. At first she had attended to Miss Anson, but that had left the younger sister waiting for up to an hour when she was tired and ready for bed, so Becky had assumed that responsibility too: in an

Edwardian household, this would have been the unmarried sister's lot had she not had the means to employ a lady's maid of her own.

The last task of a long day was for Mr Edgar to check that all the lights were off, ensure that the shutters were secured and lock all the outside doors. He bolted the servants' door at 10.30 p.m., which was curfew time for them. If they were later than that, they risked Mr Edgar's wrath, and no doubt a punishment or a withdrawal of privileges if they rang the bell for admittance, or a cold and uncomfortable night in the coal shed, as M. Dubiard had been known to resort to on a couple of occasions. But bells lined the attic corridor as well as the one in the basement, and should a member of the family or a guest require anything to help them sleep or to relieve indigestion after the servants had retired, these would jangle out and disturb their slumbers.

The only variation in this routine was on Sundays when the servants were obliged to attend church – 'to remind them of their duties of servitude and show respect to their master'. At least most were. M. Dubiard had declined, pleading that he was a Catholic and a Scottish Episcopalian service did not accord with his idea of religious practice. 'It's all one God,' spluttered Mr Edgar, but he didn't push the point.

'All things bright and beautiful' sang out the Olliff-Coopers as they surveyed their bevy of servants singing from the same hymn sheet at Harvest Festival. 'The Lord God gave them all…The rich man in his castle, the poor man at his gate, He made them high or lowly, And ordered their estate.' While the family rode to church and back in the landau, the servants had to walk the couple of miles both ways to Duns or Edron church whatever the weather. When they arrived, wearing their best clothes, they sat in a separate pew apart from the family: the social distinctions sanctioned in the sight of God as man. The mandatory church attendance signified that servants were not employed for work alone, but for status, deference and obedience, that the natural order of being should be maintained. But despite this, the servants quite enjoyed their Sunday excursion, particularly if the sermon was not too long. 'It's just nice to get out in the fresh air,' explained Antonia. 'The people are friendly – it's good to see someone different – and we get coffee and biscuits after the service in Duns church hall.' In the first week of the 'Edwardian experiment' with gruel for lunch and dinner, this had felt like a lifesaver.

Improving texts were a feature of a servant's life in the Edwardian period: 'Whatsoever thou findest to do, do it with all thy Might' or 'Sobriety is the nursemaid of industry' or 'Humility is the servant's true dignity'. As they trudged back across the fields after church on Sundays to get on with their daily work, it is to be hoped that the servants felt uplifted, reflecting on the words of George Herbert:

Teach me, my God and King,
In all things Thee to see,
and what I do in anything
To do it as for Thee.

A servant with this clause
Makes drudgery divine;
Who sweeps a room as for Thy laws,
Makes them and the action fine.

CHAPTER SEVEN

Sunlit Lawns

While money is poured out lavishly upon questionable luxuries and needless "sport",' reproved the *Berwickshire Advertiser* in 1911,[1] 'sweet charity often has to go begging. Continual effort is necessary to raise the requisite funds to carry on the humane work in which Lady Miller [the mistress of Manderston] is active and earnest.' It went to on to report on a 'garden party held on Tuesday at Manderston' to raise funds for the various local charities in which her ladyship was involved. 'The day was ideal, brilliant sunshine and a cooling breeze; and as the grounds of Lady Miller's home lend themselves to such a function, the event was a great success…and there was a large company present.' But when the reporter tried to describe these grounds, he found the challenge all but impossible: 'to write in adequate terms of the garden is beyond us: it would require one able to describe beauty as Zola is to depict horror, but they are a feast of colour and a banquet of sweet perfume that would never pall the eye nor satiate the appetite'.

Finding herself the chatelaine of this earthly paradise, Lady Olliff-Cooper was mindful of the aristocratic tradition of *noblesse oblige* – the conviction that the right to rule, and the enjoyment of rank, privilege and wealth, carried with them moral obligations of public service and benevolence towards dependants, whose gratitude, deference and submission legitimized the existing social order. In plutocratic imitation of this, she resolved to hold a bazaar at Manderston to raise money for her favourite Border charities. As Lady Tweedsmuir, writing of her own Edwardian childhood, recalled, 'Undeserved sneers have been directed at the Lady of the Manor who blandly dispensed soup and blankets, but it must be admitted by any impartial observer that she was often the one who urged her husband to carry out work on cottages…The Lady of the Manor should have her place of honour in the history of the countryside…she lent her garden for…fêtes and heroically saw the public trampling down her lawns, or her drawing room for church sales, or her dining room for the Sunday School play. It was all part of the pattern of country life that seemed as immutable as the laws of nature.'[2]

Charity work was part of the wider ideal of Christian duty; it was an aspect of women's traditional role as nurturer, and could be seen as the responsibility that the 'big house' owed to the community in which it was situated and from which it drew sustenance in the form of labour, resources and produce. A remnant of the reciprocity inherent in feudalism, it mimicked the model of benevolent patriarchy and hierarchy that ordered the Edwardian country house. It validated, in some eyes, the possession of wealth in the midst of poverty since that wealth could be seen as being put to good use. Bazaars would be regarded as part of the social calendar of the locality. In the straitened circumstances of many traditional landowners and the very different views of societal responsibility held by many of the rich parvenus, the opportunity for the population to visit country houses in the Edwardian years had become much more restricted. The 'privatization' of the country house had led the journalist W. T. Stead to conclude that 'the landed proprietors…prevent public access to their parks, treasure-houses, historical buildings, collections of art and curios in a general way…it cannot be said that any one acts generally as if he considered himself trustee for the public'.[3] Indeed, when a coach party had turned up at Manderston requesting to look round the house, Sir John had sent them away – politely but firmly. Increasingly it was only on such select occasions as a bazaar that the hoi polloi were admitted to the gracious surroundings of the wealthy house in carefully regulated circumstances. It provided the family with an opportunity to show off their fine home and grounds, potent symbols of the unbridgeable distance between the rich and everyone else.

Equally, the money raised for charitable causes such as hospitals, the sick, the old and the needy was vital in the days before the state took financial responsibility for those of its citizens who could no longer support themselves, and the only recourse for the poor or infirm would be to poor law provision and the harsh and degrading conditions of the workhouse. Most charities were run as private committees and access to them – and the agreement to do voluntary work on their behalf – would be in the hands of society ladies. To become part of this network of social patronage had cachet much sought after by the *nouveaux riches*, and provided a worthwhile way for women with time on their hands to spend it doing something useful and beneficial in congenial company.[4] Indeed, 'only as Lady Bountiful', writes Jessica Gerrard, 'did [society women] have opportunities for independent action and unfettered power over the lives of others. Women of intelligence, energy and initiative and a thirst for power, found in philanthropy a socially approved outlet for their talents and needs.'[5] If troops of servants deprived wealthy women of their roles as housewives and, to an extent, as mothers, 'it can hardly be said,' crowed Lady Greville, 'that if the ladies of England [or no doubt Scotland] are wrapped in luxury, they are idle as well'[6] as they 'attempted to transpose the values and relations of domestic service to a wider class of the poor'[7] by ministering to their tenants in time of need, visiting hospitals and workhouses, establishing saving groups, teaching in Sunday Schools, holding educational classes for the

The Union Jack flutters over the charity bazaar held on the lawns of the Edwardian Country House.

betterment of the poor, running sewing groups and childcare classes, and fund-raising by organizing dinners, balls – and bazaars.

Wealthy women's interest in charitable works was not always entirely altruistic: the 'servant problem' in the nineteenth century had been partly seen as one of the 'degeneracy' and unreliability of many of the young women in service. By involving themselves in charitable institutions for the Christian teaching, training, education and useful employment of the poor, the rich benefactors would ensure a flow of more satisfactory recruits to domestic service, which would not only be to the direct advantage of the servant-employing class (though less to the wealthy householder than to that large number of middle and lower middle-class establishments with one or two servants) but 'to the benefit of the whole social system'. By the beginning of the twentieth century there were no fewer than 1,000 charities, some 600 of them associated with girls, connected with the Reformatory and Refuge Union, a clearing house for the smaller charities, and most of these were run by women.[8]

There had been a fine Scottish rain for days before the day of the Edwardian Country House Bazaar but by mid morning the clouds had cleared, a watery sun broke through and as the day progressed its rays grew stronger. The lawns leading to the lake were filled with marquees and stalls under striped awnings with bunting strung between them. At noon the band struck up and the Olliff-Cooper family came out of the house, walking regally to stand on the balustrade above the crowds milling on the lawn below. 'I think we all felt it was a bit like royalty coming out on to the balcony at Buckingham Palace!' confided Miss Anson in the journal she was keeping of her experiences.

The vicar of Duns gave a short blessing, reading Psalm 100: 'O be joyful in the Lord all ye lands: serve the Lord with gladness, and come before his presence with a song'; and then Lady Olliff-Cooper, her voice amplified through a brass megaphone, welcomed the visitors to the house, explained that the proceeds would be going to the local hospital and to the Royal Gardeners' Benevolent Society, and urged everyone to dig deep into their pockets in a good cause. The brass band struck up with Elgar's 'Pomp and Circumstance', the first two marches of which had first been performed in Liverpool over a hundred years earlier on 19 October 1901. Elgar had not intended his marches to have words set to them but, at the suggestion of the King, Edward VII, the words of 'Land of Hope and Glory' were later added to the music of the first, part of the libretto for the 'Coronation Ode' Elgar wrote for Edward's coronation on 9 August 1902 (the first such royal occasion for sixty years). The confident words of 'Land of Hope and Glory' rang out, led by the Edwardian Country House family:

…Mother of the Free
How shall we extol thee
Who are born of thee?
Wider still and wider
Shall thy bounds be set
God, who made thee mighty
Make thee mightier yet…

And below them the visitors and servants joined in the jingoistic hymn of Empire.

'It was such a wonderful occasion,' enthused Becky. 'There was just the band playing, no blaring music all the time, and no neon lights, and all the stalls were selling home-made things, and the competitions were old-fashioned and simple and it was such fun.' All the servants were involved: Jess and Becky were in the tea tent dressed as gypsies reading tea leaves while a bemused Erika and Ellen, who had only arrived at Manderston the night before, served cream teas. Mr Edgar, correct as always in spotless white gloves, manned the tea urn while the local Duns Brownies pitched in to help clear the tables. Rob and Charlie were running the beer tent and this included selling bottles of their home-made 'Footman's Brew', lemonade and 'pop' (ginger ale), while Antonia had a sweet stall, selling home-made peppermint creams, coconut ice, toffee, fudge, humbugs, barley sugar, honeycombs, aniseed balls and other Edwardian delights for the sweet of tooth. Mrs Davies had made a fruitcake for the 'guess the weight of the cake' stall and had organized a competition to 'guess what's in the bottle' by sniffing its contents, as well as inviting fête-goers to 'guess the name of the doll': Elizabeth. Kenny was in charge of the coconut shy and Tristan was on hand to help out where he was needed, including fishing for cardboard fish with a rod and hook, and helping with the hooded falcons, kestrels and owls that had been brought by their keeper so that visitors could have their photographs taken with these birds of prey.

'We are delighted to welcome you all to Manderston…' Lady Olliff-Cooper declares the fête open.

Sir John and Mr Edgar confer in the sunshine.

In the centre of the lawns, M. Dubiard, wearing his chef's apparel, was expertly shucking oysters, though there weren't many takers. Mr Edgar in the tea tent wondered just how many cups of tea could be drunk in a single afternoon. Miss Morrison, dressed in sage green – 'one of milady's hand-me-downs, it makes me look less like a servant' – could not be off duty either while the breeze threatened to lift off Lady Olliff-Cooper's large feather-trimmed hat, which her maid had to keep tying on with a chiffon scarf.

Mr Jonathan was running one of the most popular events of the bazaar, 'tip the man off the log', whereby two contestants sitting astride a log tried to knock each other off using bolsters. There was always a queue for this feather-bedded form of wrestling, and quite a few old scores were paid off in ritualized form that afternoon. One of those who joined the contestants several times was Jonty's younger brother Guy, who, dressed in an Eton jacket and pint-sized pinstripe trousers, took part in pretty well every activity going, including watching the Punch and Judy show and entering 'racing the blind horse' which was Tristan's responsibility.

In the largest marquee, Lady Olliff-Copper was talking to the local exhibitors who had entered the various competitions for needlework: there were three categories, quilt, tapestry and 'other'. The entries had already been logged and sorted out by Miss Anson, acting as her sister's secretary. 'To my untutored eye they all looked very good, as though the patchwork and samplers and cross stitch and all the other things had taken several winters of long dark evenings in front of the fire to make.' She had spoken to all the entrants as they delivered their handicrafts so she could put some useful information on the card: something along the lines of 'Mrs…has been a staunch supporter of the Scottish Rural Arts Institute for forty-four years…' that would give her sister something to say to each person as she did her rounds. In categorizing the entries, Miss Anson had been helped by the expert eye of her sister's maid, Miss Morrison, and now the entries were being judged by the lady of the house, herself a skilled lace-maker. 'I took judging the needlework competition very seriously, because it was obvious that people had put a huge amount of effort into the workmanship, which was of a very high standard.' After much deliberation Lady Olliff-Cooper chose what she considered to be the best work, handed out certificates to the winners in each category, and watched the demonstrations of lace-making, elaborate 'Fabergé-style' egg-decoration, millinery and calligraphy that were going on in the tent.

There really was no end to the ingenuity of the Edwardians when it came to organizing competitive fund-raising events. *The Lady's Companion* in January 1911 recommended that 'few things succeed better at Bazaars than simple and amusing competitions, the small outlay necessary for materials being a great recommendation. An entrance fee of 2d should be charged for each competition, outside spectators paying 1d to "view the fun".' It went to suggest such gender stereotypical activities as 'Nail driving competition – Ladies only; Sewing on buttons – Gentlemen only; Sharpening lead pencils – Ladies only; Apple paring – Gentlemen only. Prizes awarded for the largest number of apples correctly peeled, cored and sliced; Millinery competition – Gentlemen to trim hats with crinkled paper and pins. Creations to be judged by a committee of Ladies' – and a range of other 'fun' pursuits that must have had bazaar-goers queuing up two deep on a sunny afternoon to participate in 'Pin sticking – pins to be stuck into a sheet of paper in neat and regular rows – 100 in 5 minutes; Covering books with brown paper – neatest and most workmanlike result takes prize; Match-tying – tying so many matches within a given time on a piece of string; and Candle-lighting – twenty-four candles are fixed in a row, and the successful competitor lights all with a single match'.[9]

Mr Jonathan ensures fair play in the 'tip the man off the log' contest.

Home-made sweets

Antonia, the kitchen maid, made honeycomb toffee to sell at the
Manderston Bazaar, while the housemaids, Becky and Jess,
made peppermint creams. 'They were quick and easy to make,'
said Antonia, 'and we had great fun doing so.'
The fête goers enjoyed the results, and soon all the sweets
had been sold in aid of charity.

Peppermint creams

2 medium egg whites
About 12oz (375g) icing sugar
Peppermint essence
Green food colouring
Plain chocolate for decoration (optional)

Whisk the egg whites until white but still soft. Sieve in the icing sugar, stirring thoroughly until enough has been absorbed to make a stiff paste. Add a few drops of peppermint essence and knead into a ball. Divide the mixture in half; make a hole in the centre of one half, add a few drops of green colouring and knead until it is evenly distributed.

Roll out each ball of paste, and cut shapes using pastry cutters; or mould flattened rounds about the size of a 50p piece.

Place the sweets on a baking sheet dusted with icing sugar and leave in a cool place to set. When the sweets are hard, they are ready to decorate (if wanted).

Melt some plain chocolate in a bowl over a saucepan containing simmering water. Dip the sweets into the chocolate until they are half covered and leave to set. Alternatively, pipe the chocolate on to the sweets in a pattern (M. Dubiard wrote M for Manderston).

(NOTE: in Edwardian times, the maids would have used imperial measures; metric equivalents are given here – for best results, one system only should be used consistently.)

Honeycomb toffee

Makes approximately 1lb 4oz (550g)

1lb (450g) granulated sugar
Pinch of cream of tartar
2 rounded tablespoons honey
$\frac{1}{4}$ pint (150ml) water
1 level teaspoon bicarbonate of soda

In a large, heavy-based saucepan, dissolve the sugar, cream of tartar and honey in the water over a moderate heat, stirring gently. Bring to the boil and boil gently until (if using a thermometer) the mixture reaches 310°F/155°C. Alternatively, place a blob of the mixture on a saucer and, if it sets, it is ready. If not, continue to boil for a few minutes and test again.

When ready, remove the saucepan from the heat, blend the bicarbonate of soda with two teaspoons of water and add to the mixture – be careful as it will bubble up like boiling milk.

Stir the mixture gently and then pour into a buttered tin, about 40cm x 10cm (15in x 4in), and mark the toffee into squares when nearly set.

Community effort: local people enter into the Edwardian spirit (left)
and Mrs Davies's husband dresses the part (right).

The invitation to visit the Edwardian Country House had been enthusiastically received locally and many of the visitors who flocked to the bazaar were playing the part to the full. Some had journeyed to Newcastle, Edinburgh, or even London to hire Edwardian costumes, while others had rummaged in their attics or got out the sewing machine. The results were impressive: there was a gentle rustle of taffeta on the breeze, smart, laced ankle boots tapped along the paths, large plumed hats obscured women's faces, lace *fichus* tickled their necks and their velvet skirts and cotton petticoats brushed the grass, parasols were twirled and shooting sticks punctured the lawns, hunter watches stretched across ample waistcoated male chests, and children in knickerbockers dodged among the crowds. It was hard to decide who qualified for the title 'best dressed Edwardian' but eventually the prize for the man was awarded to Mrs Davies's husband, Peter, who had at one time thought that he would have rather liked to have taken the role of butler in the house.

The bazaar was an opportunity to sample a range of Edwardian delights: Betty Snow, who lives in Bonkyl Cottage a few miles from Manderston, had a stall selling nothing but home-made jams, pickles and other epicurean delights. She had gooseberry and elderflower jelly, rowan jelly, rose petal jelly, spiced crab apple jelly, rhubarb and ginger jam, tayberry jam – a cross-breed fruit of raspberries and blackberries that had first become popular in the Borders around 1905, she thought. There were jars of lemon and orange curd, rhubarb chutney, brandied raspberries with wild strawberries, bottles of raspberry and blackcurrant vinegar – 'very good for a cold with honey and hot water' – and mixed herb and garlic oil. There was a home-made cake stall with sponges, fruitcakes, scones and dainty butterfly fairy cakes. John Murphy from Heatherslaw Corn Mill, the most northerly mill in England, just over the border, had a stall with a millstone that was used to grind his wheat, all the varieties of which were grown locally. Brenda Leddy was selling clotted cream and butter made from milk from her Jersey cows in Kelso, and Chainbridge honey farm had a stall selling honey and beeswax. There was a produce stall groaning with giant marrows, turnips and cabbages belonging to Jock Bolton from a nearby farm who also supplied the house with vegetables, a plant stall and a stall explaining the work of the Gardeners' Royal Benevolent Society, one of the charities that would benefit from the bazaar. This stall was manned by one of the society's local patrons, Lieutenant Colonel Simon Furness, from a nearby country house of the same period as Manderston, Netherbyres at Eyemouth. He had generously donated the house to the society in 1991, and moved to a smaller property in the grounds.

A particular draw was an apothecary stall of Rose & Co from Haworth in Yorkshire, which displayed a range of typical Edwardian products from the workaday, such as dolly pegs, carbolic soap and bags of Reckitt's blue, which were especially covetable to the female servants with their work-roughened hands, their faces denied creams, their bodies innocent of fragrant lotions and powders. There were tempting lavender lotions, rose water skin freshener, geranium and orange oil for the bath, herbal foot balms and mustard baths, beeswax for lips and rose and glycerine salve for hands and nails, eau de cologne, *papier poudré* 'for busy people', powder puffs and dry shampoos. Miss Morrison resolved to hunt out some recipes and try to concoct something similar from ingredients she had to hand.

And from those days before antibiotics there were medications on the apothecary's stall too: vapour rubs for colds and catarrh, rubbing ointments containing wintergreen and valerian for aches and pains, 'Zam-Buk' ointment to soothe cuts and grazes, sprains and chilblains, sasparillo pastilles for a sore throat. Gazing

Mrs Davies's recipes

The housekeeper, Mrs Davies, made this rich fruitcake for the 'guess the weight of the cake' competition at the Manderston Bazaar.

Fruitcake

8oz (225g) butter
8oz (225 g) caster sugar,
   or soft brown sugar
4 eggs
8oz (225 g) plain flour
4oz (100g) sultanas
4oz (100g) raisins
4oz (100g) currants
2oz (50g) candied peel
2oz (50g) glacé cherries
4oz (100g) chopped almonds

Cream the butter and sugar together. Add the eggs one at a time, and beat well. Add the sieved flour and all the dry ingredients together and mix well. The mixture should fall slowly off a wooden spoon. If it is too stiff, add a little cold milk.

Put the mixture in a deep cake tin that has been buttered and lined with grease-proof paper, and bake in a slow oven (325°F/180°C/gas mark 4) for one to one and a half hours. Leave the cake in the tin until it is cool, and then store in an airtight tin.

(NOTE: in Edwardian times, imperial measures would have used; metric equivalents are given here – for best results, one system only should be used consistently.)

at the display, Mrs Davies wondered if there was anything she should add to the meagre medicine cabinet that she, as housekeeper, kept in her parlour. At present it consisted of bandages, cotton wool, some castor oil, witch hazel, Sloane's Liniment, oil of peppermint, glycerine, Fuller's Earth ointment, a proprietary brand of 'pick-me-up' and some smelling salts that contained ammonia and were, she thought, 'absolutely foul-smelling, but no doubt effective in reviving anyone who felt faint'.

The housekeeper had discussed the matter with Dr McCrae, who is a Fellow of the Royal College of Physicians in Edinburgh, and has an expert knowledge of Edwardian medicine. It was he who had recommended potassium bromide as a sleeping draught for the scullery maid when the 'ghost scare' was at its height, though he had added wryly that 'as anyone who has been a soldier can tell you, a nip of that in your tea is supposed to suppress sexual appetites too'. It might have its uses, Mrs Davies thought, given a group of highly charged young people closeted together for three months. She had already tried out some traditional remedies. 'If you use witch hazel on a bruise it does seem to work,' the housekeeper conceded, 'and certainly rubbing Sloane's Liniment on strained muscles seems to bring relief and I am satisfied with Fuller's Earth ointment or Zam-Buk for minor cuts and grazes and burns. But the oil of peppermint mixed with hot water which was supposed to ease the maid's period pains didn't help at all.'

Jams and jellies for sale on Betty Snow's stall.

She had also heard that poultices were very popular in Edwardian times. These could be made from bran, bread or mustard, mixed with boiling water and spread on a flannel which was then applied to the afflicted part – a sore throat or bruised arm. Mrs Davies hadn't found them particularly effective, but the warmth was comforting. Another popular Edwardian 'cure', for a bad cold or a chesty cough, was to rub goose grease into the neck or chest, and, coming from a farming family herself, Mrs Davies recalled that that this practice had persisted into her own childhood. She could remember her mother rendering the fat from the Christmas goose and keeping it in a screw-top jar. She would rub it into the children's chests and keep it from smearing off by wrapping the patient in a red flannel bandage. Mrs Davies wasn't convinced about the efficacy of this remedy either, but again the warmth had been comforting. In her view, the only thing that really worked was Aspirin, which had been invented by a German pharmaceutical company and first went on sale in British chemists' in October 1905, so that was permissible. Dr McCrae agreed, but pointed out that the fact that the old remedies gave comfort was not insignificant, since then the patient was likely to feel better, so in that sense they did work – up to a point. Indeed, from the medical point of view, those in domestic service were usually better off than most other low-paid workers who would not be able to find the money to pay the doctor, whereas the physician who attended their employers would often be asked to take a look at a sickly servant.

As the Olliff-Coopers paraded graciously around their sunlit lawns, followed a few paces behind by Miss Anson, they picked up a trinket at one stall, some flowers at another, watched Master Guy try to win a coconut, bought a quarter of a pound of peppermint creams with a chocolate M iced on from Antonia, stopped to exchange pleasantries with their neighbours, commended the Brownies on their hard work and enjoyed the sight of the local Cub troop watching the Punch and Judy show. Finally, sitting in one of the blue and white striped deckchairs listening to the brass band play such confident airs as 'Men of Harlech' and 'Rule Britannia', Lady Olliff-Cooper reflected on what a pleasant occasion it was. How delightful it was to be able to share the family's good fortune with their staff and the local community for an afternoon. She was pleased to think that some of the money raised would be going to the local Knoll hospital that she and Miss Morrison had visited recently. It had been an amazing occasion, she recalled. As a modern day doctor she had had no qualms about the visit, but she had been startled by her reception. As she moved among the beds exchanging words with some of the patients their faces lit up visibly. 'It was a bit like being Princess Diana. The visit obviously meant so much to them, just seeing me, the mistress of the "big house" in a lovely frock, shaking their hand, seemed to have lifted their spirits. That was rather nice.' The authenticity of Lady Olliff-Cooper's experience was confirmed by a visitor to the bazaar who had nursed locally for sixty-five years, including Sir James Miller's widow in her old age. 'When Lady Miller came round the hospital,

Jess guides her blindfolded 'horse' (Master Guy) round an obstacle race.
The team that completed the course in the shortest time was declared the winner.

which she did regularly, she would make sure to wear a different hat each time. It was a tonic for the patients to see her. In my view it did them more good than any medicine.'

In the Edwardian period, cottage hospitals were the most usual form of care for the sick in rural areas. These were generally small, and care in them had to be paid for, though charges were generally modest and constituted about one-tenth of the hospital's income, the rest of which came from wealthy landowners and from local fund-raising events – like the Edwardian Country House bazaar. The elderly poor were more likely to be treated in workhouse infirmaries. Until the 1908 Poor Law, the workhouse was the only option for an old person without family or financial support, and probably at this time some 5 per cent of the population over sixty-five would be living in the workhouse – and a high proportion of that total would be those who had been in service and had no family to turn to in their old age, nor legal entitlement to a pension. The 1908 Old Age Pension Act was drafted 'to lift the shadow of the workhouse from the homes of the poor' in Lloyd George's words – though persons did not qualify unless they lived on less than 12 shillings a week (the equivalent today of about £35) and, prior to 1925, until they reached seventy years of age. The workhouse was greatly feared: it was a monotonous, prison-like regimented life, with poor food and the loss of dignity and freedom – including the right to vote.

On the day of the Edwardian Country House bazaar, the Olliff-Coopers were just about half-way through their time there. As she sat listening to the band, the sun warming her back, Lady Olliff-

A page from the Manderston album showing a bazaar at Thurston, the nearby house of
Sir James Miller's sister, in 1911. The house was the work of Manderston's architect, John Kinross.

Cooper took stock. 'It feels like a watershed. It has taken us these first six weeks to sort ourselves out, and now it's time to reflect on what we've achieved, what's gone right and what's been wrong.

'I love the house. It's just so beautiful. I still feel it's all totally magical, as if Cinderella is going to the ball,' she reflected. 'I feel that I am almost living a teenage life with all the fun and frippery, the obsession with clothes and with your appearance. But the thing that has really surprised me is how regimented my life is. The whole day seems to be taken up with getting dressed into whatever is appropriate for whatever meal it is next, then eating the meal, then getting changed again for the next meal. We have sometimes three courses for breakfast and then another three courses for lunch and maybe five or six courses for dinner. So that's a lot of time at table. It's getting better because Morrison and I are getting more adroit at getting me dressed, but I don't have nearly as time as I imagined I would to read, and write letters and write my journal and just wander round the grounds. I calculate that about five hours of my day every day is taken up preparing myself for meals and then eating them. I find it hard to relax because of this rigid timetable and the length of meals and all the formal dressing, and it doesn't help that my corset is so tight that I can never sit in comfort. I have to perch on the side of the chairs. I know that I seem to be fussing about meals and dresses, and you could well ask, "Hasn't she got anything better to do than complain? She's hardly got a life of drudgery like the servants below stairs" – and that's certainly true. When I came here I was desperate to get away from my daily life of endless hard work and chores, but of course my life of luxury here is at the expense of other people working very hard. I know that the kitchen staff are getting up at 6 a.m. and are not in bed until 11 at night. It worries me that we will come over as very callous to the people who are serving us, which is not a very nice thought.

'I have never in my entire life had such freedom from chores, yet so many restrictions in other ways. If I'm out riding, for example, and so lunch is delayed, then the schedules of everyone below stairs is thrown completely out of kilter. So you can't have any spontaneity like that at all. Having the servants around all the time is a real block on conversation. I am finding that difficult. I imagine that if you lived like it for long you would end up having practically no contact with anyone unless you made a real effort to drag them off to another room to talk privately. It could be a real emotional desert.

'It's hard for Guy, who is only ten. It's such a formal existence. We are always saying sit still, sit up straight, put that down, don't touch – and he's an ebullient child and he needs to run around and shout, and though he has the rough and tumble of school, it's not easy for him here sometimes.

'I also think that we are *very* conscious of the need to observe all the Edwardian social niceties. As *parvenus* we would have been much more conscious about etiquette than those at the very top of the social ladder who could behave as they liked because they were a duke or something and could simply say, "I'm going to do it my way" and people would accept him because of who he was. But we have to take a lot of trouble over how to behave and how to address people, who takes precedence over whom, and whether you eat jelly with a fork or a spoon, and all that sort of thing.

'But it is a seductive business and both John and I are going to find it very difficult to go back to normality. We have just had a couple of friends of Jonty's to stay and it reminded me how completely effortless entertaining can be in these circumstances. I don't have to change the sheets here or put them in the washing machine or anything. And when it comes to meals, I just tell M. Dubiard that there will be six extra for dinner and that's it. Whereas at home I rarely entertain because it's so tedious trailing round the supermarket and carting all the shopping home in the car and unpacking it and deciding what to cook, and then cooking it and washing up and balancing all that with a career and

Beauty treats

Though make-up was frowned upon as 'fast' in the Edwardian era, Lady Diana Manners (later Cooper) recalls the most her mother, a famed beauty, would use was 'a very little powder (Fuller's Earth) and a speck of Roger & Gallet's pink lip-salve', society women spent many hours at their toilet pampering themselves with creams, lotions and fragrances.

Floral bath soaks

For the Edwardian Country House maids, having a luxurious, scented bath was just a memory – and a dream – so they were delighted when Caroline of Rose Apothecary came to show them how to make decorative sachets filled with floral bath salts. All the ingredients were readily to hand: Becky, Jess, Antonia, Erika and Ellen could have taken some salt from the kitchen, asked Mrs Davies for some dolly blue from her store cupboard, and begged some lavender oil from Miss Morrison. As for the flowers, those could have been picked from the gardens when no one was looking…

1kg (2lb 4oz) coarse salt
2 tablespoons lavender flowers
20 drops oil of lavender
Tiny pinch of dolly blue powder (optional)
Small dried rosebuds

Combine all the ingredients (except the rosebuds) and stir well until the colour is evenly distributed. Divide into muslin squares, sprinkle a few rosebuds in each and tie with raffia or silver thread. These can then be dropped into the bath to scent it.

Alternatively, the bath salts can be poured into a glass jar and sealed with a glass stopper, or a screw-top covered in a pretty cotton fabric tied on with raffia or narrow ribbon.

Glycerine and rose water

This is a traditional lotion used until relatively recently to moisturise the skin on the face and body. It would generally have been made up by the chemist, but can easily be made at home.

Combine 1 part glycerine with 1 part rose water. Pour into a glass bottle, seal and shake well.

Classic cologne

300ml (12 fl oz) alcohol
1 teaspoon lemon oil
1 teaspoon rosemary oil
6 drops rose oil

Combine the alcohol, lemon oil, rosemary oil and rose oil and store in a dark place for one week. Use liberally after bathing.

motherhood. It's far too tiring. When we have dinner parties here I don't even iron my own dress, or do my own hair. It is all done for me. I am completely pampered. All I have to do is to go down and act the part. I can see how a woman of those times, if she was married to a wealthy man, could have a life of total idleness and selfishness. But I *am* conscious that I am at the top of the tree here, and that for other people it may be a much less enjoyable experience.

'I think that having a title helps too. It increases your confidence because people approach you with the attitude that they are privileged to meet you. It makes me feel more confident and more gracious. I no longer attempt to open doors myself, I just stand there until someone opens them for me. I am no longer embarrassed by my "title". In fact after a little while I began to find myself feeling mildly irritated if people didn't address me as m'lady. And Sir John has taken to his title like a duck to water. In fact I think that it has brought out the best in him. John is easily capable of running a large country house like this. He is a man of enormous abilities who would be quite capable of running Blenheim Palace. He would make a very good benevolent landlord, an aristocrat really, he would take a genuine interest in his tenants. He is not the sort of person who is happy being a member of a team. He likes to be captain of the ship, making all the decisions himself. He is a natural autocrat – though he would say he's not, everyone else around him would say that he is. I think he has seen here a lifestyle which would have suited him very well if he had been born a hundred years ago. He would have fitted in perfectly. I am sure that he would have become a much-loved squire.

An Edwardian Punch and Judy show enchants the children at the Manderston bazaar.

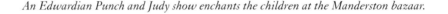

'I find it easier to be married in this environment. By and large as a wife you don't have overlapping interests with your husband, you're not in competition with him. We have our separate spheres. It's not like the twenty-first century where the roles are more mixed up and men have to adopt semi-female roles, taking out the rubbish and stuff like that. But here we're not stepping on each other's territory at all, which is very nice. One of the nicest things about this experience is seeing John really happy in his role.' But at that very moment, hairline cracks were beginning to threaten the tranquillity of Lady Olliff-Cooper's Edwardian world. In the far corner of the lawn was a striped tent in which sat a fortune-teller shuffling her tarot cards. In front of her sat Miss Avril Anson, Lady Olliff-Cooper's unmarried sister who lived with the family in the Edwardian Country House. 'You are frustrated,' pronounced the fortune-teller. 'You feel constrained and it simply went on from there…it was all completely relevant to my current situation', Miss Anson confided to her journal. 'She told me that my life was currently stretched like a piece of fabric held

The young master tucks in. Guy Olliff-Cooper at the fête.

together by pins. I had very limited options while this remained the case. It would not last long, but I should use the time *now* to consider what I wanted when my life moves into the next phase. She said that my body is stressed and that I must take care of it (good food, plenty of sleep, etc.) or else I would be quite ill. She warned me of a dark-haired woman who does not have my best interests at heart. Her description of my life at present was spot on, and I am going to monitor how accurate her predictions were.'

In the twenty-first century Dr Avril Anson, a scientist, works as a marketing consultant. She is single, in a long-term relationship, has her own home and an independent lifestyle, though she sees her sister Anna and her family, who live nearby, frequently. But in the Edwardian Country House, Miss Anson's position was less that of an independent sibling equal, and more of a financially dependent unmarried woman. And she found this inhibiting and stressful. 'I realize that Anna and John view me in the role of a poor relation dependent on John's generosity. The etiquette book I was given when I arrived explained that I am a dependent relation:

> As the unmarried sister of the mistress of the house, your status within the household is dependent solely on the good grace and generosity of the master. You should endeavour at all times to be a good companion to your sister, the mistress, and not present any kind of burden to her husband. No task should be too great for you to take on to ensure that the household runs as smoothly as possible and expresses your gratitude to them for providing you with this comfortable life. You should scrupulously examine every aspect of your conduct to make sure that you uphold the family name and position and do nothing to bring it into disrepute.

I don't find this acceptable at all. It makes my position here very difficult.'

Paper lanterns

*Paper lanterns with candles were hung from trees to
illuminate Edwardian parties and dances. These
were made of tissue paper or rice paper stretched
over a narrow wire or cane frame, and hung by a
silk cord or thread; as the breeze wafted, the lights
flickered in the night.*

The artist John Singer Sargent painted two girls hanging Japanese lanterns in his popular painting 'Carnation, Lily, Lily, Rose', which he completed in 1886. He recalled the inspiration for his work in a letter to a friend:

I am trying to paint a charming thing I saw the other evening [as he was boating at Pangbourne in Berkshire]. Two little girls in a garden at twilight lighting paper lanterns among the flowers from rose tree to rose tree'.[10]

When the Duchess of Devonshire held her legendary fancy dress ball in 1897, it was a warm, clear July evening as many of the guests strolled in...

'The garden had been as elaborately decorated as the house. In the centre of the lawn was an eight-point star flanked with tiny stars at each corner...the oak and elm trees were outlined with Japanese lanterns, while the avenues to the east and west were festooned with Venetian lamps of blue and green, and the flower beds and gravel paths were picked out in red, white and blue fairy lights. In all, twelve thousand lamps shone in the garden, and with coloured fires that burned at intervals, it was a scene of brilliant illumination.'[11]

Today, such paper lanterns can be bought cheaply in Chinese supermarkets or shops specializing in oriental crafts. Tea lights (night lights) should always be used rather than candles, and the lanterns should never be left unattended when alight.

Plain paper lanterns or globes can be decorated to fit in with a colour scheme or a themed party. A design can be painted or stencilled directly on to the paper; alternatively, a 'pocket' of thin tissue paper (cut with pinking shears to give a decorative edge) can be stuck on, and a picture or photograph (perhaps of the host or hostess) slipped inside it. The bottom edge of the lantern can be decorated with tassels, or beads strung on to strong thread or medium-thickness fuse wire.

These can then be hung from trees or tall fence posts, or knotted on to lengths of string and looped between trees or bamboo sticks pushed into the ground. Or they can be tied on to the spokes of a rotary garden clothes drier, or to those of a bicycle wheel firmly secured horizontally to the top of a square wooden post.

Miss Anson

Avril Anson is Anna Olliff-Cooper's younger sister. She has a PhD in microbiology, and was a lecturer at the University of Exeter before moving into marketing. At fifty, she is now a freelance marketing consultant. She is an intrepid overseas traveller, but she was attracted by the idea of some time travel when Anna rang her up to say that she was thinking of applying to take part of the Edwardian Country House project and would she, Avril, be interested? Before she'd even put the phone down, Avril's head was full of images of 'ladies in long dresses playing croquet against the backdrop of a stately house... Everywhere was sunshine, tranquillity and peace. Of *course* I was interested.'

After a few days in the house Avril wrote a letter to her mother in fine Edwardian style: 'I'm being as agreeable as I may to my sister and to her husband, as is proper for a guest who expects to stay for three months in her brother-in-law's home.' But it was by no means easy. She felt that she was trying to reconcile two irreconcilables: her status as an independent, educated, professional twenty-first-century woman, and that of a dependent Edwardian lady of reduced rank and circumstances within the family. She found it particularly hard that despite her education and managerial experience in the 'real world', her role in the Edwardian Country House was to be submissive, obliged to hold back from offering opinions and seek permission from Sir John, as head of the household, for many of her activities. She resolved, 'I want to find out as much as possible about the women's movement at the beginning of the century, and how they managed to change attitudes in society and move forward to take control of their lives.'

It was a battle fought with twenty-first-century sensibilities. Marriage remained the standard experience of women of all classes until the 1960s and this was particularly the case until the First World War. In 1901 nearly 85 per cent of women over forty-five either were married or were widows; in 1911 the figure was 83.2 per cent, and this continued to be the number into the 1960s.[12] The imbalance in the sex ratio, which increased gradually between 1871 and 1911, and dramatically as a result of the First World War, meant that there was a growing number of women who never married.[13] But marriage was regarded as a woman's 'natural destiny', and those who did not achieve it were regarded as 'failures', compared by the novelist George Gissing to 'an odd glove', useless without a partner, 'redundant' to the business of life, which was marriage and motherhood. Unmarried women faced an often lonely and certainly marginalized future, living with their parents or in the household of a male relative, or relative-in-law.

From 1880 elementary education was compulsory for both boys and girls up to the age of thirteen, and while the majority of upper-class girls were educated at home by a governess, increasing numbers of middle-class girls were either attending day schools, or being sent away to boarding school. Girls' grammar schools were established; the Girls' Public Day School Trust was founded in 1906 and by then the number of girls in secondary education had grown, but it was still much smaller than that of boys. It was not exceptional for school to finish at lunch time for girls so that they could spend the afternoon with their mothers at home learning 'domestic arts'.[14] As the journalist Mary Stocks recalls, even after an excellent academic education such as she had received, 'it was counted as no disgrace for a girl to pursue no profession, do no systematic work, and "come out" as a young adult female available for invitations to dances or proposals of marriage'.[15] If she did not receive, or declined to accept, such proposals, her life could be very restricted. Opportunities in higher education were limited: it has been estimated that about 15 per cent of all university students in 1900 were women, but they could not study in the same environment nor for the same qualifications as men. After the First World War, notwithstanding the carnage of actual or potential husbands on the battlefields of France and Flanders, the 'problem' of what to do with unmarried women was eased by the increasing number of opportunities for higher education, training and employment open to women. But before 1914 'excess' women were regarded as a social problem, particularly as the highest number of those 'surplus to requirements' were middle class, and it was estimated that in 1900 about a third of the daughters of peers remained single.

'We are equals and we have a close relationship,' said Anna Oliff-Cooper (left) of her sister, Avril Anson. But the Edwardian Country House experience put it under strain.

Mrs Humphry (the guru 'Madge' of the magazine *Truth*) was characteristically brisk about the matter:

In Roman Catholic countries the matter is simplified by the number of girls who enter convents…here in England we neither have, nor wish for, any such method for reducing the disparity of numbers. Nor does emigration appeal very strongly to the girls of middle-class families. A visit to friends in India has furnished many with the chance of 'settling' that seemed far enough away at home. But the old idea that a woman who remains unmarried is a social failure has long been obsolete. Some of the most popular members of London Society are to be found among its spinsters…[16]

However, a bitter anonymous tirade, *The Spinster By One*, published in the magazine *The Freewoman* in November 1911, told a rather different story:

[The spinster is] our social Nemesis…The indictment which the Spinster lays up against Society is that of ingenious cruelty…she is mothered into the world by a being, who, whatever she may be, is not a spinster, and from this being she draws her instincts…Little by little, the development of her entire form sets towards a single consummation, and all the while, by every kind of device, the mind is set towards the same consummation. In babyhood, she begins with her dolls. Why do not parents of a spinster give her a gun or an engine? If Society is going to have spinsters, it should train spinsters…Among the very poor there is no spinster difficulty, because the very poor do not remain spinsters. It is from higher up the social scale, where social judgements count, where the individual is a little more highly wrought, better fashioned for suffering, that we draw the army of actual spinsters. It is from the class where it is not good form to have too much feeling, and actual bad form to show any; where there is a smattering of education, and little interest to fill in the time that their numbers rally and increase.[17]

'Marriage was not so much an alliance between the sexes as an important social definition,' points out the historian Leonore Davidoff; 'serious for a man, but imperative for a girl. It was part of her…duty to enlarge her sphere of influence through marriage.'[18] 'Married women simply had a higher status,' explained Lady Olliff-Cooper, and Edwardian etiquette bore her out. 'If there is a married woman present, she takes precedence over any unmarried women, regardless of age or social status.' 'If there was a bride of eighteen at some occasion, she would take precedence over my sister who is fifty,' endorsed Lady Olliff-Cooper. 'Even if she was an empty-headed flibbertigibbet, her views would still count for more.'

It was a situation that Avril found increasingly insupportable. 'I have dropped status here, whereas Anna and John have increased their status. In the modern world I have a PhD and I have a lot of management skills and problem-solving skills that I am not allowed to use. I am not allowed to venture any opinion or suggest anything without being asked, and my opinion is not usually called for. I just have to keep quiet a lot of the time, and I'm not used to that, and I have learned to agree wholeheartedly with John on all kinds of subjects on which we normally have very different views.

'I have been given a room that is too small and dark with a desk that I can't use because I can't get a chair under it, and the wardrobes are too small for my clothes. So they get creased and have to be ironed all over again. It seems to me that there were only two modes for wealthy Edwardian women: the decorative or the childlike. When your husband knew best, there was no point in being educated and you couldn't handle your own financial affairs. For some women this lifestyle must have seemed absolutely wonderful, very pampered and satisfying. You had everything you wanted, you looked beautiful, had fabulous clothes and jewellery. You were an ornament on your husband's arm, and if you were willing to bear his children and act as a hostess when he required it, you had a very fulfilled and luxurious lifestyle. For many women this would have been all they wanted. But for other women surely it was not enough. I feel myself crying out in outrage on behalf of women long dead. It must have been a stultifying life if you were not allowed to express an opinion or use your brain at all. I find it very difficult living in such a way, and I am trying to discover how women managed to break free from their gilded cage…'

As Miss Anson emerged from the fortune-teller's tent, blinking in the bright sunlight, three figures pushing bicycles came along the path from the village. Climbing the grass bank, one of the men unfurled a banner bearing the words 'Clarion Club' while the woman set up a makeshift soapbox, mounted it and started to address the assembled fête-goers.

'Comrades,' she called, 'just pause for a moment before you wander round this wonderful bazaar, pause to consider a question. What do you want? Do you earn enough money? Are your working hours too long? Are you really valued by your employer? You have a right to leisure…we are told that work is ennobling, but that does not seem to apply to our masters! For too long the rich and powerful have exploited the poor and weak…we have to fight…Socialism is the only answer…we are only powerless when we stand alone. Unity is strength. Fellowship is life,' she concluded. And her fellow cyclists struck up with a rousing rendition of 'The Red Flag': 'The people's flag is deepest red…' The anthem had been written by an Irish socialist on a twenty-minute journey from Charing Cross to Lewisham in 1899. It became Labour's battle hymn which until recently concluded every Labour Party conference, even if few delegates, or those on the platform, could remember the words any more. At the time, the Fabian playwright George Bernard Shaw thought that it was a song not to drive listeners to action but 'to crawl under the bedstead'. But that afternoon at the Edwardian Country House, the stirring words of the chorus wafted gently across the sunlit lawns:

> Then raise the scarlet standard high!
> Within its shade we'll live and die.
> Though cowards flinch and traitors sneer,
> We'll keep the red flag flying here.

A dialogue of the deaf?
Mr Edgar and the Clarion proselytisers.

Self-consciously, the lower servants joined in. 'We've had a visit from a trade union come to sow the seeds of disaffection among the servants,' sniffed Mr Edgar, pursing his lips as he continued to serve cream teas to the gentry and their hangers-on.

The Clarion Club had been started in 1894, inspired by the message preached by Robert Blatchford, a campaigning journalist. When Blatchford had worked in Manchester on the radical *Sunday Chronicle* he had been appalled at the conditions in which the industrial workers of that great northern city lived. Under the pseudonym 'Nunquam Dormio' (I never sleep), he had written a series of exposés of the slums, 'sixty thousand houses and not a single decent habitation',[19] and the penurious and unhealthy lives of their inhabitants. Following a row with the paper's proprietor, Edward Hulton, Blatchford – who had been won over to socialism after reading a pamphlet written by William Morris and the founder of the Social Democratic Federation, H. M. Hyndman – resigned, declaring, 'You will not have socialism in your paper. I will not write anything else.' With four other *Chronicle* journalists, he set up a weekly penny newspaper in December 1891 addressed to the working man and woman in prose that was humorous as well as proselytizing. By 1908, the paper, whose one aim was 'to make socialists' by explaining the issues 'in the simplest and best language at our command' (though it also included articles on music, theatre, books and sport as well as a woman's section and a 'children's corner'), had moved to Fleet Street and was selling upwards of 80,000 copies a week.

Among the sports that the *Clarion* covered was cycling. In the 1890s bicycles had opened up new vistas for workers. The 'safety' cycle, a great advance on the 'ordinary' (or penny-farthing) bike had

An expedition: straw-boatered Edwardian aficionados of the new craze of bicycling.

been developed in the 1880s. Improved production methods soon brought the price down so that it was within reach of working people. A second-hand bike could be purchased for around £2: if you were a clerk, or factory worker or shop assistant, that represented about two weeks' wages. Or you could buy a new machine for around £10 on an instalment plan. Cycling was a means of transport available to men and women, young and old; and cycling clubs, previously the exclusive preserve of the middle classes, sprang up all over Britain, but particularly in the north where factory workers seized the opportunity to get out of the smoke-grimed, squalid industrial cities into the countryside. 'It meant that a luxury hitherto almost the exclusive privilege of the rich was now within easy reach of all.'[20]

But it was not only the poor to whom cycling offered pleasure and freedom: Miss Anson was finding cycling, along with horse riding, something of a salvation in the Edwardian Country House. 'I absolutely love cycling. The bicycle opens a whole new world for women. I feel the need to escape from the house from time to time because it's such a

The freedom of the road: Master Guy bicycles down the drive at Manderston.

constrained and controlling environment. It's partly the clothes, partly the etiquette and partly my position in the house and the fact that I can't make any decisions for myself. Cycling gives me such a heady sense of release. I get out into the free air and I have to take a decision whether to turn left or right, to go fast or to go slow, and these may seem very small matters but here it feels like a wonderful sense of freedom of choice and of wider horizons! Riding a bike has given me the first opportunity that I have had to be spontaneous, to wear clothes that are comfortable and practical: you have to wear your skirts shorter, or hitch them up, or they'd get tangled up in the spokes of the wheels, and you just can't wear your corset in the same way and sit on the saddle of a bike. So that's the corset gone, and the wig has to go too as I wear a bowler when I'm cycling or riding, since it might afford me a little protection if I fell off, and of course comfortable, flattish shoes for the pedals. So all that's very satisfactory.'

A century on, Avril Anson had discovered for herself the delights of 'rational dress'. The Rational Dress Society had been started by Viscountess Harberton in the 1880s in order to promote clothes for women based on 'considerations of health, comfort and beauty' – in other words, less restrictive clothing that allowed women to participate in a greater range of activities, since most current styles made 'healthy exercise almost impossible'.[21] *Punch* was predictably scornful, mocking

…gowns hygienic, and frocks calisthenic,
And dresses quite worth of a modern burlesque;
With garments for walking, and tennis and talking,
All terribly manful and too trouseresque.[22]

Oscar Wilde and his wife Constance were great supporters of the movement: she gave a lecture, 'Clothed and in Our Right Minds', to the Somerville Society; it was reported in the *Rational Dress Society Gazette* which she went on to edit in 1888–9. This advocated a loose, divided skirt as the most practical wear for active women,[23] and some advanced women did adopt this radical attempt to equalize the apparel of men and women as a first step to greater equality in other matters. But the more usual new style, though it owed a considerable debt to the riding habits that women had been wearing since the eighteenth century, was a tailored suit to be worn during the day. It proved to be eminently suited to the lifestyle of the so-called 'New Woman' (another *Punch* coinage), who was independent and earned her own living and was determined to have an active physical and intellectual life. Her clothes would be light years away from those of her more traditional sister who was all corsets and trailing garments and fussy bits and pieces at throat and wrist, all of which could be seen to sum up a languid, indulged and rather inactive way of life. The 'New Woman's' suits were tailor made, usually in wool with a tight-fitting jacket and A-line skirt (very suitable for striding around), and under this suit she would wear a high-necked, crisp blouse and sometimes even a waistcoat, the lot topped off with a straw boater. It was ideal sporting wear too, for golfing (the Ladies' Golf Union was founded in 1893); for playing team games (the Original Ladies' Cricketer Club first played in 1890 and the first international hockey match was held in 1897); and for bicycling, which by the early years of the Edwardian era had given women just the freedom Miss Anson yearned for – and the ability to outpace a chaperone, which was another sort of freedom.

Riding habits: the Edwardian Country House ladies wearing skirts designed for side-saddle horsewomanship.

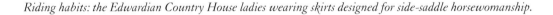

At the beginning of the twentieth century, cycling shared an affinity with socialism as well as women's liberation. Both appeared democratic and to offer freedom and a better, more equitable future, be it of the open road or of living and working conditions. One cold night in February 1904, a small meeting was held in Birmingham to discuss how best the 'pleasures of cycling [could be combined] with the propaganda of socialism'. Originally the club started by Tom Groom and five others was to be called the Socialist Cycling Club, but within a couple of months the name had been changed to the Clarion Cycling Club after the members' favourite newspaper.[24] Its activities were publicized in the *Clarion* and soon a number of other clubs had sprung up, and annual meetings were held. Robert Blatchford came along on some of the Clarion CC's regular rides at weekends, bank holidays and summer evenings. Picnics, concerts and political meetings were added to its activities, and eventually an insurance scheme, while Clarion choirs and bands were formed. Women had been admitted almost from the start, and by 1913 the 'cycling socialists', zealots with their saddlebags stuffed full of copies of the *Clarion* to distribute, numbered over 7,000 nationwide.

It was not only working people, however, who responded to the Clarion call. The Countess of Warwick recounts in her memoirs how in 'the cruelly hard winter of 1895' she had held a fancy dress ball at Warwick Castle.

> The ball was spoken of as 'the event of the season' and was a great success. The newspapers applauded with great enthusiasm, all except one obscure sheet, by name the *Clarion*. I read with indignation and amazement a violent attack on myself for holding idle junketing in a time of general misery. This 'impertinent rag' said scathingly that ours was a sham benevolence, a frivolous ignoring of real social conditions. I was so angry…I got up at once, told my maid that I was going to London by the earliest train, and, leaving my Castle without a word of explanation to anyone, I was in Fleet Street by midday searching for the editorial offices of the *Clarion*. I found this office…with the editor's name, Robert Blatchford, on the door. I entered unannounced, and there at his writing desk sat the man who had dared to attack us for indulging in legitimate amusement that had at the same time given honest work to so many unemployed…

> 'How could you be so unfair, so unjust?' I said. 'Our ball has given work to half the county, and to dozens of dressmakers in London besides.'

> 'Will you sit down?' he replied. 'While I explain to you how mistaken you are?…and then Robert Blatchford told me, as a Socialist and a Democrat, what he thought of charity bazaars and ladies bountiful. He made it plain to me the difference between productive and unproductive labour…By this new standard I found that nine-tenths of the money spent on the Warwick ball had been wasted…Of course I did not grasp all that was poured into my hungry soul, but before the end of the talk I did realize humbly that setting the poor, who themselves needed food and coal and decent housing, to build unnecessary rooms for an evening's entertainment, to cook dainties for people already overfed, and to make clothes for rich dancers was idle work. The great ball, and all its preparations, I found, had not added one iota to the nation's wealth.

> I was somewhat dazed when at last I left Fleet Street…and during the journey home I thought and thought about all that I had been hearing and learning. I knew that my outlook on life could never be the same as before this incident…I was as one who had found a new, real world…next day I sent for ten pounds' worth of books on socialism.[25]

The Edwardian Beerage: Kenny (left) and Tristan.

The Labour Representation Committee, an amalgam of trade unionists and socialists, was established in 1900 under the auspices of Keir Hardie, the leader of the ILP (Independent Labour Party) who had deplored that the *Clarion* was almost 'totally destroying...the fibre of the socialist movement...by a spirit of irresponsible levity'.[26] Its aim was to represent the working man in Parliament, but in the 1900 election, fought during the Boer War, only two Labour MPs were returned to Westminster. It was not until the secret electoral pact with the Liberal party that the renamed Labour Party managed to achieve thirty MPs in the 1906 election, and it was 1924 before the first Labour government came – briefly – to power, though by that time it was clear that Labour had eclipsed the Liberals as the alternative party to the Conservatives.

The 1884 Reform Act had extended the franchise to all male ratepayers and lodgers paying rent of £10 a year or more and this, coupled with further distribution of seats to the industrial north and Midlands, effectively gave the vote to skilled working-class men, though it still meant that an estimated 40 per cent of all adult males were not eligible to vote. Since domestic servants were neither ratepayers nor paying tenants they were not covered by the terms of the Act, though a 'servant's clause' gave employers the right to register their domestic servants. But research on this suggests that very few masters or mistresses availed themselves of the opportunity to get their servants on the electoral register. 'Gentleman's service,' complained a former footman bitterly, was suitable only 'for a man who is looking for a sure meal and a bed, and who is willing to forego his liberty as a citizen'.[27] Furthermore, while the membership of trade unions rose to around 4 million by 1914, domestic servants were almost entirely un-unionized, living as they did in their masters' houses, with little solidarity between upper and lower servants and with little 'exchange value' for their work. It had been calculated in 1873 that a housemaid's day extended from 6 a.m. until 10 p.m., and even allowing for meal and 'needlework breaks' she worked a twelve-hour day, which was two hours longer than a factory worker[28] – a fact that Becky, Jess, Antonia, Erika and Ellen could fervently testify to at the time of their Edwardian experiment some forty years later.

During the following decades, the hours of other women workers were statutorily reduced: in 1896 legislation was passed which limited women to working a maximum thirty days' overtime a year. In 1906 and 1913 Shop Acts specified the maximum number of hours shop workers could labour, and in 1909 the Trades Boards Act established wage boards to deal with the intractable problem of women working either in small workshops or as out workers in their own homes. These boards regulated rates of pay and hours worked, and in 1913 six more trades were added to the original four to be policed.[29] In 1908 the coal miner's working day was restricted to eight hours below ground while, since 1861, most industrial workers had been granted statutory days off. Yet, as Elizabeth Roberts, a historian of women's work, writes, the home remained a place about which lawmakers hesitated to legislate and in which it was very difficult to enforce legislation when passed; and throughout the period the state made no attempt at regulating the pay or working conditions of those in domestic service.[30] As she points out, it is ironic that it would have taken a Lancashire weaver about thirty minutes to make the material for a shirt, but its subsequent life required about twelve hours of washing, starching and ironing by domestic servants.[31]

There had been an attempt to found a servants' trade union as early as 1872, and the London and Provincial Servants' Union was founded in the 1890s, but neither had penetrated below stairs to any great extent.[32] It was not until 1918 that the government commissioned the first ever inquiry into the conditions of domestic servants. So in the Edwardian period, there was no organized movement to fight for improved working conditions, better pay or regular time off for those below stairs. All was dependent on the benevolence of the master.

The servants in the Edwardian Country House had no guaranteed time off; it was not unusual for their working days to last for eighteen hours when there was an 'event' or guests were staying. 'The only time off we get is when we collapse into bed at night,' sighed a weary Becky – though that looked set to improve now. Furthermore, Sir John had raised the ire of the lower servants by threatening that their relations would not be permitted to come to the bazaar as he had originally promised, when he found that some of them had broken rules by eating at a local restaurant that the family patronized. Though he subsequently retracted this harsh punishment, the servants had been incensed.

'I thought that it was really good that the Clarion people came,' said Kenny. 'Trade unions were needed to speak for people who couldn't speak up for themselves, to give them some courage to confront the people who were exploiting them. But I was a bit worried about reprisals after Sir John had so nearly not let our families come to visit, so though I shouted out a bit and joined in singing the Red Flag, that was all. I wish I'd done more.'

Antonia thought that if she had heard the speech 'as an Edwardian servant I just don't think I would have believed that it was possible to work just an eight-hour day because we work all the hours that God sends. The Clarion club literature does make sense, but I'm not sure that I would have taken any action, unless all the servants banded together, and that wouldn't have been very likely. Certainly not the upper servants, and I would have been afraid of repercussions, so I might have been a bit hesitant.'

When he should have been clearing up after the bazaar, Kenny sat in the servants' lavatory reading a Clarion pamphlet on Land Nationalization that the cyclists had left. In his book *Merrie England,* which had sold three-quarters of a million copies when it was published in 1894, Robert Blatchford pointed out that the working classes, which comprised seven-eighths of the population, received less than a third of the national income. This situation could be rectified, he argued, by nationalizing the land, industry and commerce. The Edwardian Country House in public ownership, not one man's fiefdom any more, but run by the people, for the people – now *that* really would be something, thought the hall boy.

Ale wife: Antonia takes a break at the fête.

CHAPTER EIGHT

Huntin', Shootin' and Fishin'

A. P. Herbert wrote the following lines in 1930.[1] But as Phyllida Barstow points out,[2] this would have seemed unacceptable levity about a serious matter in the Edwardian era when plutocrats were emulating aristocrats in aiming to bag as many birds as possible, and when a day out on the moors in the sleeting rain was considered what country house life was *for*.

It's really remarkably pleasant
To wander about in a wood
And kill an occasional pheasant
Provided the motive is good
And one of the jolliest features of killing superfluous game
Is the thought that you are saving the creatures
From a death of dishonour or shame.

Every bird has to die
By-and-by, by-and-by,
And they're lucky to die as they do,
For if they do not
They are probably shot
By someone who's not in Who's Who;
And I give you my word
Any sensitive bird –
A point for our foolish reproaches –
Prefers his career
To be stopped by a peer
And not by unmannerly poachers.

As in so many social matters, it was the King, Edward VII, who led the field. As Prince of Wales he had purchased the 8,000-acre Sandringham estate in Norfolk in 1862 with money accrued from the properties in the Duchy of Cornwall, to give him some independence from his controlling mother, Queen Victoria. The pleasure-loving monarch-to-be had straight away set up his new home as one of the finest hunting lodges in the country, building a railway station at Wolferton, which was two miles away, to bring his guests as near to his estate as possible and planting acres of trees and bushes to give cover to the birds he intended to shoot. Competition between landowners to bag the largest number of birds at a shoot grew intense in the years leading up to an entirely different sort of killing field in 1914. In 1913 Lord Burnham's guests in Buckinghamshire shot nearly 4,000 pheasants in a single day,[3] and Lord de Grey – admittedly a recognized expert shot – bagged 556,813 birds between 1867 and his death in 1923.

The King was not a first-class shot, thought Lord Warwick, but 'he was at least a good one, and was certainly a first-class sportsman'. According to Jonathan Garnier Ruffer, Edward was best at hitting driven partridges, and least good at potting pheasants.[4] His sons, however, were in the top league. The oldest, Prince Eddie (who died in 1892), was excellent, but his younger brother, the future King George V, was even better, and by the beginning of the twentieth century was reckoned to be one of the six top shots in the country.

When the King led a shooting party at Sandringham in November 1905, the nine or ten guns brought down a total of 6,448 birds – 4,135 pheasants, 2,009 partridges, 14 woodcock, 275 wild duck, 12 pigeons and 3 'various', plus 232 hares and 576 rabbits – a total 'bag' of 7,256 in three days.[5] The birds were beaten out of their hiding places towards the guns by the estate gamekeeper, other estate workers and local men recruited for the day's sport. The tweed-suited shooting party would raise their guns and congratulate each other on their skill in bringing down so many of the dense flock that darkened the sky, convinced that it was good 'sport' as another dead weight of feathers thudded to the ground, to be retrieved by gun dogs. A farmer who watched a Sandringham shoot described such an occasion:

> On they come in ever increasing numbers, until they burst in a cloud over the fence…This is the exciting moment, a terrific fusillade ensues, birds dropping down in all directions, wheeling about in confusion between the flags and the guns, the survivors gathering themselves together and escaping into the fields beyond. The shooters then retire to another line of fencing, making themselves comfortable with camp-stools and cigars until the birds are driven up as before, and so through the day, only leaving off for luncheon in a tent brought from Sandringham.[6]

King Edward VII shooting at Sandringham in 1907. The King would keep the clocks in his Norfolk home half an hour fast to ensure extra sport before darkness fell.

Sportsman's victuals: an Edwardian picnic basket.

Shooting at this level, rather than taking a potshot at a bird as it flew out of the hedge, was a rich man's sport. Traditional landowners, hard hit by falling agricultural rents, often managed to reduce some of their losses by renting out shooting (and hunting and fishing) rights to those of the *nouveaux riches* who hadn't quite managed to acquire a sporting estate of their own, but who nevertheless wanted the outdoor fun and social cachet that such a property bestowed. Advertisements in *Country Life* for properties for sale or rent often emphasized the sporting facilities: 'excellent partridge shooting…from 7,000 to 8,000 pheasants reared annually. Eight and a half miles of good trout fishing'[7] – rather than the agricultural possibilities, as the historian Pamela Horn points out.[8] And in November 1911, the *Tatler* estimated that the annual expenditure in Britain on shooting totalled £8,182,000.[9] In 1913 the Earl of Crawford complained about the cost of shooting grouse:

The equipment, the paraphernalia and above all the cost of grouse driving increases every year. There is a growing standard of comfort for instance in the grouse butts, which are now constructed with great care and accuracy in order the better to circumvent the birds: and the wages of the drivers, mostly boys from the surrounding villages, have largely increased. One now pays five shillings a day to these youths, and into the bargain they have to be driven to the moor…[but] when the last increase in wages was conceded, their free lunch was knocked off, which is considered a real advantage as the boys now bring their own frugal bread and cheese with them whereas previously they gorged themselves at their employer's expense, so freely as to find post-prandial walking a hard and uninviting task.[10]

To protect their precious birds from poachers, country house owners employed gamekeepers: by 1911 there were more than twice as many gamekeepers in rural areas as there were policemen.

In keeping with his Edwardian calling, and indeed his twenty-first-century country pursuits, Sir John Olliff-Cooper was determined to live up to expectations as a sporting man and his first port of call before leaving for Manderston was to a London gunsmith. 'You need a 30-inch barrel,' he was told, 'and a double trigger. In 1905 the majority of people were using double triggers, which had the advantage that you can use the choke barrel first when you are shooting grouse.' Sir John was a bit dubious since he had always used a single trigger, but he was willing to try mounting his gun and 'aiming' at a pheasant drawn on a piece of paper that the gunsmith held up for him. Some adjustment was needed with the stock, which depends on the length of the shooter's arm, so that Sir John could 'use [his] skill to the optimum, bearing in mind that it'll be cold on the moors in Scotland and [he'll] probably be wearing a thick tweed jacket, so [they would] need to make allowance for that.' The gunsmith maintained, 'It makes an enormous difference to how many birds you hit having the gun fitted correctly, because then you shoot where you think you're shooting.'

Sir John was equipped with a set of ivory position finders that he would hand out to his guests. These were each marked with a number that corresponded to a numbered stake that would be stuck in the ground at each drive. The gun would take up position by his stake and take aim as the birds were driven over his particular pitch. At the next drive each sportsman would move up to two numbers so that in theory everyone had an equal chance of shooting from the best position – which was probably in the centre. Sir John then gave instructions about the birds the party was going to shoot that day, and which to leave alone because they were trying to encourage their proliferation.

'Finally,' said the gunsmith, 'there's one thing I would recommend and that's this device called a "Norfolk Liar". It's marked for duck, grouse, pheasants and partridges. You start at zero and click each time you shoot a bird so you can keep a tally of your score. Not that you'd dream of *telling* anyone at the end of the drive, but it's nice to know.' Not all shoots were so delicate: sometimes at lunch each member of the party would call out the number of birds he had shot, whereas in other circles this was considered distinctly bad form, a vulgar variety of one-upmanship unbefitting of a gentleman.

In 1906, guns like the one Sir John was squaring up to, a royal twelve-bore, would have cost something in the region of 135 guineas a pair, and the leather and oak case to keep them in would have been around £6 15s. Nowadays a comparable pair of guns, which would be almost identical in every detail to the Edwardian gun, in a case, would set a sportsman back around £90,000, 'which was a considerable investment now as it was then' conceded the gunsmith. 'It is a testament to the design of

A page in a Manderston photograph album records the delights of a shooting party in Aberdeenshire in 1907.

the gun and to gun-making skills that it has proved timeless. Materials and technology have changed a bit – the steel is stronger, there are self-opening mechanisms and ejectors – but basically they are pretty unchanged.'

'Well, you can't really improve on perfection,' agreed the new country house tenant, watching with great satisfaction as 'his' guns were taken away to be adjusted to Sir John's fit, before being despatched north in time for his first shoot.

'I do enjoy shooting game,' Sir John confessed. 'It's the old hunting instinct, I suppose. I enjoy clay shooting, but nothing like as much as a day's shooting for the table. When we went out I found it hard at first shooting with the genuine authentic Edwardian black powder cartridges rather than the smokeless sort we use today. The noise is disconcerting – it's more of a boom than a bang – and there's a great belch of grey smoke and fire, and you are shooting at the birds through a haze of smoke.'

As host to the shoot, Sir John explained: 'There are very few rules today…no ground game, and we're not shooting woodcock.' Then the shooting party, wearing Norfolk tweed jackets – devised by tailors for the King in response to his request for a fuller style of jacket that would not impede the arms when raising a gun[11] – or waxed canvas jackets to keep out the rain, along with stout boots and an assortment of caps and deerstalker hats, set off in pursuit of their prey. Their guns were uncocked, the

A determined Edwardian lady shot (left), gun aloft, and (right) shooting clays: Mr Raj Singh (left) joins the Olliff-Coopers in potting targets on the back lawn.

cartridges in a bag. As they walked, they talked among themselves about how this was by far the best way to enjoy the countryside.

It was by no means a poor morning's score and the hunters were able to console themselves that 'the birds were flying exceedingly well for so early in the season' and were therefore adroit at missing being shot. 'I call it nature conservation when I miss,' said one of the party gamely.

It was unusual for women to shoot in Edwardian times, though a very few did, including the Duchess of Bedford who was acknowledged to be a crack shot. Queen Victoria had considered any woman who shot to be 'fast', and to most Edwardians she was 'very unconventional', but today we might think 'perverse' a better description of one who chose to trudge across often wet moors in a biting wind, deafened by the sound of gunfire, and in danger of being assaulted by dead birds crashing from the sky.

A thoughtful hostess would make sure that among the company invited for a country house weekend when sport was on the agenda (as it invariably was), a sprinkling of unsporting men would be invited. These 'darlings', or 'lap dogs' as they were known, would stay behind with the ladies, gossiping, playing card games and indulging in mild flirtations. One of the most popular of these 'sporting eunuchs' was the Portuguese ambassador, the exquisitely mannered Marquess de Souveral, who was a wonderful conversationalist (a little too wonderful on occasions for Edward VII, for whom neither witty repartee nor substantial analysis came naturally in conversation, and yet who was easily bored) and kept the ladies delightfully amused. But the women at an Edwardian country house shooting party would invariably leave the fireside and their pleasant conversation to join the men for luncheon. This could be a sandwich snatched between drives, but was much more likely to be an elaborate affair of hampers and wine coolers carried out by the servants.

Charles and Robin, as Sir John liked them to be called, did the honours for the shooting party, carrying out wicker baskets of food, champagne and glasses, and attempting to erect a tent in the middle of a field using a piece of awning and four poles which they drove into the earth. The party was thus able to sit out of the wind to ruminate on the balance between the cruelty of man and his swiftly discharged gun, as against the rawer justice of nature in the wild, red in tooth and claw, while refuelling for another drive before the light faded. As the sun went down, they all trudged back to the house satisfied with their day's sport and nonchalantly swinging their booty, a brace or two of pheasants or a couple of ducks apiece.

A day's shooting upstairs meant more work downstairs with guns to clean, muddy boots to deal with, game to be hung until it was well and truly high, and then plucked and stuffed and roasted and served up with a couple of feathers stuck in the rump, or casseroled with port or Malmsey wine. Auguste Escoffier, the great French chef, who had been *chef de cuisine* to the general staff of the Rhine Army during the Franco-Prussian War, and at the Grand Hotel Monte Carlo before being lured to London by César Ritz to cook first at the Savoy and then the Carlton Hotel, had written *A Guide to Modern Cookery* which was published in 1907. This became one of M. Dubiard's kitchen bibles, and he followed its recommendation that pheasants 'should be hung for a few days before being plucked in a moderate draught, that they may begin to decompose, and that the particular value of their flesh may be accentuated, a process which increases their culinary value. Whatever opinion may be held in regard to the gaminess of these birds, one thing is quite certain – namely, that the meat of a fresh pheasant and that of a high one are two totally different things. When fresh, the meat is flavourless, whereas when it is reasonably high it is tender, full of taste, and of an incomparable flavour.' Before going on to give no fewer than thirty-four ways to serve a pheasant, including stuffing it with *foie gras*, truffles, pork or even other birds including woodcock, Escoffier passed on a useful tip: 'If the last large feather in the wing…be pointed, the bird is young; if it be round, the reverse is the case.'[12]

Apart from birds for the table, Sir John provided hare on one occasion and fish on others. Manderston is located in fine fishing country. The Tweed, which runs close by, provides the opportunity to catch salmon, trout or grayling. The Duke of Roxburgh owns the best beats on the Tweed, including junctions – pools where two sources of waters meet – where the fishing potential is best. Salmon, however, is almost impossible to catch and even highly experienced anglers can come back empty-handed after a full day in pursuit. And these days there is a catch-and-release policy on the Tweed, so, unlike Edwardian times, when the rivers were better stocked with salmon anyway, no one catching a fish can take it home for lunch as an Edwardian country gentleman might.

As a Border plutocrat, Sir John would have employed a ghillie who knew the river well and who would take charge of the boat and carry the tackle and rods. The best weather for fishing is an overcast day after a few days' rain. Fish don't appreciate the sun. A book on fishing for salmon and trout, published in 1912, which was dedicated to Edward VII, 'the best and keenest sportsman of our time' – though the King was never a keen fisherman – explains that 'there are more differences about salmon flies than upon any other subject connected with salmon fishing. Some people assert that it is necessary to use different patterns of flies for every month during the fishing season; others that certain patterns are suitable only for certain rivers, and that it is useless to fish with any others. Another theory is that certain shades of colour must be used on certain days. Every fisherman one meets has his own ideas on this subject.'[13]

Sportsman's gear: Sir John equips himself in the vestibule for a day's fishing.

Sir John, a keen fisherman in Edwardian as in twenty-first-century times, casts his line.

An experienced fisherman would fly-fish when the conditions were clear and calm and the water low, and he would arc the feather imitation bait over the sparkling river to dart along its surface. When the river was high and the water muddy, an angler would spin the line out, and he would probably have carried rods for both conditions. Salmon fishers usually wade out into the river wearing chest-high canvas waders, waxed to make them waterproof and held up by a bib and brace. Wading can be very dangerous in fast flowing rivers and particularly so in Scotland, where the water can be freezing cold even in spring and autumn. An Edwardian angler would have rubbed his legs with goose fat to keep out the cold and made sure that he came out of the river every quarter of an hour or so for a nip of whisky. Fishing from a boat was also popular but it was considered to be more likely to scare the fish away.

Sir John was doubly blessed in aquatic endowment. As well as the nearby Tweed and its tributaries, the Edwardian Country House boasted a large lake in the grounds which was well stocked with brown trout. But salmon fishing in particular was a rich man's sport, with an increasing number of stretches of river in private hands, their fishing rights leased out so that the local population was not able to catch fish from the waters that eddied through their locality. Indeed, one of the first points of friction had come when the hall boy, eighteen-year-old Kenny, had been discovered fishing with a baited hook off the bridge that crossed the lake. 'It was absolutely fantastic. I got an old cane rod and a centre-pin wheel and half a loaf of bread which I half-inched from the kitchen and wrapped in my apron. I went down and stuck the rod in and I was just whipping out fish right, left and centre, each of them was at least three pounds and a couple were four. I might get some more later because I won't be going to church. It's not really poaching,' defended Kenny as he expertly landed a large, thrashing fish. 'I'm only going for perch and they're a nuisance fish. I'm not catching the trout.' But Sir John, who had not had such a successful day, did not see it like that. 'Why does the salmon take the fly?' was an age-old question for fishermen, and one that William Scrope's classic *Days and Nights of Salmon Fishing in the Tweed* had answered with the suggestion that it was merely for the sake of passing time and amusing itself. But whatever the answer, the salmon was not rising to the bait, and this did not improve Sir John's tolerance. 'That stupid boy!' exploded the master of the house. 'It really is not on. The lake is stocked with expensive trout for me and my guests. They are not there for the hall boy. If it happens again, his position in the house will be in jeopardy.'

Today it can cost as much as £26,000 to rent fishing rights for four rods for a week on the Tweed at the height of the season. The *Tatler* in its audit of Britain's sporting activities reckoned that the nation spent something over half a million pounds on fishing,[14] and, making a twenty-first-century contribution to this leisurely pastime, Sir John organized a small fishing party of four rods. After the success of the political dinner party he was keen to extend the range of guests invited to his table to those distinguished in the arts, and decided to venture an invitation for a weekend's fishing on the Tweed to the Poet Laureate, Andrew Motion, who admitted that 'next to poetry fishing is the thing that I enjoy most'. Sir John was honoured when he accepted.

> ## Salmon flies
>
> *'There is more difference of opinion about salmon flies than upon any other subject connected with salmon fishing. Some people assert that it is necessary to use different patterns of flies for every month during the fishing season; others, that certain patterns are suitable only for certain rivers ... another theory is that certain shades of colour must be used on certain days. Every fisherman one meets has his own ideas upon this subject.'*
>
> FROM *Fishing* BY H. CHOLMONDELEY-PENNELL, LATE HER MAJESTY'S INSPECTOR OF SEA FISHERIES (1912)
>
>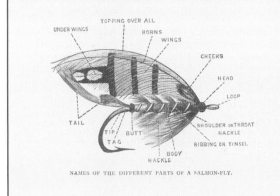
>
> NAMES OF THE DIFFERENT PARTS OF A SALMON-FLY.

The Poet Laureate is a royal appointment that carries a nominal stipend and the encouragement (though not obligation) to write a poem to mark events of national importance. Mr Motion, who is a biographer, publisher and Professor of Creative Writing at the University of East Anglia as well as Britain's official premier poet, wrote a poem on the death of Princess Diana, for example, and also one after the attack on the World Trade Centre on 11 September 2001.

Regrettably, the Edwardian period saw the tenure of the laureateship at its lowest ebb with the appointment of Alfred Austin, who held the post from 1896 until 1913. Inheriting the mantle of a line of distinguished poetic forefathers that included Ben Jonson, Dryden, Wordsworth and his immediate predecessor, the towering late Victorian figure of Alfred, Lord Tennyson, Austin was a much parodied versifier of some excruciating lines. His most memorable was penned on the occasion of the near fatal illness of the Prince of Wales in November 1871: 'Flash'd from his bed, the electric tidings came/He is not better; he is much the same'. When asked how such a lamentable appointment to this high office could have been made, the Prime Minister, Lord Salisbury, admitted sadly that no one else had applied. That evening, after dinner, the Olliff-Coopers had arranged a musical soirée to entertain their sporting guests. The family had been taking singing lessons with a local teacher, Mr Drummond, and were particularly appreciative of the fine singing that night in their own drawing room from a small choir from Edinburgh. The firelight flickered, the reflection of the lamps glanced off the jewels at the necks of the ladies, making dancing, angular points of light, the men looked well fed, content and somewhat comatose in their white tie and tails. Then, at Sir John's request, Andrew Motion stepped forward to read a few verses from one his own poems that seemed particularly appropriate after spending a day casting lines on the river that yielded nothing in return, 'A Severe Absence of Fish':

A poet entertains: Andrew Motion reads to the Olliff-Coopers and their guests.

> Even the most masterful of Zen Grand Masters
> Might lose patience and want time to run faster
>
> if, waist-deep like me in this bitterly cold river
> all week, he had cast his truest cast over and over —
>
> casting with all the passionate concentration of will
> a person can possibly have when they are trying to kill
>
> something they love…

Below stairs, Ellen had finally finished scrubbing the pots and pans from the meal that night; Charlie, Rob and Kenny had cleared the dining room table, served coffee and liqueurs, and washed the china, silver and glass. Mrs Davies had stowed it back in the cupboards and sorted out the dirty linen; Jess had checked the fires in the family and guest bedrooms while Becky had tidied up the rooms, turned on bedside lights, laid out nightwear and turned down the beds. Now at the invitation of Sir John, the servants stood in the shadows watching the evening's entertainment in the drawing room through a half open door. But not for long. Worn out after an arduous day's labour, Mr Edgar was nodding off and one by one the servants tiptoed away to their beds, while Miss Morrison resigned herself to quite a wait before Lady Olliff-Cooper would ring for her maid's help in preparing for bed.

The third sport in the triad of Edwardian country house pursuits was fox-hunting, and one autumn morning the local hunt, the Berwickshire Hounds, held their meet at Manderston. The Berwickshire Hunt is the oldest in Scotland. Records of its activities can be traced to the start of the seventeenth century, but the hunt was formally established in 1787 and has been active ever since. Sir James Miller, who rebuilt Manderston, was the Master of the Northumberland and Berwickshire Fox Hounds until his premature death in 1906 (as the result of a chill having turned to pneumonia after a day's hunting), and it was he who moved the kennels to Manderston where they remain today. His obituary celebrated that role:

There's a loud tally-ho! And Sir James is away
…it isn't a fox o'er the Merse he has followed;
It isn't the crack of a sporting gun,
Nor the shout of the Boers in a sally;
It isn't Sainfoin and it isn't Rocksand [two of Sir James's prize-winning race horses]
That has carried him over the valley.

There's a keen tally-ho and Sir James is away,
He has left all behind that is mortal,
He has gone far beyond the shadow of death,
To dwell in the regions immortal
He has gone from the scene of his earthly career,
And there's many a heart filled with sadness,
Oh the rich and the poor are as one in their grief
For he joined alike in their gladness…

Lady Palmer, the present mistress of Manderston, is joint MFH, and the hunt, which meets twice a week in the season which lasts from November to mid March, regularly sets off from there.

'Are those for the ladies?' enquired Sir John, as he watched his butler and footmen lay out silver trays full of claret glasses for the hunt. 'No, sir,' explained Mr Edgar, 'the issue is one of quality.' The smaller glasses contained twenty-year-old vintage port for those local hunt dignitaries invited *into* the house, while 'very good quality, but not vintage' port was served in larger glasses to those gathering *outside* on the gravel drive. Opening the vintage port had been quite a production below stairs since Mr Edgar had insisted that the traditional Edwardian method should be followed. Vintage port forms a crusty sediment over the years it is laid down in cellars; to avoid disturbing this, and to make sure that none of the cork crumbles into the port (which might happen if a corkscrew were used), the neck of the bottle is gripped tightly using iron tongs heated red hot in the coal fire of the range, and a feather dipped in icy cold water is passed over the neck. This is supposed to effect a clean break – and is not an easy operation, as the servants found. Once the neck has snapped off in the required fashion, the port is then poured through a silver funnel into a linen-covered sieve to further avoid contamination of the fine liquid as it drips into the crystal decanter.

The hunt was a magnificent sight as the horses trotted up towards the house, under trees with leaves an autumnal golden brown, the hounds snapping at their hooves, the huntsmen and women resplendent in hunting pink (which is red). Everyone in the Edwardian country house had a view about hunting, and as the servants ferried the trays of port along with slices of Mrs Davies's rich fruitcake to the equestrian guests, they gave voice to their opinions – but *sotto voce* to each other.

The housekeeper was in favour of hunting: she had seen all too often what foxes had done to her chickens. 'They are sly and cunning and they just wantonly kill the chickens, they don't even eat most of them,' Mrs Davies said vehemently. 'A fox doesn't have a predator now that there aren't any wolves any more. There is nothing to kill a fox now but a human being.' Ellen, the newly-arrived scullery maid, admitted that as a farmer's daughter she had grown up with hunting and found it an unremarkable rural reality, though she found it too contentious to talk about the matter surrounded by her fellow servants in the Edwardian country house. Kenny had no such inhibitions: 'I have some quite strong views against hunting. I think that it's wrong to hunt foxes because the countryside is their natural environment. What rights do we have as human beings to go and chase a fox and rip it apart using dogs? If a fox steals your chickens, fair enough, shoot it, but to hunt it down in the woods and pull it apart limb from limb, seems quite scandalous to me. As far as I am concerned, it's just a load of upper-class crap, all part of the ridiculous society that I'm living in at the moment where it is good etiquette to ride on the back of one animal in order to go and rip another animal apart. The hunt will just mean another invasion of snobby people as far as I'm concerned who I am going to have to serve. It's my job, so I'll do it, but I don't like it. It feels more and more as if I'm owned. It's Sir John's house, Sir John's hunt, Sir John's servants. If we formed a choir, say, for our own amusement, it would be Sir John's choir. All our work is just adding to his status. And the hunt is all part of that too.'

Mixing with the guests in the hall upstairs, Sir John maintained that he had 'no fixed ideas' about hunting, but felt that 'whatever the rights and wrongs of it, it is something that it would be desperately sad to lose'. And Lady Olliff-Cooper agreed: 'It is so terribly English,' she said wistfully (though they were in Scotland) as the hunt set off.

Although only 10 per cent of a sample polled by MORI in the summer of 1999 thought that 'fox-hunting is a necessary means of preserving the balance of wild life in our countryside', and 52 per cent strongly and 11 per cent less strongly supported a ban,[15] many of the respondents were town, city or suburban dwellers, rather than country dwellers for whom hunting was commonplace. Despite the act of the Scottish Parliament in February 2002, banning fox hunting, the Olliff-Coopers tried to think themselves back into the minds of Edwardian country house owners and what *their* views would have been. 'I think personally that I would probably come down on the side of abolishing hunting as being cruel to foxes,' concluded Lady Olliff-Cooper, 'but part of the point of this series is to show how far our attitudes have changed in the last hundred years. We have to realize that in Edwardian times an awful lot of humans had hardly any rights at all, ethnic minorities, religious minorities, even our servants don't have rights in the sense that we know them. They don't have the right for time off from work, or free speech, and they didn't have rights to health care, so in Edwardian times the concept of animals having rights would have seemed ludicrous to most people. By hosting the meet, we are trying to show that this would have been a normal, reasonable practice in Edwardian society.'

'Far too many people would have been dying of tuberculosis to worry about foxes,' added Sir John, and his wife agreed. 'Every generation thinks that the one before ignores the rights of some significant group,' she said. 'In the next century no doubt people will think that we were barbaric in our treatment of…'

'Ants?' suggested Sir John.

Fox-hunting was not a sport that was confined to men. Today more than half of those who regularly ride to hounds with the Berwickshire are women, and in the Edwardian years this would not have been unusual. The Duchess of Bedford, Margot Asquith, wife of the Liberal Prime Minister, and Winston Churchill's mother, Lady Randolph Churchill, were considered very fine horsewomen who enjoyed nothing more than chasing after foxes, while the Empress Elizabeth of Austria (who hunted in England, Scotland and Ireland), was a legendary huntswoman who was sewn into her figure-hugging costume, carried a large fan as she galloped, and drew 'crowds agog to catch a glimpse of her' whenever she appeared. In 1899 a Miss McClintock became the lady MFH of a subscription pack and *Country Life* praised her as 'one of the hardest riders the country [has] ever known'.[16] Women usually rode side-saddle, which made it difficult to dismount quickly and could be dangerous in an accident; nevertheless they enjoyed an exhilarating sense of freedom as they galloped through the countryside, taking jumps, flying over hedges, walls and ditches, attracting admiration for their 'good seat' on a horse. They rode elegantly, clad in a long skirt, tight fitting jacket, stock and small hard top hat, often with a veil or streamers of chiffon billowing out behind.

When she embraced socialism after her epiphany with the *Clarion*, the Countess of Warwick began to see the error of her hunting ways too. She admitted: 'Remembering the place that hunting held in my life, it is not to be supposed that my ear was open in my youth to arguments against such an exhilarating pastime…I know well the thrill of galloping on a good horse over high Leicestershire at the tail of the hounds, with no thought of the little red beast's agony, or the sickening meanness of digging him out of his only refuge, "mother earth".' She confessed to 'having a prick of shame even in my former thoughtless years when riding my horse home after the Hunt if I met tired workmen returning home after a day's work. My day's record was of precious hours spent in wasteful idleness, while these men had been adding to the productiveness of their country.' And 'Daisy' Warwick became convinced that 'the false argument of the trade in horses, and in hay and corn, and the employment given at the hunting centres bear scrutiny. These are in the same luxury category as that old Warwick Fancy Ball.' Nor was there any 'possible compensation [for farmers] for broken fences and trodden-down cereals and pasture, nor for the cattle escaping through open gates. The Hunt invariably leaves a trail of destruction behind it, and for all this merely flings a trifle to the "Poultry Fund".'[17]

But it was the First World War that convinced the Countess of Warwick that 'for women there is joy to be had in attaining skill in sports that have no trail of blood'. For since 'the time that our first train-load of wounded reached the Red Cross hospital in 1914…I have never wittingly seen hounds again… If we have learned anything from those years of carnage it is that life is sacred…I am not alone in this feeling. Men friends – themselves crack shots – have told me that although they formerly enjoyed the shooting season, they can no longer find pleasure in killing birds or ground game, from a new feeling of reluctance to take life of any kind' and hoped that now 'the horrid cruelty of this sport has been made plain…before long this evil thing will be forbidden'.[18]

Miss Anson watched the meet from her bedroom window. 'When I was a teenager I saw a fox torn apart by the hounds in front of my eyes. Since then, while I love the colour and the sounds of the meet, the tradition and all the excitement, I have never wanted to hunt myself. I am not really a hunt supporter, nor am I anti-hunting. It certainly all looked great fun today, very colourful, and a couple of the women were riding side-saddle.'

Miss Anson was not well: a viral infection had been diagnosed and she felt exhausted much of the time and was feeling increasingly frustrated by the limitations and inhibitions placed on her by her position in the family in the Edwardian Country House. But horse riding was proving a great pleasure and liberation for Avril Anson. Within a few days of arriving at Manderston, she had recorded in her journal: 'My first lesson in riding side-saddle. What a pleasure! What an amazing sense of freedom, spontaneity, control, exhilaration, discovery etc! This is what I came for. None of this nonsense about appearances, etiquette and stiff formality. The horses are beautifully schooled, the tutor is lovely, the clothes are strange and the whole experience great fun. I managed to walk, trot and canter round the paddock.' Soon she was riding every day that she could, often with her sister.

Riding side-saddle, which fell generally out of fashion after the First World War, has become popular again in recent years. The Side Saddle Association was established in 1974 with the aim of reviving the art of riding side-saddle and encouraging more people to take it up. It now boasts 1,200 members and arranges a National Championship Show, training courses, grade tests and social events. Its rules for 'turnout' are distinctly Edwardian, though: a safety bowler hat with 'an unwrinkled veil' is to be worn and the brim of the hat 'should be parallel to the ground and just above the eyebrows'. Adults are permitted to wear a silk hat – height specified in accordance with the height of the wearer – but only after midday and for more prestigious

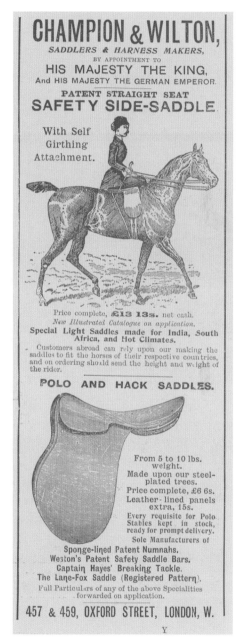

Lady Olliff-Cooper riding side-saddle.

events. The hair should be worn in a bun (real or false) 'no larger than the size of a small doughnut' and wispy strands restrained in a hair net. The habit must be 'of restrained hue tweed or discreet check (e.g. Prince of Wales) with long brown or black boots depending on the colour of the habit and hat'. The habit should be made of sufficient weight to prevent the apron blowing around in the wind.' Since 'the riding apparel is governed by what type of hat is worn' the wearing of a bowler calls for a shirt and tie whereas with a silk hat a folded silk or cotton stock is correct, but in Edwardian times women would have worn a silk or piqué stock. And in no circumstances must 'floral buttonholes, earrings or visible jewellery' be worn.[19] In the Edwardian era, as more women chose to ride, there were experiments to make riding side-saddle safer in the event of a fall. These included skirts that were looped or, would spring apart under pressure, and various patent safety stirrup designs.

As well as the horses ridden by Lady Olliff-Cooper and Miss Anson, there was Tony, the pony that Master Guy had been given for his tenth birthday and which he was greatly enjoying learning to ride. Mr Jonathan was also acquiring equestrian skills, and soon progressed from being led round the paddock on a leading rein to hacking through the quiet lanes around the estate accompanied by his aunt. The horses that the Olliff-Coopers rode were looked after by Tristan. Just as it had been essential to obtain the services of a professional chef, given the culinary demands that would be put upon him in the Edwardian Country House, so it was necessary to appoint as groom and carriage driver a person who had worked with horses for some time, and Tristan fitted the bill perfectly: 'I've worked with horses all my life.'

His role was to look after the horses, feeding, grooming and exercising them, preparing them for the family to ride, and driving the carriages – a landau, a brougham, a wagonette and a dog cart that were kept in the stables and used when the family went to church every Sunday, for visits they made in the neighbourhood and for transporting guests. Tristan lived 'above the shop' in a room above the stables, but ate with the other servants and usually spent his evenings in the servants' hall. He was sometimes pressed into service as an auxiliary footmen when the family had a large dinner party or held a ball, and his outdoor good looks (rather like Mr Darcy in the television adaptation of *Pride and Prejudice*, giggled the maids) added to the prestige of the house. His day started at around 7 a.m. when he went to feed and muck out the horses and exercise Guy's pony since his master was not able to ride him on schooldays. After breakfast and prayers at the house, it would be back down to the stables often to prepare the carriage at very short notice.

'I just don't think that the family has any idea how long it takes to get the carriage ready, the horses in harness and into the shafts,' said Tristan. 'They seem to think it's like ringing for a minicab.

The road to Duns is quite dangerous. At first the carriages were a novelty and cars would stop. But now they've got used to seeing us around and nearly force the carriage into the ditch sometimes.

'A house like this wouldn't run without its horses. Horses were still the main mode of transport, and they were a status symbol too for the upper classes. Horses just seemed a much more elegant way to travel. We've got three horses, Jack, Buck and Murphy, and they all need exercising for a minimum of half an hour a day and then they have to be rubbed down and groomed. I clean the tack in the morning once I've finished exercising the horses and put it all away and then it's time to feed the horses again and go to the house for my lunch. Most afternoons one or other member of the family wants to go out riding so I have to see that, and then I'll sweep out the yard, and clean any of the tack that's been used. I get a bit of a break then unless the carriage is needed, and then I exercise Tony again, feed the horses, do odd jobs around the stables before I go up to the house for supper. I come back down again and rub down the horses for the night and give them some hay and make sure they've got water. There's usually some maintenance work to do on the carriages too – they have to be cleaned and the brass polished, and often some paint has to be touched up. I try to keep them in tip-top condition all the time, and I need to soak the wheels because if you don't the wood shrinks and the spokes become loose. We do that by dragging the coach into the lake to soak and then winching it out again. So there's always plenty to do.

'The horses are my sole charge, so I can't have a day off because I still have the horses to think about. Who would feed them and exercise them? The best I can hope for it is to get into Duns sometimes of an evening and have a drink with the other servants.'

The stables at Manderston are magnificent. The magazine *Horse and Hound* confirmed that the house could 'probably boast the finest stables in all the wide world'.[20] 'The horses have a much better life than the servants,' was Tristan's view. 'I mean, you've only got

The groom and coachman

Tristan Aldrich, who is nineteen, had 'been around horses pretty well all [his] life' when he came to the Edwardian Country House as groom and carriage driver. At one time he had thought of going into the RAF but soon gave that up in favour of working with horses. Tristan lives and works in Norfolk, training with the Olympic carriage driver John Parker. He makes and repairs harnesses as well as being in charge of a couple of dozen horses. He has driven a variety of horse-drawn vehicles and was knowledgeable about the landau, the brougham, the wagonette and the dog cart that were housed at Manderston and that he would be using to transport the Olliff-Coopers on their social round, as well as teaching Master Guy and Mr Jonathan equestrian skills.

to compare their stables to the servants' hall to see that. All the doors down here are mahogany, they've got marble stalls to keep the horses cool in the summer, they've got underfloor heating in the stables and the coach house to keep it warm in winter, whereas in the servants' hall all we've got are the bare essentials, a couple of small fires and some running water, no luxuries at all. There's just no comparison. The horses have got it made, they've got a life of Riley down here.'

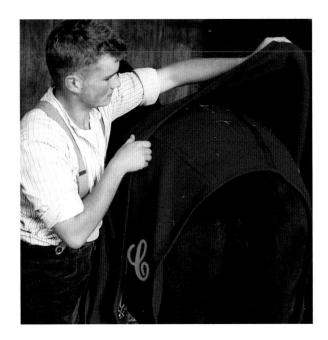

Tristan tending one of the horses in the magnificent marble-lined stalls in the Manderston stables. The horse blanket bears the monogram 'OC' for Olliff-Cooper.

As befitted a man of the turf, Sir James Miller had housing for his horses completed in 1895, nearly ten years before he started to remodel his house. The architect was John Kinross, who must have so impressed with his plans for the stables that he was commissioned to design the main house. Georgian in design like the house, the stables cost £20,000 (well over £1 million at today's prices) at a time when building costs were relatively low. They are built round three courts; the first is guarded by an arch flanked with Doric columns, and on the inside of the arch are detailed relief panels of huntsmen and hounds. To the left are coach houses and to the right loose boxes with barrel-vaulted roofs. There are also separate buildings housing boxes for foaling, a sick bay and a forge. The horses' stalls are made of teak with polished brass posts, and the names of the horses all begin with the initial M that stands for Miller and for Manderston. Above each stall is a plate inscribed with a horse's name: 'Mystery', 'Magic', 'Milton', 'Matchless', 'Malakoff', 'Monarch', 'Mango'. The large harness room, which is fitted out in rosewood and floored in Italian marble, is hung with heavy leather saddles, bridles, stirrups, snaffles, bits, and, covering the walls, a veritable flower garden of brightly coloured rosettes and certificates that the Manderston horses have been awarded over the years for various dressage events, point to points, team events and gymkhanas.

But not far from the horses' stabling at Manderston stood commodious garages and workshops for the 'horseless carriage', the motor-car, which was such striking evidence of plutocratic wealth and the slow demise of the old order. There had been considerable hostility from landowners to the coming of the railways in the mid nineteenth century, an event welcomed by Thomas Arnold, headmaster of Rugby, as 'heralding the downfall of the aristocracy'. He 'rejoice[d] to see [the steam engine] and think that feudality is gone for ever'.[21] The steam trains were noisy and polluting, like small-scale factory chimneys bringing industry into the green and pleasant lands. They compulsorily criss-crossed land previously considered inviolate and, worst of all, enabled 'masses of ordinary people to travel distances hitherto undreamed of. It was the most potent symbol of the new age of the industrial revolution, and it portended major changes in the structure of business and of wealth-holding.'[22] But such hostility became muted when it was realized how much money could be made by selling land, in an era when its agricultural value had plummeted, for railway tracks and tunnels to be laid across it.

At the end of the century, the advent of the motor car met with no less initial hostility than that of the train in some aristocratic circles since 'unlike the railway, the automobile was explicitly conceived as a horse substitute',[23] with firms that had previously made carriages switching production to automobiles. Unlike railways, which were a democratic – if stratified – form of transport, the car was a prerequisite of ostentation. By 1904, when the requirement to register car ownership was made law, there were 8,500 cars on the roads of Britain, and it was almost entirely the wealthy (or their uniformed chauffeurs) who were at the steering wheel. Like Toad in *Wind in the Willows* the new cohort of motor car owners dressed in a vulgar fashion, drove recklessly and made a great deal of noise in doing so. Owning a car meant that distances became paltry and social life was reconfigured, since the distance a horse could travel no longer needed to circumscribe a person's social round. The Edwardian plutocrat's delight, the 'Saturday to Monday' country house party, was one significant result.

But motor-cars were not generally welcomed by the 'horsey community' since they interfered with fox-hunting: the smell of petrol put the hounds off the scent while the cars frightened the horses. More soberly, as David Cannadine points out, the military implications of the combustion engine meant that the cavalry, previously the elite corps, ceded ground to the mechanized infantry in the First World War.[24] But the trend was irreversible. In 1896 the Locomotives and Highway Act abolished the requirement for a man waving a red flag to walk in front of every car, and raised the speed limit on public roads to a dizzying 14 mph. That same year the future Edward VII took his first spin in a motor-car.

There was one advantage at least that cars had over horses, muttered Kenny rebelliously, as he was instructed to clear up the horse dung after the meet had departed. But Mr Edgar saw an opportunity.

'I told Kenny that he would have to clean the forecourt after the meet and he was just about to explode when I said, "And I will come with you to help you." I had two objectives in mind. One was to demonstrate that there is no task that is too menial. It doesn't matter what it is if it needs doing. The other is a more subtle point and that was a lesson in humility that we all need to learn. The minute Kenny saw me take off my white gloves and don an apron over my Sunday best it didn't matter any more that we were collecting horse manure; we were two men together doing a necessary job. So I hope that Kenny had learned that lesson.'

The next few weeks would tell.

Edwardian motoring: the Napier car that the Olliff-Coopers used during their Edwardian séjour, and (inset) fashions for Edwardian lady motorists.

41

CHAPTER NINE

Being Edwardian

'Fine. If they want Edwardian, I'll give them Edwardian,' spat M. Dubiard, slamming a large copper pan down on the hot range. The simmering resentment below stairs had come to a head. As befits the *chef de cuisine* in a grand Edwardian country house where entertaining was as much for show as for conviviality, M. Dubiard spent nights poring over recipe books, determined to serve the correct food for the period. With a minimum of three courses at luncheon and five for dinner, frequent guests in the house and a round of dinner parties, it meant a great deal of work.

Before arriving, M. Dubiard had worked his way all through *Larousse Gastronomique* to refresh his memory, and in the house his 'bible' was Escoffier, though he consulted other sources such as Carême, Brillat-Savarin and Dugléré, whom he called 'the Mozart of the kitchen', and Mrs Beeton too, as well as drawing on his own compendious knowledge of French cookery. On their first night in the house, the Olliff-Coopers had been served a consommé followed by a tomato soup with basil and tapioca. The fish course had consisted of a petite croustade of smoked salmon and scrambled eggs; the main course had been Beef Wellington which, according to Escoffier, would have been called an *entrée* since it was 'less voluminous' than a *relévé* (literally 'to relieve' the soup), though he admitted that now that meals were served *à la russe*, rather than *à la française*, the distinction had become somewhat academic. The *entremet* (dessert) was a rhubarb and damson jelly and the meal concluded with tiny pineapple tartlets. Similar meals had followed: upstairs had dined on such delicacies as lobster and asparagus, oysters prepared in a variety of ways, quail, turbot with fennel, veal, langoustines, glazed roast pork, savoury and sweet soufflés, saddle of lamb, lamb cutlets, vegetables *provençales* (without garlic since, to M. Dubiard's irritation, Sir John had decreed that no garlic was to be used in the food served to the family as he was allergic to it), braised oxtail, galantine of duck, roast guinea fowl, sirloin steak. Then there had been a variety of sweet and savoury jellies, custards, sweet omelettes, tarts, pies and ices with praline and sugared violets. The list went on.

FANCY DISHES.

Delicious desserts as suggested by Mrs Beeton.

M. Dubiard checks whether a hare hanging in the game pantry is sufficiently high to serve.

One day the kitchen maid, Antonia, had been taken to see the specially built Manderston dairy, housed in a corbelled tower, the octagonal room designed like a cloister with a vaulted ceiling, its floor, walls and counters fashioned from marble and alabaster 'imported from seven countries'.[1] A carving on the wall depicting a dairymaid milking a cow, which was modelled on an animal in the byre, is reputed to have been removed on the instructions of Sir James Miller when he realized that the dairymaid was sitting on the wrong side of the cow. The solecism corrected, the plaque, which weighs close on half a ton, was rehung. It was in these delightful surroundings that Antonia was taught how to churn butter and how to make clotted cream, and this now featured on the dinner menu to accompany dessert or be taken at tea with scones and jam.

M. Dubiard had noticed that when he had sent up jugged hare, rich in a sauce made from its own blood, the dish had been returned untouched. Likewise when Sir John had shot game, he donated it to the kitchen staff. 'I think they only want bistro food like we eat in the twenty-first century,' the chef fumed. 'They are just not living as an Edwardian family would have done.' Leafing through his recipe books, the chef noticed the incidence of dishes that rarely figure on modern menus such as teal, ptarmigan, widgeon, lark (as a pâté, roast or in a pie), pigeon, capon, fish such as flounder, smelts, eel, pike, squab, dory, and parts of the animal not often consumed at today's table such as heart, sweetbreads, tail and cheek, not to mention sucking pig, pig's trotters and pig's ears. Stroking his chin thoughtfully, M. Dubiard's eyes began to gleam.

The issue of 'being Edwardian' had become wider than one of culinary peccadilloes. The material conditions of an Edwardian existence were clearly in place in the country house: the absence of labour-saving devices ranging from washing machines through vacuum cleaners to detergent and scouring powder; the clothes from corsets and bloomers to laced walking boots, long skirts, large, feathered hats and furs (above stairs), stuff frocks, crisp white caps and aprons (below stairs). The turn of the century was signalled by the absence of commodities too: no proprietary brands of shampoo, no deodorants, tampons, make-up; no instant coffee, sliced bread, tea bags, Coca Cola; no trainers, fleeces, felt-tip pens, video games, television, CD players, mobile phones…

The duties of the servants were spelled out in the book of rules and instructions that they had been handed on arrival, and were expected to read, learn and inwardly digest, and Mr Edgar had drawn up a timetable for everyone so they knew exactly what they should be doing and when. Upstairs the Olliff-Coopers and Miss Anson were likewise supplied with manuals of advice on etiquette, including correct forms of address, rules of precedence and dress codes, while contemporary magazines and newspapers brought the family and servants up to date with news of the outside world as it was lived then.

But 'being Edwardian' was about *living* the Edwardian experience, not just using Edwardiana as a stage set. It was about trying to comprehend the rules of engagement and etiquette of the era in order to get into its prevailing mindset. It was physically hard for the servants to have to rise before the sun, scrub pots and pans all day and be at the beck and call of their employers at all times. But what was much harder intellectually and emotionally was to shed twenty-first-century attitudes and acquire

a servility and unquestioning obedience that would have been required of an Edwardian servant. This did not mean, of course, that our Edwardian forefathers and mothers were accepting, uncritical, uncomplaining beings without sensibilities, unaware of concepts of dignity and respect. During the period before the First World War, increasing numbers of men and women chose not to go into domestic service the moment that other opportunities in factories, offices and shops became available. In his social survey, Charles Booth noted that the reluctance to take up domestic service owed less to meagre pay and poor conditions – for unskilled factory or agricultural workers endured far worse of both – than to the requisite servility. It was increasingly shunned because of the relationship between master and servant which was similar to that between sovereign and subject, demanding 'an all pervading attitude of watchful respect, accompanied by a readiness to respond at once to any gracious advance that may be made'

Master Guy, the only member of the Olliff-Cooper family to feel at home below stairs, jokes with Antonia and Becky.

A television-free zone: Jess reads, Erika plays cards and Tristan talks in the servants' hall.

without ever 'presuming or for a moment "forgetting themselves"'.[2] A butler writing in the magazine *Nineteenth Century* near the end of Victoria's reign regretted that the master of the house often assumed that his position endowed him with an innate superiority, and was likely to forget 'that the servant whom he treats like a dog may have nerves as highly strung, and may feel as acutely as the guest whom he must treat with courtesy'.[3] And most poignantly a footman's memoir cried out against his lack of freedom: 'The life of a gentleman's servant is something like that of a bird shut up in a cage. The bird is well fed and well housed, but is deprived of liberty.'[4] And indeed employers were advised that 'servants, like birds, must be caught when young'.[5]

It took a considerable leap of imagination for the servants to shed twenty-first-century attitudes and climb back into the cage of the Edwardian era. A few days after the family arrived, the first footman, Charlie, was optimistic about things in an inappropriately modern way: 'It's a bit of a "them and us" mentality at the moment because obviously we are waiting on them hand and foot, which is our job after all, but I think that in time Mr Edgar and Rob [the second footman] and I will be a position to bridge the gap. Hopefully in time, we'll be able to have a bit of banter. Well, perhaps not banter,' he conceded, 'but be a bit more light-hearted with Sir John and Lady Olliff-Cooper and the rest of the family. And at the same time we'll keep our links with the rest of the servants and tell them exaggerated stories of what's happening upstairs, I think it'll be a laugh, really.' But it wasn't.

When Charlie, in charge because Mr Edgar was unwell, tried to put in place a modern managerial solution – such as any twenty-first-century human resources consultant would welcome – to the problem of the scullery maid's exhaustion and ennui, he found it wasn't that simple. 'I thought we'd have a sort of a rota. That is, I would take it in turns to do the washing-up for a day a week and that would give Ellen [or Kelly as it was at the time] a break and allow Kenny to take over from me as footman for an evening to give him a bit of variety – and experience – too.' But this was not an acceptable situation as far as Sir John was concerned. He had no desire to know that his personable first footman was in the basement up to his elbows in greasy suds, while it was the untrained hall boy now standing before him in ill-fitting footman's livery.

It had been the same with the staff's request for a rota of regular half-days off, which had finally been granted. 'I will do my best,' Mr Edgar had responded, 'but the needs of the family have to come first, and if any one of us is required to serve them, then he or she cannot have the time off. The sole reason that we are here is to serve the family.'

As far as the Edwardian Country House servants were concerned, the family upstairs had no such constraints. They would have been uncomprehending of Henry James's observation that such Edwardian plutocrats lived lives of 'gilded bondage'. To them, the family was free to indulge its every whim thanks to *their* labour. As far as they could see, the Olliff-Coopers were living for pleasure, enjoying a pampered lifestyle – and they weren't always all that grateful for it. Rob was struck when he had accompanied Lady Olliff-Cooper on a visit to a school in Duns and she had told the children that it had only taken her a couple of days to settle into her Edwardian lifestyle. 'It dawned on me then that if you are given privilege, as they have been given privilege, it's easy to get used to that pretty well straight away. But if you have had privileges, what you deserve, your rights, all taken away as we have below stairs, that's much harder to adjust to.'

But it wasn't all one way. The family upstairs had restraints too; they were hardly ever alone. 'It's got to the point that Jonty has taken to writing an appointment in my diary just to talk to me,' said his mother guiltily. The servants were present at every meal and the presence of Rob and Charlie standing erect, staring impassively into the middle distance as the family ate, was a considerable restraint on conversation. 'Servants have eyes and ears to wag downstairs' one of their etiquette manuals had cautioned. The maids tidied the women's bedrooms when they were downstairs and any intimate secrets could be perused at leisure, journals and letters read if any member of the family was less than vigilant, or one of the housemaids or Miss Morrison proved particularly curious. 'No man is a hero to his valet' was a salutary truth that the male members of the family brought ruefully to mind sometimes, mindful, perhaps, of an inevitable indiscretion or flash of irritability. Though they employed some thirteen below stairs servants, Edwardian etiquette made it improper for the family to venture to the nether regions of their own house, and they suspected that their daily doings were the subject of servant gossip and speculation, criticism and occasional ribald jocularity. Any discontents the staff felt filtered through to the family, while uncertainty about how extensive were the lands of the lord of misrule below stairs must have made for unease on occasions.

The family's activities had to fit into the rigid timetable of the house – meals had to be served at prescribed times or the efficient mechanism of the house would be thrown into disarray. The gong sounded for luncheon, then to dress for dinner, then for dinner itself. If the servants' life was ruled by bells, it seemed to the family that theirs was by gongs. Then there were the restraints of Edwardian etiquette (the word means labelling or ticketing), and this elaborate code grew up from the early nineteenth century to delineate social boundaries. The purpose was to keep those below you at a distance, emphasize 'commensuality' with those who were your social equal, and aim to gain access to the next higher group.[6] The 'system' governed what it was proper to discuss in front of the servants, and what with the servants; the rules of precedence and address; how to start a letter and how to end it; who to invite to your house and how; and the whole fraught business of introductions, being 'at home' and paying calls.

'Inferiors' were introduced to 'superiors', and rank always took precedence over anything else. Servants were not introduced to anyone. Once a lady had been introduced (but not before, unless she was immensely grand) she might call on that person and send in her card. *The Lady* explained this labyrinthine system:

> There is a very strict etiquette in the matter of cards and calls and there is one essential difference between *calling* and *leaving cards*. It is usual on paying a first visit merely to leave cards without inquiring if the mistress of the house is at home. Thus Mrs A. leaves her own card and two of her husband's cards upon Mrs B. Within a week, if possible, certainly within ten days, Mrs B. should return the visit and leave cards on Mrs A. Should Mrs A., however, have 'called' upon Mrs B. and the latter returned it by merely leaving cards, this would be taken as a sign that the latter did not desire the acquaintance to ripen into friendship. Strict etiquette demands that a call should be returned by a call and a card by a card.[7]

Master and servant: Rob stands to attention as Sir John eats his lunch on a fishing expedition.

Lady Olliff-Cooper

*Manderston
Duns*

Once this ritual had been gone through and the notional Mrs (or Lady) A. and Mrs (or Lady) B. actually got together, there were further conventions to be observed. The first visit should be short – around fifteen minutes – and conversation should be light and impersonal; politics and religion were to be eschewed and dogs and children were not appropriate appendages. If the call was a morning one, outdoor clothes should be kept on; in the afternoon a coat or cloak could be shed, but a lady would keep her hat on (partly no doubt because it was such a kerfuffle to fix it on and off with hairpins and hatpins galore). If the initial visit was deemed to have passed off well, a dinner invitation might ensue and the tactics could be deemed to have worked. Should the family leave the area for a period, maybe to go to London for the Season, they would distribute cards marked 'P.P.C.' – Pour Prend Congé) and when they returned the whole intricate game would start up again with maybe some new players to add a little interest.

There is, of course, no entirely homogeneous society that can be simply reconstructed by consulting its manuals of instruction. There were some upper-class Edwardians who chose to ignore these social niceties, either because they had pretensions to be 'bohemian', or simply because they were so grand that they could be insouciant about what others thought of them. Yet as late as 1911 Lady Colin Campbell was quite firm:

> Visits of form of which most people complain and yet to which most people submit, are absolutely necessary – being in fact the basis on which that great structure, society, mainly rests. You cannot invite people to your house, however often you may have met them elsewhere, until you have first called upon them in a formal manner, and they have returned the visit. It is a kind of safeguard against any acquaintances which are thought to be undesirable. If you do not wish to continue the friendship, you discontinue to call, and that is considered an intimation of such intentions, and therefore no further advances are made.[8]

And for those *arrivistes* not born to the purple, such rules served as handrails around the maze that was Edwardian society.

For the Olliff-Coppers, the complexity of the situation was compounded. As newcomers to Edwardian society, not only were they having to navigate a whole atlas of unseen, confusing and sometimes contradictory behavioural maps, they were also having to think themselves back into the dynamics of that terrain. Their task was to unlearn twenty-first-century ways of behaving, speaking and even thinking, and to assume the new and sometimes uncomfortable logic of their situation.

'It is difficult for us to know how far to act as Edwardians and how far to stick to our twenty-first-century principles,' worried Lady Olliff Cooper. 'It's a very difficult, delicate balancing act and sometimes we manage it better than others. Quite a lot of the time we do actually *feel* Edwardian and hence our instinct is to act in ways that the Edwardians would have done, but of course the way that Edwardians acted is perceived nowadays as being callous and indifferent, unkind and unfeeling in many respects. So when we act like that we will appear as callous and uncaring people. And yet the rest of the time we agonize because we know that we are letting our twenty-first-century sensibilities get in the way of historical veracity, the way we *would* have acted, no matter how we might feel about such behaviour now.'

A few weeks into the project, Sir John began to feel that the balance was tilting too far one way. 'There is a natural inclination to get to know people and want them to like you, and in the twenty-first century we think that we get the best from people by having them like and respect us, but we know today that this has to be earned. It's not just there as of right. And that would not have been the Edwardian view. As a family, we have stayed at very high quality hotels, but being waited on in hotels is just not the same as being waited on in your own home by your own servants, though I am not quite sure why there is that difference. I know that I am perfectly capable of running an Edwardian country house as it would have been run in 1905, though obviously I have not been brought up to do so. And that is what I am going to do. The staff is becoming over familiar and we are allowing it to happen. We are finding it hard to detach their twenty-first-century status, the people they are, the jobs they do in the modern world, from their status here now as employees with not much status. I have spoken about this at great length to Edgar and we are both agreed that it is essential to re-establish an absolute understanding of the employer/employee relationship as it would have been before the First World War.'

His wife agreed: 'There was a feeling that people were slipping into an easy twenty-first-century familiarity that was just not authentic and could have turned the whole project into a second-rate costume drama rather than a real social experiment in Edwardian living. So yesterday morning I made a list of some of the things that need to be tightened up around the house on the female side. John has spoken to Edgar and I have spoken to Mrs Davies, and as a result things seem to be running much more efficiently. Our meal was on time last night and it was delicious as usual. I realize that we are going be seen as remarkably haughty and really rather unpleasant if we fully adopt Edwardian attitudes in this way. But that's how it has to be.'

Below stairs Mr Edgar had assembled the servants and told them of the new regime: 'Meals on time on the dot, all the china and glass and silver checked in and out by the housekeeper, a smart appearance at all times, no hands in pockets or lolling around, attendance at prayers and at church compulsory unless I give permission otherwise, no time off without my express agreement, and no familiarity,' he warned. 'This is going to be run as an Edwardian house upstairs and down.'

A person who did know how life in this particular country house had been was Mrs Whinney, who had worked at Manderston seventy years ago in the household of Sir James Miller's widow. Mrs Whinney's name was Betty, but when she had gone to work in a house where the mistress was called Lady Betty, the mistress decided that it was not at all proper that a housemaid should have the same name as she did, so in future the housemaid was always known as Elizabeth above stairs, and Betty below. Mrs Whinney was invited to meet the present-day 'servants' and answer their questions about how it had been in *her* day. She had joined the staff when she was fifteen years old; it was her second position and her wages had been £30 a year, paid quarterly as was usual. By the time she was nineteen she was head housemaid, with three girls working under her, and when she left service in her early thirties her wages had risen to £60 a year. But the servants were always trying to find ways to scrimp and save a little: when the family were away and the servants were paid 'board wages' Mrs Whinney had to buy her own sugar, so she decided that she would learn to drink tea without it.

When she saw Charlie and Rob, it had brought back vivid memories of the footmen she had worked with at Manderston: 'They used to wash their own shirts to save money rather than pay the laundry, and one of them asked me to iron his shirts, and when I refused he pushed me into the safe where the silver was kept, and he locked the door and went off to the pictures leaving me there. Luckily the housekeeper, Mrs Hall, a tall, handsome woman, very strict but very nice, met him and asked where I was and he came back and opened the door and I was lying on the floor unconscious. I suppose it was lack of air.'

Mrs Whinney's memories of the butler were not very warm either: 'He was a bit on the amorous side. One day he made an advance to me when I was cleaning a room and I just took my brush and hit him on the face with it and his cheek bled. He pretended to everyone that he'd cut himself shaving. I think that was partly why I left. I didn't feel comfortable there any more, and I couldn't talk to anyone about him, the only way to deal with it was to move on, so I did.'

A superior life. Sir John and Lady Olliff-Cooper discuss their plans for the day.

But despite that, Mrs Whinney told the servants that she would still recommend domestic service as a job for young people: 'I felt I was quite privileged. If I had gone into a factory it would have been very repetitive work, whereas in service you met a lot of new people. We had a nice place to live, we had good food and though there wasn't much time off we made our own fun. The footmen would put tapioca in between the sheets which made it very uncomfortable to sleep, and it was the devil to get rid of it. When I was promoted to be head housemaid, they used to put flour on my pillow, and I didn't see it, and the next morning I'd wake up and all my hair was white. But you got a useful training in service; you learned to do things properly and if you didn't you'd suffer the consequences because you wouldn't get a reference when you applied for another job. It was good discipline.'

But, as Lady Olliff-Cooper recognized, there were bound to be difficulties in trying to reinstate Edwardian discipline. 'There's a lot of bubbling discontent in the house at the moment,' she recorded. 'If you put nineteen modern-day people together in a house and tell half the people that they are superior and in every way more important than the other half, you are bound to have problems. In the twenty-first century we are brought up to think of everyone as being equal. In the Edwardian era people were brought up thinking that their superiors were superior, and that there was an unbridgeable divide, so you are bound to have problems with twenty-first-century people not wishing to go back to a position of servitude – which is entirely understandable.'

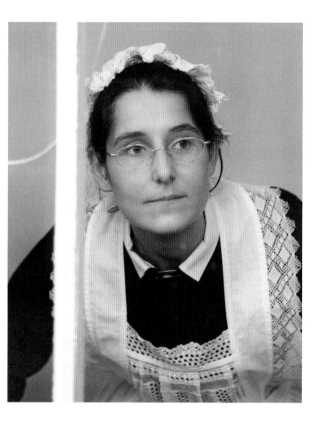

A window on another world. Becky watches guests arrive at the Edwardian Country House.

But the lower servants did not see quite like that. 'I was on my hands and knees one day drying the marble floor in the hall after I had mopped it, and I just felt so Edwardian, because literally not a soul noticed me,' Becky reflected. 'In one room people were playing billiards, and in another Sir John was singing, and another someone was snoring. It was all going on around me. The house was full of guests and people were milling about and it was as if I was invisible, and I thought this is what it was really like to be an Edwardian maid. It was the strangest feeling and yet it was good, because it seemed so authentic. It was what I wanted to experience, to really know what being a maid felt like. I was so tired, my hands were sore, my eyes ached, and my back ached. I had been up and down stairs all day long. I hadn't got to bed until 2 a.m. because there was a ball and we had loads of clearing up to do, and I was up again at 6 a.m., and now there are guests staying in all the rooms. So that's more work.'

The housemaids, the footmen, the hall boy, the groom and the scullery maid felt that they had got Edwardian lock, stock and barrel, whereas upstairs were enjoying Edwardian advantages without signing up for aspects they found distasteful. And matters came to a head over food.

The dinner gong sounded, the family went into the dining room for dinner and Charlie entered carrying a swan carved from ice, a sublime Edwardian centrepiece. 'It was amazing,' marvelled Ellen, who had watched M. Dubiard painstakingly chipping way at a large block of ice, fashioning the curved neck and feathered wings of a bird similar to those that glided on the lake. But hardly had the ooh's and ah's of delight subsided and the lamb broth had been consumed, than the footmen served a dish of curried frog's legs, and then the dining room door opened again and in came the chef himself bearing aloft a roasted pig's head on a platter. He laid it down on the serving table and proceeded to carve slices of the cheek on to plates and ladle on spoonfuls of piquant caper sauce before passing the plates around. As the family politely pushed the meat around their plates, the glazed and mutilated head sat reprovingly on the sideboard.

'It was amazing,' reported Ellen, who heard of the excitement second hand. 'As far as I can see, the family want the luxury and grandeur of the Edwardian experience, but they don't want to eat the food. They hardly ate a mouthful of the pig's head and that was an insult to Monsieur's cooking. I imagine that they are used to buying their food pre-packed from a supermarket, and don't want to know where it comes from. But it wouldn't have been like that in Edwardian times. It's their loss, but its chef's too because he's so disappointed. He puts all that work in to make authentic Edwardian dishes and the family won't eat them.'

Rob agreed: 'I think it would have been valid to send it back if they didn't like pork. It would be fair enough to veto that, but not because you could see it came from the pig. At an Edwardian table a pig's head all garnished like that would have been regarded as a spectacle to impress guests.'

'It did *not* please my husband,' reported Lady Olliff-Cooper. 'We had a discussion with M. Dubiard the next day and we appreciate that he cares strongly about cooking in an authentic Edwardian manner. It's just that we don't want to eat it. He will have to realize that in any period of history, not just the Edwardian, the purpose of the cook is to please the master, not for the master to be discomforted by the cook. We have come to an agreement that M. Dubiard can present us with his more exotic menus, and he started to talk about sea urchin soufflé. Oh dear, I have visions of pig's trotters next week. We are quite willing to try these things, but he must accept that on some occasions, they will come back down again untouched and that he must provide us with an alternative that we can eat. And he must understand that in Edwardian times, or in current times, it isn't *his* role to dictate.'

It was a difficult time for Mr Edgar: as one of the 'top ten' (as the upper servants were misleadingly called) he, along with the housekeeper, Mrs Davies, the lady's maid, Miss

The roasted pig's head that caused all the trouble awaiting decoration before being served.

Morrison, and M. Dubiard himself, often saw things differently from the 'lower five'. As far as the butler was concerned, his loyalty to the family was absolute and he would brook no criticism of them from the other servants. He greatly valued his relationship with Sir John, as did Miss Morrison hers with Lady Olliff-Cooper. These were in no sense perceived as being relationships between equals, but rather of mutual employer/servant respect, and Mr Edgar's waking hours were devoted to the comfort of his master. He did not regard it as his role to question any order but simply to execute it. But on this occasion he felt troubled.

The battle lines had been drawn – at least for the time being. Ellen and Erika, taking a stroll to Duns, had met Lady Olliff-Cooper, who had reproved them for being out in public without hats. 'I know we should have been wearing them,' admitted Ellen, 'but I felt like saying, "We will start wearing our hats when you start eating the food that Monsieur's serving you." But I didn't.'

Ellen had particular reason to be sensitive about her position. The moment she had arrived, the day before the bazaar, Kenny's gloom had lifted. 'She's actually quite stunning,' he thought and within days was able to report: 'I'm getting on with Ellen really well. She is a real cracking bird. She is simple, that is, she doesn't wear make-up or anything. She's an absolute stunner and she's a good laugh and laughs at everything I say.' The other servants began to remark on Kenny's new-found commitment to work, but noticed that he was particularly anxious to help out in the kitchen where Ellen was always to be found. With a couple of weeks the chef reported, 'I have a couple of lovebirds in my kitchen,' and Kenny was exultant. 'I just can't say how happy I am. I am enjoying the whole Edwardian thing more than ever and that's down to a particular female. Everything is going really well and she's fantastic in

Ellen, the scullery maid, refilling plate warmers with oil in the butler's pantry.

every way, she is just amazing, she's funny, she's clever, she's just ace. We went out for a walk through the woods and we ended up at the South Gate and stood looking over the fields to the Cheviot Hills. It was beautiful evening and we ended up snogging. I didn't think that I was going to get through this Edwardian stuff, but now I think I'm going to just breeze through. I am just so happy it's untrue and I'm feeling very, very lucky.'

The hall boy

The thought of being able to walk in the footsteps of a person who lived before my time would be a great adventure,' wrote Kenneth Skelton to Mr Edgar in his letter of application to the Edwardian Country House. 'I would love the opportunity to be a member of your staff and I am offering my services as hall boy.' Eighteen-year-old Kenny is a care worker from Stoke on Trent, looking after people with Alzheimer's, Parkinson's and senile dementia. 'It's hard work and can be stressful. The pay's not much but it's very worthwhile.' He soon found that the authentic Edwardian experience could be tough going too. 'I have *never* worked so hard in all my life,' he groaned. Kenny found the below stairs hierarchy and discipline particularly irksome, and was soon in revolt against the privileged lifestyle it was designed to support. But there were compensations. 'I like maids,' he had ventured before he joined the project, and soon there was one in particular…

But the course of true love, Edwardian style, was not a smooth one. It was hard for Ellen and Kenny: 'We haven't really had much of a chance to get to know one another, we don't have any time on our own. We must get on average about half an hour a day when it's just me and Ellen and nobody else. Everybody is always around and Mr Edgar walks in and you can't even sit with your arms around each other.' It wasn't just the jobs they had to do, their long working hours and the fact that their free time hardly ever seemed to coincide that made life difficult for the young couple. It was also that romance below stairs was frowned on, and if discovered usually led to dismissal. Mr Edgar, who was by no means unsympathetic, called Kenny into his office to warn him to make sure that the romance did not interfere with his work, and to remind him that it was essential that he and Ellen were discreet. 'If the mistress gets to hear of it, it'll be Ellen that has to go,' the butler warned.

It was not easy to see how servants would ever marry since so many obstacles were put in the way of the usual progress of courtship. 'Followers' were not permitted, partly because they were a distraction from work and daily routine and partly because they were considered likely to be 'undesirable', careless or even light-fingered with property. The only men that the women servants were likely to meet were their fellow servants, tradesmen who came to the kitchen door or the servants who came to the house with guests and were billeted below stairs for the duration of the visit. The limited time off did not help either and the most a maid might hope for was a wander through country lanes with a suitor during her half day off. In more benevolent families, a female servant might be allowed to invite a young man to tea in the servants' hall, but this was an unusual dispensation from the mistress of the house. As Margaret Powell, herself a housemaid, recalled:

The business of getting a young man was not respectable and one's employers tended to degrade every relationship. It seemed to me one was expected to find husbands under a gooseberry bush. *Their* daughters were debs, and they could meet young men at balls, dances and private parties, but if any of the servants had boyfriends they were known as 'followers'…a degrading term… You had to slink up the area steps and meet on the corner of the road on some pretext like going to post a letter. And on your night out when you came back you couldn't…bring him in to say goodnight to him…he wasn't a young man, he was a 'follower'. They made you feel there was something intrinsically bad in having a member of the opposite sex interested in you at all.[9]

Getting acquainted: Kenny interrupts his firewood chopping to talk to Ellen.

Obviously, not all servant romances became public knowledge – some were kept quiet by an understanding butler or housekeeper, and sometimes employers could show generosity, allowing the couple to marry and remain in their employ, maybe even giving them a cottage on the estate. But as with most Edwardian sexual mores, it was the female servant who suffered. A maid who got pregnant was invariably summarily dismissed, sent packing at once without a reference, to face a grim future. 'I insisted on her [a pregnant kitchen maid] leaving the house at once,' reported an Edwardian country house owner, Henry Polderoy. 'One cannot be too careful or too quick in these matters: a man of my standing must avoid the very shadow of a slur on his reputation or judgement. Although the girl declared that she would be unable to reach her mother's home…on the same day, I would not allow her to remain…It would never do to encourage vice by making things comfortable and easy for the sinner.'[10] And when Sir James Miller's brother-in-law, the urbane and worldly Lord Curzon, discovered that one of his housemaids had allowed a footman to spend the night with her, 'I put the little slut out into the street at a moment's notice,' he wrote to his wife.

Unless she was able to return to her family, which rural poverty made impossible in many cases, the girl's options were extremely limited. At the end of the nineteenth century, the figures told a sad story. In 1900, 60 per cent of all unmarried women applying to have their children admitted to London Foundling hospitals had been in domestic service, and of those 35 per cent were drawn from 'the higher ranks of service'.[11] And it was believed that a large proportion of the prostitutes in London had 'chosen' life on the streets in preference to the only other alternative for the unemployed – and unemployable – domestic servant, the workhouse. Small wonder that any servant who found herself 'in the family way' would resort to desperate measures such as swallowing quinine, penny royal or handfuls of Beecham's pills, taking scalding mustard baths, volunteering to move heavy furniture or clamber up precarious ladders, or throwing herself off tables and down stairs in order to abort her unborn child. The father of the child may well have been another servant or tradesmen, but it was also possible that it could have been the 'young master' – or even the older master – who regarded a comely female servant as his property in sex as in other forms of service. A sexually predatory employer could make a servant's life insupportable since she was likely to be disbelieved and dismissed if she reported him, and she would be sacked if she became pregnant. A pornographic eleven-volume memoir, *My Secret Life*, published in Amsterdam in the decade before Edward VII came to the throne, reveals the extent to which the author considered the servants in his mother's house to be there for his priapic delectation, referring to them as if they were blood stock: 'clean, well fed, full-blooded', 'has not been used, ridden or raced for a week, and is ready for service'. In the now famous case of Arthur J. Munby, a barrister and civil servant, it was revealed when he died in 1910 that he had been secretly married to a parlour maid, Hannah Cullwick, for nearly forty years. Despite the fact that she was his wife, Hannah continued to act as her husband's servant, waiting at table, scrubbing the floors, valeting his wardrobe and addressing him as 'sir' in company, while he delighted in taking photographs of her in this subservient, grimy role.[12] He wrote a poem that expressed his feelings:

> *Her strong, bare, sinewy arms and rugged hands*
> *Blacken'd with labour, and her peasant dress*
> *Rude, coarse in texture, yet most picturesque,*
> *And suited to her station and her ways;*
> *All these, transfigured by that sentiment*
> *Of lowly contrast to the man she served;*
> *Grew dignified with beauty and herself*
> *A noble working woman, not ashamed*
> *Of what her work had made her.*[13]

Standing in for Charlie at lunch one day, Kenny could not help overhearing the conversation at table. 'If you weren't particularly enamoured of your husband you could always seek diversions,' Lady Olliff-Cooper suggested. 'And vice versa,' chipped in a male guest eagerly. 'And that was basically all right because most of these were arranged marriages to an extent,' her ladyship continued doubtfully. 'But of course servants weren't allowed to have relationships with other servants. A footman could not have had a relationship with a maid. Or if they did I imagine they would both have to leave and get married.' 'No,' contradicted Master Guy, 'if they did and the master of the house found out, they'd be chucked out,' he concluded with relish.

It increased Kenny's resentment of his masters and the double standards he felt operated above and below stairs: 'The family came into this project from a wealthy background already – the only difference for them is that they are a bit more pampered with a period twist. Whereas the people downstairs have come from comfortable backgrounds into something which is absolutely disgusting. They have one bath a week, they have horrible food and the Edwardian experience is infinitely more profound for the servants than it is for the family upstairs. I don't see how anyone can make a comparison between our struggle and their struggle because it's just not the same. The ladies upstairs moan about having to wear a corset, but the girls downstairs have to clean fires and mop floors and bend over and scrub out baths in theirs, so how those upstairs can moan about having to sit and eat tea in their corsets is absolutely beyond me. I don't think they have the slightest comprehension of how we live downstairs.'

One night, when the Sir John and Lady Olliff-Cooper had gone to the opera and had taken Mr Edgar, Mr Raj Singh and Miss Morrison as their guests, the young downstairs servants decided to sample life upstairs. Creeping up the backstairs, the uninvited guests burst into the marble hall and hurried from room to room, sampling the delights of gracious living. The lower servants took turns at the billiard table, 'that essential plaything for every Edwardian gentleman', situated in what was originally the library at Manderston until, after Sir James's death in 1906, his widow had been persuaded by her brothers to move in the games table. Schooled in pub pool, the servants potted shots across the seeming acres of green baize – 'the slate bed of a full-sized billiard table measures 12ft by 6ft ½in, and as an allowance of 2in in width must be made for the projection of the cushions, the *playable* bed of a table is 11ft 8in in length and 5ft 9 ½in in width, and consequently is practically double as long as it is wide', explained the chapter 'Games of Skill' in the 1904 edition of *Cassell's Book of Sports and Pastimes*. While declining to get into a discussion about the origin or longevity of the game, the book insisted that 'recent improvements…have so changed its character that, practically speaking, it may be considered a game of modern date'.[14]

They lounged guiltily in the comfortable morning room sofas, while Rob picked out a tune on the piano. The servants peered into the card room before flinging open the double doors to the ballroom and sliding across the highly polished floor as if it were an ice rink, glistening under the crystal chandeliers. 'It was really weird,' said Antonia, for it was a rare chance for her to see how the family she served lived, as it was for Ellen – the kitchen staff neither needed to go nor were invited above stairs other than for daily prayers. 'It was like a dream, or a scene from a novel. It was really, really magic.' They tiptoed up the famous silver staircase and then stood outside Lady Olliff-Cooper's bedroom, before realizing how late it was getting and how far they had strayed beyond their boundaries. The world turned briefly upside-down, the 'lower five' hurried back to the servants' quarters and their narrow iron beds, thin strips of carpet on the floor of their attic or basement rooms, their tin baths and dawn start the next morning.

The upstairs/downstairs divide in the Edwardian Country House found its image in national politics. In 1906, after 'the most exciting general election for years', magic lanterns supplied by Lord Northcliffe's new popular *Daily Mail* projected the results on to massive screens in London's Trafalgar Square and on the Embankment: it was a landslide victory for the Liberals. The Conservative and Unionists had been reduced from 400 to 157 members while the Liberals won 400 seats, including 24 Lib-Labs; there were 83 Irish nationalists and 30 Labour members were returned.[15] With an unshakeable majority and broad, geographically based support, the victorious new government saw itself as poised to 'sweep away the last relics of feudalism' in the name of the politics of 'the People'. In 1908, H. H. Asquith, 'the first non-landed Prime Minister in the nation's history',[16] succeeded Campbell-Bannerman as Prime Minister and appointed the Welsh solicitor turned politician David Lloyd George as Chancellor of the Exchequer.

Lloyd George was a 'political genius who cast spells rather than won debates';[17] his exuberant and exhilarating rhetoric could 'kindle an audience into flame' and the object of his invective and exhortation were the '[upper] classes' as opposed to the 'masses'. His intention was to 'rob the hen roost' of the wealthy to 'raise money to wage implacable warfare against poverty and squalidness'. In 1906

Campbell-Bannerman had promised that Britain would become 'less of a pleasure ground for the rich and more of a treasure house for the nation': in other words, the glaring inequality between rich and poor, which was the subject of so much contemporary comment, was to begin to be redressed. The Old Age Pensions Act of 1908 introduced non-contributory pensions 'as of right' (though it was means tested) by which everyone over seventy years of age was entitled to an income of five shillings a week (at a time when less than half the population lived beyond sixty-five).[18] In the words of the Fabian socialist, Beatrice Webb, it guaranteed 'an enforced minimum of civilized life' for the very old.

In 1911, Lloyd George introduced his proposals for a contributory insurance scheme by which 'the employer and the State should enter into a partnership with the working man in order as far as possible to mitigate the burden [of unemployment and sickness] that falls upon him'. The provisions of the bill covered manual workers, including domestic servants. In the case of female servants this required a contribution of 3d a week from the master or mistress, who was also obliged to collect the servant's contribution which was an equal amount, purchase a National Insurance stamp and stick on the card. In some households this was regarded as an intolerable interference by the state into domestic life. Pamela Horn tells how petitions and demonstrations were organized in opposition to the bill which, in the words of the *Daily Mail* – which was in the forefront of orchestrating the campaign against this 'obnoxious legislation'[19] – 'creates a new tax of 26/- a year for every servant [and] will destroy happy domestic relations in hundreds and thousands of homes'.[20] Despite the protests, the scheme came into force in July 1912. Every insured female worker was entitled to medical care by a doctor, free treatment in a sanatorium or other institution 'when suffering from tuberculosis', weekly sickness benefit of 7s 6d a week for twenty-six weeks and a disablement benefit of 5 shillings thereafter should she still be unable to work. The provisions were the same for male servants, but the contributions were a penny more and the sickness benefit was 10 shillings.[21]

It is hard to see why numbers of servants also petitioned against the introduction of this Act. It may speak of employer intimidation, or a pragmatic wish on the part of the servant not to displease the master and mistress in whose house he or she lived; it may suggest that such servants were confident of their treatment in sickness as in health; or it may indicate that the model of paternal (or maternal) benevolence that characterized the Edwardian household was deeply embedded in servant as in employer consciousness.

At the same time as they were introducing sweeping social welfare reforms, the Liberals were, with some considerable reluctance, entering into an

Potting the black. Mr Jonathan concentrates on a game of billiards.

Epsom racecourse: The Derby was the greatest national carnival of the Edwardian year - the House of Commons went into recess for the day, and the King only missed the occasion if the Court was in mourning.

escalating naval arms race with Germany. The government finally committed itself to building eighteen new Dreadnought battleships. This costly imperative posed a stark choice: either cut spending on social welfare, or raise taxation. Lloyd George was in no doubt which it should be. He had plans to open Labour Exchanges for the unemployed; the growth in cars necessitated an ambitious road-building and improvement programme; and child allowances were to be introduced. In his so-called 'People's Budget' of 1909 the Chancellor raised duties on spirits and tobacco, the top rate of death duties was increased to 15 per cent, income tax rose from 1 shilling to 1s 2d, and a super tax of sixpence in the pound on incomes over £5,000 was introduced for the first time. Most startling was the direct blow at the landed classes: a capital gains tax on land. Whenever an estate changed hands due to inheritance or sale, a 20 per cent tax was to be levied on the unearned increment (an increase not due to development or investment) of the land's value. And a 10 per cent tax was to be charged on any increase in land value when a lease was transferred or renewed, plus an annual 10 per cent tax on undeveloped land.

In fact, these taxes were not particularly successful revenue-raising initiatives since the value of land was not rising significantly, nor had it been since the 1880s, and the duties were repealed in 1920, but they were symbolic of Lloyd George's assault on the landed classes – and those who had acquired land. And the landed classes and their representatives fought back. Though the budget was passed in the Commons on 4 November 1909 by 379 votes to 149, when the bill came to the Lords, it was thrown out. Lloyd George picked up the gauntlet with alacrity. 'Savage strife between class and class' predicted the young politician Winston Churchill, who was President of the Board of Trade in the Liberal administration. Lloyd George toured the country, denouncing the peers as 'five hundred men chosen accidentally from among the unemployed' pitted against 'millions of people who are engaged in the industry which makes the wealth of the country'. Edward VII was appalled at what he regarded as dangerous rhetoric

215

'calculated to set class against class, and to inflame the passions of the working and lower orders', and, from the other side of the divide, the Labour politician, Ramsay MacDonald, concurred. 'Never before have the rich as a class ranged themselves so completely on one side as they have done this time. Loafing and industry were never so well divided.'[22]

Up and down the country stormed the fiery Welsh orator, denouncing the rich as parasitical and past their sell-by date for the modern world. Home after a day's shooting, Sir John read an account of Lloyd George's speech made to a gathering of 4,000 at Limehouse in East London on 19 July 1909 in that day's copy of *The Times*. The Chancellor had begun by reminding his audience how, in the face of growing Anglo-German antagonism, the City of London had urged the government to commit itself to an expensive rearmament programme and promised financial support for such an enterprise. 'But when we sent in the bill…these gentleman say, "Perfectly true; somebody has got to pay, but we would rather that somebody was somebody else [laughter and cheers]…but…it is not so much the Dreadnoughts that we object to, it is the pensions".' He continued in the same vein, naming and shaming rich landlords whose wealth was unproductive, yet who were extorting money from their tenants in ways that made his proposed taxes to finance the welfare programme seem modest: 'Oh those dukes [loud laughter], how they harass us! [more laughter]' At the end of Lloyd George's long speech 'the audience rose and sang "For he's a jolly good fellow".'[23]

In his simulacrum of Edwardian life from the position of a plutocrat whose talent for making money had allowed him to assume the style, if not the responsibilities, of the landed classes, Sir John was not in the front line of Lloyd George's sitting duck targets. These were the 'Tory backwoodsmen', peers who had thrown out the 'people's budget' and were now resisting to the last ditch the government's efforts to reform the Lords and to diminish their political power in the land. But there were straws in the wind. The hike in death duties was unlikely to end there,

Tips

The following remarks apply to guests who are in the same set as the host who is supposed to be a man of the wealthy upper classes. The butler will expect a sovereign for a few days' visit…a woman week-end guest will give five shillings to the maid who looks after her room, half a crown to the footman…who carries down her luggage, and a similar amount to the coach driver who takes her to the station…for longer visits the tips would be in proportion to the length. A girl is not expected to give such liberal tips as her married friends. Married couples pay their tips separately, the man gives something to the butler, his wife to the parlour maid and housemaid, sometimes to the housekeeper if she had availed herself of her services in any way. Should a man-servant have valeted the husband, the latter should give him a tip. At the conclusion of a ten-days' visit to a house where there has been no shooting [which would have upped the bill considerably] the money spent on tips sometimes amounts to five pounds [around £300 in today's terms].

Everywoman's Encyclopaedia (1910)

Mr Edgar kept a careful account of all tips he was handed for his staff at the Edwardian Country House, and handed them out accordingly.

and would inhibit a rich man's ability to pass on intact to his heirs what he regarded as their rightful inheritance. Taxation was rising and now that the principle of a super tax had been introduced, how much longer would fabulous riches be permitted to fructify in the vaults of Lombard Street, or, more likely, be lavished on an excess of 'fevered [Edwardian] luxury'?

It was deuced worrying, and the 'servant problem' wasn't getting any easier. In 1911, the year that the Parliament Act limiting the power of the Lords over the Commons to one of delay rather than outright veto was finally forced through, it was a particularly glorious summer, when day after day the sun shone from a cloudless sky, caressing the lawns of the great country houses where the soft thud of tennis balls and the thwack of croquet mallets passed the long days; where ladies, in elegant, wafting tea gowns and large picture hats conversed softly as they took tea under shady trees; where men discussed the generally buoyant nature of the stock market and the excellent prospects for grouse.

The year 1911 epitomizes a view of the Edwardian era as a 'long golden garden party' – but it is misleading, and it was changing. Under those spreading trees on stifling afternoons ladies might be reading a novel by one of those Victorian 'queens of the circulating library' who were still so popular in Edwardian times: Mary Braddon, Mrs Henry Wood, Marie Correlli or Ouid, or reading aloud Beatrix Potter's *Peter Rabbit* or Rudyard Kipling's *Puck of Pook's Hill* to a child sprawled at their feet. But it was during this era that the unsettling writings of Ezra Pound, Virginia Woolf, James Joyce and D. H. Lawrence were first published. It was, as Samuel Hynes has written, both a Garden Party World and a Labour Party World.[24] Beyond the nation's gently rolling lawns, the international situation was unstable and unsure, and British isolation in Europe no longer seemed such a glorious option; women (at least some) were demanding the vote, while Ireland, far from being pacified, was making increasingly insistent demands for Home Rule.

In 1901 the social reformer Seebohm Rowntree had estimated that a third of the urban population fell below the line of subsistence and that a working man with three children was likely to spend ten years unable to feed and clothe his family adequately.[25] There is debate among economic historians about the relative rise or downturn in the economy between 1901 and 1914, but it seems clear that economists and politicians at the time regarded conditions as stagnant or worse, and that working people felt that their wages were not keeping pace with rises in the cost of living.[26] But now the working man was directly represented in Parliament and his needs were being forced onto the political agenda; trade union membership had more than doubled from 1.97 million in 1905 to 4.15 million in 1913.[27] The number of men in domestic service had been declining for decades and increasingly women were waiting at table and appropriating other previously male functions, particularly in middle-class households.

As she hurried purposefully round the guest bedrooms changing the sheets and towels one day, Becky, who had been reflecting for some time on what 'being Edwardian' really meant was suddenly hit by an obvious fact. 'The family make a big thing about how we are dependent on them for our livelihood. How we wouldn't have a roof over our head, or food in our stomachs without them, and I've realized it is actually the complete opposite. The truth is they wouldn't be able to manage without us. They need us to run the house, put food on the table, even dress them. They think that they are the powerful ones, but really it's they who need us. Maybe at some level they know that and that's why they have be so dominant and so officious because they are worried deep down that we might realize that we have rights too and might rebel against them. There many more us downstairs than there are of the family upstairs. If all of us servants find a single voice, then the family are going to be in deep trouble because there is actually nothing they can do in that situation…'

CHAPTER TEN

The Fast Set

'Death of the King' proclaimed a black-bordered *Daily Mirror* on 7 May 1910. Edward VII had 'breathed his last' at 11.45 p.m. the previous night in the presence of Her Majesty Queen Alexandra, and their children: the Prince and Princess of Wales, the Princess Royal (the Duchess of Fife), Princess Victoria and Princess Louise (Duchess of Argyll) – all except their daughter Maud, Queen of Norway, who was on her way. 'The Whole World Sorrowing…the nation plunged into mourning…the period of Court mourning will last at least six months,' reported the paper.

Sir John summoned the family and servants to announce the news, and Rob and Charlie removed Edward VII's portrait from the walls of the Edwardian Country House, and reflected on what the news might have meant to them in the early summer of 1910.

The King's body lay in state in Westminster Hall for three days as 250,000 of his subjects filed silently past. Eight kings and an emperor attended the funeral at Windsor, which was held on 20 May. Edward's terrier dog, Caesar, trotted behind the coffin, much to the irritation of the German Kaiser, who was disinclined to yield precedence to a small, rather scruffy, dog.

When Queen Victoria died, commentators had proclaimed the end of an era. 'It will mean great changes in the world,' predicted Lady Battersea, a member of the Rothschild banking family. 'Black garments, crape, black bows on whips – all black!…Black, mourning London, black, mourning England, black, mourning Empire – those facts are text and sermon. The emptiness of the great city without the feeling of the Queen's living presence in her Empire, and the sensation of universal change haunted me.'[1] It seemed significant that Edward should come to the throne at the very dawn of the twentieth century, and court and country waited in anticipation for the metaphorical heavy chenille drapes of Victoria's reign to be flung wide open, for a relaxation in manners and moral codes, a less fussy etiquette and a less rigidly hierarchical society. They were not to be entirely disappointed.

Edward both granted licence to his eponymous era and was perfectly in tune with it. He was a monarch for the plutocracy, surrounding himself with men of money (which he frequently needed) who were invariably from a background in trade or finance and several of whom were Jewish. In the words of George Dangerfield's elegant book *The Strange Death of Liberal England*, 'He represented in a concentrated shape those bourgeois kings whose florid forms and rather dubious escapades were all the industrial world had left of an ancient divinity.'[2] The King practised conspicuous consumption to a fine art at home and abroad (where he particularly favoured the casinos of Biarritz and Monte Carlo). He was 'the first English sovereign of whom it could be fairly said that he knew the world [which was more than could be said for most of his ministers]. King Edward had met the Americans in America, the Indians in India [unlike his mother who as Empress of India had never visited the subcontinent]'; he had travelled in Spain, Italy and Russia; he was at home in Denmark [which was the homeland of his wife] and Germany; he especially enjoyed Austria and he loved Paris and the French'.[3] As Prince of Wales, he had been pro-French and wary of German intentions, and as King liked to see himself as having been instrumental in forging the *entente cordiale* between England and France in 1904.

The king who gave his name and set the style of era that was to linger on for another four years after his death had had a long period of apprenticeship for his brief nine-year tenure of the throne. He was fifty-nine when his mother, Queen Victoria, died on 22 January 1901, the longest reigning monarch in British history. It had been a mortifying time waiting in the wings (perhaps not unlike the situation with the present royal family). The imperious mother had infantilized the wayward son, keeping him at arm's distance from the affairs of state for decades and failing to appreciate the qualities he *did* have of diplomacy, personality, and a modernizing view of his role – whether in revitalizing the dreary mausoleum that Buckingham Palace had become (which he had christened 'the Sepulchre' when he moved there as King), riding round London incognito in 'common' hansom cabs, clamping down on the excessive drinking of the household at Balmoral, or recognizing Britain's place in Europe.

As Prince of Wales, Bertie, as he was known within the family, had the reputation as a playboy, a *bon viveur*, a gambler and something of a *roué*. He was a prince in the most acute contrast to his late father, Victoria's 'beloved Albert', who had been a model of middle-class moral probity, constitutional application and the very personification of the Puritan ethic. His mother used to sigh, 'What will became of the poor country when I die? If Bertie succeeds he would…spend his life in one whirl of amusements.'

'A strong Conservative, and a still stronger Jingo', in the words of the radical Charles Dilke, the King was convinced that the Liberal government's proposed social reforms would destabilize society. Yet he expressed concern for the poverty in which so many of his citizens lived, and, having sat on a Royal Commission concerned with the housing of the working classes, showed sympathy for their

The Coronation of Edward VII, 9th August, 1902. The King's appendicitis had delayed the ceremony by seven weeks and most foreign dignitaries had returned home, but the London crowds were enthusiastic.

Sketch of Sir James Miller's horse, Sainfoin, which he had only bought two days previously,
winning the 1890 Derby 'by three parts of a length'.

'perfectly disgraceful' conditions (though he was forced to concede in a speech to the Lords in 1884 that the conditions in which his own tenants lived were equally disgraceful).

Edward could be boisterous in male company. He had purchased Sandringham in Norfolk out of his own rents, and relished its rural environs and opportunities for sport. He enjoyed a bachelor lifestyle long after he had ceased to be one, and most nights could be found at the theatre, opera or music hall before going on to dinner. Yet he was a fond father, indulgent grandfather, and was courteous, and generally considerate to servants, though he could fly into rages if all was not to his liking. His superstitious nature, which grew more pronounced as he grew older, caused problems for his staff and those of the houses he visited. The King slept with his bed festooned with good luck charms and tokens, while his servants were forbidden to turn his mattress on a Friday and he was discombobulated at the sight of crossed knives at table. He refused to dine with thirteen at table, and one of his biographers, Christopher Hibbert, tells of a visit abroad when this had happened three nights running. When the King computed the numbers, his sense of foreboding was assuaged only when he realized that one of the guests was pregnant so those at table could be counted as fourteen.[4]

But though Edward was a monarch resolutely disposed to the pursuit of pleasure, he was not, in the practice of his trade of kingship, either dissolute or irresponsible. He was, in Dangerfield's words, 'a good king after his fashion…he combined duty with indulgence…he was never tyrannical, he was never loud or ill-mannered; he was just comfortably disreputable. How right, it seemed, under his kindly dispensation, that humanity's fondest sins should be drummed from church and chapel only to find refuge in the Throne!'[5] But Edward could be rigid in his observance of status and the correct behaviour that paid tribute to it. He was meticulous and demanding in his strict observation of dress codes. Delighting in pageantry, he took every excuse to dress up in full military regalia, and was happy to 'receive princes and ambassadors and open museums and hospitals, and attend cattle shows and military shows and shows of every kind'.[6] He was pernickety and vocal in his criticism of small errors in the dress of others, chiding the Duchess of Marlborough for wearing a semi-crescent of diamonds in her hair rather than a full-blown tiara at dinner, upbraiding England's premier duke for wearing an order pinned on upside-down, and reproving his Prime Minister, Lord Rosebery, for turning up at a function wearing plain trousers rather than silk stockings, charging that he was dressed like an American ambassador.

The King was also regal in the announcements of his progress to various country houses, when an impending visit flung the host establishment in a state of near panic. Nancy Astor (the wife of the American millionaire, Waldorf Astor), who in 1919 was to be the first woman to take her seat in the House of Commons, recalled a visit of the King to their fabulous Thames-side mansion, Cliveden, in July 1908: 'On Sunday a.m. Lady Desborough telephoned Waldorf that the King wished to come over so he came followed by 16 courtiers for tea and stopped 2 hours & went over the house and garden and seemed v. pleased with it all…The nephews and nieces were furious at his coming as it broke up their tennis. He was v. pleasant and thought Cliveden the prettiest place in England…only I do think it slightly strong bringing 16 people, it made us 40 for tea.'[7] The Countess of Warwick, whose Essex home was central to the circuit, recounted: 'I could tell stories of men and women who had to economize for a whole year, or alternatively get into debt that they might entertain royalty for one weekend.'[8] The King would expect to feast to excess, drink his favourite tipple, champagne, smoke a large number of the highest quality cigars, shoot prolific numbers of game, gamble heavily late into the night and have his latest mistress accommodated in royal style. It could also be exhausting: the King was a martinet in matters of royal etiquette and ruled that no lady could retire before the Queen and no gentleman could take to his bed before the King chose to take to his. This could be a taxing regulation for fellow guests and the unfortunate man in whose house the monarch was being entertained.

Edward was not a handsome man: he had the long Coburg nose of his father (someone kindly said his was a profile particularly well-suited to depiction on coins of the realm), a somewhat receding chin which was disguised under a sharply trimmed beard, heavy-lidded, protuberant eyes, and he was stocky running to corpulent when he came to the throne (his friends' nickname – never used to his face – was 'Tum-tum'). He was, however, a very natty dresser and soon became a sartorial role model for tailors all over Europe, and the demands of his own wardrobe made his tailor-in-chief a rich man. The King always travelled with two valets, leaving several more at home to keep his wardrobe – which included over a hundred pieces of headgear and a designated room for all his uniforms and regalia – spruce.

If not blessed with dashing good looks, his ample form and somewhat sensuous visage gave Edward a certain physical presence that combined well with the seductive attraction of power and rank. As Prince of Wales, he had been involved in a number of scandals involving women and gambling.

On 10 March 1863, Edward married a Danish princess, Alexandra, when he was twenty-one and she was eighteen. The Queen was still in deep mourning for Albert and the wedding was a low-key affair held at St George's Chapel, Windsor.

Alix (as she was known) was reputed to be the most beautiful princess in Europe – certainly the most beautiful <u>Protestant</u> princess, which was a requirement – and her looks and elegance lasted into her old age. She was exceptionally kind-natured, increasingly deaf, not at all clever or witty, violently anti-German, unremittingly unpunctual, and unswervingly devoted to her husband. The Prince was granted a civil list income of £100,000 a year by parliament and the couple moved to Marlborough House in London. Here, Edward was seriously underemployed, his mother consistently refusing to let him get anywhere near the reins of royal power, denying him his wish for an army career, and vetoing any suggestions that he might fill an ambassadorial post. So the Waleses' life fell into the grooves of the smart set routine that it was to follow for decades: yacht racing at Cowes in August; in September the Prince went abroad, usually to one of the fashionable German or Austrian spa resorts; in October he would be deer-stalking in Scotland, and from November until early spring would be based at Sandringham hosting shoots and doing the round of other people's country house sporting parties. In May he would be in London for three months for the season, having spent a month or so on the Riviera in early spring. And then the restless carousel started up again, interspersed by visits to Paris and race meetings at Goodwood and Ascot, the Derby and the Grand National, none of which the Prince was inclined to miss.

Alix, meanwhile, spent rather a lot of her early married life pregnant (the couple were to have five children) and at home with the children she so enjoyed. She swallowed her pride over her husband's deviations from the path of marital fidelity, providing she was not humiliated by them in public (as she felt she was over his long affair with Daisy Brooke – later the Countess of Warwick – in the 1890s), recognized that she could not expect him to be at home from *cinq à sept* (the traditional hours for paying calls), and that he might absent himself from functions and not return home until the small hours. As he grew older the King 'settled down' with a series of sequential 'official' mistresses, who at least did relieve his constant tendency to boredom and assuaged his unpredictable flashes of irritability.

The first was the daughter of the Dean of Jersey, Emily (Lillie) Le Breton, who had married a not terribly satisfactory and not terribly wealthy widower, Edward Langtry. Lillie was heart-stoppingly beautiful and soon *tout Londres* knew it when she was painted first by the artist Frank Miles, and then by John Everett Millais who thought that she was 'quite simply the most beautiful woman on earth' and captured her on canvas holding a species of amaryllis that gave her the epithet 'Jersey Lily'. Edward Burne Jones, Edward Poynter and Whistler painted her too. Photography was a relatively

A record from the Manderston album of a house party held there, signed by the hostess, Eveline Miller, and her guests.

A leisurely afternoon on the lake: Mr Jonathan rows his aunt and Miss Morrison.

new art, and when likenesses of Mrs Langtry as a 'professional beauty' were printed, they sold like wildfire and the instant celebrity found herself invited to the smartest houses. Oscar Wilde fell in love with her too – in his fashion – admiring her less for her beauty than for her 'charm, her wit, her mind', and was fascinated to meet the *maîtresse en titre* of the Prince of Wales. For on 24 May 1877 Lillie Langtry had met the Prince, who was then thirty-five, at a supper party in London. He was enchanted by her and asked if he might call on her the next afternoon. According to Theo Aronson, this was the accepted courtship by a married man of a married woman since her husband was likely to be out at that time, and, as was the fashion, she would be wearing a tea gown to receive visitors.[9] Tea gowns, as Lady Olliff-Cooper found, were a delight: they were diaphanous, floaty creations, underneath which a lady did not wear a corset. This was not a signal of sexual availability like going naked under a fur coat: women as ultra respectable as the Duchess of York (later Queen Mary) wore a tea gown, as did hundreds of other society ladies, for such apparel represented leisure and tranquillity. It also made illicit sexual congress much easier and quicker with less fumbling.

The Prince's affair was pursued through afternoon calls and country house weekends, and it soon became apparent to hostesses that should the Prince of Wales be invited to dinner or a ball, he would be much more likely to attend if Mrs Langtry was invited too. He showered her with jewels and furs; he arranged for her to be presented at court (which unlocked more social gates including balls at Buckingham Palace), and Princess Alexandra invited her to Marlborough House and Sandringham, and treated her husband's mistress with dignified courtesy and kindness.

The enterprising Mrs Langtry eventually became a successful actress, and though the affair with the Prince of Wales cooled, he remained fond of her, seeing her often and always making a point of attending the first night of her performances, but in 1890 he fell in love again. This time it was with the spirited woman who is best known as the Countess of Warwick. Frances Maynard (always known as Daisy) was an aristocrat, another legendary beauty 'who drew crowds to watch her take her morning ride in Rotten Row or her afternoon drive in the Park',[10] and also a wealthy woman in her own right when she married Francis Brooke, heir to the 4th Earl of Warwick in 1881 at 'the most brilliant wedding of a dozen seasons'. But it was a fairly semi-detached marriage. 'From the beginning of our life together,' Daisy wrote, 'my husband seemed to accept the inevitability of my having a train of admirers. I could not help it. There they were. It was all a great game.'[11] And in any case 'good old Brookie' found 'a good day's fishing or shooting second in point of pleasure to nothing on earth'[12] which made him perhaps rather dull for a woman.

Sporting Edwardians from the Manderston photograph album: two country house guests eager for a game of tennis…

The Brookes were on the fringes of the Marlborough House 'set' and occasional visitors to Sandringham, and Daisy was already adept at 'Saturday to Monday' house party behaviour. Country house parties were the fulcrum of Edwardian smart society. They were an opportunity to meet friends at leisure, to discuss politics and business, to dine well and take part in sporting activities. And it was the perfect opportunity for people who were married to other people to pursue an illicit affair.

In the Edwardian period it would not have been acceptable to pursue such romances by dining in restaurants or staying at hotels and, though such affairs were usually common knowledge among the country house set (and reputedly condoned by the 'injured party'), they were subject to social conventions. Divorce was not an attractive option: it ruined a woman's reputation, deprived of her place in society, usually her home and her means of support and often her children. Divorce proceedings were expensive and thus confined to the well-off, and until 1923, though a husband could divorce his wife for adultery, this was not considered sufficient grounds for a woman to divorce her husband: she had to prove adultery aggravated by desertion, cruelty, incest, rape, sodomy or bestiality before she could divorce. In 1913 there were only 577 divorces in England and Wales (though the total was higher if Scotland was included since divorce was easier and much cheaper under the Scottish legal system) and marriage, at least in the contractual sense, was for life for almost everyone.

Hostesses of country house weekends thus needed to make sure that they were *au courant* with current romantic attachments when they allocated bedrooms. Each door had a small brass holder attached, and names were written on cards and slipped into these with due concern given to the sexual traffic flow. The hostess would ensure that the royal suite of rooms was sufficiently close to that of Edward's current *inamorata* (his wife often did not accompany him to country house parties, centred as they were around shooting). There were all sorts of conventions to lubricate such nocturnal trysts,

…and 'Well played, Sir': spectators at a cricket match.

assignations whispered over the lighted candlesticks that guided guests to their room, notes passed by the suitor's valet to be slipped on to the lady's tray by her maid, a sign left outside a room to indicate that a midnight call would be welcome – a flower was the most usual since sandwiches could be scoffed by a passing hungry guest who had mistaken their semiotic purpose, and this could result in a disappointing night for both parties. In most houses a bell would be rung at 6 a.m. to give the straying time to get back into their own beds before maids brought up the tea tray, and many were the hilarious stories of bed-hopping misadventures, including that of Lord Charles Beresford who had tiptoed into what he thought was a willing conquest's room and leapt on her bed shouting a predatory 'cock-a-doodle do', only to find that he had landed in bed with the startled Bishop of Chester.

Lord Charles, a close friend whose brother managed the Prince of Wales's stud, soon became the lover of Daisy Brooke and when that relationship came to an end in acrimonious circumstances (among other things, Lord Charles had made *his own wife* pregnant) Daisy turned to Edward for help and they in turn became lovers. It was a passionate affair: he called her 'his darling Daisy wife' and felt he could discuss anything with her for she had a quick mind and firm opinions, and was an excellent huntswoman. Soon the couple were inseparable in public as in private. They were seen together at the races, at Cowes, at the opera, in private rooms in discreet restaurants such as Rules in Maiden Lane, the Café Royal or Kettners, posing for group photographs on the terrace at innumerable country house parties, in Paris where he shopped with her at the couturiers as she was fitted with spectacular dresses, 'violet velvet', 'gauzy white gowns', 'purple grape-trimmed robes and veils of pearls on white'.[13] He also paid frequent visits to the Brooke home at Easton Lodge near Dunmow in Essex, arriving with a retinue of valets and mounds of luggage, equerries and loaders for his guns.

In December 1893 Daisy Brooke's father-in-law died and she became Countess of Warwick and châtelaine of the magnificent Warwick Castle (where one of her first acts was to design a special suite for visits from her royal lover). Her friend and neighbour, the romantic novelist Elinor Glyn, believed that she had 'never seen [a woman] who was so completely fascinating as Daisy Brooke…hers was the supreme personal; charm which I later described as "It" because it is quite indefinable, and does not depend on beauty or wit, though she possessed both to the highest degree'.[14] But by 1897 the affair between the 'It girl' and the King was effectively over, though again a warm friendship remained for a time, and if Daisy missed anything it was less the King's 'goggle-eyed' devotion which could be 'boresome',[15] and more the status of being royal favourite.

In 1898, the Edward was fifty-six – but still not king. He remained a philanderer and sexual opportunist, but it was in this year that he met the woman who was to become the last of his 'official' mistress, the twenty-nine-year-old Hon Mrs George Keppel. Alice Keppel was sensuous, vivacious and passionate, and spoke with a deep, throaty, mesmerizing voice (she was rarely seen without a long cigarette holder, which epitomized her sophistication). She was also intelligent, articulate, informed, kind, tolerant and tactful and someone once compared her to a Christmas tree 'laden with presents for everyone'. She had been married to the third son of the Earl of Albermarle some seven years before she met the King, and though they had married for love, Alice also had wealthy lovers, which she rather needed in London society, she and her husband having very little money of their own. Indeed, her first daughter, Violet, was probably not her husband's child; she grew up to be a novelist and lover of Vita Sackville-West, the doyenne of Sissinghurst, who so captured the period in her novel, *The Edwardians* in which the character Romola Cheyne is based on Mrs Keppel. Mrs Keppel was the great-grandmother of another royal mistress, Camilla Parker-Bowles.

As befits a royal mistress, the Keppels moved from their house in Knightsbridge to a grander establishment in Portman Square. But it was not very grand because the Keppels were not very rich, and one of the indices by which this could be judged was the ratio of servants they kept. The really wealthy would employ eight or even more indoor servants for each member of the family: the wealthy employed four and the Keppels had two.

In 1901 Queen Victoria died and now Mrs Keppel was the *King's* mistress, '*la favorita*' as she was known, and a leading participant in the lavish hospitality that now transformed the royal round with splendid parties, balls and levées. She stayed with him in the South of France, he called on her frequently at home arriving in a green brougham, played with her two small daughters who curtsied to the portly monarch, sat on his knee and addressed him as 'kingy'. Nancy Astor shrewdly assessed the importance of Alice Keppel: 'She is the medium through which one approaches the King. They say she absolutely rules him. She reigns supreme and is treated with all the dignity of a Pompadour.'[16] But though the liaison was fully accepted by the King's 'fast set'– indeed, the multi-millionaire Sir Ernest Cassel was a great friend, adviser and benefactor of both – the alternative royal couple were not welcome in all the great houses in the land. Lord Salisbury refused to entertain Mrs Keppel at Hatfield, as did the Catholic Duke of Norfolk at Arundel, and the Duke of Portland at Welbeck,[17] but the less traditionally minded landed classes, and above all the *nouveaux riches*, passionately desired the King to grace their house parties. They wanted him to enjoy himself, and if that meant inviting his mistress too, that accorded very well with their understanding of the new spirit of Edwardian society. And on the day of the King's coronation (postponed because of His Majesty's attack of appendicitis) on 9 August 1902, a pew in Westminster Abbey, irreverently referred to as 'the King's loose box', contained a selection of Edward's current and ex-loves including the actress Sarah Bernhardt, Mrs Ronnie Greville and, of course, Mrs Keppel; the Countess of Warwick was there in her own right as a peeress. Meanwhile, splendid in a dress of golden Indian gauze embroidered with diamonds and pearls with an embroidered, ermine-lined train, sat his queen, Alexandra, in a throne adjacent to his.

At the revamped Buckingham Palace life followed a similar pattern to that at Marlborough House, though with far more official entertaining, state business and foreign visits. Edward was not an intellectual; he did not read books, his penchant for music was more Gilbert and Sullivan than Bach, his visual taste was untutored bordering on the tacky, his conversation was hardly discursive and he did not pore over his official boxes in the way that both his parents had, and he was less than assiduous in mastering the intricacies of governance. But the new king had a sharper political sense than his mother and 'more usage of the modern world', so Sir Charles Dilke decided, while Sir Edward Grey, the Foreign Secretary, commended the new King for his rare combination of 'bonhomie and dignity'.

On his accession Parliament had increased the King's annual income of £100,000 per year to £450,000, which with the £60,000 a year he received from the Duchy of Lancaster totalled over half a million pounds. But it was not enough. The King had expensive tastes and some exceedingly wealthy friends, who were akin to 'a race of gods and goddesses descended from Olympus upon England [living] on a golden cloud, spending their riches as indolently and naturally as the leaves grown green'.[18] His appetites were prodigious, his caprcious generosity legendary.

In the Edwardian era, London was the financial capital of the world: between 1890 and 1914 the City controlled almost half the international flow of capital, and in the era when capitalism was moving from its primary stage of production to the secondary one of finance, an axis operated between London, Paris, New York, Johannesburg and Frankfurt. London was an increasingly cosmopolitan city and millionaire

'O for the wings of a dove' … Lady Olliff-Cooper and Master Guy in harmony.

entrepreneurs settled there from America, South Africa, Australia, Germany, Baghdad and Holland. And, as Joe Mordaunt Crook points out, these wealthy immigrants did their business in London and had smart establishments in Park Lane, Eaton Square or Grosvenor Square, but most also bought country estates and thus became part of the country house circuit of which Edward VII was the well-upholstered leader. Many of the arrivals were Jews. In 1903 T. H. Escott noted in his book *Society in the New Reign*: 'social control [of London is now divided between] the Yankee and the Jew…say what you will, the Jews are the salt of smart society'.[19] There was predictable, if unpleasant, patrician hostility. Although the Jewish population of Britain before the First World War was only 0.3 per cent, it has been estimated that over one-fifth of all non-landed millionaires were Jews.[20] But the anti-

Conduit of romance? Discreet tiptoeing along the bedroom corridor was a supposed feature of an Edwardian country house party.

Semitism went wider than the impoverished landed gentry. Hilaire Belloc complained that the House of Lords had become 'a committee for the protection of Anglo-Judaic plutocracy' while the newspaper magnate, Lord Northcliffe, predicted that 'we shall soon have to set the [society] columns in Yiddish'.[21]

'We resented the introduction of the Jews into the social set of the Prince of Wales,' wrote the Countess of Warwick, and went on to justify her prejudice 'not because we disliked them individually…but because they had brains and understood finance. As a class, we did not like brains. As for money, our only understanding lay in the spending, not the making of it.'[22] It might be true that the King did not feel a particular affinity with brains, but the working of capitalism was a different matter: the City fascinated him and he followed the roller coaster of the stock market with great interest, though he also understood – in spades – how to spend money. He counted among his circle of wealthy men 'tradesmen' like Sir Thomas Lipton, a tea merchant and grocer who was a yachting companion; the furniture manufacturer with a shop in the Tottenham Court Road, Sir John Blundell Maple; and Jews such as the Beits (whose money came from diamonds and gold) and the Wernhers (Sir Julius Wernher was the owner of the magnificent Luton Hoo which Beatrice Webb castigated as a 'machine for the futile expenditure of wealth'),[23] both from South Africa.

Even closer friends were the Rothschilds. Nathaniel ('Natty') Rothschild, the grandson of Nathan Mayer Rothschild who had come from Frankfurt to found the English Rothschild family fortune, had been a friend since Edward's undergraduate days at Cambridge, and Edward was also a frequent visitor to the luxurious homes of Nathan's brothers Alfred and Leopold, where he joined his hosts in a day's stag hunting – though this was not a particularly favourite sport of his. Their uncle, Sir Anthony de Rothschild, advised Edward on his finances and arranged for the family bank to advance him money on occasions, as did Baron Maurice von Hirsch auf Gereuth, who was known as 'Turkish Hirsch' because that was where much of his money had been made building railways for the Ottoman sultan (Victoria would never receive Hirsch at court despite his generosity to her son and other rather better causes). In 1875 the then Prince of Wales paid a visit to India where he met the 'Rothschilds of the East', the Sephardic Jewish Sassoon family of merchants, notably Albert Abdullah (who had been knighted and given the freedom of the City of London for the role he had played in the acquisition of the Suez Canal). Arthur and Reuben Sassoon subsequently moved to London, where they became part of Edward's close circle of friends, advisers and occasional helpmeets.

But Edward met his closest and most trusted Jewish friend five years before he became King. Sir Ernest Cassel was a Cologne-born financier who had made his money in Sweden, in North American and Mexican railway construction and in Egypt where he financed the Aswan dam on the Nile (at the time the largest civil engineering project in the world) and set up the Egyptian National Bank and also one in Turkey.[24] In London it was Cassel who largely funded the construction of the London Underground (after the Rothschilds had withdrawn) and, with Lord Rothschild, acquired a number of companies out of which grew Vickers, which was to become the foremost armaments manufacturer and the Allies' main arsenal in the First World War. A close friendship sprang up between the King and the fabulously wealthy but socially awkward and lonely Cassel, and it was with Cassel that Edward had the final appointment of his life. 'I am very seedy,' the King told him, 'but I wanted to see you.' When Sir Ernest (whose granddaughter Edwina would one day marry Queen Victoria's great-grandson Lord Louis Mountbatten, the last Viceroy of India) died in 1921, he left £7 million, having already given away £2 million.

The historian Anthony Allfrey suggests that Sir Ernest Cassel was:

> the last of the new breed of financiers mainly of Jewish and mostly of German origin, who
> played such a pre-eminent part in English social, political and economic life of the Edwardian
> age, a position they owed to the unprejudiced, if not disinterested, patronage of King Edward.
> None contributed more to the flow of capital and diffusion of trade at a time when the industrial
> strength of Great Britain was ebbing: few contributed as much to the giddy social whirl or to the
> delectation of their Prince and King. Without them the short-lived, exotic, agitated and often
> anxious Edwardian era would never have achieved its full flavour and texture.[25]

At the King's insistent request, Mrs Keppel was admitted to his bedroom as he lay dying of bronchitis and a series of heart attacks, and to their discomfort the King insisted that she and the Queen should kiss and make their peace before he lapsed into a coma and died at a quarter to midnight on 6 May 1910, aged sixty-eight. Mrs Keppel had to be led away in hysterics, repeating as she went, 'I never did any harm, there was nothing between us. What is to become of me?' as Princess Victoria, the King's youngest child, tried to calm her. But she recovered and, invited to the funeral, went, dressed from head to toe in what might have been construed as 'widow's weeds'. The Queen, though 'unable to cry…was in a terrible state of despair' and insisted 'he was the whole of my life, and now he is dead, nothing matters' while his oldest son, soon to be proclaimed King George V, wrote in his diary: 'I have lost my best friend and the best of fathers. I never had a [cross] word with him in my life. I am heartbroken and overwhelmed with grief.'

There were the conventional tributes in parliament and the press, and the nation, to whom the King's death had come as a surprise, wondered what life would be like under the new, almost unknown George V who, it was rumoured, was a very different man from his father.

But if pieties were to be expected, there were many more for whom Edward's lifestyle did not serve as a template: it was not only the poor, the working classes or the middle classes who neither could, nor in many cases had any desire to, emulate the royal round of pleasure. There were landed establishment figures who considered the King to be a vulgar disgrace, acting like a *parvenu* in a society of which he was at the summit and supposed to be the supreme exemplar, and there were the intellectuals and the administrators for whom Edward VII was a disastrous waste of regal space in an age when so much needed address and redress. The novelist of subtle social observation, Henry James, disapproved of him as an 'arch vulgarian, Edward the Caresser'. The poet Wilfrid Scawen Blunt wrote perceptively in his diary:

> Everyone has gone into black for the King's death, and some enthusiasts talk about going into
> mourning for a year. It is all very absurd considering what the poor King was, but the papers
> are crammed with his praises as if he had been a saint of God. All the week since his death has
> been one of storms and tempests attributed to a comet so diminutive that nobody has seen it yet,
> and last night one of the great beech trees was thrown down in the park. I saw it lying uprooted
> on my way to the station this morning, a symbol of the dead King, quite rotten at the root, but
> one half of it clothed with its spring green.[26]

And within two years of the King's death, the authoritative *Dictionary of National Biography* included an entry written by the editor, a Tudor historian, Sir Sidney Lee, which spoke scathingly of the King as 'no reader of books. He could not keep his mind upon them…he lacked the intellectual equipment of a thinker, and showed on occasion an unwillingness to exert mental power'. It charged that the

From the Manderston stable: Sir James Miller owned two Derby winners, Sainfoin (1890) and Rock Sand (1903).

King had had 'no personal control of diplomacy' and had 'no conception of any readjustment of the balance of European power' and even for that diplomatic masterstroke commonly attributed to him, the *entente cordiale*, with France 'no direct responsibility for its initiation or conclusion belonged to him'. Reading the entry, the Labour leader, Keir Hardie, professed to feel duped. 'Now we know that whilst he was supposed to be labouring abroad for the country's good, he was simply enjoying himself as a very amiable, pleasure-loving man of the world, who was bored with politics and had not the capacity to understand foreign relationships.'[27]

Edwardian views of Edward thus mirror the complexities and tensions of his eponymous era. This was at a time when industrial strife was mounting, when it was becoming increasingly obvious that Irish nationalism was unanswerable within the existing frame of nineteenth-century political solutions, when Parliament's hereditary chamber was about to lose some of its power, and when the international situation was growing ever more threatening. Legislation introduced by the Liberal government, the growth of the Labour vote, and the stuttering, uneven advance of trade union power were evidence that the pendulum which had been inexorably swinging since the 1880s was taking an ever wider arc into the lives of the British people. The state was gradually assuming more systematic responsibility for its citizens, and private fiefdoms of money, property and privilege would not be left untouched in this halting progress towards a measure of the redistribution of resources – and thus inroads into a person's freedom to spend entirely as they would what they had or could acquire.

In the meantime, however, the people took their pleasures. As his father lay dying, the Prince of Wales brought the King the news that his horse Witch of the Air had won the 4.15 race at Kempton Park. 'I have heard of it,' murmured the dying sovereign, to whom the news had been telegraphed. 'I am very glad' – the last coherent words he spoke before lapsing into a coma. That summer the women going into the Royal Enclosure at Ascot races wore mourning clothes for what was known as 'black Ascot'.

Country Life's sporting audit published in 1911 estimated that the nation's annual expenditure on racing outstripped that of any other sport at £10,593,000 and that was in addition to capital expenditure of £8,320,000. And terrible were the tales of losses on the turf. The father of Oscar Wilde's infamous *inamorato*, 'Bosie', Lord Alfred Douglas, reckoned that between them his father, the deeply eccentric 8th Marquess of Queensberry, and his brother lost more £700,000 on various racing activities. And he obviously inherited the gene himself since it took him a very short time to get through his inheritance of £16,000 in a similar manner. In seven years Lord Rosslyn had managed to bankrupt himself, dissipating an inheritance of £50,000 and an annual income of £17,000 largely on buying racehorses, betting and gambling. George Cornwallis-West, one of the royal circle, confessed that his 'chief recollection of racing in Edwardian days is wondering how I could pay the bookies on Monday morning',[28] and no doubt he spoke for legion. Racing was one of the King's passions too. It had been one of his mother's many complaints about him that as a young man he spent far too much time at the races, but Edward continued to grace every major event on the racing calendar with his presence – and often one of his horses was running after he bought his own stable. The King's trainer, Marcus Beresford (brother of the infamous Sir Charles), 'was among the best known men in the racing world'.[29] The major races were those held at Newmarket, Ascot, Sandown, Goodwood, Doncaster and Epsom, and house parties were frequently arranged around those meetings by those with homes nearby. The Duke of Portland gives a flavour of such a weekend at Newmarket:

> We were called at seven in the morning. At eight, our hacks were waiting at the door, and in full enjoyment of the usual cold east wind…we rode to the Heath to see the horses at exercise. Having done so, and perhaps tried some of them, we returned, either uplifted or downcast but in any case, terribly hungry, to breakfast on prawns, poached eggs, bacon and muffins.

> …After attending the races…we rode home to tea, at which there were usually still more shrimps and prawns, but alas no plovers' eggs. At six we went to the stables, for the evening inspection of the horses. When this was over, it was usually time for dinner, either at home or with our friends. When we dined out, we often finished the evening in the Jockey Club Rooms.[30]

One of Edward's biographers, Philip Magnus, recounts how the King was one of the few men in England to make racing pay over the years. Between 1886, when he began to race his own horses and his death in 1910, his stallions earned him £269,495 in stud fees, and his horses won £146,345 in stake money: a total of £415, 840.[31] In June 1896, when still Prince of Wales, his horse Persimmon won the Derby and in 1900, the year before he became king, Persimmon's brother Diamond Jubilee won it again. That year, his stable went on to win the Grand National, the St Leger, the Eclipse Stakes and the Two Thousand Guineas as well. After that he had a run of bad luck until 1909 when his horse Minoru won the Derby in a photo finish, the first time that a reigning sovereign had ever had a Derby winner. The crowds on Epsom Downs went wild with excitement, calling for 'Three cheers for good old Teddy', while the band struck up with a rousing rendition of the National Anthem. 'The Prince of Wales is loved,' Lord Granville had commented dryly, 'because he has all the faults of which the Englishman is accused.'[32]

In keeping with Edwardian pleasures, the Olliff-Coopers went racing too. A chauffeur-driven car took a party from the Edwardian Country House to Kelso races where Sir John's horse, Indian Wings, was running. Some servants accompanied the family too, to enjoy a day's sport – and serve a picnic hamper and glasses of champagne. In a flamboyant gesture, Sir John laid a bet of 20 guineas on his horse coming in first.

Not only was the day out in keeping with the Edwardian age, it was particularly appropriate to the Country House where the Olliff-Coopers were living their Edwardian lives. Sir James Miller had been an important figure on the national racing scene and was the leading owner in the country in prize money when he won £24,768 in 1903. When he died *Sporting Life* had paid fulsome tribute to his prowess since, like the King, Sir James had been lucky with the turf, making some £118,000 in his lifetime.

'It was a fabulous day,' recounted Miss Anson. 'Two of my fantasies came true when we went to Kelso races. Because we were owners, we were allowed into the paddock to watch the horses being saddled for the race. We met the trainer and the jockey. We were invited to give the jockey last-minute instructions so we said, "Gallop all the way and see if you can win." because we didn't really know what else to say. And that's exactly what he did and Indian Wings was the clear winner. So then my other fantasy came true when we went into the winners' enclosure and were able to go up and pat our horse and congratulate the jockey. I was absolutely over the moon. We talked to the trainer again and all had champagne and I felt tremendously privileged – and lucky. I would love to own a racehorse. In fact I realized how much I would like a lifestyle for real that meant that the family could keep a string of race-horses and go to meetings to watch our horses run.'

Horse-racing might be a sport of kings, but the working classes enjoyed it too. It was, as Ross McKibbin has pointed out, possible to call it a 'national' sport 'only by a somewhat skewed definition of "national". What made it "national" was popular betting which linked a mass of working-class betters to a sport that was, in fact, aristocratic and plutocratic. Without betting, it would have been no more national than 12-metre yachting or deer-hunting.'[33] Indeed, betting on horses was almost the only sport on which organized working-class gambling took place before the First World War; betting on the dogs and football pools came later. The House of Lords select committee set up in 1902 came to the conclusion 'that betting is generally prevalent in the United Kingdom, and that the practice of betting has increased considerably in late years especially among the working classes'.[34] 'Racing held the rabid interest of millions,' recalled an Edwardian. 'It bound the labourer with cap-touching loyalty to the aristocrat. There were those who would only back King Edward's, Lord Derby's or Lord Rosebery's horses. In winning they felt for a brief moment a glow of unity with the greatest in the land.'[35] By the Edwardian era, *Sporting Life*, the *Sportsman* and the *Sporting Chronicle* each had a circulation exceeding 30,000 and there was a host of lesser imitators.[36] But it was not clear how widespread betting was nor what the figures involved were. In 1851 it had been claimed that £1 million had changed hands at the Chester Cup meeting, and by 1913 an entry in an *Encyclopaedia of Religion and Ethics* put the figure at £100,000,000 a year.[37] But proof was hard to come by, though undoubtedly the spread of the sporting press and the technology that enabled odds to be telegraphed to the race course had aided this rise.

'Did you enjoy yourself at the races, Kenny?' asked Sir John benignly later.
'Yes, thank you, sir,' replied the hall boy.
'And did you have a little flutter?'

'Yes, sir,' said Kenny, adding, under his breath, 'but not a 20 guinea bet.' Which, considering that Kenny's annual salary was in the region of £12 a year, was hardly surprising.

But those who won – and lost – money on the racecourse usually found other ways to do so too. Indeed, it was while staying at a country house party near Doncaster for the St Leger races that the then Prince of Wales was involved in a serious scandal that threw a very adverse light on the gambling and drinking set that revolved around his royal person. A visitor to Sandringham in 1890 had found it 'a shocking affair for the Royal Family to play an illegal game every night. They have a real table, and rakes, and everything, like rooms at Monte Carlo'.[38] The Prince, who had once enjoyed dancing but had grown too portly to trip the light fantastic in comfort, relieved the inevitable boredom of the country house circuit, and the same people in different combinations and settings, with a little indoor sport as well as shooting, racing and hunting. He always carried a set of baccarat counters that had been given to him by his friend, Reuben Sassoon. They were in denominations varying from five shillings to ten pounds and were engraved with the Prince of Wales's feathers.[39] They were also illegal currency.

During the St Leger race week in September, the Prince usually stayed with his friend Christopher Sykes, 'the great Xtopher' as he was known, but Sykes was one of those for whom the carousel of extravagant entertaining had brought near bankruptcy, and he was no longer in the position to host a St Leger house party at his home, Brantingham Thorpe, near Doncaster. So in 1890 this was held by the ship owner Arthur Wilson, who Edward did not know well, at his home, Tranby Croft. That first evening, another guest, Lieutenant Colonel Sir William Gordon-Cumming of the Scots Guards, was observed cheating at baccarat by upping or reducing his stakes after he had managed to covertly look at his cards – a sleight-of-hand the French called *la pousette*. Sir William was kept under close surveillance the next night and was seen to cheat on a number of occasions, winning £225 over two evenings, usually from the Prince of Wales, who was the banker. When confronted with his crime, the redress traditional among 'gentlemen' was agreed: those present swore 'to preserve silence' on the matter in exchange for a solemn promise from Sir William that 'I will undertake never to play cards as long as I live'. This was intended to protect the reputation of the Prince of Wales, who kept a copy of the agreement signed by all those present and left Tranby Croft sharpish next morning.

But too many people knew – it was soon common gossip among the smart set (the Countess of Warwick – Daisy Brooke – earned her nickname 'Babbling Brooke' for her part in spreading the news) and Gordon-Cumming announced his intention to sue five of his accusers for the slur on his character. When the case came to court, the country would know that the heir apparent to the throne was a gambler and a participant in illegal games. In the event, the jury found against Sir William, who was dismissed from the Army, blackballed by his clubs and effectively expelled from society. 'The light which it has thrown on [his habits]…alarms and shocks the people,' wrote Victoria of her errant son, but he did not see it quite like that and declined her suggestion that he should send a missive to the Archbishop of Canterbury condemning gambling as a social evil. In his view, gambling was what took place between consenting adults who could well afford it. Finally, he decided to take up bridge in place of baccarat (and one of the many attractions of Mrs Keppel was to be that she played a good hand of bridge, though she once confessed ingenuously that she could 'not tell a King from a Knave' when Edward challenged her at the card table).

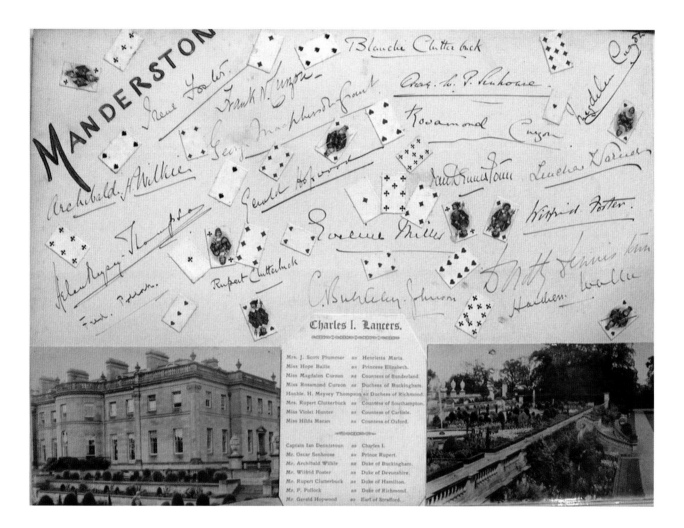

The record of a popular Edwardian evening at cards at Manderston.

After dinner, the Olliff-Coopers would sometimes play games. Particularly if they had company, there was bridge and whist and parlour games; the one they most enjoyed was 'the feather' (which could also be played with tissue paper). 'The players must draw their chairs in a circle as closely together as possible. One of the party begins the game by throwing the feather into the air as high as possible…the object of the game is to keep it from touching anyone, as the player whom it touches must pay a forfeit… it is impossible to imagine the excitement that can be produced by each player preventing the feather from lighting on him [by means of blowing and swotting]. The game must be heartily played to be fully appreciated.'[40] But that night the Olliff-Coopers recalled the Tranby Croft affair as they played baccarat in the chinoiserie-furnished card room by the fire, with the red-lacquered grandfather clock ticking, a chalk line carefully delineating the space so that no repeat of the affair was likely at *their* table. The stakes were high, and again Sir John was lucky as he scooped his winnings into a pile.

Dinner cleared, the servants were in the servants' hall downstairs playing cards too. Sometimes they played dominoes or cribbage, or games such as Old Maid or Loo, but that night their game was poker, a recent import from the United States. The excitement was raucous but the stakes were paltry.

CHAPTER ELEVEN

Imperial Might

A large cloth map of the world, its surface veined with a network of almost imperceptible cracks, hung on the wall of the Edwardian Country House alongside a blackboard, the mounted stuffed head of a startled rabbit, a likeness of the new King, George V, botanical drawings and multiplication tables, while on the desk and windowsills jostled a collection of birds' eggs, a disintegrating nest, some pressed leaves, a fossil, a writing slate and exercise books, reading primers, steel-nibbed pens, lead pencils and wax crayons – all the appurtenances of an early-twentieth-century child's education. It was the domain of Mr Raj Singh, who had been engaged by Sir John to tutor his ten-year-old son, Guy, while the family was living the Edwardian experiment.

Pointing at the map with a ruler, Mr Singh, a teacher in London in the twenty-first century, showed his pupil the island of Fiji where he had been born, and India where his family came from. 'When George V came to the throne, the British Empire had almost reached its apogee,' he explained. 'You can see, all these countries that are coloured pink are British possessions and they spread right round the globe, large parts of Africa, Australia, New Zealand, Canada, India. It was said that the sun never set on the British Empire.'

In January 1911 the newly crowned King and his wife, Queen Mary, set off for India. It was the only visit made to the subcontinent by a reigning King Emperor and it was commemorated 'by a durbar [assembly] of unprecedented scale and extravagance'.[1] The highlight of the Delhi durbar came when the King and Queen, wearing jewel-encrusted crowns of freshly minted imperial gold and ermine-lined robes of purple, sitting on golden thrones in a crimson marquee, received a long procession of Indian princes who came to pay homage to their imperial majesties. They were, wrote the correspondent for *The Times,* 'remote but beneficent, raised far above the multitude [it was estimated that there was a crowd of 100,000 spectators], but visible to all'.[2] After the ceremonials, the King went hunting in Nepal over the New Year, bagging twenty-four tigers and a bear, while eighteen rhinoceroses were also shot by the hunting party.

It was not the first time that George V had visited India: in October 1905, the then Prince and Princess of Wales had left England in the battleship *Renown* for a four-and-a-half-month-long visit of the subcontinent that took them from Bombay to Delhi, to Calcutta, Mysore, Hyderabad and Jaipur. It was an exhausting and exhilarating 9,000-mile tour by train, car and carriage of the 'jewel in the crown' of Britain's Empire. On their arrival in Bombay they were welcomed by Lord Curzon, who had been Viceroy for seven years, but three months earlier had been forced to resign in a bitter row with the British government over the military administration of the subcontinent. George Nathaniel Curzon was the brother of Eveline, who married Sir James Miller, the rebuilder of Manderston, home to the Edwardian Country House experiment. As Manderston owed a profound architectural debt to the Curzon family seat, Kedleston Hall in Derbyshire, so was the Government House in Calcutta modelled on Kedleston.

Though he no longer occupied the top job, in recognition of his meticulous planning of the royal visit, Curzon was grudgingly permitted to welcome the royal couple on their arrival in Bombay, before handing over to his successor, the Earl of Minto, a week later. It was a painful humiliation for the 'very superior person' who was the embodiment of ceremonial pageantry. In

January 1903 Curzon had orchestrated a durbar to proclaim the accession of George's father, Edward VII, to his Indian subjects – a quarter of a billion of them. It was to be 'the biggest show that India will ever have had'. In the early Victorian period the British had been anxious to 'contrast their honest, plain black frock coats with the pretentious glitter of the oriental monarchs they controlled'.[3] But following the Indian mutiny of 1857–9 against the rule of the British Governor General, Lord Dalhousie, its brutal suppression and the assumption by the Crown of responsibility for the governance of India (which had previously rested with the East India Company), British policy in India had changed: its intention now was to present the colonial rulers as the legitimate successors to the deposed Mughal Emperors. Far from being 'reformed', the traditional Brahmanic hierarchies of caste (which had become more extensive and rigid during the period of control by the East India Company) were to be respected as 'capable of integrating into a single hierarchy all [the Empire's] subjects, Indian and British alike' so that social status equated with official position in British India. The model, according to the historian David Cannadine, was that of British metropolitan society in which local government depended on the aristocracy and local gentry 'so their chosen partners in South Asia were the "natural leaders": large landowners, men of "property and rank", of "power and importance", "who exercised great influence" in rural society' – rather like 'the position once occupied by the English Squire'[4]. This in theory meant that the imperial enterprise in India could be administered from Britain in 'collaboration' with 'dependable allies' doing the work of the imperialists much as local government at home implemented the policies of parliament. The third of India not governed directly by the British (first from Calcutta and later Delhi) was divided into some 500 or 600 princely states – 'personal fiefdoms ruled over by rajas and mahrajas, nawabs and nizams', who were no longer to be regarded as strange and reviled but welcomed as a sort of 'feudal social order' that would enable the British to rule that section of India indirectly in a way that they understood.

Queen Mary and King George V at the Delhi durbar in 1911.

Disraeli had created Victoria Empress of India in 1876 and new orders of chivalry along British lines were created for the Indian princes – and for the imperial administrators. In 1893 and 1900 an equivalent to *Burke's Peerage* for India was published: *The Golden Book of India: A Genealogical and Biographical Dictionary of the Ruling Princes, Chiefs, Nobles and Other Personages, Titled or Decorated, of the Indian Empire*.[5] It was dedicated to the Queen Empress.

Curzon's Edwardian viceroyalty was the summit of the ostentatious display of the British Raj which had appropriated what were believed to be Mughal court ceremonials and invented their own peacock displays of sovereignty, convinced that this was expedient since what was termed the 'oriental mind' equated such pomp and excessive splendour (far grander than any pageantry that surrounded the British monarch at home) with authority. The durbar was a spangled spectacle of unprecedented magnificence that lasted two full weeks. It demonstrated that the imperial administration could combine 'oriental exuberance' with 'western precision', reported *The Times*.[6] But, as David Cannadine points out, in a country where poverty was endemic and which had recently endured a decimating famine, this 'Curzonation'[7], far from reinforcing the unity of India, which the Viceroy had proclaimed was one of the purposes of the durbar (along with a demonstration of British prestige which was inextricably interlinked with his own) 'merely served to reinforce an unequal division of wealth, and to demonstrate that India was a nation ruled by others'.[8] For the Indian population it was a '*tamasha*', an empty entertainment.[9]

'As long as we rule India we are the greatest power in the world,' Lord Curzon had argued in 1901. 'If we lose it we shall drop straight away to a third-rate power.'[10]

'It is people like you,' said Mr Raj Singh to Master Guy in the Edwardian Country House schoolroom, 'who are educated to go out and govern places like that' – as he pointed his ruler in an arc that took in India and Ceylon. 'How do you feel about that?'

Ten-year-old Master Guy, who in his 'real life' expects to follow his older brother to Winchester and then to Oxford or Cambridge, looked insouciant. An Edwardian public school education would have prepared a boy to take a commission in the army or navy, become a clergyman perhaps, or a senior civil servant, a barrister, or join a branch of the Indian or colonial administration. Since the days of Dr Arnold of Rugby School, more than half a century before, the public school system had been organized to produce just such men. In the words of one historian of the Raj, Lawrence James, such a pupil would have grown up to be 'a Christian gentleman with a stunted imagination, who played by the rules and whose highest aim was to serve others'.[11] The headmaster of Harrow, who was later to become Bishop of Calcutta, was convinced that 'if there is in the British race, as I think there is, a special aptitude for "taking up the white man's burden"…it may be ascribed, above all other causes, to the spirit of organized games'.[12] Geography lessons learned by trainee teachers at college in Cambridge consisted almost entirely of lists of colonies, details of how they were acquired, the products the colonies produced and the accounts of the life of their native inhabitants; and when these teachers went out into their schools, this was part of the rote learning they would instil in their pupils. A booklet produced for schoolchildren gave 'facts and figures' on the Empire, asserting that from 'the spacious times of Great Elizabeth'…our colonial expansion has gone steadily on, and, with the exception of the American States, our efforts everywhere have been crowned with success' – and resulted in the present situation in which 'the sun never sets upon the British Empire, which is far larger than any that the world has ever seen. The British Isles contains just over 121,000 square miles, but for every one of these there are

90 square miles in other parts of the Empire, making a total of nearly 11½ millions of square miles, or one-fifth of the habitable surface of the globe. The population of this immense expanse of territory is over 400 millions, i.e. about one quarter of the all the inhabitants of the earth.'[13] Or, put another way, in 1912, one in four people was a subject of King George V.

The Empire might well have caught such a pupil's imagination. Since the end of the nineteenth century there had been a proliferation of popular books and magazines written expressly to enthuse boys with ideas of Empire. There were the thrilling novels of G. A. Henty with such titles as *By Sheer Pluck*, *The Young Colonists*, *With Buller at Natal*, and *Through the Sikh War*, often awarded as school or Sunday School prizes, and copies of some of which Master Guy had found in his school room. There were the works of Rudyard Kipling, who had been brought up by an Indian ayah and had felt exiled when he was sent back to school in Britain: *Kim* (1901), *The Jungle Book* (1894) and in particular his tale of public school pranksters who would one day run the Empire, *Stalky & Co* (1899). 'India's full of Stalkies,' a character explains. And there were sensational tales of imperial derring-do to read in such weekly magazines as the *Boy's Own Paper*, *Chums*, *Young England*, *Pluck* and *Union Jack*.

The tutor

Reji Raj looked forward to his role as Mr Raj Singh, tutor to the youngest Olliff-Cooper. Born in Fiji to Hindu parents from India, Reji is a convert to Christianity. He has been a primary school teacher for the last twenty years, and currently teaches history and religion at a Church of England school in Paddington, London. His pupils are multiracial – for many, English is their second language. A number of them are refugees, and have sometimes been deeply traumatized by events in their young lives. Helping these children to settle in their new environment, and to catch up with their learning, is challenging and demanding work.

Reji is currently studying for an MA in theology, and is very interested in India's cultural heritage. 'I can never be an Englishman – I am Indian and I am proud to be that. I want to explore Indian religion and culture and customs, and one of the ways I can do that is by studying Indian classical dance, which expresses so many things about Indian culture and beliefs.'

It was this interest in India's past that drew him to the Edwardian Country House project. He was particularly curious to know why the Nehrus and other distinguished and highly educated Indian families had tried to emulate the British Raj during the Edwardian period. 'But there really was no choice: to get anywhere you had to be like the British, your masters, who considered themselves to be the superior race. I feel that the British held a mirror up to the Indians and saw a sort of harmony between their class system and the caste system. So I decided that I wanted to see what it would have been like a hundred years ago for an Indian to live with an upper-class English family.'

The position of Guy in the Edwardian Country House could be a lonely one. 'We volunteered to do this,' Sir John said. 'He didn't.' Although a child brought up in a prosperous county house in the Edwardian period may well have been educated at home by a tutor or governess before he was sent away to public school at thirteen, it would have been an experience shared with other siblings, the children of neighbouring families, or even estate workers' offspring. Master Guy learned on his own with the tutor his father had engaged, and in spite of playing games and taking nature walks in the extensive grounds, it was a long, tiring and isolating experience for a boy used to the companionship of day school.

It was hardly surprising that the downstairs servants were to play an important role in Master Guy's life. As a very bright child of considerable initiative, he had an Edwardian appreciation of how the system worked. 'You were supposed to wear your hat low down over your eyes so when you looked at the servants – it would make them look inferior. Before I came here I really liked the idea of saying, "Oi, servant, bring me a cup of tea", and I know that you are supposed to think that servants are under you but when they come round serving dinner I say to my dad, "You are just itching to say thank you," but you know that the best compliment you can pay them is just to accept that they have given it to you and just let them pass by. The servants really are my friends here.'

The second footman, Rob, had been charged with the care of Master Guy: 'I get on with Rob really well, probably because he's a bit like me, but much older, and he is really helpful and clears up my clothes, he picks them up off the floor and tidies my room, and he's generally in good spirits.' Rob

Lord Curzon, Viceroy of India from 1890 to 1905, having shot a tiger and a leopard.

would take up Guy's supper in the evening and sit with him while he ate it, and the two would play card games like Trumps, or Snap or Cheat and finish off with a game of draughts rather than Guy's twenty-first-century stalwarts, his Gameboy or video games. Rob would read to Guy before he went to bed at night: they particularly enjoyed *The Arabian Nights Entertainments* (and Ali Baba and the Forty Thieves) best of all and Kenneth Grahame's *Wind in the Willows*, published in 1908.

And the child had sussed out straight away where there was fun to be had in the Edwardian Country House – and that was in the servants' hall. If he was ever missing, he was most likely to be found there where he found the atmosphere much more conducive than the stiff formality that pertained upstairs. 'I run around a lot downstairs because it is sometimes so boring and so formal upstairs so I go downstairs to be normal and relax. It's not all, "Mother, you should go first", "No, no, Avril must go first, Guy". Down here people will just talk to me and play cards and I just hang around. I lie on the sofa and listen to the servants' conversation and add little bits until Mr Edgar usually tells me to go back upstairs after a while.' The ten-year old enjoyed the footmen's horseplay and the maids were kind to him, telling him about what they were doing and letting him 'help' them with their daily work. 'Becky and Jess are really good and sing together and I join in and they give me sweets. I can help Jess light the fires and Becky clears up after me, so they are both amazing.' Mrs Davies usually managed to find Master Guy some biscuits she'd made, and though he was sometimes rather in the way given the servants' tight schedule of chores, particularly if there were guests staying, the servants felt rather sorry for Guy with his confined and isolated life; they grew fond of

Master Guy

Guy, who had his tenth birthday as the Olliff-Coopers arrived at the Edwardian Country House, had no trepidations about the 'Edwardian experiment'. Though he knew he would miss his friends and his Gameboy, he very much fancied the idea of just ringing a bell and giving orders to servants. But he soon found that it wasn't quite like that. 'I have never had a servant friend before. Servants are very expensive in the twenty-first century, but here I spend a lot of time in the servants' quarters where there's much more going on and it's much more fun. When I go back home and we do Edwardian history at school, I'll be able to say to my teacher, 'Actually, sir, I lived that.'

the child and went out of their way to keep him amused below stairs. This would have been a familiar pattern in an Edwardian house with a number of servants. In many cases, the children of the house were familiar both with the domestic staff and the part of the house where they worked in a way that was entirely remote to their parents, and many an afternoon was spent in the kitchen 'helping' cook, or listening to the male servants' badinage in the butler's parlour. In an age when children were still to an extent regarded as apprentice adults who needed strict discipline to train them for their roles in life, and were thus expected to be seen but not heard in formal adult company, the licence and more casual manners enjoyed below stairs would draw a child to the community like a moth to a flame.

Wind in the Willows

When Ratty, Mole and Badger reached the carriage drive of Toad Hall, they found, 'just as the Badger had anticipated, a shiny new motor-car, of great size, painted a bright red (Toad's favourite colour), standing in front of the house. As they neared the door it was flung open, and Mr Toad, arrayed in goggles, cap, gaiters, and enormous overcoat, came swaggering down the steps.'

Kenneth Grahame's *Wind in the Willows* (with illustrations by E. H. Shepard) anthropomorphizes Edwardian life with its story of the leisured, landed gentry. Toad, the 'Terror of the Highway', lives in the local great house and 'squanders the money' his father left him, and drives so recklessly that he is sent to prison, leaving Toad Hall standing empty. It is then invaded by distinctly proletarian stoats and weasels whose normal habitat is the Wild Wood beyond.

Although Guy usually obligingly followed the routine of the Edwardian country house and wore the appropriate clothes – Eton suits, stiff collars and pint-sized top hats or sailor suits for smart occasions, or scaled-down tweed jackets and knickerbockers for every day – after a few weeks in the Edwardian Country House, he was clearly finding the demands of his enforced time travel hard to cope with on occasions. The Olliff-Coopers decided that their son was suffering from not having any friends of his own age to spend time with, and that Master Guy should go daily to school in nearby Berwick-upon-Tweed. It was arranged that his tutor would accompany the child to school and back again, supervise his homework in the evenings and devise activities and small expeditions which would maximize the Edwardian experience for him and take advantage of Manderston's superb rural surroundings. And there would still be the opportunity to ride his pony, a pleasure previously unknown to him at home in the New Forest.

This arrangement, however, made the position of Mr Raj Singh even more uncomfortable than it already was. He had been engaged to teach the son of the master of the house. His role was not simply to impart facts and school Master Guy in mathematics, grammar, the sciences, Greek and Latin so that he would pass the common entrance examination to his public school; it was also to inculcate the manners and attitudes of a gentleman, a possible future ruler of the Empire, of which Mr Raj Singh himself was a subject in this scenario. Sir John had made it clear that Mr Raj Singh, as his son's closest companion, was not a servant, and must not be treated like one. He was to enjoy the same treatment and privileges as the family. He took his meals with the Olliff-Coopers, was introduced to their guests and accompanied them on several outings. His bedroom was on the same floor as the family's, he had his own bathroom – and a bell pull in his room to summon the servants. And this was to be a source of tension. As far as the butler and the footmen were concerned, the tutor was in danger of abusing his position, ringing for help in finding things and summoning them with frequent requests for tea or glasses of water, requiring to be woken by a footman instead of using an alarm clock. In their view he kept himself aloof from them and treated them with disdain – indeed, as servants.

But as far as Mr Raj Singh was concerned, his situation was very difficult. Sir John had instructed him that he must observe the same etiquette as a member of the family in order to set an example to his son. It was true that Mr Raj Singh was invited to eat with the family, join in their activities and meet their guests, but he still felt constrained. It was clear that he was not expected to venture an opinion unless expressly invited to do so, and his role was analogous to that of Miss Anson, the dependent spinster sister, so the two decided. They were both formally within the magic family circle yet an ancillary member of it without equal conversational rights and with little cognisance taken of their preferences – which they were unable to express anyway.

The tutor felt his position particularly acutely since it resonated both of class and of race. 'The family are extremely kind to me. They treat me like a gentleman. I partake of all the things that go on around here, and it's all superb and very elegant and lovely. I go with them in the carriage to church, I sit in the family pew, I take music lessons and dancing lessons with the family, they invite me to eat with them and always try to include me in their conversations. Sir John can be very sensitive to my position. He always makes me feel absolutely welcome and he asks my opinion and listens to what I have to say. And her ladyship is so gentle and kind too. But there is an invisible barrier. I feel very constrained here. I am always a step behind the family and I find the protocol and the etiquette amazingly restricting, though in a way it's a safety net, you know exactly where you are because it is all so prescribed. I have to act with dignity and decorum at all times. I have to know my place at all times. I don't say anything unless I am asked. I just smile politely and listen to the conversation. Sir John and her ladyship have both complimented me on my impeccable manners, and that's nice to know, but inside I feel just like a volcano.

'It is so frustrating, there is no one who I can really talk to intimately, have a heart to heart with. I am very isolated because I am in limbo. I am betwixt and between. I am with the family, but I am not a member of the family, but I am not a servant either, and I can't go downstairs and make friends with them and spend time in their company. I empathize with the servants running up and down stairs all the time. They look very tired sometimes, so I try to do what I can for myself, but I once volunteered to go down to fetch something, and I was stopped at once and told, "No you can't. You are not a servant. You are a tutor and companion to my son. I do not wish a servant to teach my son." So I can't even do what my pupil does! And that means of course that the servants see me as arrogant and stand-offish and acting above my station in not wishing to associate with them. It means that I am on my own a great deal – particularly now that Master Guy goes to school. And I think that there is a particular distance between the butler and me. He can be

Ready for bed: Master Guy and his teddy bear prepare to retire.

Mr Raj Singh, the tutor, and Sir John take a walk.

very icy towards me. I think he resents the fact that I am treated like one of the family, whereas to him, I am just another servant of the family.

'It makes me empathize and sympathize with tutors and governesses throughout history, men and women who were highly intelligent, often well qualified. They were respected to a certain extent, but many doors were closed to them. And in the end they were always employees no matter how well they were treated.

'It is particularly poignant for me because I come from the Fiji Islands and my parents both came from India, though we have lived for four generations in Fiji, and because Fiji was a British colony it is still at least two decades behind Britain. This Edwardian country house reminds me of my childhood. We all had this goal of trying to be terribly English. We lived in an Edwardian way really with strict etiquette and a code of manners and dress, and always taking afternoon tea and things like that, and when I first came to England it was quite a culture shock for me. So coming here to the Edwardian Country House is like coming home because the etiquette and sense of propriety are as they were in my childhood. I think that living in the Edwardian Country House has brought back the colonial experience very vividly to me. We lived in a country controlled by an outside power, the sense of status and hierarchy was very strong, and we lived by somebody else's rules and regulations, and that is exactly how it was for somebody in my position in Edwardian times. But it does amaze me when I see the system in action why Indian people with their thousands of years of culture could somehow have decided to forsake this and try to emulate Edwardian British culture which was so stifling that it smothered freedom and creativity and expressiveness. Why did they want to be like their colonial masters? What was so attractive about something that put them down and debased their culture and made it seem inferior to western ways? I just don't understand.'

Mr Raj Singh was also troubled by the notion that at the time of the Raj an Indian tutor could have been something of a 'trophy' for an English family, an exotic exhibit of 'otherness' in the way that Queen Victoria had had her Munshi (teacher), Abdul Karim from Agra, who had become her trusted and indulged companion/servant, much resented by other members of the royal household. There had not been much encouragement from the British for Indian aspirations: in 1909 only 65 of the 1,244 members of the Indian Civil Service were non-British.[14] There was a small Indian community in Britain by the start of the Edwardian period. Since at least the eighteenth century, the British had imported Indian servants and ayahs (nannies for the children) on their return to the homeland, and a number of lascars (sailors) who were employed on ships that sailed between Britain and India settled in Britain – despite laws that forbade this. Their life could be very hard and little protection or help was offered to them in many cases. In the early years of the twentieth century, the number of Indians coming to Britain to study – mainly law and medicine and for entry to the Indian Civil Service – rose from around 300 in 1900 to roughly 1,750 in 1913.[15] In 1892 the first Indian, Dadabhai Naoroji, was elected to Parliament as a Liberal, and in 1895 Manchererjee Bhownagree was returned as Conservative Member for Bethnal Green.[16]

Duleep Singh, the son of the founder of the Sikh nation, had been forced to renounce his claims as Maharajah of the Punjab (and hand over the famous Koh-i-Noor diamond as a 'gift' to Queen Victoria) when it was annexed by the British in 1849. He subsequently settled in Britain on a stipend. In 1863 Duleep Singh purchased Elveden Hall on the Norfolk/Suffolk borders and soon was part of the Prince of Wales's shooting set, but his extravagant lifestyle, and feeling of betrayal by the British, led him to renounce his Christian faith and set off back to India. He did not get there but died in Paris in 1893. His body was brought back to Elveden Hall (which had been purchased by the Earl of Iveagh) for burial.

Aware that Mr Raj Singh too felt lonely and misunderstood at times, Sir John suggested an occasion that would celebrate aspects of his culture and tell others in the Edwardian Country House more about India both today and under British rule at the start of the twentieth century. He decided to step out of the frame of what would have been likely in an Edwardian Country House in order to hold what he called a Raj supper at Manderston. Mr Singh was enthusiastic about the idea and volunteered to invite some friends of his who would perform traditional Hindu dances for the occasion. Meanwhile the Olliff-Coopers drew up a list of distinguished guests who had close connections with the subcontinent and views both on Empire and issues of race and culture in contemporary Britain.

Mr Edgar serves Mr Raj Singh at dinner.

Unfortunately, the challenge proved greater than anyone had anticipated when the chef, M. Dubiard, fell ill with a gastric infection and was unable to cook the meal. It was soon apparent that the rest of the servants had only the sketchiest concept of authentic Indian cooking, confined mainly to takeaway curries and the odd samosa or onion bhaji at a party. If they had consulted the 1901 edition of *Mrs Beeton* they would have found a short, bracing section on Indian cookery, but from the tenor of the remarks it appeared that the recipes were to be cooked by the Englishwoman in India (where 'mangoes are a taste only acquired by those who have not a prejudice against turpentine') rather than imported for the home table. It warned that 'Indian cooks are clever, and, with very simple materials will turn out a good dinner; whereas the same food in the hands of an ordinary English cook would resolve itself into the plainest meal', though since the key ingredient seemed to be curry powder rather than a rich mix of ground spices as was required for authentic Indian cooking, this was not surprising.[17] But necessity being the mother of invention the staff worked out a system whereby Mrs Davies the housekeeper, Antonia the kitchen maid, Ellen the scullery maid, and Kenny the hall boy would take instructions from the bedridden chef and cook the meal themselves. It was hard work and nerve-racking but eventually a vegetarian meal was assembled for the dance troupe and a series of curries – chicken, lamb, beef and vegetable complete with raita, spinach aloo and dhal served with pilau rice, nan bread and chapatis – were prepared for upstairs to be followed by a platter of mangoes, paw paw, pineapple, kiwi fruit and melon.

'It was a memorable night,' said the butler. 'It really was fantastic. We all had to work very hard. We did not really have the experience or the precedents to produce a dinner like that. We had to work it out for ourselves and it was all a great success. We had been without a chef for two days, and everyone was very overworked and tired because we had a number of visitors over the weekend. But I take my hat off to M. Dubiard [which was not always the case]. He couldn't come into the kitchen, but although he was ill he directed operations so we had the benefit of his expertise being put to use by staff who had never done anything like this before. Everybody lent a hand. They were magnificent. It all went perfectly and I get puffed up on occasions like this and feel about eight feet tall with pride for my staff. The table looked beautiful. It was glittering with candles and flowers, and when Lady Olliff-Cooper came downstairs in her wonderful new gown she looked absolutely radiant, she outshone all the other guests and that gave us a real sense of pride as her servants. The Indian dancers were excellent and no superlative can describe how good the musicians were. It was a fantastic occasion and it transported us all back to the Edwardian era. We really felt that we were in an Edwardian household, having an Edwardian entertainment, and it was quite unforgettable.'

But not everything ran quite so smoothly. Mr Raj Singh was not pleased when he heard that the performers were to be shown in through the servants' entrance and were to be served dinner in the servants' hall. 'In India dancers are very highly valued. Young girls in the temples performed ritual dances full of religious meaning, but when the British came they did not approve. They called them nautch girls which is insulting. And it does not seem right to me that at Manderston the dancers and the musicians should be treated like servants rather than as guests of the house.'

The company that sat down at table was indeed illustrious. 'We are having royalty tonight,' Sir John had explained to Guy, and promptly at four o'clock Prince Moshin Ali Khan, of Hyderabad, arrived. A financial consultant who has lived in Europe for half a century, the Prince, who is very active in charity work in Britain and is the founder of One Nation which seeks to promote unity between Muslims, Jews and Christians in Britain, still keeps close links with his home state. Master Guy, who had been given a book published to celebrate the 1911 Indian durbar, was delighted to find in it a photograph of Prince Ali

Khan's uncle, the Nizam of Hyderabad, which he showed to their guest. Another distinguished guest, Yasmin Alibhai-Brown, arrived in Britain from Uganda in 1972 when Idi Amin expelled all Asians from the country, and is now a journalist, broadcaster and writer who advises the Home Office and various other institutions on matters of race. Her most recent books, *Who Do We Think We Are?* and *After Multiculturalism*, are both critical analyses of issues of race and ethnicity in British society today. The third distinguished guest, Krishnan Guru-Murthy, is also a journalist and broadcaster. He was brought up in Lancashire, educated at Oxford, and is now a presenter and reporter on Channel 4 news.

Unsurprisingly, the discussion at table soon turned to matters of Empire, race and ethnicity and in particular to Mr Raj Singh's contention that the structure of the Edwardian Country House resembled that of colonial domination: 'In many ways the house holds up a mirror to the colonial system in terms of power and a rigid sense of place.'

'In India we have twenty-four castes,' explained Ms Alibhai-Brown, 'and they are rigidly differentiated.'

Lady Olliff-Cooper nodded. 'We have a strong sense of hierarchy here too. The whole structure in this house is to ensure that everyone knows their place, and keeps to it. That way the whole machine runs very smoothly.' It sounded like the view from the top.

'Our positions in the house are similar'. Mr Raj Singh and Miss Anson dancing in sympathy.

'Are your servants happy?' demanded Ms Alibhai-Brown.

'Oh yes,' replied Sir John complacently.

'But how do you know?' persisted his guest.

'Because they have smiles on their faces,' concluded the host.

Ms Alibhai-Brown turned to Mr Raj Singh: 'What do you do in the house?' she asked.

'I was shocked by his answer,' said Mr Edgar. 'It was a straightforward question. He could have replied that he looked after the child when he was not at school, but instead he chose to say what he was *not* allowed to do. He spoke of his lack of freedom and of the animosity shown to him by the servants. He said that he was made to defer to the family and not allowed to speak at table. I felt really affronted by that because Sir John has always taken such pains to make it clear to me that Mr Raj Singh is like a member of the family and must be treated as such. I wanted to say, "What animosity are you speaking about? It is you who set yourself apart. Why don't you ever take the hand of friendship when it is extended to you by those down below?" But because I am the butler I had to keep quiet. I was on duty so I just had to stand there and not say anything. But I was very concerned that those at the table would get the impression that both the family and the servants have excluded him, maybe on the grounds of race. And that simply is not true. It's not true at all.'

Evening bag

The narrow silhouette of Edwardian clothes made a little bag an essential fashion accessory for ladies. Called 'Dorothy' bags and often used to carry dancing slippers, these drawstring reticules were very similar to many of today's fashionable evening bags and are simple to make.

The material most often used in the Edwardian era would have been velvet or satin, usually lined in silk and decorated with a tassel, silk embroidery, beadwork or lace as here.

To make a similar bag, you will need a piece of firm fabric such as cotton, velvet, taffeta or satin, and silk, polyester or linen with fine cotton for the lining.

Materials

Two squares of fabric, about 28cm x 28cm (11in x 11in), for the bag and the same amount for the lining
120cm (48in) narrow (0.5cm/¼in diameter) silk cord, cut into two equal lengths for the handles, plus 30cm (12in) for the bottom of the bag
A decorative silk tassel in a matching or toning colour
Decorative trim, of silver, gold or lace, or motifs or small beads (optional)

Method

Lay each square of fabric on its lining, outer faces together. If you are using a decorative trim (as in the illustration), apply this to the right side of the outer fabric before joining it to the lining. (The trim lies between the top and bottom drawstring casings – see below.) Alternatively, beads or a motif can be sewn on to the outside of the finished bag.

Sew the lining and outer fabric together along the top and bottom edges. Turn right side out and press lightly. Now run a line of stitches along the bottom of each square, 1cm (½in) from the edge. This will form the casing for the bottom cord. Then run three parallel lines of stitches along the top of each square, 3cm (1in), 4cm (1½in) and 5cm (2in) from the edge. These will form the casings for the two drawstring handles.

With right sides facing, sew the side seams together, between the bottom and the top rows of stitching.

Thread the 30cm (12in) of silk cord through the bottom casing (using a safety pin); pull tightly and knot firmly. Cut the ends off to 3cm (just over 1in).

Turn the bag right side out. Attach the silk tassel to the centre bottom of the bag.

Insert one of the 60cm (24in) lengths of silk cord in one end of the upper casing at the top of the bag; thread it through to the opposite end, then back through the casing on the other half of the bag. You should now have two ends of cord on one side of the bag. Knot them together firmly about 2cm (just under 1in) from their ends. Repeat this procedure in the lower casing, starting at the other side of the bag. Pull the two sets of knotted cord handles together to close the bag.

In the schoolroom: Master Guy and Mr Raj Singh.

The imperial drum had beaten loudly during the Boer War (1899–1902) – the manufacture of patriotic souvenirs, the proliferation of images of Empire in advertising from Bovril to England's Glory matches to Colman's Mustard, music hall songs and even an ABC for babies:

> C is for Colonies
> Rightly we boast,
> That of all the great nations
> Great Britain has the most.

Newsreels of victories were shown at fairgrounds and at the newly popular cinemas that were opening up in towns and cities across the country. The painted, musket-carrying red-jacketed lead soldiers that Master Guy lined up in the school room may have been produced to capitalize on the jingoistic fervour generated by the battles of Spion Kop and the siege of Mafeking, but boys would have continued to use them to re-enact these British triumphs, as real-life soldiers of the Royal West Surrey Regiment had reprised the fighting on the North-West frontier at a display at the Crystal Palace in 1898.[18] But while the Conservative party (on the whole), the armed services and the popular press remained imperial-minded throughout the first decade of the new century, uncertainties about the imperial project (including particularly the question of indentured Chinese labour in South Africa that became a political issue in the 1906 election, and the real potential for colonial rivalry with Germany) troubled many Liberals. Although the infant Labour Party was divided in its attitude towards Empire, many of its supporters felt a natural affinity for struggling and oppressed nationalist movements that were stirring across those parts of the globe coloured pink. As the *Clarion*'s Robert Blatchford (who was both a socialist and an Imperialist) observed, while it was said that the sun never set on the British Empire, there were many city slums over which it had never risen. Indeed, the poor physical state of many working-class recruits for the Boer War had awakened the British social conscience to the appalling conditions of many of its own population, and hastened the beginnings of the welfare state.

It was not hard to see how the idea of Empire appealed to those above stairs, many of whom might have investments in South African diamonds or gold, in Indian tea and spices, and would provide the officers fighting to retain the Empire and the administrators sent out to run it, but what about those below stairs? How were they to be associated with the imperial idea? How could they be induced to feel a pride in Empire – and believe that they benefited from Britain's far-flung possessions, since they might one day be called upon to defend them?

Empire Day had first been celebrated in 1902: it was the inspiration of the Anglo-Irish imperialist the Earl of Meath, who campaigned for schools throughout the country to glorify the Empire every year on the birthday of Queen Victoria, 24 May. But in the face of Labour opposition, it was not officially sanctioned by Parliament until 1916, during the third year of the Great War. In one of his messages 'to the children of the Empire', Lord Meath had urged children to 'remember that a great future awaits you, however humble may be your station in life, for no one can take from you the great honour and privilege of being citizens of the British Empire. Your heritage is far greater than the youthful heir to the largest landowner or greatest millionaire. The estate to which you succeed is 12 millions of square miles in extent, much of it undeveloped, and awaiting your industry to make it

'It's got to run like clockwork'. Mr Edgar briefs Charlie
(who has exchanged his usual footman's livery) on the night of the Empire Ball.

The Olliff-Coopers and their guests watch the Empire Day pageant.

fruitful…'[19] A pamphlet issued by the Empire Day League in 1912 had been found in the Edwardian Country House, and it proved the inspiration for pageant to be staged during the Empire Ball, the most glittering event of the Edwardian Country House experience.

The occasion was to be a fancy dress ball on the theme of Empire: there were plenty of precedents. In 1842 Queen Victoria and Prince Albert had thrown a Plantagenet Ball at which Victoria was dressed as Queen Philippa wearing a diamond stomacher (bodice) estimated to be worth £60,000, while Albert masqueraded as Edward III. Encouraged by the success of this venture, the royal couple held a royal *Bal Costume* in 1845 to which guests were required to wear costumes that would have been worn in the decade from 1740 to 1750. In 1874 the artist Sir Frederick Leighton designed a magnificent ball to be held at the home of the future Edward VII, Marlborough House, at which the Princess of Wales, dressed as a grand Venetian lady, led a quadrille with 'Harty Tarty', the Marquis of Hartington. And then, of course, in 1895 there was the Countess of Warwick's ball where the theme was the reigns of Louis XV and XVI, and which led, indirectly, to her conversion to socialism. But perhaps the most famous fancy dress ball of all was the one held by the Duchess of Devonshire to celebrate Queen Victoria's Diamond Jubilee in 1897.

This event was held at Devonshire House, one of the grandest houses in London, which faced on to Piccadilly and looked out over Green Park, to which the guests were instructed to wear any 'allegorical or historical costume before 1815'. This included the servants, who were dressed in Egyptian or Elizabethan outfits hired from theatrical costumiers.[20] The Duchess, a portly woman, was dressed by Worth as Zenobia, Queen of Palmyra, while the Duke paraded as the Holy Roman Emperor, Charles V, as painted by Titian. The then Prince of Wales was togged up as the Grand Master of the Knights Hospitallers of St John of Jerusalem and Chevalier of Malta, which involved an Elizabethan-style costume consisting of a black doublet and hose, a large, feather-plumed hat and silver-spurred boots, while his Princess came positively dripping with pearls as the daughter of Henry II of France and Catherine de Medici, Marguerite de Valois, who married her cousin, Henry of Navarre in 1572. Mrs Keppel, very soon to be *la favorita* of the King, looked customarily beautiful as Madame de Polignac.

Among the rest of the guests could be found almost every historical character of note: some played tribute to their ancestors: the Duke of Somerset reprised his forebear Edward Seymour, 1st Duke and Lord Protector of England in the reign of his nephew Edward VI, while his duchess portrayed the first Duke's sister, Jane Seymour, the third of Henry VIII's six wives. Others rose above themselves: Lady Tweedmouth led a procession as Elizabeth I to her husband's Earl of Leicester; Lady Randolph Churchill elected to be Theodora, wife of the Roman Emperor, Justinian; Countess de Grey dressed as Cleopatra; the Countess of Warwick seemed strangely retrograde as Marie Antoinette (the costume she had worn at her own ball two years earlier); while Viscountess Raincliffe was presumptuous as Catherine the Great, Empress of Russia. Others took classical or metaphysical references: Sibyl, Countess of Westmorland went as Hebe, goddess of youth and culture, as portrayed by Sir Joshua Reynolds (and found the huge stuffed eagle perched on her shoulder something of an inhibition when the dancing started); Lord and Lady Rodney dressed as King Arthur and Queen Guinevere; the Hon. Mrs Reginald Talbot was a Valkyrie; the Countess of Mar and Kellie represented Dante's Beatrice; Lady Doreen Long wore a costume embroidered with the moon and stars as Urania, goddess of astronomy. Others were more modest, representing 'Venetian gentlemen', a 'courtier at the French Court' or 'two Highland gentlemen, 1745', while others were frankly wacky: Margot Asquith came as an oriental snake charmer replete with papier mâché snakes (while her husband, the future Prime Minister H. H. Asquith – who hadn't much wanted to go anyway and didn't stay long – thought it might be held against him if he appeared as Oliver Cromwell, so put on the kit of an ordinary Roundhead soldier); and George Cornwallis-West blacked up as his idea of a slave and donned 'garments like multi-coloured bed quilts'[21] to appear in the retinue of his sister Daisy, Princess of Pless, rather a favourite of Edward VII's, who went as the Queen of Sheba.

The sister-in-law of Lady Miller of Manderston, Mary Curzon (née Leiter, the American heiress to the Marshall Fields Chicago department store fortune), was invited to the Devonshire House ball and went dressed as Valentina Visconti of Milan, though the Curzons were still on their way back from India when the great Manderston ball was held in November 1905. The occasion was the completion of the

Miss Anson enthroned as Britannia, the central figure of the Empire Ball pageant.

The Empire Ball floral displays

The flower arrangements at the Empire Ball were
flamboyant – they had to compete with a myriad of decorations
and colourful costumes. Today, they would be suitable for
a large party, though the table decorations could be
adapted for a dinner party.

Around the stage where the Empire pageant was performed stood box clipped into conical shapes, kentia palms and garlands of moss and white rosebuds, fashioned in wire and raffia in a similar way to the table wreaths (see below), but without the ends being joined up, and these were coiled round the pillars and hung from the candle sconces.

In the dining room, large lead urns stood on either side of the buffet table, each containing tall Asiatic lilies in peach and yellow and matching stems of alstromeria. On every table was a wreath about 10 inches (4cm) deep, made by twisting wire into a circle and winding raffia round it and then covering the raffia with layers of moss. Tiny crab apples and tight red and orange rosebuds were then pushed into the moss so that there was a layer of green and then a layer of floral colour. To complete the arrangement, a tall silver candelabrum was added to the centre of the arrangement.

'At the present time there is quite a rage for floral decorations for the dinner table. Even at old-fashioned dinner parties, where all the dishes are put upon the table, a good deal of space is devoted to the vases and other receptacles that are used to hold the flowers; but for the dinners that are served à la Russe, it is absolutely necessary that the table should be covered by artistic and pretty decorations. Fashionable dinner-givers vie with each other in the quality and arrangement of their flowers as much as the dinners themselves, or the wines served; and we see new ideas for this purpose chronicled day by day. So varying is the fashion, in fact, of our tables that only a weekly journal could give any idea of the charming blends of colour, the exquisite grouping of foliage and flowers, the beauty of form of the baskets, vases, &c., in which they are arranged; or the pretty wreaths in which they are tied to lay upon the silk or damask of the dinner tables of the wealthy.'

MRS BEETON'S COOKERY BOOK

Darcus Howe converses with his fellow guests at the Empire Ball.

'palatial new residence…a form of a "house warming" entertainment', suggested the *Berwickshire News*, 'which afforded an opportunity to the large assembly present – representing the leading families on both sides of the Border, as well as friends from more distant parts – of conveying hearty congratulations to Sir James and Lady Miller. The guests numbered nearly 350, and for their enjoyment and comfort elaborate and princely preparations had been made, to the successful carrying out of which the splendid mansion admirably lends itself.'[22]

The dancing started at 10 p.m. after a supper (detailed in the newspaper) which comprised such delicacies as pheasants in aspic, *mousses de jambon à la* Rothschild, salmon with pink shrimps, ices, jellies, cream trifles, petits fours, and, for those still hungry at 2 a.m (the dancing did not finish until an hour later), devilled game and lamb was provided.

It was an awesome precedent for the Edwardian Country House Empire Ball set in 1912. The house looked surely as magnificent as it had in 1905 when 'the superb permanent furnishings were given additional charm by a wealth of judiciously arranged palms, lilies, white and yellow chrysanthemums and other flowers [while] the spacious ballroom…and the drawing room…were most tastefully adorned with orchids of exquisite beauty'. Flambeaux stuck into the verges guided the carriages and cars up the drive and the whole house glittered into the night as the guests arrived dressed in costumes that invoked various empires in history – the Roman, the Egyptian, the Ottoman, the Napoleonic, the Elizabethan mastery of the high seas and the Victorian and Edwardian empires.

Sir John looked commanding as Nelson; Miss Anson was sinuous as Cleopatra and, since she was obliged to wear a headdress, was delighted to be able to abandon her wig for the evening; Jonty was dressed as Bonnie Prince Charlie, but the *pièce de resistance* was Lady Olliff-Cooper who came majestically down the silver staircase dressed as Marie Antoinette (just as the Countess of Warwick had), complete with a high galleon wig (which she removed for the dancing). As they arrived to be greeted by their hosts, the guests were handed a glass of 'Empire champagne' spiked with 'gunpowder' (which Health and Safety regulations insisted had to be saltpetre instead) by the footmen wearing turbans and sarongs made by Miss Morrison. These clothes made the young men waddle 'like penguins', their bare feet padding along the cold marble floors; the material was really too thick for the Indian-style dress Miss Morrison was seeking to re-create – 'But it's all I could find.'

Everyone had been pressed into service on that important night. Mr Edgar darted hither and thither checking that all was going smoothly; Charlie and Rob, helped by Kenny and Tristan, served drinks to the guests and waited at table for the dinner; while Mrs Davies and Miss Morrison, Becky and Jess helped where they could, carrying coats, directing guests, doing emergency repairs to fragile clothes. It was to be a twenty-hour day for most of the staff, and they had not managed to have a rest before the festivities began. With a houseful of guests, the servants would have to be up early the next day to serve breakfast and minister to their needs and whims. But it was the kitchen that was the real hive of activity – and had been for several days. M. Dubiard had prepared a spread that would have outshone the 1905 buffet: he had spent until five in the morning of the ball locked away in the ice house carving a model of Britannia as the centrepiece for the buffet and had worked right round the clock to provide a sumptuous feast for the Olliff-Coopers and their guests.

'It was completely magic,' marvelled Ellen and Antonia who had helped with the preparation. 'It was just the most fantastic spread you have ever seen and Monsieur was completely exhausted by the time it was ready, but he was also really pleased. He was going round with a huge smile on his face and every time one of the footman carried a tray of food upstairs, he punched the air with pleasure. He's a chef in a million. He deserves so much praise. I just hope that the family appreciate what a wonder he is.'

The table was laden with dishes: for fifty guests there was duck, langoustines, cold turbot, dressed lamb cutlets, a lobster reclining on a bed on 'rocks' made of gelatine, ostrich Wellington, a suckling pig, oysters, hams, salads, minted new potatoes, a selection of English cheeses, sweet soufflés, ices, jewel-coloured fruit jellies turned out from elaborate copper moulds so they looked fairy castles, ices, a selection of chocolate mousses – all served to the guests as they drank champagne sitting at 'small round tables' that had been arranged in the dining room just as they had been in 1905, 'each with its own silver candelabrum and gilt chairs'. And as at that ball, when 'hanging baskets of flowers hung around the five massive thirty-light ormolu and crystal chandeliers, these being flanked on either side by an equal number of hanging baskets of flowers, whose ground work was asparagus sprengeri, set with blooms of lilium longiflorum albium and lilium roseum, the suspenders of these, as well as of the candelabra, being swathed in smilax',[23] flowers were banked around the room.

There was dancing in the ballroom: the family had taken lessons with a local teacher, Mr Morrison, and they led the company in a selection of waltzes, polkas, and, in concession to their locale, a couple of turns of the Gay Gordons. Every lady had been given a small, silver-edged, tasselled dance card with a silver pencil attached, and it was gratifying to see how quickly these filled up and how soon Sir John no longer needed to exhort his guests to take to the floor.

But this was an occasion with a message, and before the guests went into dinner they gathered in the hall to watch the Empire pageant. Dressed as Britannia with trident and Union Jack shield, a helmeted Miss Anson (who was to transmogrify into Cleopatra later when the music struck up) sat at the centre of a *tableau vivant* celebrating the British Empire. She welcomed the guests, and then Master Guy, as First Minister, read out a speech proclaiming, 'Tis the day of Empire, and we meet to do thee homage' to which 'Britannia' replied, 'And who are my subjects, noble lord?'

Master Guy in the role of Britannia's 'first minister'.

'All those, madam, who have given their lives by noble deeds to found thy mighty Empire, these two thousand years,' replied Guy, as a way of introducing the children who were mainly friends of his from the school he was attending in Berwick. These young actors represented 'ancient Britons', 'King Alfred', 'the sea-dog, Sir Francis Drake', 'the great explorers of the North-West passage', and a roll-call of other British 'heroes' culminating in 'thy warriors who guard thy menaced throne and lead thy men to victory', 'thy mighty sailors, who defend thy shores and keep off all who, through jealousy and world-lust, would ravage thy fair island home'. And finally 'These, madam, are thy aeroplanes, whose wings mount the clouds, making thee supreme in air, as on sea,'[24] as small boys zoomed on to the stage each in a cardboard cockpit with flapping cardboard aircraft wings. The children had been kitted out by Miss Morrison 'with Erika helping out', as Master Guy explained, 'going treadle, treadle, treadle, sew, sew, sew until late into the night for three weeks.'

'Britannia' rose and thanked 'you all, troops and Ministers. Our past, and present and future are secure. Our past granite; our present steel; and our future' – she paused – 'what you make it. With duty, love, and honour as our guide, our Empire still shall hold; and like summer roses perfume the world with freedom's gladsome fragrance. Be bold, be brave, do right! And as long as ye do this, I, Britannia, will proudly be your Queen!' Miss Anson declared with a flourish. As the finale, the stage led a rousing chorus of 'Rule Britannia', which most of the guests joined in singing enthusiastically. But at least one did not.

'I could never sing "Rule Britannia, Britons never, never shall be slaves" because implicit is that other people can be slaves,' explained the broadcaster and writer Darcus Howe. Darcus, who came to Britain from Trinidad in 1961, was intrigued to find out how the essence of Englishness in the first years of the old century was being interpreted in the Edwardian country house. Impressive in the costume of a naval commander in recognition of the Empire's long role in fighting for British causes (or the fact that it was naval power that overthrew British rule in the West Indies), he came to Manderston for the Empire Ball. 'I was interested to see how the young people in the house who came here as servants had adjusted to the mores of a time 100 years ago, and how the middle-aged master of the house and his wife from a typical middle-class English life adjusted to this much more privileged and grander life style,' he explained.

Like Mr Raj Singh, Darcus had been educated in English ways, in his case at his school in Trinidad. 'I enjoyed my education tremendously, but I was in constant revolt against the Edwardian snobbery and prejudices that were still prevalent in the colonial education system. As far as I am concerned, the Empire was a battleground, but when you fight your enemy he becomes part of you, you become like him in many ways because you can't help but admire the way he dresses, his military strategy, his culture even. Those who founded the Empire tried to establish white supremacy, but they never fully succeeded and I think that the impact of the imperial tenancy on Africa, India, the Caribbean, has been exaggerated, it really did not have a lasting cultural impact. At my school, for example, there was no real flag-waving or singing "Rule Britannia" or anything like that, and that was because a lot of the English people who taught there had fought in the Second World War, and they had fought shoulder to shoulder alongside black men, so they couldn't believe in that old idea of imperial superiority any more, and in a way they were subverting it from within. And looking back, I don't think that the Empire was built in order to civilize uncivilized people. In my view it was about the pursuit of wealth. Undoubtedly a number of imperialists *did* transform whole areas of the globe, but now that's over. We are in a post-colonial period, and out of that conflict has come a two-way process. It isn't just that there is a lot of Britain in India, Africa, the Caribbean, but there's also a lot of Africa and India and the Caribbean here in Britain today.

'Sir John is seriously circumscribed by the times he's living in. And he's not an aristocrat any more than the original owner of this house was. So it's not aristocratic licence in his case, it's the assumption of autocracy. It's 1912 and in only two years the most terrible war is going to break out, but already things have changed. We are on the cusp of real change. The rise of working-class consciousness seems to be threatening the old order, and it isn't any longer possible to imagine that the "servant problem" will go away. In fact it will get more acute. And so Sir John may well decide to treat his servants with greater generosity. When those in power are forced by changed circumstances to make concessions, they tend to portray it as generosity. But it isn't. It's that they are losing their power. And they know they are.'

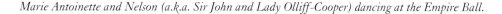

Marie Antoinette and Nelson (a.k.a. Sir John and Lady Olliff-Cooper) dancing at the Empire Ball.

Men of the 1st Nava

Winners
and Losers

'The servants' hall is a little world of its own,' reckoned Samuel and Sarah Adams in their book of guidance, *The Complete Servant*, 'in which the passions, tempers, vices and virtues are brought into play.'[1] It was in this 'little world of its own' that the final drama of the Edwardian Country House was to be played out.

The servants' hall had proved to be the centre of their daily lives for those who worked below stairs. There were a couple of battered old sofas that had certainly seen better days standing at right angles to the fireplace, and it was into these that the servants would gratefully sink to snatch a moment of relaxation between chores. At such times they might skim a newspaper or magazine, or talk, or just close their eyes for a blessed moment's snooze. In the evening when they had finished work, they would often all gather in the servants' hall to have a game of cards, play dominoes or to read. One of the pleasures of the Edwardian experience, Antonia reckoned, had been the nights when the lower servants had huddled round the fire to read aloud John Bunyan's *Pilgrim's Progress*, taking it in turns to read a chapter a night ('Come with me, Neighbour, there are such things to be had which I spoke of, and many more Glories beside. If you believe me not, read here in this Book...'). 'I couldn't believe it. You'd never find me doing something like that at home. I'd be watching television, but here it was really nice to all gather round together to read a book like that. It almost made me nostalgic for the Edwardian way of life. *Almost*,' she qualified.

There was an upright, almost-in-tune piano in the corner and both Rob and Erika, the third housemaid, were accomplished pianists and would sometimes sit at the keyboard in the evening picking out tunes – Rob even managed Beethoven's 'Moonlight Sonata', which impressed everyone. Most of the servants enjoyed music. Becky had a fine soprano singing voice – her clear, high rendition of 'Pié Jesu' was inclined to bring a tear to most eyes – and Jess loved to dance. One night the servants had had a ceilidh in their hall with Scottish fiddle players. Everyone agreed that it had been a splendid evening with plenty of opportunity for energetic reels, fairly inauthentic 'Scottish' cries, and plenty of noisy clapping in time with the music. It had been refreshing to see the 'upper ten' join in with gusto – Miss Morrison was soon breathless with all the charging across the room, arms folded, and Mrs Davies was puffing a bit too, while the butler, Mr Edgar, smiled benignly as watched what he liked to consider as his 'family' having a good time. All, that is, except M. Dubiard who, disenchanted with the demands of the Edwardian Country House, sat alone in the kitchen plucking a grey partridge and reflecting on the solitary nature of life – and death.

But the servants' hall was not always a warm and friendly place. It could be much as the Adamses had described, a battle ground resulting in misunderstandings, hurt feelings and wounded pride, as thirteen people who had never met before, and really did not have much in common (as Charlie pointed out), lived in very close proximity to each other as they struggled to make sense of the Edwardian experience.

It could also be a confusing place. On the one hand, it had all the elements of a family in the warmth and sympathy that each often expressed for the others. There had been a natural pairing: Becky and Jess worked as a team cleaning the house and almost instantly became very good friends, delighting in how much they shared in their attitudes towards life, and Jess was always interested to hear about Becky's grandmother's experiences in service, and how the first housemaid regarded her time in the Edwardian Country House as a form of homage to her much-loved relation's hard life. Mrs Davies and Miss Morrison soon found that they too had a natural affinity, as upper servants inclined to feel that the younger generation really didn't know the meaning of hard work, though Mrs Davies was always very protective of 'her girls', recognizing how onerous their duties were, and regarded herself as a mother figure and confidante to them. Rob and Charlie were a duo too, sharing a bedroom as well as their footmen's duties, though this could lead to friction at times. And then there were Ellen and Kenny whose burgeoning romance made them a couple, snatching moments alone together whenever they could, but still joining in the general life of the below stairs community.

The situation had all the tensions of family life too, and could erupt into angry accusations, flare-ups, tears and sulks before peace was restored, since, just like a family, they were all in it together for the duration.

But the servants' hall also presented a social microcosm far removed from this family model. It was here that the rigid distinctions of status were enforced with a hierarchy that sharply divided upper and lower servants, with further calibrations woven through the two categories. At first the lower servants had found it hard to comprehend the notion of instant obedience ('discipline, discipline, discipline' was Mr Edgar's mantra), of not speaking until you were spoken to, of the insistence on correct address – 'Sir' for the butler, always *Mrs* Davies, *Miss* Morrison, *Monsieur* Dubiard – and had been bemused and not a little insulted by the strict emphasis on precedence at all times, filing into prayers, sitting in order of rank at all meals, walking the two or three miles to church every Sunday and the same number back whatever the weather, while the upper servants rode in a trap. But gradually the lower servants had come, if not to accept, then to be resigned to the fact that that was how things were, and would be so long as they lived in their Edwardian personas.

M. Dubiard relaxes in the servants' hall by picking out tunes on the battered piano.

Kenny's theory was characteristically to the point. 'It goes right through the ranks in Edwardian society: you've got the rich people upstairs who dump on the footmen, and then the footman dumps on whoever is below him, which happens to be the hall boy in my case. And I know that I should be working hard and showing respect to try to earn promotion to third footman or something, but basically I'd rather be at the bottom of the pile than doing with all these people who are always pulling rank, because they consider themselves to be a notch above the person below them.' As one of the footmen, Rob could see how Kenny had constructed his paradigm, but surveying the dynamics of the hierarchy from *his*

Letters home. Mrs Davies recounts her experiences in the Edwardian Country House.

place on the ladder enabled him to recognize why there was so little solidarity at times among those in the house who might have been thought to have common cause. 'The people at the top don't deal with the people at the bottom. They give their orders to the people half-way down, who then tell the people at the bottom what to do. And that can create animosity between the upper and the lower servants and among the lower servants too.'

On the night of 5 November the entire cosmos of the hierarchy of the Edwardian Country House was created *multum in parvo* right there in the servants' hall. The previous week Sir John had announced at prayers that he had decided that as the Edwardian experiment was coming to an end he would throw a party for the servants. The food would be supplied by caterers, they would be waited on by outside help employed for the occasion, they would eat off the family's china ('the everyday stuff', Mr Edgar interjected hastily), they would be served wine from the family's cellar rather than their usual jugs of beer, and there would be dancing 'exactly the same dances as were danced at the Empire Ball' to the music of a two-piece 'orchestra', and the evening would be rounded off with fireworks and a bonfire. 'I hope that pleases you, thank you and good morning to you all,' the master of the house concluded.

It sounded wonderful. 'I am going to invite some guests,' Mr Edgar announced later at dinner in the servants' hall. 'I am going to invite the family. That's exactly what would have happened,' he added hurriedly, looking around the table at the startled faces of the lower servants staring at him.

Within the limited range of clothes available to them, the servants made an effort for the occasion. 'It's much easier for the boys,' sighed Antonia, who admitted that whatever she did, she did not find that her corset made her feel curvaceous and sexy, but more like 'a frumpy, dowdy, androgynous workhorse that needs a bath'. Nevertheless, like the other maids, she brushed out her hair and found a length of ribbon, and all the servants enjoyed the novelty of sitting at table in their own hall eating food that had been neither cooked nor served by them and talking freely to each other without waiting to be asked. 'To Edwardiana,' Mr Edgar proposed, and they all raised their glasses and repeated enthusiastically: 'To Edwardiana.'

'Sir John and Lady Olliff-Cooper,' announced Mr Edgar a few minutes later, conducting the upstairs family to their own basement to join in the servants' ball. As would have been expected, Sir John led the dancing with the housekeeper, and the butler partnered Lady Olliff-Cooper, while Mr Jonathan asked the first housemaid if she would care to dance and Master Guy made a beeline for the second housemaid, his companion in fire-making. The upper servants seemed delighted to entertain their employers and took them on a tour of the mysteries of the engine rooms of their ship of luxury. For Sir John and Mr Jonathan it was the first time that either had ever ventured below stairs, and Sir John gamely drew a comparison between Kenny's shambolic end of corridor that served as his bedroom, and their own son's 'teenage' room. Lady Olliff-Cooper and Miss Anson had already had a lightning tour of the kitchens when they had been almost forcibly dragged down there by the chef at the height of the servants' discontent, but they tactfully did not refer to that occasion. Master Guy, the only upstairs habitué of downstairs, took a proprietorial pride in showing off his knowledge of the servants' labyrinthine quarters to his parents.

The Titanic

The British liner *Titanic* was built in Belfast for the White Star Line. It was one of the largest liners in existence at the time, and its safety features – including watertight compartments in the hull – were supposed to mean that it was unsinkable. But on 14 April 1912, four days out from Southampton on its maiden voyage to America, the *Titanic* hit an iceberg some 400 miles off the coast of Newfoundland, and sank within two and a half hours. Over 1,500 people perished out of the 2,224 aboard.

The liner was plying the highly competitive Atlantic route and its speed appears to have been excessive for the icy conditions. The ship was also equipped with far too few lifeboats – in all, a shortfall of over a thousand places.

The *Titanic* has become another symbol of Edwardian inequality, since 63 per cent of the 'top deck' first-class passengers were saved, as compared to 38 per cent of the 'below deck' third-class passengers, and 24 per cent of the crew.

But the evening was not an unqualified success: when the chef, looking baleful, approached his master and embarked on a harangue, Sir John's response, 'I really can't understand what you are saying,' resounded with a deeper lack of comprehension. When Miss Morrison intervened, pointing out that 'There is a time and a place for everything and this is neither the time, nor the place', it was difficult to imagine when and where that would be. Then, when asked what lessons he would take away from his time at the house, Kenny replied: 'Well, I've learned how to cut up mashed potatoes into neat squares.'

As family and servants stood in the cold night air watching the fireworks explode across the Manderston façade, it was hard not to notice that the straw guy on the top of the blazing bonfire was wearing a mask that made him look remarkably like Sir John.

There were more complex and profound things, though, that the servants admitted they had learned in the Edwardian Country House than the practical skills, most of which they would be unlikely ever to use again. All had found reserves of physical and emotional strength that had surprised them. And no matter how reluctant some were to admit it, they had found how dependent they were on one another: how they worked like a team or nothing worked at all. This was an insight that had been crystallized for Charlie when Robert Swann, an explorer who had followed in the footsteps of Captain Scott to the Antarctic, came to the house to show lantern slides and talk about his expedition that had sought to recreate Scott's heroic but tragic expedition through ice and snow in 1912. Sir John had extended an invitation to those below stairs too, and most had accepted. For Charlie there were 'lots of parallels between what he did in the Antarctic, and what we are doing here. In his case it was reaching the South Pole, in our case it's becoming Edwardian. Becoming Edwardian seems a small achievement compared to traversing the Antarctic, but we still had to go through many of the same sort of difficulties. His team all had very different personalities, just as we have here, but if everyone is actually working towards the same goal then that you have to put your trust in each other that you will make the thing work to get there. They achieved their ambition because they did it as a team, and that's how we'll do it too.'

If the servants were prepared to buckle down to their lowly position in the great chain of Edwardian being, it was because they acknowledged (without accepting) that in such an unequal, highly specified society, a structure as rigid as steel was needed to keep everything in place and that once one plank was removed, the whole would wobble precariously. 'Hierarchy is essential to running a house like this,' Rob had concluded. 'If you dispense with it everything would fall into complete chaos.' When he reflected later on his experiences, even Kenny might come to realize that frequently what he was railing against was less the actions of his individual masters – whether the family or the upper servants – and more the assumptions that pertained less than a century ago that underpinned the whole social edifice. In the words of Gwen Raverat, who was sixteen when Edward VII came to the throne:

> Ladies were ladies in those days; they did not do things themselves, they told other people what to do and how to do it. My mother would have told anybody how to do anything: the cook how to skin a rabbit, or the groom how to harness a horse; though she had never done, or even observed, these operations herself. She would cheerfully have told an engine-driver how to drive his engine, and he would have taken it quite naturally, and have answered, 'Yes, ma'am,' 'Very good, ma'am,' 'Quite right, ma'am,' and then would have gone on driving his engine exactly as before, with hardly even an inward grin at the vagaries of the upper classes; while my mother would certainly have thought his driving much improved.[2]

Captain Scott

In 1910 Captain Robert Falcon Scott was chosen to lead a scientific expedition to the Antarctic. It was not the first time he had journeyed to these icy wastes: in 1902 he and Ernest Shackleton had travelled by sledge to the highest latitude yet reached in Antarctica. But this second expedition was to end in failure: on 18 January 1912, Scott and four members of his expedition reached the South Pole, only to find that a Norwegian expedition led by Roald Amundsen had beaten them to it by more than a month. Scott and his companions perished in the snow on their trek home in terrible weather conditions, probably from lack of food.

The heroic tragedy caught the imagination of the Edwardian public, but it had been a mismanaged attempt. The gravest mistake was to use men to pull the sledges carrying the heavy scientific equipment and supplies, rather than huskies as the Norwegians had.

She concluded: 'Of course I disapproved of having servants on principle, even when they were treated with affection and respect as ours were [though a housemaid had once been dismissed for not mending her mistresses' gloves properly]. But this was just an abstract theory; for I had never considered in the least how we should get on without them; in fact it seemed to me quite inevitable that they should be there, a necessary and very tolerable arrangement, both for them and for us.'[3]

But this 'very tolerable arrangement' was beginning to seem a great less so. Becky, in particular, had thought about the demand for change in Edwardian society, and in this she had drawn closer to Miss Anson, the predicament of their sex overcoming the barriers of class. Acting as Miss Anson's personal maid, Becky had come to understand many of the older woman's frustrations at the restricted life she led, and her need to get away on occasions from the etiquette and what she saw as her inferior position in a household that could oppress and exhaust her. But as she read in the newspaper about the death of Emily Davison – a martyr to the cause of women's right to the vote, who, waving a suffragette banner, had run out in front of the King's horse during the Derby in June 1913 and had been fatally injured by its hooves – Becky knew that this was not a personal struggle: it was a political and economic one for all women. She and Miss Anson studied the report, appalled to see how the popular press trivialized the outrage with no mention of Emily Davison's educational achievements or political beliefs. 'If enough people feel strongly enough to give their life for a cause' (though it was not entirely clear that Miss Davison *had* intended to die), Miss Anson predicted, 'things will change. They just will.'

In the provisions of the first Reform Act in 1832, women had been left out of the process of democratization because their 'natures' were considered to exclude them from public life and keep them in the domestic sphere. By 1914 some eight million men, around 60 per cent of the population, were enfranchised and no women were. The battle was for the vote: but women wanted the vote so that their demands for equal access to education and for legal and economic rights would be forced on to the nation's agenda. The 'women's movement' had a history stretching back into the nineteenth century, and notable reforms for their campaigns included the Married Women's Property Acts in 1870 and 1882; rights in the custody of children in 1873; the right to judicial separation and maintenance in 1878; the raising of the age of consent to sexual intercourse to sixteen in 1885; in 1886 the repeal of the Contagious Diseases Act (legislation introduced in the 1860s in garrison and port towns to combat the spread of venereal disease among enlisted men by identifying and registering 'common prostitutes' who could then be forcibly interned in hospital for up to nine months, while

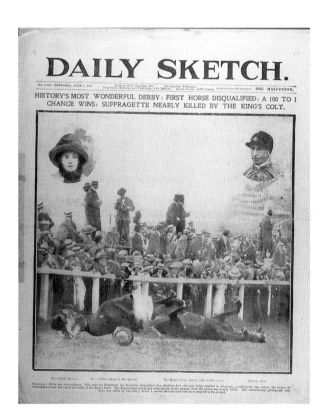

no action was taken to curb the sexual proclivities of men, and often non-prostitutes were degraded); and the gradually widening of access to employment in shops, schools, offices, the civil service and even the medical profession.[4] In 1869 women were granted the right to vote in local government elections; elementary, secondary and university education was extended to women from the 1870s; and propertied women could vote for school boards (1875), county councils (1888) and parish and district councils (1894) – since these were regarded as a legitimate extension of women's concerns for health, education and welfare.

In the Edwardian period 55 per cent of single women and 14 per cent of married women were in paid work; women were active in such organizations as the Mothers' Union (which had 40,000 members), the Girls' Friendly Society (some quarter of a million members and associates), and such bodies as the Women's Council for the Primrose League and the Women's Liberal Unionist Association, which were formed as auxiliaries to the main political parties; they were prominent canvassers and organizers at election time, sat on school boards, were elected as local councillors, and under their auspices free school meals, subsidized milk for children and outdoor relief for the elderly were introduced. Yet women still laboured under considerable economic and legal inequalities and they did not have the vote in elections to parliament. The largest of the Edwardian suffrage organizations was the National Union of Women's Suffrage Societies (NUWSS), which consolidated sixteen constituent societies under the leadership of Millicent Fawcett in 1897. It was independent of any political party and believed in constitutional means to gain the vote. The WSPU (Women's Social and Political Union) had been founded by Emmeline Pankhurst in 1903: its motto was 'Deeds not words', and during the 1906 election it moved centre stage, challenging the constitutional suffragist movements which the Pankhursts (Emmeline was joined by two of her daughters, Christabel and Sylvia) and their supporters regarded as 'all very polite and very tame'. The WSPU adopted the designation of 'suffragette' scornfully coined for it by the *Daily Mail*, and decided on militant action intended to force the hand of the Liberal government which was, in principle, sympathetic but dilatory.

However, although it was a national demand with activity all over Britain, women's suffrage was not high on the political agenda of the triumphant Liberal Party and when, in 1908, H. H. Asquith, who was an intransigent opponent, succeeded Campbell-Bannerman as Prime Minister, the suffragettes decided that 'argument [was] exhausted'. They escalated their campaign – which had previously consisted of heckling at meetings, refusing to pay fines, and sporadic attempts to storm the House of Commons – into a militant action, the aim of which was to 'to set everyone talking about votes for women, to keep the subject in the press, to leave the government no peace from it'. These tactics, which included throwing stones at politicians' windows, hurling eggs, chaining themselves to railings, scattering marbles under the hooves of police horses and setting fire to pillar boxes, divided the movement. The constitutionalists favoured peaceful lobbying as the way to persuade their political masters that they were sufficiently responsible to have a say in the affairs of the nation, while a more militant wing were convinced that without dramatic and disruptive action, their cause would be disregarded for ever.

For their civil disobedience, many suffragettes were imprisoned. In gaol a number went on hunger strike and, fearful of what it would do to public opinion should one of these women die, the Liberal government ordered forcible feeding and then introduced the infamous 'Cat and Mouse Act' in 1913. Under its terms, women were released from prison on licence when their refusal to eat had weakened them, and were then taken back into custody as soon as they had regained their health.

How would a person in Miss Anson's position have felt about the campaign for votes for women in the Edwardian period? In her role she certainly had the time to organize meetings, get up petitions, write letters and pamphlets, help to sew banners or raise funds if she so chose. Though her brother-in-law had admitted that 'there is no reason on earth why women shouldn't have the vote', he had declared unequivocally 'I will have no suffragettes in this house,' so, without independent economic means, she would have been confined to activities of a gradualist nature. But as an upper-class woman (or certainly living the life of an upper-class woman), resident mainly in the country, she might have been expected to be more conservative in her approach to such matters than her urban, middle-class sisters. They were in the vanguard of modernism and change, benefiting most from new educational and professional opportunities and most eager to link emancipation to social change and be treated as capable citizens with a voice in their governance.

And what about Becky and other working women like her – what would have been their opinion of 'the cause'? The vote might hardly seem a pressing concern to working-class women, more concerned with getting enough to eat for themselves and their families and a roof over their heads than bothering with abstract talk about 'rights', though in fact there were considerable numbers of radical suffragists among women factory and mill workers in the north of England fighting for a range of women's rights, including the vote.[5] The suffragists argued that the vote would raise women's wages and improve their positions, and drew a direct parallel between women's disadvantaged and exploited industrial position and their exclusion from both trade unions and the vote.[6] But in any case the WSPU had little interest in mobilizing the working classes or active concern for their social conditions (other than Sylvia Pankhurst, who in 1912 broke away and set about establishing a mass movement that would link the emancipation of women to the concerns of working women in the East End of London). If she had had the vote, how would an Edwardian housemaid in Becky's position have voted? Would she have deferred to the political opinion of her employers, even though the Secret Ballot Act of 1872 was intended to loosen to grip of landlord over tenant, or in Becky's case, employee? Or, 'unorganized and un-unionized' as she and her fellow domestic servants were, what policies would have won her vote? It was not until the Representation of the People Act in 1918 that all women over thirty were enfranchised, as were all adult males, so it was an academic question in the Edwardian Country House.

On 4 August 1914, Britain declared war on Germany. The Edwardian era was at an end. Less than two weeks later, *The Times* called for those employing 'men in unproductive domestic occupations, both in and out of doors' to encourage them to join up:

'Women admire the brave young men as they march away to death or glory'.
Painting by Reginald Higgins, May 1915.

There are large numbers of footmen, valets, butlers, gardeners, grooms and gamekeepers, whose services are more or less superfluous and can either be dispensed with or replaced by women without seriously hurting or incommoding anybody…the well-to-do classes are, as a whole, responding finely to the call…but many of them may not perhaps have realized yet how large a reserve of the national manhood is represented by those who serve their personal comforts and gratifications.[7]

Pamela Horn quotes the estimate that between 1914 and 1918 nearly 400,000 servants left domestic service for the armed forces, or to work in various areas of war production – transport, engineering, commerce and the land.[8] In the spring of 1915, women started to be recruited to work in munitions factories, and between then and the end of the war, around a million went on to do such work; a contemporary estimate suggests that around a quarter of this number had been domestic servants. As women were employed in industry and commerce in place of men (invariably at a lower rate of pay), so they were in domestic service and the percentage of female domestics to male increased, and snobberies about preferring footmen to parlour maids had to be forgotten. In one household at least the butler's duties 'fell on the head parlour maid, and [the employer's] valeting was done by the second parlour maid'.[9]

The pay for war work was higher: Pamela Horn quotes a domestic servant who had earned 2s 6d a week before the war, and was able to take home £3 a week from her wartime job in a cable factory, plus enjoying greater companionship and freedom.[10] Consequently, those who wished to employ domestic staff were obliged to increase their rates too: a parlour maid who was paid £16 a year in 1914 could command £24 in 1918.

In 1914, all fighting men were volunteers. Conscription was not introduced until January 1916, when the first Military Services Act inaugurated conscription for single men aged eighteen to forty-one (later, married men in that age bracket were conscripted). In these first eighteen months of a war that had been confidently predicted to be over in five, 2.4 million men joined the British Army of their own volition, increasing its size tenfold.[11] Masters were encouraged to let servants go. In January 1915, *Country Life* sternly quizzed its readers:

> Have you a Butler, Groom, Chauffeur, Gardener, or Gamekeeper serving you who, at this moment should be serving your King and Country? Have you a man serving at your table who should be serving a gun? Have you a man digging your garden who should be digging trenches? Ask your men to enlist TO-DAY.[12]

Country house owners, urged to be patriotic, usually guaranteed to keep a man's job open while he was away fighting, and to pay an income to the man's wife and children if he had them. It is quite possible that Charlie, Rob, Tristan and Kenny would have all volunteered, and Tristan's expertise with horses would have been particularly valuable to the still indispensable cavalry. Charlie expressed some doubts: 'I can see why those upstairs would volunteer. They were fighting to keep all this going,' he said, indicating the kitchen staff hard at work preparing another lavish meal, 'but I'm not so sure about why we might want to go and fight.'

'If Sir John had said you should enlist, you would have said, "Yes, sir", there would have been no argument,' insisted Mr Edgar. And if they had not volunteered (or been volunteered) the young men would have been conscripted in 1916.

In the first weeks of war, as many as 30,000 men a day flocked to enlist, queuing all day outside recruiting offices. All classes were united in the patriotic fervour with which they welcomed the war.

Young patricians were eager to get to the front as soon as possible. 'Our one great fear,' recalled Oswald Mosley, 'was that war would be over before we got there.' Lord Tennyson dressed and packed 'in feverish haste, so anxious was I not to run any chance of missing the war'. The poet Rupert Brooke declared 'the one central purpose of my life, the aim and end of it, the thing God wants of me, is to get good at beating Germans', and he wrote to another friend: 'Come and die. It'll be great fun.'[13] Lord Derby, touring the country to raise volunteers, told a meeting of the Territorial Association that 'If I had twenty sons, I should be ashamed if every one of them did not go to the front when his time came.'[14] But Mary, Countess of Wemyss, who was to see two of her sons killed in the war, was more realistic about the prospect in 'the last days of the Era of Peace'. She described her youngest son, Yvo Charteris, who was killed at Loos when he was just nineteen, reading the Declaration of War posted in the streets in August 1914: 'How many youths must have gazed with innocent, untroubled eyes, and pleasurable thrills of interest and excitement at their own death warrant, as they read the fatal Declaration which was to destroy so many millions of lives, shaking all things to their foundations, wasting the treasures of the past and casting its sinister influence far into the future.'[15]

Country house ladies organized clothing and food parcels for the troops and for prisoners of war, convened knitting parties, ran canteens at railway stations where troops were marching off to war, and some actually crossed over to France. The Duchess of Westminster ran a Red Cross hospital in a former casino at Le Touquet; Mrs Keppel helped in a field hospital in Étaples; Lady Angela Forbes ran a military canteen at Boulogne, while the Duchess of Sutherland organized an ambulance unit in Belgium. Young upper-class women trained as VAD nurses and performed such tasks for strangers as emptying chamber pots, changing soiled sheets, and dressing and washing the wounded – tasks that in pre-war years they would not have dreamed of doing for themselves since servants would have always done it for them – and grieved as their lovers, brothers and friends were killed.

By the end of 1914, six peers, sixteen baronets, ninety-five sons of peers and eighty-two sons of baronets lay among the dead on the Western Front. And so it continued throughout the Great War. Lord Rosebery spoke of 'the fountain of tears [being] nearly dry. One loss follows another until one is dazed.' 'Truly,' wrote Lady Curzon at the end of the war, 'England lost the flower of her young men in those terrible days... there was scarcely one of our friends who did not lose a son, a husband, or a brother.' Although, as David Cannadine points out, the majority of the notables who served did return home, not since the Wars of the Roses had so many 'patricians died so suddenly and so violently'. In *relative* terms, it was on the landed classes that the greatest sacrifice fell.

In the Edwardian Country House, Sir John would have been too old for active service (the upper age limit was extended to fifty-one in April 1918, but he was fifty-six), and if Master Guy could still be thought of as aged ten in 1914, he would still be too young by 1918. But Mr Jonathan was a different matter. Aged eighteen in 1914, he would most likely to have been a member of the legendary 'lost generation' of that terrible war. In the first year of the war 86,000 British fighting men were dead, wounded or missing (compared to 850,000 French and 650,000 Germans in the same period). By the end of the Great War the death toll was not far short of three quarters of a million (722,785) men. One in eight was killed: one in four was injured. The highest losses were in the army among soldiers fighting in the trenches in France and Flanders. Those who served in the army had only a one in two chance of surviving the war without being killed, wounded or taken prisoner.[16]

In absolute terms, because a greater proportion of the population and thus of fighting men was working class, these were the majority of those killed. In the First World War, 450,000 infantrymen died. Only 4 per cent of the infantry who died were commissioned: 96 per cent were from the ranks. But the war mirrored Edwardian social inequalities: many of the working-class men who volunteered were rejected as unfit for active service. Over one million of those examined between 1917 and 1918 were considered to be physically unfit for combat duty and of those from urban industrial areas around seven out of every ten men would be assessed as Grade III or IV, meaning that they were fit only for clerical work. In effect, the humbler a man's social origins were, the less likely he was to see active service, whereas the wealthy who were passed into the services as Grade I – 'men without any disabilities' – were deemed healthy enough to die.

The army hierarchy replicated the social hierarchy: officers were predominantly drawn from the middle and upper classes. In the conditions of trench warfare, junior officers led their men into battle: they were first 'over the top'. Whether they were leading an attack, a night patrol, a *reconnoitre* expedition or crawling out of their trenches to repair a barbed wire fence, they were first in the line of fire. This ideology of glory and sacrifice had been inculcated at home, in church, on the school playing fields, at university, and in books and magazines that recounted Britain's heroic imperial role in the world. Now the tab had to be picked up. There was a direct correlation between age and mortality, and between class and mortality: young officers were the most vulnerable category, the men least likely to survive the war. As J. M. Winter points out, 'Casualty rates among officers were substantially higher than among men in the ranks, and the most dangerous rank in the army – the subaltern – was recruited throughout much of the war from current pupils or old boys of the public schools and ancient universities: the finishing schools of the propertied classes.'[17] Between 1914 and 1918, 37,452 officers were killed and the rolls of honour of the fallen of the universities of Oxford and Cambridge were disproportionately heavy, as were those of the public schools. One in four men under twenty-four in 1914 from these universities would be killed: approximately one in five public school boys would perish.[18]

When he arrived at the Edwardian Country House, Jonathan Olliff-Cooper had just left Winchester school, and that autumn he went up to Magdalen College, Oxford, to read history. Winchester lost 500 boys in the First World War: the fallen from Magdalen College were 200.

Mr Jonathan

When eighteen-year old Jonathan (who is known to his family as Jonty) arrived at the Edwardian Country House, he had taken his A levels and was about to go up to Magdalen College, Oxford, to read Modern History. He was confident that living in the Edwardian period was going to be 'a very interesting historical experience'. But he was apprehensive too: 'I can't just nip down to the pub when I want to, or listen to the sort of music I enjoy, or send e-mails or watch television, and I have to ask my father's permission to do anything since he is the master of the house.' And he wondered how he would find life with servants. 'I ran the Cadet Force at school, so I'm used to telling people what to do, but maybe I will be embarrassed by servants waiting on me, and restrained because I can't be familiar with them. I won't be able to get to know them even though a lot of them are around the same age as I am.'

During the war, numbers of country houses were turned over to nursing the wounded; serried rows of beds filled former ballrooms while exquisitely plastered dining rooms became operating theatres. Others were used as convalescent homes. When the war was over many of the heirs were dead; others, squeezed by higher taxes and falling incomes, were forced to sell. A fifth of the land in Scotland, some 4 million acres, came on the market after the First World War. Death duties were increased to 40 per cent in 1919 and would continue to rise, while changes in the way that land was valued made this levy still more punitive.

And in many ways, the peace was not to bring all that people had fervently hoped for either. Most women munitions workers were laid off at the end of the war and only a limited number of women retained their jobs in aircraft factories and other industries, or moved into jobs that had previously been categorized as 'men's work' in the iron and steel industry, or as labourers in the docks, leather works, sawmills and brewing. Though some were retained as booking clerks and delivery drivers, and many women kept their jobs in shops and offices when peace came, most were dismissed from jobs they had had on the railways or buses. The government was fulfilling its pledge to those men who had left their jobs to go to war under the Restoration of Pre-War Practices Act. which had promised that such work would revert to men when the war was over.[19]

They were reminded that 'their first duty was to the soldier – the man who had done his bit for the past four years – and would now be wanting to return to his normal occupation', and were pressurized to take up traditional 'women's trades': laundry work and domestic service, with assurances that being a servant would be different now since mistresses had learned to 'appreciate' good servants and treat them with consideration. But many women were unconvinced and were determined to resist a return to domestic service even if this had been the work they had done before the war. An interview in the *Daily Chronicle* with a munitions worker who was prepared to take any job 'except domestic service', and employers were obliged to offer higher wages and guarantees of free time and even in some cases a written agreement of working conditions (including an end to the demeaning practice of calling servants by their first name or surname only), and even then 65 per cent of women said they would not go back into service whatever the inducements.[20]

'One day all this will be yours'.
As the elder son, Mr Jonathan contemplates
what might have been his future.

But frequently there was little choice. Unemployment benefit was cut after three months, and if women refused domestic work (whether they had ever done it before or not) their benefit was stopped. The 1920 Unemployment Insurance Act covered all manual workers except agricultural workers and domestic servants, and it was not until 1946 that domestic servants of both sexes were protected by national employment insurance.[21] The slump of the 1920s hit the manufacturing trades hard and reduced women's employment opportunities further. Nevertheless, the number of servants never again reached pre-war levels.

Despite the government's belief that domestic service was the answer to women's unemployment, there was a shift towards non-residential jobs and an overall slow decline until the Second World War, after which the decline was terminal. The number of women in domestic service fell by 46 per cent between 1931 and 1951, and by the latter date there were fewer than three-quarters of a million women domestic servants employed in England and Wales.[22]

It was much the same with men servants: despite government propaganda, the younger ones did not see that the 'home fit for a hero' that they had been promised meant someone else's house, and had no wish to return to life below stairs and replicate their wartime experience of scrubbing, peeling, scouring, polishing and standing to attention when spoken to. Many of the older demobilized men had difficulty finding a job since so many landed families in straitened post-war circumstances were forced to prune their domestic establishments drastically. The 1921 census recorded that of a total of 61,006 male indoor servants, only 48 per cent were working in private houses; the rest were employed as waiters or worked in institutions or commercial organizations.[23]

As the rain poured down on a dank, dark Scottish afternoon, Sir John Olliff-Cooper stood under a dripping umbrella looking out of the Cheviot Hills as the mists rolled around their bracken-covered slopes, and reflected on how difficult he was going to find it to leave the Edwardian Country House. In three months he had grown accustomed to the life and deeply attached to the house where he and his family had lived their Edwardian experiment. Now he was about to leave it for the twenty-first century, and he found that his feelings of proprietorial pride and anxiety conflated with those that he imagined his Edwardian counterpart might have felt in 1914.

Inside the house, sitting in his room with the table lamp throwing a soft pool of light on to the books he was leafing through, Sir John's heir was in a reflective mood too. 'If you had survived the First World War [and he knew how heavily the odds were stacked against that possibility for his age and class], and you had come back to this,' Mr Jonathan mused, 'you would probably view your inheritance with disgust. You would have seen young men who had been your footmen or hall boy or groom fighting shoulder to shoulder with you, going through the same hell in the trenches that you were going through, and being incredibly brave. And then you would come back to a rigid social hierarchy like this and you would think: "This isn't fair and it isn't right. It's not what we were fighting for".'

Julian Grenfell, who was to be mortally wounded at Ypres, acknowledged the debt as a metaphor in a poem he wrote in 1915, two months before he was killed, 'Prayer for Those on the Staff':

Fighting in the mud, we turn to Thee,	But not on us, for we are men
In these dread times of battle, Lord,	Of meaner clay, who fight in clay,
To keep us safe, if so may be,	But on the Staff, the Upper Ten
From shrapnel, snipers, shell and sword.	Depends the issue of the Day.[24]

Footnotes

INTRODUCTION

1 John Betjeman, 'Architecture' in Simon Nowell-Smith (ed.) in *Edwardian England: 1901–1914* (Oxford University Press, 1964), p. 362.

CHAPTER ONE

1 Samuel Hynes, *The Edwardian Turn of Mind* (Princeton University Press, 1968), p. 4.
2 Wilfrid Scawen Blunt, *My Diaries: Being a Personal Narrative of Events, 1888–1914: Part II* (Martin Secker, 1920), p. 1.
3 Jose Harris, *Private Lives, Public Spirit: Britain 1870–1914* (Oxford University Press, 1993), p. 2.
4 Cornelius Rozenraad, 'The International Money Market', quoted in David Kynaston, *The City of London. Volume II: The Golden Years, 1990–1914* (Chatto & Windus, 1995), p. 7.
5 Kynaston, p. 7.
6 Marghanita Laski, 'Domestic Life', in Simon Nowell-Smith (ed.), *Edwardian England, 1901–1914* (Oxford University Press, 1964), p. 141.
7 Harris, p. 97.
8 W. D. Rubenstein, *Men of Property: The Very Wealthy in Britain Since the Industrial Revolution* (Croom Helm, 1981), pp. 30–41.
9 Harris, p. 100.
10 W. H. Mallock, *The Old Order Changes* (London: 1886), p. 28.
11 John Betjeman, 'Architecture' in Nowell-Smith (ed.), p. 353.
12 E. S. Turner, 'Gilded Drainpipes', *London Review of Books*, 10 June 1999, pp. 31–2.
13 Lady Frances Balfour, quoted in J. Mordaunt Crook, *The Rise of the Nouveaux Riches: Style and Status in Victorian and Edwardian Architecture* (John Murray, 1999), p. 65.
14 Quoted in Crook, p. 59.
15 J. B. Priestley, *The Edwardians* (Wm. Heinemann, 1970), p. 61.
16 Martin Daunton, *Trusting Leviathan: The Politics of Taxation in Britain, 1799–1914* (Cambridge University Press, 2001), p. 21.
17 Parliamentary Debates –3rd series 125, 18 April 1853, quoted in Daunton, p. 230.
18 Elizabeth Roberts, 'Women's Work, 1840–1914', in L. A. Clarkson (ed.), *British Trade Union and Labour History: A Compendium* (Macmillan, 1990), p. 231.
19 Pamela Horn, *Life Below Stairs in the 20th Century* (Sutton Publishing, 2001), p. 10.
20 Vita Sackville-West, *The Edwardians* (The Hogarth Press, 1930, reprinted Virago Press, 1983), p. 55.
21 See Peter Mandler, *The Fall and Rise of the Stately Home* (Yale University Press, 1997), in particular Part II: 'Fortresses of Barbarism, 1867–1914', pp. 109–52.
22 [Berwickshire newspaper]
23 Clive Aslet, 'Manderston, Berwickshire', *Country Life*, 15 February 1979, pp. 390–3.
24 Clive Aslet, *The Last Country Houses* (New Haven and London: Yale University Press, 1982), p. 124.
25 From Kinross's obituary in the Council of the Royal Scottish Architects' annual report for 1931, quoted in Aslet (1982), p. 122.
26 *Manderston*: guide book to the house, no named author (Norman Hudson, n.d.), p. 3.
27 Aslet (1979), p. 393.
28 Mordaunt Crook, p. 55.
29 Aslet (1979), p. 126.
30 Aslet (1979), p. 126.

CHAPTER TWO

1 Quoted in Frank Dawes, *Not in Front of the Servants* (1973, the National Trust in conjunction with Random House, 1989), pp. 16–17.
2 Dawes, pp. 16–17.
3 Anon, *The Duties of Servants: The Routine of Domestic Service* (1894: facsimile edition Copper Beech Publishing, n.d.), pp. 73–4.
4 *The Duties of Servants*, p. 73.
5 *A New System of Domestic Cookery* (1860), quoted in Elizabeth Drury, *The Butler's Pantry Book* (A. C. Black, 1981), p. 83.
6 Dorothy Henley, *Rosalind Howard, Countess of Carlisle*, p. 87.
7 *Manderston* guide book, p. 19.
8 Jill Franklin, *The Gentleman's Country House and Its Plan, 1835–1914* (Routledge & Kegan Paul, 1981), pp. 88–9.
9 Margaret Powell, *Below Stairs* (Peter Davies, 1970), p. 156.
10 Margaret Fishenden, *House Heating* (1925), quoted in Franklin, p. 91.
11 J. J. Stevenson, *House Architecture* (2 vols, 1880).
12 K. F. Purdon, *The Laundry at Home* (1902), p. 18.
13 Pamela Sambrook, *The Country House Servant* (Sutton Publishing, in association with the National Trust, 1999), pp. 144–5.

CHAPTER THREE

1 *Beeton's Book of Household Management* edited by Mrs Isabella Beeton (S. O. Beeton, 1861; facsimile edn Jonathan Cape, 1968), p. [?].
2 E. S. Turner, *What the Butler Saw* (Michael Joseph, 1962), p. 158.
3 'Williams', *Footmen and Butler: Their Duties and How to Perform Them* (Dean & Son, n.d.), p. 88.
4 *The Servants' Practical Guide* (London: 1880), quoted in Drury, p. 13
5 Beeton, p. 278.
6 Beeton, p. 963.
7 *The Duties of Servants*, p. 53.
8 *The Duties of Servants*, pp. 52–3.
9 Christina Hardyment, *Behind the Scenes: Domestic Arrangements in Historic Houses* (The National Trust, 1997), p. 45, quoting Viola Bankes of the butler at Kingston Lacy in Dorset.
10 *National Review*, vol. XVIII (1892), pp. 812–20.
11 Sambrook, p. 20.
12 Charles Booth (ed.), *Life and Labour of the People in London*, vol. VIII, 'Population Classified by Trade' (Macmillan, 1896).
13 Drury, p. 33.
14 Beeton, p. 964.
15 Albert Thomas, *Wait and See* (Michael Joseph, 1944), p. 69.
16 Laski, pp. 162–3.
17 Hardyment, p. 35; Sambrook, p. 36.
18 Anne Cobbett, *The English Housekeeper* (1842).
19 Hardyment, p. 35.
20 Samuel and Sarah Adams, *The Complete Servant* (1825: reprint, Southover Press, 1989), p. 144.
21 James Williams, *The Footman's Guide*, quoted in Drury, p. 35.
22 Adams, p. 144.
23 Williams, quoted in Drury, p. 35.
24 Beeton, p. 996.
25 Hardyment, p. 178.
26 *Manderston* guide book, p. 20.
27 Adams, p. 143.
28 Turner, p. 170.
29 Eric Horne, *What the Butler Winked At: Being the Life and Adventures of Eric Horne (Butler) for Fifty-Seven Years in Service with the Nobility and Gentry* (T. W. Laurie, 1923), p. 78.
30 Horne, p. 143.
31 Juju Vail, *Rag rugs: Techniques in Contemporary Craft Projects* (Apple Press, 1997), p. 8.
32 Adams, p. 150.
33 Williams, p. 5.
34 Williams, pp. 5–6.
35 Market Harborough Museum oral history transcripts, quoted in Horn (2001), p. 5.

CHAPTER FOUR

1 Lady Greville, *The Gentlewoman in Society* (Henry & Co. 1892), p. 85.
2 Greville, pp. 88–9.
3 Greville, p. 90.
4 Sackville-West, p. 43.
5 Sackville-West, pp. 43–4.
6 *Punch*, 1843, pp. 40, 59.
7 Mark Girouard, *Life in the English Country House: A Social and Architectural History* (Yale University Press, 1998), p. 301.
8 Mordaunt Crook, pp. 3–4.
9 Dorothy Nevill, *Under Five Reigns* (Methuen, 1910), p. 151.
10 Rubinstein (1981), p. 41.
11 W. D. Rubinstein, 'New Men of Wealth and the Purchase of Land in 19th-Century Britain', in *Past and Present*, no. 92 (1981), p. 135.
12 Mordaunt Crook, p. 17.
13 Girouard, p. 300.
14 David Cannadine, *The Decline of the British Aristocracy* (Yale University Press, 1992), p. 96.
15 Oscar Wilde, *The Importance of Being Earnest* (London: 1895).
16 Cannadine, p. 119.
17 *Estates Gazette*, 15 October 1910, quoted in Cannadine, p. 110.
18 Cannadine, p. 108.
19 Cannadine, pp. 100–101.
20 Mordaunt Crook, p. 239.
21 Richard Wilson and Alan Mackley, *Creating Paradise: The Building of the English Country House, 1660–1880* (Hambledon Press, 2000).
22 Mandler, p. 120.
23 *The Studio Yearbook of Decorative Art*, 1908, pp. xi–xii, quoted in Aslet (1992), pp. 1–2.
24 Quoted in Aslet (1992), p. 19.
25 Thorstein Veblen, *The Theory of the Leisure Class* (Macmillan, 1899).
26 John Cornforth, 'Manderston, Berwickshire: The Seat of Lord Palmer', *Country Life* (26 August 1993), pp. 38–42.
27 Aslet (1979), pp. 466–9.
28 *Country Life* (26 August, 1979), p. 40.
29 Anon, *Etiquette: Rules & Usages of the Best Society* (1886; reprinted Leicester: Bookmart, 1995), p. 110.
30 Mrs Humphry ('Madge' of *Truth*), *Manners for Women* (Ward Lock, 1897), p. 83.
31 Mrs Humphry, pp. 83–4.
32 Mrs Humphry, p. 111.
33 *Etiquette*, p. 113.
34 *Etiquette*, p. 116.
35 Beeton, p. 12.
36 Beeton, pp. 18–19.

37   Sir Bernard Burke, *The Book of Precedence. The Peers, and Knights and the Companions of Several Orders of Knighthood Placed According to their Relative Rank* (London, 1881).
38   Leonore Davidoff, *The Best Circles: Society: Etiquette and the Season* (Croom Helm, 1973), p. 47.
39   Gwen Raverat, *Period Piece: A Cambridge Childhood* (Faber & Faber, 1952), p. 78.
40   Beeton, p. 13.
41   Beeton, p. 13.
42   Greville, p. 91.
43   Quoted in Drury, p. 134.
44   Sarah and Samuel Adams, p. 141.
45   Sabine Baring-Gould, *Royal Court* (1886), p. 47.

CHAPTER FIVE
1   Sarah and Samuel Adams, p. 83.
2   Sackville-West, p. 36.
3   Elizabeth Ewing, *History of Twentieth Century Fashion* (B. T. Batsford, 1974), pp. 8–10.
4   Cecil Beaton, *The Glass of Fashion* (Weidenfeld & Nicolson, 1954), p. 7.
5   Valerie Steele, *The History of the Corset*.
6   Sackville-West, pp. 39–40.
7   Frances Hodgson Burnett, *The Making of a Marchioness* (1901: reprint Persephone Books, 2001), p. 95.
8   *The Duties of a Lady's Maid* (London: 1825).
9   *The Duties of a Lady's Maid*, quoted in Drury, p. 103.
10   Greville, p. 135.
11   Sackville-West, p. 39.
12   Jane Ashelford, *The Art of Dress: Clothes and Society 1500–1914* (The National Trust, 1996), p. 250.
13   Ashelford, p. 250.
14   Alison Adburgham, *Shops and Shopping, 1800–1914* (George, Allen & Unwin, 2nd edn, 1981), p. 249.
15   Quoted in Ashelford, p. 262.
16   William Morris, *Hopes and Fears for Art* (London: 1880), p. 170.
17   Arthur J. Taylor, 'The Economy', in Simon Nowell-Smith (ed.), p. 107.
18   C .E. Montague, *Disenchantment*, (Chatto & Windus, 1922), quoted in Taylor, p. 106.
19   Greater London, Inner London Population and Density History: http://www.demographia.com/dm-lon
20   Ewing, p. 5.
21   Quoted in Ewing, p. 7.
22   Mrs Humphry, p. 64.
23   Laurel Brake, *Subjugated Knowledge: Journalism, Gender and Literature in the Nineteenth Century* (Macmillan, 1994), p. 132.
24   Janice Winship, *Inside Women's Magazines* (London: Pandora Press, 1987), p. 27.
25   Ros Ballaster, Margaret Beetham, Elizabeth Frazer and Sandra Hebron, *Women's Worlds: Ideology, Femininity and the Woman's Magazine* (Macmillan,1991), pp. 98–107.
26   Adburgham, p. 101.
27   Adburgham, p. 249.
28   Adburgham, p. 257.
29   Adburgham, p. 125.
30   Ashelford, p. 259.
31   Ewing, p. 6.
32   *Etiquette*, p. 116.
33   *Etiquette*, p. 118.
34   Mrs Humphry, p. 91.
35   Mrs Humphry, p. 90.
36   Beeton, p. 954.
37   *Etiquette*, p. 119.
38   Sackville-West, p. 44.

39   *The Footman and Butler*, p. 43.
40   *Etiquette*, pp. 120–8.
41   *Etiquette*, p. 119.
42   Mrs Humphry, pp. 91–2.
43   Mrs Humphry, p. 92.

CHAPTER SIX
1   Franklin, p. 1.
2   Jessica Gerrard, *Country House Life: Family and Servants, 1815–1914* (Blackwell, 1994), p. 45
3   *A Few Rules for the Manners of Servants in Good Families* (Ladies' Sanitary Association, 1901).
4   Gerrard, p. 143.
5   John Burnett (ed.) *Useful Toil: Autobiographies of Working People from the 1820s to the 1920s* (Penguin, 1977), p. 154.
6   Robert Kerr, *The Gentleman's House, or how to plan English residences from the Parsonage to the Palace* (1864), p. 223.
7   Roberts, pp. 218–19.
8   Gerrard, p. 168.
9   Mary Russell Mitford, *Our Village* (Harrap & Co., 1947; Oxford University Press paperback edn, 1982), p. 29.
10   Laski, p. 143.
11   Roberts, p. 231.
12   Quoted in Horn (2001), p. 3.
13   Nina Slingsby Smith, *George: Memoirs of a Gentleman's Gentleman* (Jonathan Cape, 1984) p. 35.
14   Dawes, pp. 103–5.
15   *Warne's Model Cookery* (London: *circa* 1899), p. 75.
16   Sambrook, p. 89.
17   Alexis Soyer, *The Gastronomic Regenerator* (1846) quoted in Drury, p. 155.
18   Gerrard, p. 11.
19   Beeton (1901 edn), p. 1456.

CHAPTER SEVEN
1   *Berwickshire Advertiser*, 1 September 1911.
2   Susan Tweedsmuir, *The Edwardian Lady* (Duckworth, 1966), pp. 84–6.
3   Quoted in Mandler, p. 206.
4   Leonore Davidoff, *The Best Circles: Society, Etiquette and the Season* (Croom Helm, 1973), pp. 56–7.
5   Jessica Gerrard, 'Lady Bountiful: Women of the Landed Classes and Rural Philanthropy', in *Victorian Studies*, Vol. 30, No. 2 (Winter 1987), p. 206.
6   Greville, pp. 155–6.
7   Anne Summers, 'A Home from Home – Women's Philanthropic Work in the Nineteenth Century', in Sandra Burman (ed.), *Work Fit for Women* (Edward Arnold, 1979), p. 39.
8   Frank Prochaska, 'Female Philanthropy and Domestic Service in Victorian England', *Bulletin of the Institute of Historical Research*, 54, 1981, pp. 79–80.
9   *The Lady's Companion*, 28 January 1911, p. 266.
10   Elaine Kilmurray and Richard Ormond (ed.), *John Singer Sargent* (Tate Gallery Publishing, 1998), p. 144.
11   Sophia Murphy, *The Duchess of Devonshire's Ball* (Sidgwick & Jackson, 1984), pp. 161–2.
12   Census, Registrar General's Annual Reports, 1971. Age, Marital Conditions and General Tables: Table 6 (HMSO, 1974), p. 13.
13   Jane Lewis, *Women in England, 1870–1950* (Wheatsheaf Books, 1984), pp. 3–4.
14   Sue Bruley, *Women in Britain since 1900* (Macmillan, 1999), p. 16.

15   Mary Stocks, *My Commonplace Book* (Peter Davies, 1970), p. 6.
16   Mrs Humphry, p. 56.
17   *The Freewoman*, 23 November 1911, quoted in Juliet Gardiner (ed.), *Women's Voices, 1880–1918: The New Woman* (Collins & Brown, 1993), pp. 200–203.
18   Davidoff, p. 50.
19   Denis Pye, *Fellowship is Life: The National Clarion Cycling Club, 1895–1995* (Clarion Publishing, 1995), p. 6.
20   Pye, p. 3.
21   Quoted in Ashelford, p. 236.
22   *Punch*, 2 June 1883.
23   Richard Ellman, *Oscar Wilde* (Hamish Hamilton, 1987), pp. 244, 268.
24   Pye, pp. 9–10.
25   Frances, Countess of Warwick, *Life's Ebb and Flow* (Hutchinson & Co., 1929), pp. 89–92.
26   Henry Pelling, *Origins of the Labour Party, 1880–1900* (Oxford University Press, 2nd edn, 1965), p. 173.
27   Eric Horne, *More Winks: Being Further Notes from the Life and Adventures of Eric Horne (Butler), for Fifty-Seven Years in Service with the Nobility and Gentry* (T. W. Laurie, 1932), pp. 215–16.
28   Roberts, p. 230.
29   Roberts, pp. 256–7.
30   Roberts, p. 257.
31   Roberts, p. 229.
32   Dawes, p. 164.

CHAPTER EIGHT
1   A. P. Herbert, *Tantivy Towers* (London: Ernest Benn, 1930).
2   Phyllida Barstow, *The English Country House Party* (1989; Sutton Publishing, 1998), p. 85.
3   Barstow, p. 86.
4   Jonathan Garnier Ruffer, *The Big Shots: Edwardian Shooting Parties* (Debrett-Viking Press, 1977), p. 21.
5   Ruffer, p. 134.
6   Christopher Hibbert, *Edward VII: A Portrait* (1976; Penguin, 1982), pp. 94–5.
7   *Country Life*, 21 January 1911.
8   Pamela Horn, *High Society: The English Social Elite,1880–1914* (Alan Sutton Publishing, 1992), p. 138.
9   Horn (1992), pp. 138–9.
10   John Vincent (ed.), *The Crawford Papers: The journals of David Lindsay, twenty-seventh Earl of Crawford and tenth Earl of Balcarres, 1871–40* (London, 1984), entry for 6–10 August 1913, p. 316.
11   Ashelford, p. 240.
12   A. Escoffier, *A Guide to Modern Cookery* (Wm. Heinemann, 1907), pp. 549–50.
13   H. Cholmondeley-Pennell, *Fishing* (Longman, Green & Co., 1912), p. 197.
14   Quoted in Horn (1992), p. 138.
15   MORI poll conducted for the *Mail on Sunday*, 14–15 July 1999, p. 1.
16   Pamela Horn, *Victorian Countrywomen* (Alan Sutton, 1991), p. 54.
17   Countess of Warwick, pp. 95–7.
18   Countess of Warwick, pp. 96–7.
19   The Side Saddle Association, *Member's Handbook, 2001*, p. 58.
20   *Manderston* guide book, p. 23.
21   Quoted in David Cannadine, *Aspects of Aristocracy* (Yale University Press, 1994), p. 56.
22   H. J. Perkin, *The Age of the Railway* (Panther, 1970), pp. 171–2.
23   Cannadine (1994), p. 62.
24   Cannadine (1994), p. 63.

CHAPTER NINE

1 *Manderston* guide book, p. 22.
2 Booth, vol. VII, p. 224.
3 'A Butler's View of Menservice' in *Nineteenth Century* (1892), XXXl, p. 925.
4 William Taylor, *Diary 1837* (ed. Dorothy Wise, 1962), quoted in Franklin, p.106.
5 Franklin, p.106.
6 Davidoff, p. 41.
7 *The Lady, a Magazine for Gentlewomen*, 9 February 1893.
8 Lady Colin Campbell, *Etiquette of Good Society* (1911), p. 63.
9 Powell, pp. 146–7.
10 C. E. Vuillamy (ed.), *The Polderoy Papers* (London: 1943), quoted in Gerrard, p. 251.
11 John R. Gillis, 'Servants, Sexual Revelations and the Risks of Illegitimacy' in Judith L. Newton, Mary P. Ryan and Judith R. Walkowitz, *Sex and Class in Women's History* (Routledge & Kegan Paul, 1983) pp. 145-6.
12 Derek Hudson (ed.), *Man of Two Worlds: The Life and Diaries of Arthur J. Munby, 1828–1910* (1972).
13 *Ann Morgan's Love: A Pedestrian Poem* (A. J. Munby, 1896), quoted in Leonore Davidoff, 'Class and Gender in Victorian England: The Diaries of Arthur J. Munby and Hannah Cullwick', *Feminist Studies*, 5, No. 1, Spring 1979, p. 87.
14 *Cassell's Book of Sports and Pastimes* (Cassell & Co., 1904), p. 334.
15 Chris Cook and John Stevenson, *The Longman Handbook of Modern British History* (Longman, 1983), p. 68.
16 Mandler, p. 174.
17 Mandler, p. 80.
18 Paul Johnson (ed.), *Twentieth-Century Britain: Economic, Cultural and Social Change* (Longman, 1994), p. 1.
19 Horn (2001), p. 17.
20 *Daily Mail*, 20 November 1911.
21 Horn (2001), pp. 17–18.
22 B. K. Murray, *The People's Budget of 1909–10: Lloyd George and Liberal Politics* (Oxford University Press, 1980), p. 256.
23 *The Times*, 31 July 1909, p. 9.
24 Hynes, p. 5.
25 Johnson, p. 80.
26 Johnson, pp. 66–7.
27 Johnson, p. 68.

CHAPTER TEN

1 Lucy Cohen, *Lady de Rothschild and her Daughters* (John Murray, 1935), pp. 269–70.
2 George Dangerfield, *The Strange Death of Liberal England* (1935, MacGibbon & Kee, 1966), pp. 40–41.
3 Roger Fulford, 'The King' in Nowell-Smith, p. 5.
4 Hibbert, p. 294.
5 Dangerfield, pp. 41–2.
6 Blunt, p. 320.
7 Quoted in James Fox, *The Langhorne Sisters* (Granta Books, 1998), p. 116.
8 Frances, Countess of Warwick, *Afterthoughts* (Cassell, 1931), p. 39.

9 Aronson, p. 41.
10 Antony Allfrey, *Edward VII and his Jewish Court* (Weidenfeld & Nicolson, 1991), p. 8.
11 Countess of Warwick, p. 77.
12 Hibbert, p. 155.
13 Aronson. pp. 125–6.
14 Elinor Glyn, *Romantic Adventure* (Ivor Nicholson & Watson, 1936), pp. 74–5.
15 Quoted in Aronson, p. 177.
16 Fox, p. 115.
17 Fox, p. 217.
18 Keith Middlemas, *The Life and Times of Edward VII* (Weidenfeld & Nicolson, 1972), p. 68.
19 T. H. S. Escott, *Society in the New Reign* (1904).
20 Rubinstein, *Men of Property*, p. 156.
21 Quoted in Mordaunt Crook, pp.156–7.
22 Countess of Warwick, quoted in Allfrey, p. 23.
23 Beatrice Webb, *Our Partnership* (ed. Barbara Drake and Margaret Cole) (Longman, 1948), pp. 412–13, 27 July 1908.
24 Allfrey, p. 12.
25 Allfrey, p. 15.
26 Blunt, p. 318.
27 Quoted in Cowles, p. 361.
28 Cornwallis-West, p. 159.
29 Cornwallis-West, p. 150.
30 The Duke of Portland, *Men, Women and Things* (London: Faber, 1937).
31 Philip Magnus, *King Edward VII* (London: John Murray, 1964), p. 254.
32 Magnus, p. 210.
33 Ross McKibbin, *Classes and Cultures: England 1918–1951* (Oxford University Press, 1998), p. 353.
34 Quoted in Ross McKibbin, *The Ideologies of Class* (Oxford University Press, 1990), p. 104.
35 McKibbin, (1990), p. 132.
36 McKibbin, p. 120.
37 J. L. Paton, 'Gambling' in *Encyclopaedia of Religion and Ethics*, 12 vols (Edinburgh, 1913), vol. VI, p. 164.
38 Miss Winifred Sturt to her fiancé, Charles Hardinge, quoted in Magnus, p. 222.
39 Magnus, p. 223.
40 *Cassell's Book of Sports and Pastimes* (London: Cassell & Company, n.d.), p. 764.

CHAPTER ELEVEN

1 Lawrence James, *Raj: The Making and Unmaking of British India* (Little, Brown and Co., 1997), p. 320.
2 Quoted in James, p. 321.
3 Bernard S. Cohen, 'Representing Authority in Victorian England', in Eric Hobsbawm and Terence Ranger (eds.), *Inventing Tradition* (Routledge & Kegan Paul, 1981), pp. 165–210.
4 David Cannadine, *Ornamentalism: How the British Saw their Empire* (Allen Lane, The Penguin Press, 2001), pp. 43–4.
5 Cannadine (2001), p. 45.
6 *The Times*, 30 December 1902.
7 Quoted in David Cannadine, 'Lord Curzon as Imperial Impresario', in *Aspects of Aristocracy: Grandeur and Decline in Modern Britain* (Yale University Press, 1994), p. 85.
8 Cannadine (1994), p. 90.

9 Quoted in Cannadine (1994), p. 90.
10 Lawrence James, *The Rise and Fall of the British Empire* (Little, Brown and Company, 1994), p. 204.
11 James (1994), p. 207.
12 Quoted in James (1994), p. 207.
13 *The Empire Book of Patriotism* (1912), p. 12.
14 James (1994), p. 347.
15 Shompa Lahiri, *Indians in Britain: Anglo-Indian Encounters, Race and Identity. 1880–1930* (Frank Cass, 2000), p. 5.
16 Rozina Visram, *Ayars, Lascars and Princes: Indians in Britain, 1700–1947* (Pluto Press, 1986), pp. 78–96.
17 Beeton (1901 edn), p. 1263.
18 James (1994), pp. 210-11.
19 *The Empire Day Book of Patriotism* (1912), p. 3.
20 Sophia Murphy, *The Duchess of Devonshire's Ball* (Sidgwick & Jackson, 1984), p. 47.
21 Murphy, p. 138.
22 *The Berwickshire News*, 14 November 1905.
23 *The Berwickshire News*, 14 November 1905.
24 *Empire Day Book of Pageants* (London: 1916), p. 10.

CHAPTER TWELVE

1 Samuel and Sarah Adams, p. 23.
2 Raverat, pp. 75–6.
3 Raverat, p. 49.
4 Martin Pugh, *Women and the Women's Movement in Britain* (Macmillan. 2nd edn, 2000), pp. 1–2.
5 Jill Liddington and Jill Norris, *One Hand Tied Behind Us: The Rise of the Women's Suffrage Union* (Virago, 1978).
6 Lisa Tickner, *Imagery of the Suffrage Campaign, 1907–14* (Chatto & Windus, 1987), p. 179.
7 Quoted in Horn (2001), p. 20.
8 Horn (2001), p. 20.
9 Rosina Harrison, *Rose: My Life in Service* (Cassell, 1975), p. 22.
10 Horn (2001), p. 24.
11 J. M. Winter, *The Great War and the British People* (Harvard University Press, 1986), p. 27.
12 *Country Life*, January 1915, quoted in Horn (2001).
13 Christopher Hassal, *Rupert Brooke: A Biography* (Faber & Faber, 1964), pp. 471, 480.
14 Quoted in David Cannadine, (1990), p. 72.
15 Quoted in Angela Lambert, *Unquiet Souls: The Indian Summer of the British Aristocracy, 1880–1918* (Macmillan, 1984), p. 166.
16 Winter, p. 72.
17 Winter, p. 66.
18 Winter, pp. 98–9.
19 Gail Braybon and Penny Summerfield, *Out of the Cage: Women's Experiences in Two World Wars* (Pandora Press, 1987), p. 120.
20 Braybon and Summerfield, p. 123.
21 Horn (2000), p. 27.
22 Horn (2000), p. 191.
23 Horn (2000), p. 30.
24 Quoted in E. L. Black (ed.), *1914–18 in Poetry* (Hodder and Stoughton, 1970), p. 102.

Further reading

A selection of the books available on the Edwardian era. Further books and articles referred to in the text can be found in the endnotes.

RECENT HISTORIES
These include the 1905–14 era and/or discuss the context of the Edwardian Country House.

Aslet, Clive, *The Last Country Houses* (Yale University Press, 1982)

Barstow, Phyllida, *The English Country House Party* (Thorsons, 1989; Sutton Publishing, 1998)

Cannadine, David, *The Decline and Fall of the British Aristocracy* (Yale University Press, 1990, Macmillan Papermac, 1996)

Cannadine, David, *Aspects of Aristocracy: Grandeur and Decline in Modern Britain* (Yale University Press, 1994; Penguin, 1995)

Cannadine, David, *Class in Britain* (Yale University Press, 1998; Penguin, 2000)

Cannadine, David, *Ornamentalism: How the British Saw their Empire* (Allen Lane: Penguin, 2001)

Clarke, Peter, *Hope and Glory: Britain 1900–1990* (Allen Lane, 1996; Penguin, 1997)

Cowles, Virginia, *Edward VII and His Circle* (Hamish Hamilton, 1956)

Dangerfield, George, *The Strange Death of Liberal England* (1935; MacGibbon & Kee, 1966)

Daunton, Martin, *Trusting Leviathan: The Politics of Taxation in Britain, 1799–1914* (Cambridge University Press, 2001)

Davidoff, Leonore, *The Best Circles: Society, Etiquette and the Season* (Croom Helm, 1973)

Dawes, Frank, *Not in Front of the Servants* (Wayland, 1973; the National Trust in conjunction with Century, 1989)

Drury, Elizabeth, *The Butler's Pantry Book* (A. C. Black, 1981)

Franklin, Jill, *The Gentleman's Country House and Its Plan, 1835–1914* (Routledge & Kegan Paul, 1981)

Gerrard, Jessica, *Country House Life: Family and Servants, 1815–1914* (Blackwell, 1994)

Girouard, Mark, *Life in the English Country House: A Social and Architectural History* (Yale University Press, 1998)

Hardyment, Christina, *Behind the Scenes: Domestic Arrangements in Historic Houses* (The National Trust, 1997)

Harris, Jose, *Private Lives, Public Spirit: Britain 1870–1914* (Oxford University Press, 1993; Penguin, 1994)

Hartcup, Adeline, *Below Stairs in the Great Country Houses* (Sidgwick & Jackson, 1980)

Hibbert, Christopher, *Edward VII: A Portrait* (Allen Lane, 1976; Penguin, 1982)

Holden, Edith, *The Country Diary of an Edwardian Lady* (Michael Joseph, 1977)

Horn, Pamela, *Ladies of the Manor: Wives and Daughters in Country-House Society, 1830–1918* (Sutton Publishing, 1991)

Horn, Pamela, *High Society: The English Social Elite, 1880–1914* (Sutton Publishing, 1992)

Horn, Pamela, *Life Below Stairs in the 20th Century* (Sutton Publishing, 2001)

Hugget, Frank E., *Life Below Stairs: Domestic Servants in England from Victorian Times* (Book Club Associates, 1977)

Hynes, Samuel, *The Edwardian Turn of Mind* (Princeton University Press, 1968)

James, Lawrence, *The Rise and Fall of the British Empire* (Little, Brown, 1994)

James, Lawrence, *Raj: The Making and Unmaking of British India* (Little, Brown, 1997)

Kynaston, David, *The City of London*, vol. II, *The Golden Years, 1890–1914* (Chatto & Windus, 1995)

Lambert, Angela, *Unquiet Souls: The Indian Summer of the British Aristocracy, 1880–1918* (Macmillan, 1984)

Magnus, Philip, *King Edward VII* (John Murray, 1964)

Mandler, Peter, *The Fall and Rise of the Stately Home* (Yale University Press, 1997)

McKibbin, Ross, *The Ideologies of Class: Social Relations in Britain, 1880–1950* (Oxford University Press, 1990)

Mordaunt Crook, J., *The Rise of the Nouveaux Riches: Style and Status in Victorian and Edwardian Architecture* (John Murray, 1999)

Nowell-Smith, Simon (ed.), *Edwardian England, 1901–1914* (Oxford University Press, 1964)

Plumptre, George, *The Fast Set: The World of Edwardian Racing* (André Deutsch, 1985)

Priestley, J. B., *The Edwardians* (Heinemann, 1970)

Pugh, Martin, *Women and the Women's Movement in Britain* (Macmillan, 2nd edn, 2000)

Rose, Kenneth, *George V* (Weidenfeld & Nicolson, 1983)

Rubinstein, W. D., *Men of Property: The Very Wealthy in Britain Since the Industrial Revolution* (Croom Helm, 1981)

Ruffer, Jonathan Garnier, *The Big Shots: Edwardian Shooting Parties* (Debrett-Viking Press, 1977)

Sambrook, Pamela, *The Country House Servant* (Sutton Publishing, in association with the National Trust, 1999)

Thompson, F. M. L., *Gentrification and Enterprise Culture: Britain, 1870–1980* (Oxford University Press, 2001)

Turner, E. S., *What the Butler Saw* (Michael Joseph, 1962)

MEMOIRS AND MANUALS
The memoirs cover the Edwardian period, or have relevance to it, and the advice manuals are among those used in the Edwardian Country House.

Adams, Samuel and Sarah, *The Complete Servant* (1825; reprint, Southover Press, 1989)

Beeton, Isabella, *The Book of Household Management* (S. O. Beeton, 1861; also 1901 edn; facsimile edn Jonathan Cape, 1968)

Blunt, Wilfrid Scawen, *My Diaries: Being a Personal Narrative of Events, 1880–1914* (Martin Secker, 1920)

Campbell, Lady Colin, *Etiquette of Good Society* (1911)

Cassell's Book of Sports and Pastimes (1904)

Cassell's Household Guide, 4 vols (*c*1900), vol. 5, 1911

Cornwallis-West, G., *Edwardian Hey-Days, Or a Little About a Lot of Things* (Putnam, 1930)

Duties of a Lady's Maid, The (1825)

Duties of Servants, The: The Routine of Domestic Service (1894; facsimile edn Copper Beech Publishing, n.d.)

Escoffier, A., *A Guide to Modern Cookery* (Heinemann, 1907)

Etiquette: Rules & Usages of the Best Society (1886; reprinted Bookmart, 1995)

Everywoman's Encyclopaedia, 8 vols (1910)

Glyn, Elinor, *Romantic Adventure* (Ivor Nicholson and Watson, 1936)

Greville, Lady, *The Gentlewoman in Society* (Henry & Co., 1892)

Horne, Eric, *What the Butler Winked At: Being the Life and Adventures of Eric Horne (Butler) for Fifty-Seven Years in Service with the Nobility and Gentry* (T. W. Laurie, 1923)

Humphry, Mrs ('Madge' of *Truth*), *Manners for Men* (1897: facsimile edn Pryor Publications, 1993)

Humphry, Mrs, *Manners for Women* (1897: facsimile edn Pryor Publications, 1993)

James, Mrs Eliot, *Our Servants: Their Duties to Us and Ours to Them* (1883)

Keppel, Sonia, *Edwardian Daughter* (Hamish Hamilton, 1958)

Ladies' Sanitary Association, *A Few Rules for the Manners of Servants in Good Families* (1901)

Raverat, Gwen, *Period Piece: A Cambridge Childhood* (Faber & Faber, 1952)

Servant's Practical Guide, The (1880)

Warne's Model Cookery (*c*.1899)

Warwick, Frances, Countess of, *Life's Ebb and Flow* (Hutchinson & Co., 1929)

'Williams', *The Footmen and Butler, Their Duties and How to Perform Them* (Dean & Son, 8th edn, n.d.)

EDWARDIAN NOVELS (RELEVANT TO THE THEME OF THE BOOK) IN REPRINT EDITIONS
Burnett, Frances Hodgson, *The Making of a Marchioness* (1901; reprinted Persephone Books, 2001)

Leverson, Ada, *The Little Otleys* (1908–16; reprinted Virago Press, 1962)

Sackville-West, Vita, *The Edwardians* (1930; reprinted Virago Press, 1983)

Wells, H. G., *Tono-Bungay* (1909; J M Dent, Everyman's Library, 1994)

Timeline

1899
Outbreak of the Second Boer War.

1900
Labour Representation Committee formed.
Conservative–Liberal Unionist coalition
under Lord Salisbury returned to power in
'khaki election'.

1901
22 January: Death of Queen Victoria, aged
eighty-one, after a reign of sixty-three
years. Edward VII succeeds to the throne.
September: Taff Vale judgement, a landmark
in the development of the Labour Party.
Workers on the Taff Vale Railway took
unofficial action to gain the right to join a
trade union. The dispute was then made
official by the Amalgamated Society of
Railway Servants but, after the strike was
settled, the railway company sought
damages from the union for losses
incurred during the strike. This was
rejected on appeal, but in July 1901 the
House of Lords reversed the appeal and
granted £42,000 plus costs against the
union. The judgement severely limited the
right to strike and convinced many
working people of the need for an
independent political party to support the
interests of labour. The Labour
Representation Committee made
immunity from prosecution for trade
unions a condition of joining the 'LibLab'
pact made before the 1906 election.
October: Britain's first submarine launched.
December: First Nobel Prizes awarded.

1902
January: Smallpox outbreak in London.
March: Cecil Rhodes, 'the architect of
Empire', dies.
May: Boer War ends.
July: Arthur Balfour succeeds Salisbury as
Conservative Prime Minister.
9 August: Coronation of Edward VII,
delayed from July because of the King's
appendicitis.
Charles Booth's survey of poverty, *Life and
Labour of the People of London*, published.
Windsor Castle opened to the public.
Beatrix Potter's *Peter Rabbit* published.
Rudyard Kipling's *Just So Stories* published.

1903
1 January: Edward VII proclaimed Emperor
of India.
October: Formation of the suffragette
Women's Social and Political Union
(WSPU), by Emmeline and Christabel
Pankhurst.
December: Marie Curie the first woman to
win the Nobel Prize.
Orville and Wright make the first successful
flight in a petrol-powered aeroplane.

1904
February: War breaks out between Russia
and Japan when the Russian fleet attacks
at Port Arthur.
April: Entente Cordiale signed with France.
Licence plates for cars compulsory.
May: Rolls-Royce car manufacturing
company formed.
November: Figures released reveal that
poverty is rising dramatically – 122,000
people in London and 800,000 in England
and Wales are in receipt of poor relief,
with a quarter of a million in workhouses.
December: J. M. Barrie's *Peter Pan, or The Boy
Who Wouldn't Grow Up* opens in London.

1905
January: 'Bloody Sunday' in St Petersburg,
when Tsar Nicholas II's troops fire on
demonstrators led by Father George
Gabon, killing 500 people.
By popular demand, Arthur Conan Doyle
brings his famous detective back from the
'dead' in a new book, *The Return of
Sherlock Holmes*.
April: More than 10,000 people perish in an
earthquake in Lahore, India.
May: Women's Suffrage Bill 'talked out' in
Commons.
June: Mutiny of Russian sailors on battleship
Potemkin.
Automobile Association founded.

July: Einstein's Theory of Relativity
proposed.
August: Lord Curzon resigns as Viceroy of
India.
October: Christabel Pankhurst and Annie
Kenney arrested: start of the militant
phase of the Suffragette movement.
Aspirin on sale in Britain.
December: Balfour resigns; Henry
Campbell-Bannerman invited to form a
government.
First motorized ambulances for traffic
accident victims introduced by London
County Council (previously ambulances
were used only for people suffering from
infectious diseases).
John Galsworthy's *A Man of Property* (the
novel that becomes the first part of *The
Forsyte Saga*) published.

1906
February: Liberal landslide at General
Election; Labour wins thirty seats.
HMS *Dreadnought* launched.
Formation of the Labour Party.
Trade Disputes Act overturns Taff Vale
Judgement.
Free school meals introduced for children in
need.
April: Mount Vesuvius erupts, killing
hundreds.
San Francisco earthquake: 800 die.
SOS becomes the international distress
signal.

1907
Women can stand for election in county and
borough election and can take the office of
mayor.

April: War Office objects to plan to construct a Channel tunnel: Bill withdrawn.

Baden-Powell founds the Boy Scout movement.

Entente Cordiale becomes Triple Alliance when Russia joins.

New Zealand achieves dominion status.

1908

April: Ill-health forces Campbell-Bannerman's resignation; Herbert Asquith succeeds him as Prime Minister.

Old Age Pensions (with a means test) introduced for a minority of old people.

Coal Mines Regulation Act legislates for a maximum working day of eight hours underground.

Territorial Army (volunteer home defence force that could be mobilized in the event of war) founded. By 1914 it had over a quarter of a million members.

England plays the first ever international football match, against Austria – and wins 6–1.

June: Edward VII visits Russia.

Olympic Games staged in London.

National Farmers' Union founded.

December: Professor Ernest Rutherford awarded the Nobel Prize for Chemistry for his work on radiation and the nature of the atom.

E. M. Forster's *Room with a View* published.

1909

Labour Exchanges established.

Trade Boards Act establishes minimum wage in some of the lowest-paid trades.

July: Blériot makes the first cross-Channel flight, taking forty-three minutes.

November: The House of Lords throws out Lloyd George's 'people's budget' – the 'most radical budget in the nation's history'.

1910

Liberals under Asquith win general election in February and December.

Union of South Africa formed.

21 May: Death of Edward VII; succeeded by George V.

July: Dr Crippen arrested at sea for the murder of his wife, the first criminal suspect to be caught by radio. He was travelling with his mistress Ethel Le Neve, disguised as a boy.

20 August: Florence Nightingale dies.

Osborne Judgement bans trade unions from funding political activities.

Girl Guide movement founded by Baden-Powell and his sister, Agnes.

1911

February: Ramsay MacDonald succeeds Keir Hardie as chairman of the parliamentary Labour party.

March: Shops Act legislates for sixty-hour week and all employees entitled to a half-day holiday each week.

Parliament Act restricts power of the House of Lords.

Payment of MPs introduced.

23 June: George V crowned in Westminster Abbey.

July: Agadir crisis when Germany sent a gunboat to Moroccan port allegedly to protect German trading interests against the French. Britain was concerned at this possible threat to Gibraltar. Although Germany and France negotiated a settlement, the incident fuelled Britain's concern about Germany's expansionist aims.

November: Balfour resigns as leader of the Conservative Party; succeeded by Andrew Bonar Law.

Period of industrial unrest from 1911 to 1914.

1912

January: Captain Scott's expedition reaches the South Pole – Amundsen has beaten them. All perish on the return journey.

April: The 'unsinkable' *Titanic* sinks after hitting an iceberg, with the loss of more than 1,500 lives.

May: Irish Home Rule Bill introduced.

September: Edward Carson organizes the Ulster Volunteers to resist Home Rule for Ireland.

British Board of Film Censors established.

Royal Flying Corps (precursor of the Royal Air Force) established.

1913

March: Cat and Mouse Act introduced in an attempt to deal with the problem of suffragettes' hunger strikes in prison.

May: Stravinsky's *Rites of Spring* performed to shocked audiences in Paris.

June: The suffragette Emily Davison throws herself under the King's horse at the Derby and dies from her injuries.

The zip fastener patented by a Swedish engineer.

Trade Union Act reverses Osborne Judgement.

September: Ulster Volunteer Force established.

D. H. Lawrence's *Sons and Lovers* published.

1914

Immigration, already restricted since 1905 Act, further restricted

March: Velazquez's *Rokeby Venus* slashed in the National Gallery by a suffragette with a meat cleaver.

Wyndham Lewis's Vorticist magazine, *Blast*, signals arrival of modernism in Britain.

April: George Bernard Shaw's *Pygmalion* opens in London, starring Mrs Patrick Campbell.

James Joyce's *Dubliners* published.

Edgar Rice Burroughs' *Tarzan of the Apes* published.

28 June: Archduke Franz Ferdinand of Austria assassinated by a Serbian nationalist in Sarajevo.

1 August: Germany declares war on Russia and, on the 3rd, France.

4 August: Britain declares war on Germany when it violates Belgian neutrality. Fighting continues on the Western Front until 11 a.m. on 11 November 1918. By this time, 772,000 British have been killed, and 1,676,037 wounded.

Index

Author's acknowledgements

Writing any book incurs debts: in a book such as this they are manifold and direct. My first thanks must go to those who peopled the Edwardian Country House: the 'upstairs' family of John and Anna Olliff-Cooper, Jonathan and Guy, and Avril Anson; the 'tutor', Rejit Singh; and the 'servants' downstairs: Tristan Aldrich, Carly (Ellen) Beard, Charlie Clay, Rob Daly, Jean Davies, Denis Dubiard, Hugh Edgar, Eva Morrison, Erika Ravitz, Jessica Rawlinson, Kenneth Skelton and Rebecca Smith. Without their willingness to share their experiences and to supply a mass of information and advice, this book could not have been written. Nor could it of course without the Wall to Wall team to whom I am most grateful: I am particularly indebted to Caroline Ross Pirie, the series producer and director, to Melanie Lindsell and to Fiona Blair with whom I seem to have been in almost daily contact. My thanks too to Nick Murphy, co-director, and to Emma Willis, executive producer, to Mark Ball, Rachel Bliss, Joyce Cope, Andrea Kohn, Amy Leader and Donna Luke.

At Channel 4 Books Charlie Carman and her team have, once again, been exemplary publishers and my thanks are due to Emma Tait, Annie Schafheitle, Verity Willcocks, and particularly to Sarah MacDonald for efficient and encouraging editorial support; to Christine King for meticulous and tactful copy editing; and to Isobel Gillan for inspired design solutions, and thanks to my agent Deborah Rogers.

Dr Peter Mandler and Daru Rooke have both read the manuscript and I have hugely benefited from their comments and suggestions, though any errors and omissions of course remain solely my responsibility. Rosalind Ebbutt has been a mine of information on costume and effects, and I am also most grateful for the help of Polly Bell-Hughes, Simon Berry, Robin Darwell-Smith, Dr John Davies, Guy Dymond, Mike Everett, Neil Freeman, Professor Henry Horwitz, Arthur Inch, Patrick MacLure, Jim Matthews, John Ormiston, Jane Pryor, Caroline and Patricia Rose, and Professor Richard Sheppard.

No book like this can be written without drawing on the work of those who traversed the terrain before: my debt to them is acknowledged in the endnotes and the suggestions for further reading.

Producer's acknowledgements

This project would not have been possible without the kindness and enthusiasm of the people who live and work in and around Duns. For their help throughout filming, Wall to Wall would like to thank Lord and Lady Palmer, Reverend Donald Gaddis, Rona and Andy Lang, Geoffrey and Valerie Dymond, Sarah Gash, Tommy and Helen Noon, Mr and Mrs Grant, Agnes and Robert Crawford, Mark Dawson, Bill Hardie, Marion Smith, John and Joan Bimson, Brenda Leddy, Johnny Rutherford, Diane Youngman, Mary and Bill Bryson, Maggie and Brian Gray, David and Marlene Young, the Knoll Hospital, the Gardeners' Royal Benevolent Society, the Berwickshire Hounds, Ronald Drummond, Christina Cowan, Sarah Hogg, Jenny Leggett, the Whip and Saddle, Christine Taylor, Gordon Morrison, Neil Mountain, Kay Melville, Roxburgh Lacemakers, Langton Rural, Dorien Irving, Professor Jimi Langley, Madame Christine Quick, Sheila Massie, Joan Russell, Robert Allott, Nan Eddy, R. Welsh and Son, Fred Baxendale at Howe and Blackhall, Richard Landale at Kelso Races, the staff and pupils at Longridge Towers, the Brownies, Guides and Cubs of Duns and the Greggs Bakery Band.

The Edwardian Country House was graced with a number of visitors. The producer would like to thank Merlin Evans, Sandy Broadhurst and Graham Pearce from the Clarion Cycling Club, Dr Morrice McCrae, Arthur Inch, John Myatt, Lady McEwen, Colonel Simon Furness, Simon Berry, Mrs Elizabeth Whinney, David Liddell Grainger and Lady de la Rue, Mr and Mrs Richard Baillie, Judith Linton and her ceilidh band, Shearings, Prince Mohsin Ali Khan of Hyderabad, Yasmin Alibhai-Brown, Krishnan Guru-Murthy, Priya Pawar, Sushma Mehta and the dancers and musicians she brought with her, Jeffrey Bates of Bates and Hindmarch antiquarian books, Darcus Howe, David Mellor, Lord Deedes, Lord and Lady Steel, Alan Beith MP, Baroness Maddock, Lady Chelsea, Robert Swan OBE, Andrew Motion, the Edinburgh University Savoy Opera Group, the two 'chauffeurs' Don Moore and George McCartney, John Adderley and everyone else who came to the fête, dinner party or Empire Ball.

For restoring the house to its Edwardian splendour, thanks are extended to our art director, Maggie Gray, who was ably assisted by Fiona Gavin with Craig Dewar, Bill Purvis, Ronnie Thompson, the two Neil Jordans and Jim Louden all helping to get the house ready on time. Special thanks to costume designers Ros Ebbutt and Amanda Keable, Pat Farmer and Lesley Docksey who made some of the clothes. Thanks also to Fran Needham and Heather Squires.

Wall to Wall researched this project with the help of our historical consultants Daru Rooke, Peter Mandler and Paul Atterbury. Further help came from Pamela Horn, David Moore, John Davis, Neil Freeman, Bill Leader, Martin Pugh, Derek Scott, Judith Lask, the Museum of Labour History, Northern Herald Books, Dr Harvey Osborne, Sara Paston-Williams, Dennis Pye, Adrian Greenwood, Jim Spencer and John Macmillan at Historic Newspapers, Dinosaur Disks, the Victorian Society, Whitechapel Art Gallery, the Working Class Movement Library, the National Library of Scotland, the Yorkshire Car Collection, the British Library, Eyemouth Museum, John Hayes at the Museum of Childhood in Edinburgh and the Victoria Research web. Thanks also to all who applied to take part, particularly those who took the time to write to the production team with country house stories of their own.

Finally, thanks to Camilla Deakin and Janice Hadlow at Channel 4 Television.

Suppliers

Stationery: Smythson of Bond Street; pens: Parker; chinaware: Josiah Wedgwood & Son; glassware: Stuart Crystal; toiletries: Rose & Co Apothecary, D. R. Harris & Co Ltd, Trumpers (for razors); Edwardian hospitality: Gore Hotel, London, Caledonian Hotel, Edinburgh; silverware: Robbe & Berking; diamonds and pearls: Hamilton & Inches; packaging: Robert Opie, Unilever; magazines and newspapers: Vinmag Archive, Historic Newspapers; wines: Berry Bros & Rudd; art materials: Windsor & Newton, Fired Earth; spectacles: Specsavers; guns: Holland and Holland; flowers for special occasions: Banks Florist, Edinburgh; ball gowns: Angels & Berman Costumier, Cosprop. LOCAL PRODUCE: Vegetables: Betty Snow (herbs), Thisselcockrig Farm, Reiver Country Farm Foods, Wild Tastes, Dicksons; eggs and dairy: Stichill Jerseys, Oxenrig Farm; fish: Waddells of Eyemouth, D. R. Collins of Eyemouth, Lindesfarne Oysters; meat: Prentice Butchers, Duns; game and poultry: Burnside Farm Foods; other products: Heatherslaw Corn Mill, Campbell & Neill (ice), Chainbridge Honey Farm, Crema (tea and coffee), Beers of Scotland, Theakstons, Pam's Flower Box.